Elton Jones grew up in the State of Paraiba (Brazil) and, after graduating from a Federal university, he took part in the MA programme at the University of Leeds (England). It is from his experiences learning, teaching, and relearning English – and about English – that he drew inspiration to write the accounts within the following pages.

Note

This work draws inspiration from actual experiences. A few characters were only inspired by actual people. Most names have been changed. Some dramatisation was created or reinterpreted. Records (pictures, videos, letters, emails) confirm the honesty of the narrative.

Published by New Generation Publishing in 2012

Copyright © Elton Jones 2012

First Edition

The author asserts the moral right under the Copyright, Designs and Patents Act 1988 to be identified as the author of this work.

All Rights reserved. No part of this publication may be reproduced, stored in a retrieval system or transmitted, in any form or by any means without the prior consent of the author, nor be otherwise circulated in any form of binding or cover other than that which it is published and without a similar condition being imposed on the subsequent purchaser.

www.newgeneration-publishing.com

 New Generation **Publishing**

The Book is on the Table

Elton Jones

I dedicate this publication to:

my mother, Valdelice, *who always helped me with her prayers and financial support*;

my father, Andrade, *who supported me financially (and reluctantly)*;

and Clifford, *who always believed in my ideas and helped me with English in so many ways.*

Part One

1

There is a sixth dimension, beyond that which is known to man... went *The Twilight Zone* pilot episode intro.

Rod Serling's series was the first television show which aroused my fascination with the world of imagination, fiction, and mystery. Then, I grew up to learn that the weird, the odd, and the bizarre can be much more real and much closer than the small screen shows. Siamese twins, human freaks, psychopaths, zombies, possessions, poltergeist, witches, satanists, sacrifices, torture chambers, mad scientists, sharks, piranhas, flesh eating worms, hurricanes, volcanoes, massive holes on the ground, and many other things which scare me to death do really exist. Furthermore, Gods, spirits, ghosts, angels, holy people, fairies, aliens, vampires, werewolves, chupacabras, wizards, enchantments, vanishings, abductions, spontaneous human combustion, time travel, screaming skulls, and many other unexplained well-known stories, mostly documented, do challenge our perspective of reality.

Somehow everyone has experienced, or knows someone who has, a paranormal incident, and ultimately all and sundry must wonder what's beneath the cloak of the Grim Reaper.

I myself have seen a human shaped shadow moving across a room right in front of my eyes. Yet, a moving shadow means nothing when compared to the amazing chain of coincidences which led me from a rather ordinary routine, living in the easternmost end of South America, to my participation in an exceptional ceremony at the heart of West Yorkshire in England.

"Rise..." commanded the Presiding Officer, prompting all participants and guests to stand up.

Following that cue, an organist started controlling the keys and pedals of a pipe organ, making its music to reverberate within the chamber walls.

The ceremony could well be mistaken for a scene from a *Harry Potter* film. The gothic style chamber where the ceremony happened was decorated with flowers and mostly illuminated by the sunlight which descended perpendicularly from above through a great arched window behind the balcony. With a pounding chest, I stood amongst other participants in between the benches to the left of the row of benches reserved to the guests.

A formal procession entered into the chamber. The members of the procession moved slowly through the narrow isle between the two rows of benches. Two wood ceremonial maces were carried by two mace-bearers ahead the procession. The way the members of the procession dressed was symbolic of their hierarchical status. The standard feature of the ceremonial dress was a black gown topped with black velvet cap or bonnet. The hierarchical distinctions were more evidently represented by the hood colours: some were dark green, or red, or scarlet, or turquoise, or white, or golden, or blue, all lined with and with bindings of a different colour. Two other wood maces and a metal more ornamented mace were carried by the last members of the procession. The procession members took their place in the stage facing the participants and guests. They attracted high reverence and admiration from everyone within the chamber.

When the organ music stopped, the Presiding Officer addressed and welcomed the participants and guests. Then, as a Senior Official started announcing the participants' names, these were brought forth onto the stage individually. After briefly queuing behind other participants, my turn to come forth arrived.

In a flash, it all came back: the self-esteem struggles, the financial difficulties, the limited resources to improve my English skills – the challenging elements that had, consistently, made my participation in that ceremony something seemingly impossible. They were about to be converted.

"In Linguistics and English Language Teaching…" When the Senior Official completed that sequence of words uttering my full name, all I could hear was a magic spell echoing against the walls of the Great Hall, transforming my entire self.

Hearing that cue, I proceeded towards the Presiding Officer, made a quick courteous bow, and received from the Presiding Officer's hands my certificate of Master of Arts. "Thanks."

It's complete. With that, I knew it. I'd consciously tapped into the *principle* – or as some call it, the *secret* – and managed to spin another turn of the *Rota* to my favour.

I'd officially become a graduate of the University of Leeds.

2

After all of us graduates had been admitted to our degrees, the Presiding Officer spoke: "I now declare this congregation closed." And then she joined the academic party, which began recessing out of the ceremonial chamber by the music of the reverberating pipe organ.

The atmosphere was heavy with emotion and although those feelings were ephemeral that graduation ceremony in the Great Hall would remain forever in the graduates' memory. The so dreamed ceremony made me extremely happy and proud. I was living a perfect life moment except for one thing: as a non-European graduate carrying a passport with a long expired student visa, I had no legal right to remain much longer in the UK.

"Hey Mr," hollered the photographer from Ede and Ravenscroft, who was waiting outside the Great Hall. "Give us a smile!" He used a tone of voice that probably meant that my expression reminded him of one of those lethargic looking faces pictured in black and white in the charity poster of the *Myasthenia Gravis Association*.

That is what I got from allowing my thoughts to wallow in my visa predicament. I'd been refused a student visa extension owing to an intricate of coincidental mistakes, which culminated with my failure to include a visa letter from University among the stack of forms sent along with the visa application to the UK Border Agency. Then, I had to leave my job because continuing to work without a regular visa could bring serious implications for my employer, who might be prosecuted, face court proceedings, and be obliged to pay heavy fines to the State. With no perspective of getting a new job and no source of income, I was left with nine hundred pound sterling (£900) in a NatWest account – sufficient to pay two months' rent, buy some food and little else. I'd had my passport returned just over a month ago, in the middle of November, whilst the study year had ended in September.

I wasn't entitled to apply for any further extension and since my passport contained no stamp, I went from a full-blown student at a British university straight to the realm of illegality as an overstayer.

So, visaless… yes, jobless… yes, but bold and beautiful baby. I'd dieted hard and walked the treadmill solid the entire week to look slim and young for Big Brother's affiliates. No cloud would throw its shade on my graduation photography. And that photographer would most certainly not have a chance to photograph me holding an MA degree certificate and looking like a mug.

"How about this?" I slapped a bright smile on.

"Proper grad grin." The photographer said with a cheeky wink before clicking the shutter.

3

To slap that glow on my face, I brought to mind *Monty Python's Life of Brian* and broke into a smile that said, "Always look on the bright side of life."

Indeed, I was trying to look on the bright side – after all, I'd just graduated from a British institution. But it was hard to remain optimistic with the wheel of fortune reversing over my dreams.

Truthfully, I still had the option of going back home for a fresh start within the time limit the UK Border Agency set for my departure from England. Sure that wouldn't be as simple as hopping into a hot air balloon, or as fancy as tapping the heels of ruby slippers three times, but the £900 from my reserve account was enough to pay for a flight ticket to the country where I came from and mostly lived during thirty years of my existence. Being the holder of degree from a British university was something good to consider, mainly if the Degree concerns the English language – there's no better place to study the English if not in its very cradle, in the land of the greenest grass and fields where invasions and bloody battles gave birth to the myriad of English dialects and accents which are now scattered throughout the world's surface. That degree would entitle me, with some effort, to obtain a place as a tutor in one of the country's State schools which offered stable jobs for life and a pension plan.

All would be well and good, if not for the fact that I preferred to learn what was in room 101 than to return to the country where I hailed from. There's nothing essentially wrong with the country itself; no starvation, natural disasters, religious extremism, or social oppression. Nevertheless, my latest experiences back there hadn't been particularly enjoyable and as I grew less and less fond on my own State I truly struggled to recognise my roots with its social values. Certainly there are plenty positive things to say about those who battle to survive and take a dignifying social place there; but I grew resentful with somewhat devastating personal experiences there and so, could do nothing to feel otherwise.

I honestly hoped that all that was gone with the wind, and just like Scarlett O'Hara under that oak tree, I saw myself as a shadow with a clenched fist raised toward heaven, promising that I was going to live through that, and when that was all over, I'd never be hungry again.

4

"...Are you enjoying the cocktail El-Jay?" Amy interrupted my thoughts.

Suddenly, the red dawn of Tara fade away and Max Steiner's grandiose music dissolved into a hubbub of voices from the guest and participants who were enjoying the free cocktail offered at the Terrace of the Union building by the School of English and the School of Modern Languages and Cultures.

Amy was one of the only five mates from our postgrad class who attended the graduation ceremony; she was there along with the only other English mate, Sophie from Wakefield. Except for Ching-Ma from China, Samira from Saudi Arabia, and Malgorzata from

Poland, all the other mates from our class had already returned to their countries of origin.

I felt blessed to have a chance to be there at the cocktail, feasting on crisps, nachos, breadsticks, sliced vegetables, and all sorts of pâté, drinking white wine and fruit cocktails, and, the best of all, lavishly surrounded by English. So, I answered to Amy, "Hell yeah I'm enjoying it. All this opulence serves to remind me of the hunger I experienced before coming to England."

"What... Serious?" Amy raised her eyebrows.

"Not hunger of food. My humble parents provided me the best they could. It was hunger of another kind. I actually starved for the English language for a long, long time."

"I should know. Such a drama queen you are..."

What's dramatic about that? If a language doesn't appear to be a sensible thing for one to long for, one sure can wonder what reason some individuals have in their minds to climb the peak of the highest mountains, or to run long distances, or swim across channels, or to break any kind of record like those weird ones from the *Guinness Book*, or to collect any sort of thing, or to scrutinise the infinitude of universe, or spend years working on an intellectual project with no profit in sight. The reason for my longing for English must be of a similar nature.

And in the onset of this longing, during adolescence, whilst I yearned to learn, listen, and live the English language, my only source of English came from a collection of twelve books and four magnetic audio tapes, produced in 1981, entitled *English at Home*. Although the journey from this initial moment to graduating at the University of Leeds had been pretty adventurous already, after the graduation ceremony I still felt there was something missing to satisfy this hunger. And even though the immigration agents could perhaps call into my flat and force me to leave the country, I'd rather run that risk, altogether with running out of money and food, before allowing myself to be taken away from English.

"...So, as I was saying, they offered me a place to teach down there and I might be flying soon." Amy was pretty excited, sipping a guava cocktail, telling me about her plans from then on.

"Good for you Amy." I realised that I had totally tuned out of the conversation. But before I could properly follow Amy, the sound of her voice gradually faded amid the hubbub of the Terrace as my thoughts turned a little theatrical again.

Such ominous thoughts made me shudder. Off and on I pondered if staying in England was a massive mistake. But, if there is something that I learned along every step of that journey learning English is that what we normally judge to be wrong is generally just a little off of our understanding of rightness. So, I strongly believed that the unfortunate situation I found myself into would eventually lead me to triumph. After all, up to the graduation ceremony day I'd battled against a few adversities and won all the battles. Nothing would dissuade me from pursuing my ultimate desire which was, among other things, to continue an academic education on English in the UK.

And whenever doubts assaulted me lately, I flipped through a few recent issues of the *Metro* and skimmed intros like *a heated row between two men over the last packet of dry roasted peanuts boiled over into brawl involving fifty people in a gentlemen's club*; or *over twenty-two thousand freakily-dressed Jacko fans gathered in thirty seven countries around the world to stage a synchronised version of Michael Jackson's 'Thriller'*; or *thirty-five year old regular church goer has made five hundred thousand pounds miming along to medleys of Cher*; or *someone has paid two hundred thousand pounds for a virtual space station and is set to make a bumper profit on the digital investment*; or yet *a fifteen pound leg of Iberico ham costing one thousand and eight hundred pounds goes on sale today.* News like those reminded me that I couldn't be going madder than the whole world itself.

"...Different strokes for different folks, and so on and so on scooby dooby dooby." Amy said with a naughty smile, just before turning down a big gulp of her guava cocktail with a campy gesture that emphasised her closing statement.

"I agree a hundred percent." I didn't have the slightest idea of what the hell Amy was talking about, or why Scooby Doo ended up in that conversation. Amy had that habit of purposely making her English sound a little more cryptic for non-natives speakers.

"I'm glad you understand me." Amy still added.

"How could I not? I'm with you, Amy." I ventured, praying Amy didn't ask me anything further in detail.

Up to the point where her words still made sense to me, I understood that she'd made up her mind to go and teach English for a charitable organization in some country from Central America. In a moment like that, it was a relief to learn that someone like Amy, whose shrewdness was indubitable, also had daring plans on what to do after our academic adventure. Alas, her intrepid aspirations didn't make me feel much more fortunate.

I grew used to being unbelievably unlucky. It didn't matter what my next step was, Ms Fortuna always had a trap specially crafted to torment me. So, I could justifiably bemoan, revolt, and despair about my visa situation, but the truth is that, trap after trap, I'd developed the stubbornness of a donkey and the intuition of an escapologist. And these were essentially the two attributes that made me cultivate a passion for English as an instrument of self-affirmation and salvation. The more things turned grim, the more I cling on to English. For some time by now, I hadn't allowed anything to push me away from this passion, and to manage that, I'd strongly persuaded myself to believe that whenever bad luck struck it could only push me into a better direction – a direction which organically had to do with English. And the direction from then onwards was to obtain extra legal time in the UK by appealing to the Immigration and Asylum Chamber in the hope of overturning the refusal of my tier four Student Visa.

For this, I counted on the help of an Englishman. A man named Clifford.

5

"Sorry to interrupt ye." Clifford had attended the graduation ceremony and remained patiently by my side during the cocktail as Amy chatted away. Actually, Clifford had made me company throughout that entire postgraduate course – a period during which he offered me support and assistance. "The cocktail is lovely bu' ah 'av t' dash now." Clifford lightly touched his wrist watch to remind me that he still had to work that day.

"I'm coming with you." I turned to Amy as she picked her fifth guava cocktail. "Amy, success and happiness for you… for us actually, from now on."

"Oh, thank you." Amy had a warm smile. "B-bye then… and success."

I mouthed farewells to the classmates who I saw on the way out of the Union building, as I left the Terrace along with Clifford to pick up his vehicle, parked opposite Hyde Park, at Monument Moor.

"Mah angel was particularly gorgeous at t' ceremony." Clifford threw that comment almost casually, knowing that I'd be fully flattered.

Even though his words quite failed to convince me of the true intentions of that comment, I felt truly grateful. "Thanks. N' thank especially for being here. I'm way happier 'cause you managed to come today."

"Ah wouldn't miss it fur nowt." He emphasised and dropped into a silence which, I strongly suspected, would last for a good while.

After some metres, I knew how much longer that silence would last, and where it was going to lead. It was my obligation, then, to fill the silence and avoid that Clifford sudden change of mood spoiled the bliss of that occasion.

"I'm going to start today…" I made a brief pause just to choose my words a little more carefully. "…Writing, you know… With all this paper work, appealing to the Immigration office, and getting ready for the graduation ceremony, I managed to draft next to nothing on paper."

Still, no response from Clifford.

"You know all the things I believe. You know the whole thing. Just you being here this morning, as I see, is part of the *magic*. What you've just witnessed at the Great Hall was much more than just a graduation ceremony. It's much more meaningful. I mean, not even ten years ago, I had roughly £50 saved in the bank, no proper job, or any secure source of income whatsoever. Just imagining a moment like this would sound absurd a few years back. And I'm not saying only in terms of funding. Back then, all the English I knew came almost totally off a collection of course books and cassette tapes printed in the Eighties, and off the scarce hours of lessons offered at the State-funded school." I caught my breath for a second, trying to slow down my excitement. "I'm aware of the huge gap between the level of English I knew then, and the English I master now. You sure realise the shortcomings of my English. But, hear me, all English speakers, even native speakers, even the Queen herself, are continuously improving their own English; and there's always aspects of the language everyone still fails to master. I'm aware that I still got a lot to learn, but I'm also aware that I learned a lot; especially a lot about certain aspects of language that most natives, like you, ignore…"

Despite of that deliberate provocation, Clifford still kept his upper lip stiff. "…And I just graduated from a postgraduate course that helped me to understand further the workings underlying what I did to improve my English, to increase my vocabulary, to amplify my listening proficiency, to enhance my grasp of meaning, and to turn what was mostly stutter, poor pronunciation, n' crippled grammar into a fully fledged command of a language."

Clifford still kept quiet; but at least he didn't have that vague gaze of who isn't bothered. "There're certain things we must do, a pattern of behaviour and attitudes that, I believe, effectively accelerate an individual's real command of English. The level of my command of English now and what I managed to do with such level is undeniable evidence of the success of my English learning journey. And best of all: I now understand better the grounds of the success of my English learning journey and its link with the classic philosophy on the nature of language, and with the modern theories on language and on second language learning."

Quite hesitant, earnestly immersed into Clifford's blue eyes, I gathered the courage to add. "You also know well the things I believe regarding our reality. Listen, I'm reasonably sceptic about lots of things. But

I do want to write on how the grounds to learning a second language are somehow connected to certain principles that supposedly pervades our reality. You know... *Law of Attraction*, the thought that like attracts like; basically the principles of *faith* revisited by some American authors in the first half of the Twentieth century... Reality n' language seem to be engulfed by a principle that has to do with such *attraction*, and it isn't difficult to notice this idea in mainstream academic theory on linguistics and second language learning".

With an almost dying breath, I concluded. "And I want to share these ideas. I want others to understand them n' apply 'em to their own English learning goals."

Probably sensing my hardly contained despair for some sign of support, Clifford stopped abruptly. "Listen," he said firmly, making me turn, at an arm's length ahead of him. We were right at Hyde Park's entrance, just metres from the statue of Queen Victoria, who seemed to watch us from her pedestal, with a vigilant gaze of stone. "Ah believe in you." Clifford then gripped my lower jaw making me my eyes meet his unblinking stare. "Ah'm here to support you, whatever's that you have in mind."

"Thank you." I replied, almost sheepish.

Clifford then let go of my jaw and we crossed the Woodhouse Lane towards car park at Monument Moor.

To ease the tension, I added feigning indignation: "Listen, you're twice my size; your biceps must be what... 'bout sixteen inches? You know how strong was that grip on my jaw? I was about to yell *fire*!

Clifford – amused, and visibly smug – replied. "Shoo' oop."

6

After taking his time in the car hand-rolling a Golden Virginia, Clifford drove up toward Clarendon Rd. and stopped at the traffic lights at the top of University Road.

"Ah ye alright fur today mah angel?" Clifford said between two puffs on the Golden Virginia.

"I'm alright. You're coming tonight?"

"Ah'll let ye know as it goes." Clifford answered as I jumped off the vehicle swiftly before the traffic lights turned green.

Clifford, wouldn't turn up at night, I knew it. That's why he became silent all of a sudden soon as I expressed my happiness with his presence.

Don't lose it now. Keep on shinning.

From here, I walked through the university towards my flat, grinning blissfully, recalling the glory of hearing my name echoed in the Great Hall and already envisioning the prospect of becoming a published writer in English.

Yes, writing was an old aspiration and now I had a great story to tell. I'd set myself off to write about my journey learning English, and the wonderful things I'd learned along that journey. I wanted to write about my passion for English, a passion that justified my resolution to remain temporarily in the UK despite my visa situation.

And if I managed to succeed, as I believed within my heart, and if I managed to pull that off, as I'd done other times, that would prove one thing: when we pursuit to experience the full potential of a passion we can trigger the human mysterious power to make a desire to take form on the surface of the world.

Well, it was truth that, although pursuing my passion for English had given me a lot of success, things hadn't gone quite as I desired until here. Writing about my journey learning English had rumbled round my mind right after I started the Master at the University of Leeds, but the academic workload and the working schedule wouldn't allow much time for that.

Had I not been dismissed from work, a month of overtime would have helped me to afford a laptop with a modern Word processor as I'd planned. But my only source of income was gone and whoosh, up over and wham-o on my original thought. Nonetheless, if I really desired to become a published writer in English I still had within reach, on my flat, all the necessary tools to start off: paper and a ballpoint pen. Nothing could stop me now. So, determined to succeed, I wielded that pen like a sword, prepared to fight, and started to write for the sake of my dear life.

"Fuck!" I yawped, after realising that the ink cartridge in the pen had dried out.

7

In the days after that I went on wrestling with both my fortune and my literary abilities. And I'd honestly seen Turkish men greased in oil display more grace at Kirkpinar tournaments than me, as I struggled to write. Things didn't get any prettier every time Clifford turned up at night. He'd give me plenty excuses to keep procrastinating with my literary endeavour as I crossed off the calendar the final days of the Noughties.

At the end of each programme broadcast on BBC television and most Hollywood productions it is still marked in the Roman numerical system, MMIX. Everywhere else it is mostly printed in Arabic numerals, 2009. The last two letters, in the former, or digits, in the latter, is about to change because the year of two thousand and nine is coming to an end in the United Kingdom and every country where the days are based on the Christian calendar.

Along with the end of the year's celebrations, the last days of December brought temperatures below zero and heavy snow showers. The mouldy black of the rooftops, the red-bricks of the houses, the gray of the pavements, the cobblestone streets and the roads, the greenish of the trees, and proper green of the parks, pastures and the hills, all the variety of colours had faded out under the white spectrum of a sub-zero atmosphere and a thick layer of snow powder on the ground.

On the morning of Christmas Day, BBC One and BBC News showed images of the snow on the roof of the London Weather Centre. "This year in Britain, we officially have a White Christmas."

I watched the announcement in my *Matsui HD Ready* telly on the digital channel one while opening the presents Clifford had left two days before. Lindor chocolate truffles, Fox Wonders chocolate biscuits, Thinsulate gloves, George stripped jumper, Calvin Classic underwear, N-spa blueberry shower bath gel and raspberry body scrub, and an eau de toilette. As Clifford couldn't be with me during holidays, the *Freeview* channels kept me company. BBC Three showed countdown programmes like *Most annoying people of 2009* and the review of interesting facts of the decade called *The Noughties... was that it?* ITV Three showed the *On the buses* spin-off films, *The Best of Benny Hill*, and some *Carry On* spoofs. Channel Four showed countdown programmes under the title *The hundred greatest...* Four Music showed the last *Top Twenty* of the year.

On the thirty-first, most tv channels presented the *New Year's Eve Countdown* against the backdrop of the Big Bang, the London Eye and Buckingham Palace, with fireworks scattering a myriad of sparkling bright colours over the white falling snow and the dark of the night.

Before going to bed, as I usually did most nights since my arrival in England in 2007, I ended the day praying on my knees, asking for mercy, strength, faith, and glory.

When I was about to hit the pillow, the screen of my mobile phone flashed. *Clifford*.

"Appy new yea' mah angel."

"Appy new yea' babes…" I imitated Clifford's accent.

"'Ow a' ye this mo'ning?"

"I'm alright. What made you call?"

"Just to wish ye a good yea'." Clifford knew I could tell that he was lying. So, he got to business. "Lis'en… Ah can't stay long in t' mobile. I called to tell that today ah'll try n' get a temporary solution to yer job situation. I'm calling in soon as I can wi' another surprise for ye…"

"Oh, don't let me trying to guess it. I want to…" Before I had a chance to ask the line went dead.

8

2010 started with a fresh… no, chilling… actually, freezing New Year's Day in the UK. The newspapers around the country issued weather warnings: 2010 will bring along with January the longest cold snap of the last three decades, with temperatures plummeting up to minus eighteen degrees and up to almost eight inches of snow in some areas.

What a wonderful time to start writing. Flat seven at Six Springfield Mount in Leeds, the place where I lived since July, only had electrical heating, which would cost a fortune in electricity if I dared to turn it on. Also, a sub-zero temperature wasn't very helpful as I strived to keep one bare hand free to write whilst all wrapped in a duvet. Clifford had come to the rescue with an old fashioned, nonetheless efficient, personal computer that had Microsoft Office Word 97. Still, typing the keys of a keyboard using gloves slowed me down a little. I tried turning on a portable halogen heater. After a minute, instead of warming up, all it did was to make me feel like my face was ablaze.

Besides me everyone else seemed to be adapting themselves to the new struggles of the challenging weather. Papers' headlines brought in bold letters the word *whitemare*, reporting the consequences of the wave of snow. Major roads were closed, train services delayed or cancelled, and many airport runways were shut. Drivers were skidding and crashing their cars. Many were trapped while snow ploughs were battling to keep motorways and main roads open. On the icy street pavements and parks of the towns, adults and children alike were sledging, sliding, slipping, falling, snapping, and gashing. Hospital admissions had increased as a result of traffic accidents and injuries suffered by sledgers. The snow was even causing a headache for City Councils, as compensation claims flooded in citing their failure to grit pavements as the cause for a string of ice related injuries. The front page of *Metro* reported that, to keep warm during those arctic days, hard-up pensioners had resorted to large hardback books as efficient cheap slow-burning fuel substitutes for coal, which cost many times more per bag. It was relieving to know that others were solidary with me in such a bitter time.

The shivering weather drew so much attention that the media even referred to it with a specific name: *The Big Freeze*. It was a fresh new item of language which I learned totally from contextual experience, whilst immersed in a world pervaded with English.

In the years of my experience learning English as a second language, absorbing the meaning of new items without resorting to dictionaries, asking others, or making a wild guess, was something that I immensely appreciated. Naturally, as nothing is free these days, the price to absorb each item of English in such a precious manner was considerably dear. And so it was surrounded by the biting cold of the Big Freeze that I was about to plunge into a deeper and denser layer of English, where I'd have to haggle over the price of yet another word from English. *Valeting* is the word.

9

EWAN

On the morning of fourth of January, the first Monday of a new decade, a blizzard howled its way along the A19 on the route to Doncaster as the whiteout gained new momentum at the beginning of the year. An even thicker layer of fresh snowfall covered the fields stripping the green belt of the natural colour that gave it its name. That snowy landscape however gained mild tones of grey and blue when reflected in the hopeful eyes of Ewan as they absorbed that scenario from behind the windscreen of his Vauxhall Omega.

On the way to work, after the end of the year holidays, Ewan enjoyed the precious moments of warmth and comfort which the vehicle's heater provided. Already a little impatient with the weather he mentally repeated to himself his new year's resolution as a mantra to reinforce his determination to put in practice a plan to give his business a well deserved boost.

As the wind blew snow with more strength Ewan turned the windscreen wipers on to full power making them run more swiftly, wiping the snow off his field of vision with the same force that it hit the windscreen. From behind the wheel of his Vauxhall, at the simple command of a dashboard, Ewan let the weather have a piece of his strength, of his power and control over the world immediately around him, reassuring to himself that no Big Freeze out there was enough to dissuade him from his new year's resolution and that he was no less determined that morning than in New Year's Eve.

Just some nights before, at Ewan's house in Snaith, a New Year's Eve celebration was in full swing. Whilst Big Ben gazed out from the blaring television, counting down the remaining seconds of the Noughties, a bottle of champagne held aloft by unsteady hands swayed in time to its sonorous tolls. "Fourteen! Thirteen!" Those hands shared the same pale complexion, belonging, as they did, to Ewan's relatives.

Ewan stood close by, observing, detached, unable to share in the excitement of his extended family. Their expression of happiness and thankfulness for another year lived in the good grace of the Lord was at odds with Ewan's pessimistic view of what the Noughties had brought to the lives of himself, his family, and by extension to the people of England itself.

Distant popping sounds drifted in through a half open window; their pre-emptive flashes smeared against its misted pane. "Twelve! Eleven!" As everyone counted down the final seconds of the year with gusto, Ewan only half noticed lost in a glum recollection of the passing decade.

"Six!" Ewan's sense of patriotism had been undermined by the scandalous news printed in the daily papers. He wondered how much of the country's tax revenue was selfishly misused by high profile hustlers hidden within Whitehall and its far-flung outposts. Thinking of the effects these facts had on people's values countrywide revolted Ewan. A turn of the page of the *Daily Mail* revealed how the outbreak of corruption was spreading across the population. The number of Britons currently living off state handouts surpassed the 5 million mark. More than a million had lived on benefits for more than 12 years and almost 2 million for 7 years. The latest occupation of British youth was parenting. The country was welcoming a second generation of idlers. A generation being rewarded to do little but scratch their arses, procreate, and with a little bit of luck enjoy fifteen minutes of fame, under the limelight with Trisha Goddard or whilst facing Jeremy Kyle's moral bashing. A generation without role models, neither parents nor government, to light the way.

"Five!" Shame wasn't the only damage that a generation of bums had wrought on Ewan's country. A worse effect was both inevitable and evident in the complexion and language of the people: the soaring immigration of the last years had literally changed the face of Britain. As the English people received incentives to stay at home sitting on their backsides, immigrants filled the job market and kept the country moving on but not without an unconsidered price to British society. In Ewan's daily routine hearing a clear, proper British accent of English was fast dying out.

"Four!" Ewan's view was that this trend would continue unabated if the country relied on its government for intervention. Since UK's integration to the European Community and its consequent open borders policy the whole European populace seemed to be flooding onto English soil. The situation would grow direr as the European Union constantly incorporated new, often poorer, countries. Ewan knew that being part of the EEC was economically necessary and brought some advantages to Britain; but he was sure also that at some point, unchecked, it'd have negative consequences. Perhaps his pride in his country clouded his judgement, but still he couldn't shake the certainty that accepting all the rules handed down by Europe was wrong. If the government didn't impose limits to the trade it surely sent a clear signal that England needed the European Union far more than they needed England to expand their effective base of power. Ewan also feared the possibility of conversion to the Euro currency, which would doubtlessly involve a devaluation of sterling.

"Three!" When reading about the non-European immigrants, Ewan could barely contain his frustration. Was he, an Englishman born and bred, soon to become part of an ethnic minority in the country that his family had called theirs for generations? Could he blame and condemn an individual who immigrated looking for happiness? After all, many of his customers were of an obvious overseas origin and thus he derived a good part of his income from them.

"Two!" What really irked Ewan was that more and more he was getting used to hearing people speaking languages other than English with each other right to his face. Some of his customers would rudely switch from English when not addressing him directly. As a customer himself in the cafés, pizzerias, shops, and local groceries, he came across staff who displayed this same behaviour with no regard as to whom they served. Were it restricted to certain particular immigrant residential areas, he'd just ignore. Yet, for some,

10

"Ten!" Downing Street. Prime Minister Tony Blair and Gordon Brown. The two successive leaders of the Labour Party, the political party in power for almost thirteen years, still yet to garner a single vote from Ewan or any member of his family. Ewan's fears concerning the Labour Party's rise to power in the 1997 General Election had proved to be well founded.

"Nine!" What a wretched year that was. A perfect conclusion to, and summary of, everything that went wrong in a decade of Labour government. A year that brought a revelation to Ewan: the party he so fervently supported, the Conservative (Tory), had proved that it shared in some respects the same disappointing nature as the Labour. Many Conservative Members of Parliament found themselves involved in the infamous MPs parliamentary expenses scandal back in May when the *Daily Telegraph* denounced MPs for abusing the lax expenses system from which they, mainly within the rules, claimed public funds to pay for an alarming catalogue of private, in some cases very personal, items. The sordid list of questionable claims ranged far and wide, all at the British taxpayers' expense: second housing allowance, council tax, phantom mortgages, housekeeping, repairing, refurbishing, furnishing, gardening, pool cleaning, moat dredging, life insurance premiums, personal services, personal accountancy, private babysitters, professional photo shoots, tv licences, *Sky Sports*, *Sky Movies*, *Adult Channel*, *Television X*, DVD players, flat-screen tvs, massage chairs, toilet seats, kitchen sinks, washing machines, electrical equipment, coal, fireplaces, heaters, light bulbs, restaurant meals, *Kit-Kat*, *Jaffa Cakes*, manure.

"Eight!" Anger. Ewan remembered the times that, over a pint of *Guinness* at the local pub, he'd debated with his pals how Labour gave parliament a bad name, how the Conservatives would've done a much better job. He'd backed the Tories to the hilt, and now felt a fool. Labour and Tory MPs were equally involved in the expenses debauchery. He felt betrayed, thinking how he worked 12 hours, sometimes more, Monday to Saturday, to live a life not of luxury but of make do and mend, as he got by on a mix of prudence and DIY. His sole luxury was health insurance, though this was in truth to avoid the possibility of any long and costly period off work on some endless NHS waiting list. All this whilst the political elite lived it up on taxes taken from his hard earned pay pocket.

"Seven!" While only a few MPs were threatened with prosecution, he could face court proceedings if he refused to pay the compulsory £145 yearly tax for owning a telly. At least the licence fee gave him quality tv. For him, quality tv, for the BBC executives, quality lifestyle. The *Daily Mail*'s facts and figures regarding the BBC only added insult to Ewan's injured taxpayer's pride. 5 of the 10 biggest pensions in the public sector belonged to BBC executives. 47 of the BBC's top executives were paid more than the Prime Minister. Lavish receptions and massive parties with six figure budgets were sponsored by the tv licence. Hundreds of jobs were axed and programme budgets were squeezed in the recession of 2008 but the 17.5 million paid in bonuses remained untouched. The BBC staff even managed their own mini expenses scandal, claiming for swanky dinners in Las Vegas, innumerable restaurant lunches, vintage champagne, luxury cakes, bouquets, private transportation. No wonder the expenses scandal was exposed by an independent newspaper rather than by the independent journalism of the BBC.

English seemed to be a minor inconvenience, to be articulated only when absolutely necessary. Ewan was also frustrated to observe how some immigrants, purposely spoke, behaved, and dressed in such a manner as to make a statement of their ethnical difference; they should be worshipping the culture and traditions of the country that provides them with opportunities and social dignity. Why on earth they showed pride for the culture and traditions of a land they very likely fled from?

"One!" Whilst beggars pestering passers-by for a change had become a common sight in the city centre it struck Ewan that none of them appeared to be foreign. He grew angry with the realisation that whilst the richness of his land appealed to a world abroad many English folks didn't seem to understand the potential that such richness offered for their personal prosperity. Long ago whilst studying for his GCSEs Ewan learned during a History lesson that, in the five hundreds, invaders referred to the native Celts or Britons as *Wealas* which means *slaves* or *foreigners*. It felt odd that at what was to become the first second of 2010, under a corrupt government and the prospective of becoming the social odd, the word *Wealas* seemed so appropriate to explain how Ewan felt about himself.

Pop! The blast provoked by the pressure from within the champagne bottle combined with the cheering of Ewan's relatives startled him out of his gloomy trance. If he didn't think of something soon to give a better direction to his fate as an Englishman in that social context, he could end up, in the not too distant future, being pushed to the bottom of his own society, paying taxes to support social idlers, whilst also being overshadowed by the immigrant newcomers. He vowed not to let that happen, no matter the cost. That was to be his new year's resolution.

11

And that resolution gained further tangible form within Ewan's thoughts, just like the white fizzy bubbles of the champagne morphed into the icy flakes which now – as the New Year's Eve faded to but a memory – settled on Ewan's waterproof steel-toe boots when he stepped out of his Vauxhall Omega.

Ewan didn't know where to start from exactly to make the business grow but he knew that he needed extra help because soon there would be extra work to do and he'd be even busier than usual.

Coincidentally, on New Year's Day, one of Ewan's nephews had rung asking if he might be able to find a job for a lad he knew.

"Bring t' lad wi' you Monday morning. He can start straight away, we'll see 'ow 'e do" was Ewan's answer.

And so his nephew duly delivered the fine young lad who despite having an obvious foreign accent could speak reasonably clear, and obviously educated, English.

Though immediately curious about the lad's origins Ewan preferred not to start drilling the newcomer with personal questions right away.

And so day's work began. Ewan grabbed an empty black gallon bucket, handed it to the lad and told him to half fill it with water then asked "Have you experience in valeting?"

12

Just off Wheatley Hall Road, towards the end of Whittington Industrial Estate, in Doncaster, a number of warehouse units housed second hand vehicles waiting to be repaired and prepared by the various tradesmen therein. Throughout the day the dusty potholed wasteland in front of these units – covered in snow at that time – is used both as a parking lot for the vehicles awaiting work and as a sales pitch.

The vehicles facing Unit twenty, all due to be advertised that week, formed two neat rows of six in total and belonged to Bodyshop UK. Those vehicles varied in shape size and colour; nevertheless all shared an unloved sheen. Years of acidic rain and bleaching sun had dulled once gleaming paintwork and played havoc with rubber and plastic trims. Layer upon layer of road grime left untouched by their previous owners did little to improve matters. Orange blooms of rust, the odd dent, and some signs of long forgotten vandalism competed for attention on that sorry collection. Within the next hours, these sad looking vehicles should come to resemble the "high quality pre-owned vehicles", which the already written adverts laid claim to. Quite how, I had no idea. All I knew was that starting from the first week of the new decade, when I began working for a local tradesman named Ewan, the responsibility to get those vehicles pristine clean would be mine.

"Aye oop, cock! 'ow are we this morning?" Ewan greeted me with those ritual words, as he did every morning when I arrived in Whittington Street.

He approached me with a tone of enthusiasm which didn't match my response. Not that I wasn't excited about working at his garage.

On the contrary; every time Ewan uttered "Ready to crack on with the lasses!" – with his hoarse voice quality that seemed to be produced entirely with the back of his throat – just listening to his English gave me chills that made the thin hair on my forearm completely erect.

The problem was that Ewan's English contrasted so much with my English that, no matter how much attention and effort I put on my articulation and intonation in those first days, when I opened my mouth to respond I sounded like an alien that had just learned a few words of English.

"I am… ready." I replied, out of tune, quietly cursing myself because I definitely could sound much better than that. And if that wasn't enough to shake my linguistic self-confidence, still there were Ewan's official instructions.

"Got that?" Ewan always finished his instructions with those two confirming syllables, which sounded more like *go' a'*, and immediately moved away to "crack on" with something else. During Ewan's instructions in those initial mornings I spent half of the time admiring the different words he used to express himself and how naturally he articulated all those glottal sounds; the other half of the time I tried to guess what on earth Ewan was telling me to do exactly.

Ewan came from a family that had lived in the civil parish of Snaith and Cowick for generations; a common occurrence in the area. The lack of populace movement around those areas had distilled the local dialect to a virtual sublanguage all its own, a dialect Ewan spoke fluently and, to make matters worse for me, quickly. After years of ceaseless effort learning English, I believed to possess a comprehensive knowledge of vocabulary. The moment Ewan uttered the simplest task he obliged me to face my linguistic Waterloo.

"Start 'oovering the Daihatsu Terios afor' owt." Ewan said, pointing at an industrial Hoover at the back of the Unit twenty.

As Ewan swiftly shifted away, I swear that, despite being covered by layers of flesh, tissue, and clothing, I could hear each bone of my body rattling.

13

Day one at the Bodyshop UK, I had to rely mostly on Ewan's body language to follow his instructions. Fortunately, two years working in Leeds train station – where one can hear accents from all over the country, though with a bias towards Yorkshire – had bestowed to my auditory skills a kind of fine tuning to the way the vowel sounds were pronounced in other areas. So, after an initial period of bewilderment, with a little concentration and a couple of "beg your pardon", I adjusted my ear canal to Ewan's accent and began to grasp the odd word he barked at me above the industrial noise prevalent in the area. But that was just the prologue.

The real challenge commenced when Ewan assumed – probably misled by my polite and phonetically mechanical responses to his questions – that he could refer to any vehicles parked in front of Unit twenty using their brand names, then issue a list of commands in what could be described as tradespeak, and expect that I'd immediately jump to it.

"Dahiatsu what…?" I mumbled to myself.

Apart from the lovely Mini Coopers – the type Hugh Grant drives in the opening sequence of *Four Weddings and a Funeral*, or more famously, those used in the getaway sequence of *The Italian Job* – all vehicles looked the same to me; different shapes, sizes and colours but all just vehicles. Never had the concept of hyponym made so much sense as an aspect underlying and shaping the way language is used.

That would bring me back to the Roger Stevens Lecture Theatre at the University of Leeds – week four of the undergraduate module *Language, Text and Context*, the first time I came across with concept of hyponymy.

"Hyponym refers to a lexeme of more specific meaning…" It was Dr Gupta, full name Anthea Fraser Gupta, with her very English manners, and her highly educated Northern English accent, who presented the concept of hyponym to a half excited half anxious audience of both British and Overseas students. "…Hyponym is actually a lesser known term used to describe sense relationships between words – like synonym or antonym."

In the blur of my memory, Dr Gupta proceeded with the lecture explaining how the concept of hyponym applied to my current pickle trying to pick which vehicle in the Unit twenty I was supposed to hoover.

"The term synonym refers to words related to another by a similarity of meaning – like *vehicle, car,* or *automobile*. The term hyponym refers to words related to another (more broad, categorical word) by a specificity of meaning. So, instead of using the general word *vehicle*, a person may use the hyponyms *cabriolet, convertible, coupe, estate,* or *station wagon, hatchback, roadster, saloon,* or *sedan* in other English speaking areas other than UK, or yet more specifically *Omega, Ford Ka, Laguna, Peugeot, Seicento*."

As the topic of a lecture on Semantics, *hyponymy* was just another item of the linguistic terminology. In the academic environment back then, the term *hyponym* felt so distant to practical life, almost meaningless or useless outside the linguistic lingo. At the garage, faced with a choice of twelve different vehicles (simply cars from now) and just one hot hyponym to choose from, it had an epiphanic importance to me.

Before resorting to Ewan's help, I gazed around the parking lot hoping to identify the Daihatsu. In the front row, all I could see was a green car with sharp edges and colour coded bumpers, a blue car with rounded blunt edges, another green one with even more rounded edges, a really round and smooth light blue car, another one blue just slightly taller but with square edges, and another one black also square yet taller with large wheels. Had Ewan used those adjectives, taught at elementary levels of English, he'd have greatly helped me to identify any car. However, such a descriptive, non-economical, use of language would be bizarre to Ewan because, as an experienced tradesman, he conceived those cars as completely distinct entities, which he acknowledged using single identifying hyponyms.

"Oh, simples; tha's a Hyundai Accent, a Peugeot 206, an Alfa Romeo, a Fiat Brava, a Volkswagen Golf, and yer babe, the Daihatsu Terios". Incredibly, when I eventually gathered courage to ask "which of those cars were the Dahiatso", Ewan listed those names without pointing or nodding, as if to intentionally confuse me as to which direction, left or right, he was referring to.

Noticing the chaff on Ewan's expression, I took a light breath to dissimulate my impatience, and humbly murmured: "Can you say the plate number, please?"

14

And just like that, I began a crash course in what to me felt like a whole new English: the English of the Bodyshop UK.

That very specific English labelled every little thing within, and adjacent to, the world of the garage; a world of English that Ewan introduced me to whilst I followed him through his instructions like Alice followed the White Rabbit – except that I ended up falling down to an intricate labyrinth of hyponyms related to cars, body parts, tools, tasks, and tricks. With few exceptions, there seemed to be not one thing in the garage with a name that I'd heard before, yet Ewan referred to each single item in sight using a specific identifying word. And each new word Ewan used would immediately lead to another range of vocabulary that referred to items and actions within the garage routine. This is how I came to learn that the meaning of *valet*, which is defined with a seven word entry in the *Concise Oxford English Dictionary*, becomes considerably more complex in the real world.

"...'fore we get this totty wet, first off y'll need to giy it a strong 'oover out."

The beginning of the valeting process started with the Hoover, I already knew that. Ewan himself had formally introduced me to this word before the Daihatsu.

"What's an *'oovah*?" I asked, when Ewan first told me to fetch one for him.

"'Oover... vacuum cleaner. Never 'eard that b'for? The'..." Ewan pointed to the Hoover at the back of the Unit twenty. And as I went to retrieve it, Ewan continued. "'Oover's a tradema'k of vacuum cleaner. It's named after t' American manufacturer William H. Hoover."

Surprisingly to me, Ewan coughed up the initial '*h*' sound of the name American's name. Unsurprisingly however, Ewan, like most Englishman I've ever met, talked like he'd learned by heart the whole of ten volumes of *The British Encyclopaedia*.

The Hoover in the Unit twenty was a Henry – with a smile and funny eyes printed on its body and the nozzle in place of a nose. I already had this Hoover in hands for the Daihatsu, ready to follow Ewan's directions, which he, wasting no time, kept shooting.

"Driver n' passenger carpets, t' upholstery, seats n' dashboard. Don' forge' hatch an' boot. Use t' vac 'n a brush to do t' dash." Ewan meant business this time, pointing and touching at every command of his instruction, and confirming with his *go' a'* before saying *crack on* and leaving me inside the Unit twenty.

He returned a minute after I'd turned the Hoover off. "Now, y'll need a bucket three quarters full o' wa'er; chuck in a glug of TFR (traffic film remover) an' 'bout three or four capfuls of finish (*finish* is a cleaning chemical tagged *Brisk Extra*). Then, dip a piece o' rag, like this," – Ewan dipped his bare hand in the cold solution, under a temperature alternating around zero degree, without a single twitch on his face. As for me, Clifford had provided me protective rubber gloves. – "an' wet the upholstery sections nearest you; say, on driver's side n' seat. Scrub it with a brush... this one's best" – he threw a blue brush with short stiff bristles towards me as I kneeled by the door opposite to him, next to the driver's seat – "to get ' muck off well. Do t' same to carpets n' floors. An' don't forget t' boot." Before leaving again, Ewan reminded me: "If the wheel an' dashboard is too mucky, wet n' scrub'em. An' after scrubbin' each section, vac'em straight back off t' get rid o' t' suds." Then, he came back for the last time before I finished. "See 'ow t' roof lining is mucky? Grab a dry rag, soak it wi' thinners an' wipe. Giy it a good rub over, till it get anything out. Once y've wet clean'd it, leave it dry a bit, so y' can come n' gerra wa'm in t' office – it's a bit bloody freezing today – an' ah'll come n' 'ave a look ow' you'v done."

When not instructing me, Ewan constantly alternated between *bloody* and *fucking* to warm his blood up. Unlike him, I wasn't proficient in English enough to ward off pain and cold through the use of taboo language, so I was really glad to have a chance to warm up for some time in the office.

To reach the office I had to waddle through a thick blanket of newly fallen snow that turned the irregular ground of Whittington Industrial Estate into a smooth surface. Behind me, I left a trail of hardware boot prints deeply etched in the snow across the parking lot all the way to Unit eighteen, where the office was located. Unit eighteen was larger than Unit twenty and was used to store most of the cars at night. The office had a small fan heater – that made it really cosy – and was situated right at the back of Unit eighteen – what kept the snow out of sight. Ewan left me alone there for a while and I almost forgot all about the cold burden of the Big Freeze.

The warmth of the office even helped me to engage in a more positive thinking. *Valeting in the cold isn't all that tough if I can have warm breaks.*

But, as if the Big Freeze wanted to make sure I'd never dared to disregard its bigness, when I returned to Unit twenty again, it manifested its presence through a fresh blast of snow.

"*Oh eM Jee.* Please my Lord, tell me Ewan is being funny right now." I murmured in cold shock.

Maybe it was just snowflakes hitting my face, or I had frozen tears running down my cheeks. Whatever that was, I really hoped that the falling snow was deceiving my senses: The Daihatsu that I had to continue valeting was now parked in front of Unit twenty, already accumulating a layer of snow on its roof.

15

"Are'y' reet?!" Ewan half spoke half grunted, midway through lifting a large container of thinner and carrying it to the back of the garage, visibly proud of showing off his vigour.

I just nodded my head, not really knowing if he'd made a question or affirmed something about me.

Are'y' reet not even close sounded to my ears the *Are you all right* from *Standard English* – the English that one learns in the formal courses of English as a 2nd language. The most colloquial expressions Ewan used would still remain a mystery to me for some time. But at that moment, I knew whatever I didn't understand with the power of my once thought to be *advanced* English, I'd understand with the urgency of the situation. And Ewan would wait nothing – or should I say *nowt* – when he noticed the word *clueless* all over my beautiful mug.

"Now it's clean, we'll mek it look good." He started again, coming along with me towards the Daihatsu he'd reversed and parked outside, at the entrance ramp of the unit. Ewan then rubbed his hands, handed me a piece of fabric, and continued: "Use a clean dry rag t' apply bumper gel or vinyl shield o'er t' wheel, dashboard, an' any other plastic, rubber, or leather upholstery sections to mak'em shine n' wa'erproof." – I imitated his procedure. – "Done tha', crack on wi' the outside o' the body. Spray *Smart Wheels* (acid free wheel cleaner) on t' alloys; leave it for a bit so it eat through t' rust be'er. B'fore y' jet'em off, go over'em wi' this brush. Watch yeself wi' tha' stuff tho, if yer gerr't on yer skin it'll sting like buggery. If t' rust is stubborn an' thes owt left use wheel acid, an' it'll get rid of owt tha's left."

Concentrated as I was, squatting down to the wheel level to brush well the inner parts of the alloys, I hardly noticed Ewan had paused his coaching and had gone back inside the unit. For a brief while, as the noise from other units died down, I enjoyed a momentary stillness contemplating how beautifully the white snowflakes contrasted with the black paintwork of the Daihatsu. That stillness changed into a thrill when I raised my head and saw Ewan standing a little further opposite me, feet slightly apart to keep balance on that slippery ground, pointing a sub-machine gun-like nozzle on my face whilst the snow swirled smoothly around him.

"Move or ah squirt?" Ewan said with a devil smirk, twitching his forefinger threateningly in the trigger assembly of what was actually the lance of a pressure washer. "'ave used one o' this b'fore?"

"Ever" I replied with an affected accent that I judged to be witty.

"So 'av a bash then." Ewan said handing me the gun together with a large yellow sponge. "First jet t' sponge off to ge' any grit off, not t' scratch the paint when y' rub it over. Then, keep t' nozzle three feet from the paintwork." – As he realised I hadn't the slightest notion of distance in foot Ewan grabbed the nozzle and gently pushed the gun, and me with it, to the right distance. – "Y' do too close, y'll rip the painwork. We don't wan' tha'. Now, press t' gun n' giy it a jet off to ge' rid o' t' worst of it." Ewan's commands worked in conjunction with his hand motions which functioned as if he was pulling invisible strings attached to me. "Now, giv' us t' sponge, pour some *Duet* on it." He poured the car shampoo on the sponge as I held it towards him. "An' give the car a good rub down all over n' jet it off agin straigh' away or y'll end up wi' suds marks." This time Ewan handed me a plastic wiper. "Finish with a blade off, then leave it dry a bit."

Whilst I wiped the water with the blade, Ewan vanished again. When he returned he brought with him a large portion of chips wrapped in a brown paper. "Come 'ave a wa'am agin. I go' this from t' chippy fur'oos." He said and marched firmly off towards Unit eighteen.

But just before Ewan disappeared into the unit, he shouted back: "Ah still have a bone to pick up wi' ye. 'Bout yer nacionality…"

16

The valeting process wasn't completed yet, as I'd learn later. At least, the wet procedure was over. Valeting under low temperatures was pretty harsh at first, but Ewan's gentleness and patience made the working routine more bearable. And because Ewan was so kind, it was hard not to tell him where I'd come from originally the first time that he couldn't really restrain his curiosity – he'd been warned that I was rather reserved on that issue from day one, when Clifford introduced me to him. Soon after the *Daihatsu*, when Ewan brought that issue bluntly but – seeing me so reticent – didn't really insist on it, he tried a more subtle approach.

"I bet Fiat Seicento is common in yer country, right?" Ewan asked, patting the snow covered roof of the messy car I was about to start valeting.

"I don't know." I answered honestly.

"Seicento, Italian. It's quite common in I'ly, huh?" He continued with a straight face.

"Oh, you know I'm horrible with car names." I told a bit edgy, feeling the inevitable question approaching.

"But, y're from I'ly, right?" Ewan finally dropped the question.

"Oh God," I mumbled, thinking what to say. "I'm not... comfortable about that. I mean, to talk about that, if you don't mind." I said, almost begging for him to excuse and understand me.

"Go on tell us. Ah won't tell anyone, cross me 'art". He insisted, tracing an x with his little finger on the left side of his chest.

"I don't mean to..." – I started excusing myself, choosing carefully my words – "...disrespect your authority," Then I tried to actually make him understand my reasons. "But it's that I prefer not to talk about this subject because I believe that if no one associate me with a foreign country, people will think of me less as a foreigner, and I'll be less conscious about being a foreigner, and this generates a beneficial effect on my English proficiency."

After listening to my explanation Ewan pulled a puzzled expression and started saying, "Wha' ye focking on...?" And then, as he promptly realised that I was serious about that, he burst into a big laughter and said: "Oh, yo're crackers n' the 'ead, you are. Me missus won' believe when ah tell'er. Oh!" Then he trod off towards Unit eighteen, leaving me to question why I insisted in putting myself through that whole situation.

Despite the awkwardness, quick exchanges like that with Ewan felt incredibly enticing to me. And during those initial days that was pretty much how I felt about everything else within the world of the garage. I felt blessed and blissful for being there, overindulging in the language experience that the garage routine afforded. At times, as I struggled through the valeting routine, I grew dejected and frustrated with the cold weather.

The virtually ceaseless swirling snowfall which accompanied my daily toil kept falling on throughout January.

The Big Freeze imposed a few breaks amid the wet procedure of the valeting routine when either the hoover's nozzle froze up and blocked as I vacuumed water from the cars' interior or when the water sprayed at the bodywork formed a sheet of ice as it landed on the cold metal. Either way, I had to go inside to defrost the equipment and, as a happy by product, my numb hands. In order to keep my hands warm longer during the wet procedure I had the idea to use a woolly glove underneath the rubber ones – all it did was to tighten the blood circulation and cause my hands to go numb faster. Then, when my hands went painfully numb and my thoughts turned as bitter and bleak as that wintry weather, I raised my head, gazed at the falling snow, and remembered that just a decade ago, under the tropical climate of the Brazilian Northeast, wishful to experience what snow felt like, I used to scrape frost from inside the freezer, throw the frost upwards, and wait underneath for it to fall.

Back in that time, just as my experience with snow was reduced to a millisecond cascade of melting frost, so too my experience with English was reduced to that English available on tv networks. At least, cable and satellite tv offered plenty options of shows with their original English soundtrack. Unluckily for me, cable had yet to reach the neighbourhood where I dwelt, and satellite was a luxury that my parents couldn't afford. So, adding to the category of unaffordable luxury video cassette recorder and television with SAP, the actual alternative left for me was open television. And open television broadcast scarce alternatives of non-dubbed programmes: a black and white film that the main network showed on Sundays at 2 a.m., two *South Park* episodes that *MTV* showed on Saturdays at 12 p.m., and two *The Addams Family* episodes that *Record* network showed on Tuesdays around 3 a.m.

At such odd hours, a bleeping bedside alarm clock would wake me up so that I could record the audio track of *South Park* and *The Addams Family* using an audio cassette recorder connected to the tv – an 80's technology legacy. I usually lingered snoozing by the recorder to flip the cassette, which only recorded twenty-three minutes per side, so as not to miss the following episode. At that stage I'd gained elementary proficiency in English through reading a twelve-book course and listening to four cassette tapes which accompanied the books. So, after revising the twelve books in all combination sequences possible and having learnt the sentences from the cassette tapes by heart, moving on to listening to the English from those programmes certainly characterised a progress on my language learning journey. And I listened to those audio recording from the moment I got up, many and many times throughout the day, to the moment I got myself tucked into bed again. I listened to some episodes again and again, flipping the cassette over and over, praying for Saturday and Tuesday to come so there would be new material to listen to. I did that for months, in the belief that if I heard English throughout the day persistently my brain would become attuned to English as the tongue from my daily routine, and not as some distant foreign language.

Holding tightly to the memory of the initial miles of that journey learning English helped to pound life back into my numb hands and to sweeten and brighten up my thoughts during the many valeting sessions, amid that insistent falling snow. And that memory approach greatly improved my confidence that morning whilst I valeted the Fiat Seicento, making me go from a state of anxiety and gloom to a sudden burst of joy.

"Yes." I repeated to myself. "I am on the right track."

This is my yellow brick road, and I'm off to meet the Wizard, I thought, reminding myself that I'd gasped for that scarce and artificial English before and now I could breathe abundant and genuine English along with the fresh air of the Big Freeze. "I'm on the right way. If ever a wonderful way there was, that wonderful way was the one *b'cos, b'cos, b'cos, b'cos, b'cos, b'cos...*"

"Ye like singin' then." Ewan suddenly appeared behind the Seicento and caught me half murmuring half singing my thoughts aloud. "Is it benefecial t' yer English?" He emphasised the word *beneficial* with a pretentious intonation, probably giving me a hint which I quite didn't grasp immediately. He then laughed and again entered the Unit twenty.

"No. I like singing just to improve my mood a bit."

"Ah know wot ye mean. Foocking weather crawl up inside oos."

"You say *fuck*. I say *follow the yellow brick road*." I tried to sound fancy.

"Ye like t' *Wizard* then." Ewan's intonation blurred the line between question and statement. Then, without warning, he dropped it. "N' all that magic bullcrap."

"I like the film, yes. And I believe real life is a bit magic sometimes."

"Ye want magic, do it thee-sen... by workin' 'ard, ah say." Ewan laughed and again entered the unit.

After getting a little more used to Ewan I began to laugh along with him. At times sadness would strike when I allowed my thoughts to rumble around the visa situation and the fact that I was working illegally. Then I'd bring myself to remember that thanks to my visa situation I had that opportunity to be at Whittington Street undergoing an experience that reinvigorated my English. And indeed, that experience under the Big Freeze refreshed the parts of my English other academic experiences couldn't reach.

17

"How is mah angel this morning?" greeted Clifford, who had been waiting for me inside his car, parked in the short-stay parking at the entrance of Wakefield Westgate station.

"I'm alright," I replied handing to him a medium white filter coffee and chocolate chip shortcake that I'd just bought from the Pumpkin Café inside the station.

"Ta." Clifford thanked midway through gobbling the shortcake up.

After washing the shortcake down with two big gulps of the filter coffee, Clifford started the ignition, drove off the short-stay park, turned left on to Westgate End, and continued towards the M-one. That was the first leg of a forty-minute ride on the road to Doncaster – a daily ride that Clifford gave me since he first introduced me to work with Ewan in the Bodyshop UK, and that had become an essential part of a new morning routine commuting from Leeds to Doncaster.

Like all aspects related to that new morning routine, I found it quite stimulating and easy to adjust myself to. Having to wake up at a quarter to seven in the morning gave me a chance to become acquainted with *The Basil Brush Show*, which started just after seven on the CBBC channel, and that I watched while getting dressed and having a cuppa. Then, I'd proceed down to Leeds City station – trying out some amateur slides along the accumulating snow on the pavement – to catch the seven fifty-one Northern Rail train to Blackpool North. After queuing shortly to purchase a one-way ticket to Wakefield Westgate, I'd pick up a free copy of the *Metro* paper before crossing through the electronic gates.

During the ride to Doncaster I had a chance to discuss the newspaper's articles with Clifford, who generally enlightened me regarding the meaning of some words that were new to me.

"Oh, here is one: *Def jam*... what that means?" I asked holding the paper upright.

"Def jam what?" Clifford replied, taking his eyes momentarily off the road and peeking at the paper in my hands.

"It's not here. I heard it yesterday on ITV, an' just remembered. It was *def jam comedy* something and there..." I interrupted my words, noticing that Clifford had began to hand-roll the second Golden Virginia of that morning whilst doing around 60 miles in the snow covered M-one – a stunt that he did holding the wheel with his thighs.

"Oh, you know you make me nervous doing this. Wait till we get to a station." I suggested, a little hesitant, afraid to be giving further reason for him to show off his driving stunts.

"...Def jam comedy, summat to do with black culture. Black comedians, I reckon." Clifford mumbled with a light smirk, jamming his foot on the accelerator.

"I know you can drive, please don't." I appealed to his good sense, a bit confuse with the words, feeling my heart beginning to race faster as the speedometer pointer reached seventy. "Please stop doing this Clifford."

"Doing what...?" He continued, pretending to ignore the cause of my apprehension, but reducing the speed immediately after my appeal.

"I'm not amused." I said, using a tone of disappointment that certainly didn't convince him – as I could tell just by observing the manner he flicked the lighter on to light the hand-rolled cigarette which he now squeezed on the lips with a smug expression.

"Fear not my angel, the road is gritted." Clifford said through his teeth, which he kept clenched to hold the cigarette firmly in the right corner of his mouth.

Though the cause for apprehension had passed, my heart continued racing as I gazed at the way Clifford blew the smoke slowly upwards. He knew that, even though I feigned anger, his provoking behaviour thrilled me. Indeed, for me, being with Clifford by my side on a daily basis on that road to Doncaster was adventurous like in the films of Bing Crosby and Bob Hope, only with no women involved and no singing number. I enjoyed admiring the snow along the M-one and chatting playfully with Clifford all the way to Whittington Street. But our double act didn't always end when we arrived there.

"Do you have any valeting work to begin this morning?" Clifford asked as soon as he pulled into Whittington Street.

"Not that I know." I replied as Clifford started hand-rolling the third Golden Virginia of that morning.

"So, go and check with Ewan, 'cause you're staying with me today." Clifford said in his usual calm tone, and started licking a king size blue Rizla leisurely.

18

Clifford worked on a much smaller unit next to Ewan's. He usually had two or three cars advertised on line, but the main source of his income came from the painting and body work he did for other local traders – chiefly Ewan. Since the beginning, Ewan had assigned me to helped Clifford out on the paint side of the garage work, untangling the airline, masking up, cleaning the paint gun with thinner, flatting the primer, covering the car to be painted with masking film, flatting the paint, and other minor tasks which generally involved cleaning and organising. Clifford also guided me through other activities of the garage routine as necessary. Still, my number one priority was valeting.

In the start of that morning, I left Clifford enjoying the warmth of the car and sauntered on the snow covered ground towards Unit twenty – wishing I had another jumper on – to confirm with Ewan if there was any urgent valeting to do. When I appeared at the unit Ewan was warming up his hands in front of a small fan heater.

"Aye oop." Ewan greeted me when I appeared at the unit, sounding less cheerful than usual. "I'm feelin' a bi' poorly. I belled Cliff fur 'im t' be in charge t'day."

"Alright." I responded and continued listening.

"Ah 'aven' gone wi' you through t' proper finish bi' ye'. Tell'im to show you 'ow t' do it. Ah'll stay in t' office if ye need." He said and continued grumbling – "Foocking cold, foocking cold weather." – as he trudged off to Unit eighteen, barely lifting his feet.

Soon after Ewan entered into Unit eighteen, Clifford turned up at the Unit twenty still puffing some smoke clouds. "So, the boss isn't well, huh. Wot did 'e tell?"

"He said you'd be in charge." – Clifford nodded his head indicating that he already knew that – "And that you should show me how to do the finish bit. What finish bit? We've done that."

Clifford opened a roguish smile, as he did sometimes after I said something but he wouldn't tell me why. "Rubber dressing and polish – it's the last bit of work you do when you valet. Ewan likes doing this last bi' 'imself. Ah'll show you, don't worry."

I wanted to ask Clifford why he'd smiled, but as soon as he flicked the *fag end* – as he called it – into the snow, he moved to the back of the unit to get some pieces of clean cloth.

When he returned, he tossed one to me straight. Clifford then approached one of the two cars which I'd wet cleaned the day before, opened the front door, and removed a fan heater that was usually left inside overnight to dry the interior of the car.

"Do as I do, right? Get the vinyl shield bottle first." I followed his instruction. "Just tick a bi' of vinyl shield on a rag, and now rub it smoothly over the bumper. Bumpers with this appearance are called colour coded bumpers, right. Do t' same for wipers, plastic antenna, handles." I followed Clifford. "Now it's ' tires. Use this brush here." He showed me a brush with long soft bristles. "Get the Highstyle, 'cause tires ought t' be dressed wi' Highstyle to turn'em black and shiny." I followed him around just looking. "Now grab tha' li'le blue sponge over there. We'll do the polish. Actually, a ligh' quick polish – a proper polish 'ave to be wi' the buffer. Mind to jet the sponge off first to get any grit off not to scratch the paintwork. Then wring it out – it need to be damp, not wet. Now, the white bottle over there – the wax, yes – get it o'er 'ere. You pour a bit o' wax on the sponge and rub it over t' paintwork, including in the door shuts. Do it all over." Clifford was incredibly quick doing that. "By t' time you done, the wax'll be dry and you can start rubbing the wax off with a clean dry rag."

"I've waxed some times, but it took me ages to clean, and the paint was all stained." I actually wanted to ask Clifford about that before.

"Wet sponge. It 'av to be just lightly dump. You get with time." Clifford continued, throwing another fresh piece of cloth to me. "To finish, you'll buff the windows, windscreen n' mirrors. Get that grey bottle. That's glass polisher. Pour on a clean rag, like this. Go around t' windows 'n windscreen, outside and inside, mirrors. Then, just wipe it all off with a clean rag."

Whilst we finished dressing and polishing the cars I asked Clifford what was wrong with Ewan that morning.

"Business is quiet n' the weather go' the best of 'im." Clifford used a slightly mocking tone. "He's jus' a bi' glum, don't worry. Later 'e'll be 'ere to pester you."

"By the way, he asked me 'bout my nationality again."

Seeing concern in my expression, Clifford quickly put me at ease. "We'll come up wi' a solution for tha' later. Don't worry about it; today it just oos." Clifford then changed his tone to deeper voice and gave me an impish look. "N' you know what that means…"

I wasn't always comfortable when Clifford used that tone with me. So, I answered with my usual over-played outraged manner. "What?"

"You'll find out later…"

And so, without Ewan, we continued the partnership throughout that day. And when night came, and Ewan had long been gone, and the cars were all parked inside the units, and we were ready to call it a night, Clifford didn't seem much eager to leave the garage.

19

In the next day, Ewan was all smirks and wisecracks again, and that routine remained the same through the following weeks. Occasionally, Ewan just disappeared and left Clifford in charge. I continued honing my valeting skills, and helping Clifford out. As I gained more proficiency in all the phases of the valeting process, more often I'd hear Ewan shouting "spot on" or "split fire" every time he reversed the car from the Unit twenty back to its parking spot.

When the snow showers finally stopped, and the snow started melting away, business in the garage improved gradually, and so increased the number of cars that I had to valet and help Clifford with. Whenever I had to do any work inside the unit that didn't involve making much noise – like dressing, polishing, or flatting the primer – I usually turned a CD player on with a soundtrack in English so that my ears were constantly attuned to English, thus preventing me to engage in thoughts in a non-English language.

Here was a valuable habit I'd cultivated on my journey learning English: much of our thoughts boil down to memories of conversations, imaginary dialogues with people of our daily lives, and memories of something that we hear in our mother tongue; all this maintain our language skills anchored to a remote reality of the language we want to learn – in my case, English. Another language is, some scholars argue, another habit. So, I'd consciously cultivated a habit of engaging my thoughts in English.

And if it's true that that old habits die hard, then that old habit of mine was still alive and kicking. So to keep my thoughts engaged on the right idiom, I did fill every hour of silence with some sound in English – preferably something that I could hear repeatedly and so end up learning expressions and words I hadn't noticed before.

And to feed that listening habit I listened to anything available, from *Radio Times* promotional releases like *Doctor Who*, *The Resurrection Casket*, to Retro Audio dramas like *Wuthering Heights* and *The Third Man* released by Alten8. I also had a chance to listen to BBC audio titles about English like *Eat Shoots & Leaves*, and both series of *Fry's English Delight*. That habit of listening to radio programmes soon drew attention from other traders and workers on the site, and a few good humoured jibes ensued.

Once, whilst polishing a car, I remained enthralled by *The Joy of Gibberish* – a bonus episode from the second series of *Fry's English Delight* – which was playing at full volume in the background. At some point the programme illustrated a sound poem: Kurt Schwitters' *The Ursonate*.

"*...Fumms bö wö tää zää Uu, pögiff, kwii Ee. Dedesnn nn rrrrr, Ii Ee, mpiff tillff too, tillll, Jüü Kaa? Rinnzekete bee bee nnz krr müü? ziiuu ennze, ziiuu rinnzkrrmüü, rakete bee bee, Rrummpff tillff toooo? Ziiuu ennze ziiuu nnzkrrmüü...*"

Right then, Dave, a local mechanic from a neighbouring garage, wandered into Unit twenty and yelled from the top of his lungs.

"Wo' t' foocking 'ell ah ye listening to?!" Dave awakened me from a deep concentration.

A bit dazed, I lifted my head from the paintwork and replied hesitantly. "It's just a programme about gibberish."

"Oh, I thought tha' was ' tongue from yer country!" Dave, still holding a straight face, shouted over the loud voice of Stephen Fry that continued playing in the background.

Other times, the person who came to taunt me about my listening habit was Dave's son, Daniel, a thirty year old who shared the garage with his father. Daniel behaved like, and had the appearance of, a teen; always speaking loudly, frankly, and always referring to Ewan as "fatty" and Clifford as "rusty". Daniel himself was known as "big ears". Happily, he didn't nickname me after anything. But he'd promised me that he'd forever greet me by asking "wher'you come from, 'ow old ar'you" until he learned that information from me. The only times that Daniel wouldn't greet with the usual "wher'you come from, 'ow old ar'you" was when he thought of something more annoying to comment on.

"Morning – are you listening to your religious sermon today?" Daniel said, whenever he met me early morning, referring to a collection of six CDs entitled *The Power to Influence*, published by Anthony Robbins & Associates, which I listened to repeatedly those days.

Those CDs, as far as I could understand, contained the recordings of a series of lectures, directed to a salespersons group, presented by Anthony Robbins about persuasion. Daniel referred to those lectures as religious because Mr Robbins constantly repeated the word *beliefs* using an American preacher-like intonation. The second CD, for example, starts with the question: "What's the real difference between success and failure?" To which Mr Robbins himself answers: "Beliefs!"

Daniel never missed an opportunity to make fun of me referring to the CDs from *The Power to Influence*. He did that since the day I tried to explain to him that the way I had found those CDs could be understood either as a massive coincidence or as some sort of supernatural manifestation.

"Dan, I swear on the holy Bible! I found these CDs scattered on the ground, shining under a sunny day, next to a car Ewan had just parked up for me to valet, without a single scratch." I told with my usual excitement whenever I talked about suchlike ideas.

"Whoa. A sunny day! Tha's a miracle. It smell in 'ere." Daniel said scratching his nose, and then, pretending to sneeze, added. "Bullshit! Excuse me. Perhaps, they fell from sky."

"That's not the case Dan. Ewan knows I like to keep the CDs I find in the cars, so he must have found them and left for me there." I continued, ignoring Daniel's cynical sneer. "The thing is, I found these CDs in a day I was feeling doubts about being here, about working here. And you know that I have a purpose to be here."

"Yeah, wha' is it?" Daniel posed that question, as he usually did whenever he found an opportunity. "Wha' brough' y' 'ere? Why y' don' tell us?"

"I told you. The experience I have with English here, I couldn't have anywhere else." I made an effort to be as earnest with Daniel as I could without going into further details. "And I have an idea on what to do with this experience that will give me what I really desire."

"Wha' is it? Wha's t' idea?" Daniel fished again.

"Alright, this I cannot tell until it's done. But that's exactly what I'm trying to explain, Dan." I really had to make a bit of juggling to maintain a conversation with Daniel without being dragged into his fishing game. "I was telling that I was going through a moment of strong doubt about this purpose because it will need some good time to make it happen. And that's when I found the CDs. Now, listen to this. Just bear with me."

I put the disk number two in the player and advanced two minutes and eight seconds into the first track. We began listening to the audio.

20

"*...how hard would you really work, if you absolutely knew – how hard would you work in this course, how hard would you work on any course of study, to really master this stuff, to stay present, to take notes, to manage your state – you'd been seating for a while – how hard would you really work, if you knew that by mastering the tools of influence and persuasion – that you could literally create, be, do, have everything you want for the rest of your life? If you believed that, in your gut...*"

Then I pressed the stop button. "See what I mean?"

As Daniel remained quiet I continued. "I'm working here because I believe that I'm digging the means to reach my purpose. So it's a massive coincidence that in a moment of strong doubt I found these CDs that talk exactly about believing and working hard towards a purpose. But, this is no meaningless coincidence; this type of coincidence seems to communicate with us, and must have something to do with the divine, some invisible force that is connected with us."

When I made my point, Daniel looked at me and said: "You're 'way wi' fairies."

"Wha'…" I stuttered, already sensing what was coming, and finally found the courage to complete. "What that means?"

"I' means y're…" Daniel pointed his index finger to his head and, drawing circling motions with that finger, imitated the cuckoo whistle loudly. And as if that hadn't been clear enough, he added. "You're foocking barmy."

"See? I learned one more." I said, fortunately feeling enough confident about myself to eschew embarrassment with Daniel's contribution to the conversation.

"So, y' wan' to use y'r English t' be promoted from valet to salesperson. Tha's y'r idea?" Daniel continued poking fun.

I have to confess that Daniel's frank choice of words made conversing with him during my spear time one of the most delightful perks of working in the Bodyshop UK. All that verbal exercise, having to duck and dive Daniel's questions and witticisms to maintain a conversation going on, felt extremely exciting to me. I couldn't refrain from taking pleasure in working my English out to maintain the details of my identity and purposes undisclosed against Daniel's constant attempts to uncover them with his sly choice of words.

"...Bu', serious, 'ow come y' wi' a degree in English, end up 'ere in t' garage?" Daniel couldn't miss the opportunity to sneak that question into the conversation.

"Oh my God, this again Dan? Listen, working here for me is worth the same as working anywhere else in England using my degree. Actually, let me rephrase. Working here for me is a blessing. This free contact with a native speaker, like you, I would never have working as a teacher, or behind a counter anywhere."

"Bu' a teacher can make way mo' than 'ere." Daniel counter argued.

"Well, one, I think I'd have to be a local citizen to get a well paid job as a teacher. And two, the English I have here is all the riches I need – at least for now." I used a little theatrical tone to feign a forced sincerity to Daniel, although I truly felt that, or at least wanted desperately to believe in that.

"Suit yeself. Boo'... Can I be 'onest?" Daniel made a pause and a straight face, preparing himself for another remark.

As he never usually thought much before saying anything, I thought *goodness me*, nodded, and braced myself to hear what he had to say.

21

"There's summat dodgy 'bout you."

"Dan," I said after some silence. "I don't expect you to understand my reasons to work here. But, by now, you know a little about what I believe, right."

Daniel shrugged lightly.

"You know what I believe about having found these CDs?"

Daniel drew a gentle smile and continued quiet.

"So, I believe that the circumstances that brought me here are not just coincidental. Those CDs were brought to me because I needed those CDs. So, I was brought to Whittington Street because I needed Whittington Street. Does that make sense?" I said that with a pause before each word, making an effort to put that idea together to Daniel.

"You're 'way wi' fairies." Daniel told in an unusual low tone, smiling only slightly, like he felt sorry for my sanity. He then found an excuse and went back to his unit.

It was quite disappointing that I'd failed to make Dan understand that. But the truth is that, although I didn't really want to tell Daniel the latest circumstances that made me resort to working at Ewan's garage, I earnestly thought that telling Daniel about that wouldn't make him fully understand the complexity of circumstances that impelled me to embrace that experience instead of battling for another alternative. And what truly impelled me to embrace that experience was a strong belief that being there at the Bodyshop UK was a fundamental part of a chain of coincidental incidents – incidents which were organically bound to a deep passion I felt for English and triggered by a firm resolution I'd taken to fulfil that passion just about ten years ago.

At that time, I worked behind the counter of a street stall in the easternmost city of South America. At 6 a.m. I had to be at the stall, ready to open its shutters, and those shutters wouldn't come down until four p.m. I had to stay behind that counter for ten hours, with no break, either on busy or quiet days. During those hours I'd work preparing fast food, like grilled cheese sandwich or ham and cheese sandwich, and serving traditional deep-fried snacks, or slices of butter cake, or cupcakes. I generally offered these along with coffee, soft drinks, mineral water, or coconut water. Apart from these items, I still sold mints, sweets, chewing gum, and that is all folks.

In order to run that business at the stall I had to pay a monthly rent. So, after paying the debts I'd end up with an equivalent to eighty US dollars or fifty British pounds per month. That was a reasonable profit, considering that such amount of money was virtually the official minimum wage of the country at the beginning of the Noughties. That was enough to afford cinema on weekends and buy second-hand film soundtracks – the type of music that I loved. What bothered me most about that stall was that there was no running water and, because the plates used to serve the food needed to be washed constantly, I had to go and fetch water from a tap two hundred metres away – three or four times a day. But my routine didn't end there.

At night I attended classes at the local State University. So, after closing the stall at 4 p.m., I had to go home, have my only decent meal of the day, shower, then get dressed and be on my way to the university campus on a bus joyride of nearly fifty minutes. I had been stuck in that Monday to Friday routine for almost a year. I was twenty going on twenty-one, and the only fellows falling in line were the ones waiting to be served at the stall. I was watching life pass me by and getting a little worried about that.

That little worry gradually grew towards the end of 2000, when business in the stall started going downhill. The customers of the stall came mostly from the community who attended a publicly funded paediatric hospital across the road. Since it was usual for public servants to protest for better salaries quite often, the hospital staff went on strike from time to time; and so, the business in the stall slowed down intermittently.

Certain weeks I made enough to afford public transportation. And that seemed to be more than a hint for me to start thinking on a strategy to break the hell out of that stall.

To start putting that strategy in action, I had first to change to another undergraduate course. I could graduate in Social Communication within 2 years but, after that graduation, counting on a promising career prospect was out of the question. I had an academic curriculum with no work experience in the area of Social Communication and a school record filled with roughly above-average grades – a symptom of the little relevance that such course had to my intellectual inclinations and of my general lack of academic enthusiasm. Alas, I'd ignored my general feelings of unhappiness with that course for quite a while.

So, to start all over in a different undergraduate course, with intention to follow it through successfully, this time I had better hit the bullseye. To begin with, I thought of a course that entitled me to a comfortable number of job prospects. Then, I thought that a course that had to do with literature would be consistent with my ever-present writing aspirations. Finally, I thought of my passionate long-standing relationship with English, and decided that it was more than time to make a commitment to it. After playing that thought game of sense and sensibility I had a perfect match: Letters – Major in English Language and Literature.

22

"Ar' y' goin' t' do yer dancin' routine fur us t'day Jonesy?" Ewan asked loudly, with a slight tone of malice, smirking as usual, and elbowing Daniel who was right by his side.

On a Thursday evening like that, when the garage work had practically ended for Ewan and Daniel, they definitely had nothing better to do with their idle time other than turning to me for their amusement. And as they seemed to have grown tired of making prying questions, they found a new approach to assert their sentinelling presence: by winding me up about my habit of exercising and dancing whilst washing or polishing cars.

I'd adopted that habit under the premise that, if nothing else good could spring from working in a garage – besides the indisputable benefits to my English – at least it was a great opportunity to get in shape and keep fit. So, I developed a method of sponging and polishing cars that helped me to work out. Instead of moving just the arms in circular motions over the paintwork, which is the most comfortable manner to either sponge or polish a car, I'd move the entire upper part of my body along the arm movement while keeping the hips and lower limbs still. Instead of either bending the spine or crouching to reach lower parts of the car I'd stretch one leg and flex the other, assuming something close to a *trikonasana* position, otherwise known as triangle pose, until my hand reached the required point. By sponging and polishing with such movements I hoped to accelerate fat burning around the hips, waist, and abdomen, and strengthen muscles from the calf, hamstrings, thighs, buttocks, chest, shoulders, and arms. All those body movements were done with much more pleasure, more efficiency, and constant rhythm when accompanied by dance music – dance music with lyrics in English naturally. In which case, some serious hip-wiggling and pelvis-thrusting was involved.

Luckily I'd found inside a car the CD *Now That's What I Call Music! 63.*

And so, opportunely, I worked – or should I say worked out – to the sound of *Beep* by Pussycat Dolls and *My Humps* by Black Eyed Peas which played endlessly on a loop. As I usually did all the exercise and dancing inside the unit, away from human eyes, I felt free to dare some wild moves à la Shakira and Elvis Presley around the cars.

But that Thursday evening, I loaded the CD player with another of my favourite findings: disc 2 of *A Hundred number one hits*; then, I programmed the CD player's memory *Rubber Bullets* by *10cc*, *Yes Sir I Can Boogie* by Baccara, and *Ring my Bell* by Anita. And when I prepared myself to start polishing two cars, Ewan and Daniel decided to recline comfortably against the car that was parked at the entrance ramp of Unit twenty and to keep watching me.

"Ah'll guess whe' 'e come from by t' way 'e jiggles." Ewan said to Daniel, loud enough to make me hear – as usual, he managed to join the best of two worlds in terms of taunting.

"Shoo' oop Fatty. Y' mak'im shy." Daniel joined Ewan in his teasing.

"C'mon. Shek i' Jonesay!" Ewan said insolently, as I waxed the car oblivious to their presence.

That'd be a perfect intro to a Jean-Daniel Cadinot film, and I couldn't feel more flattered than posing as the leading role. But there in the garage, in the real world, it just made me feel extremely embarrassed and lightly outraged. Ewan and Daniel really left me in a difficult position – it was bullying, Yoga-style. I just couldn't let them realise that they had the power to embarrass me with their attitude. Likewise, I couldn't offer them the display they might be expecting to enjoy. So, I polished quietly, doing my version of the *trikonasana* position, moving up and down lightly, leg-flexing and leg-stretching, but no wiggling or thrusting.

"Told you'd scare 'im." Daniel said as I finished wiping the wax off the first car and moved to the next one.

"I'm no' tippin' ye Jonesy." Ewan insisted a bit louder as I continued to ignore them.

Despite feeling embarrassed and a little uneasy with Ewan and Dan, I couldn't avoid finding their behaviour amusing. In all truth, I secretly enjoyed their attention and their insinuations. I could never take that as an offence. If I'd learned something about the behaviour of straight men until there, it is that sexual innuendos, teasing, taunting, and even light insults, are generally their friendly manner to approach a gay man. I learned that after engaging in so many unpleasant arguments in my younger days, when I was easily offended by this type of approach. Straight men, most of the time, don't really understand much about their own homoerotic feelings, and having a gay man close to them generally arouse their curiosity. Daniel, who was a husband and a father, was a typical example. After we met at the garage, he didn't wait long to come up with indirect questions about my sexuality.

"D'you 'ave a bird?" Daniel started after having just mentioned about his wife.

"What kind of bird?" I answered, pretending not to know that *bird* meant a girlfriend.

"No, I mean a swee'eart, a girlfriend, an inamorata." Daniel explained patiently, but eager to get my response.

"What? No." I replied with a shrug and an expression that insinuated that his question didn't even make sense.

After a one second of hesitation Daniel took the risk of going further, trying to impress a witty tone to his question. "A boyfriend then?"

I, pretty casually, replied: "No. I'm single and free."

"No, 'cause tha's normal." Daniel tried to explain himself as if I cared.

Daniel had insisted in that same sequence of questions at least three times, as if I'd suddenly open up and say I had a boyfriend.

In all honesty, never had I heard from any Caucasian English person the slightest word of prejudice against a gay person; and I was aware that the English society was light years ahead of civilisation regarding the gay issue: the first open gay kiss on a television soap opera, *Eastenders*, was broadcast in 1989; the first lesbian kiss on another tv soap opera, *Brookside*, was broadcast in 1994; the ban on individuals serving at Her Majesty's Armed Forces openly as homosexuals was lifted in the year 2000; same gender couples were granted the right to form civil-partnership and adopt children in England and Wales in 2004; these facts only reflect the reality that gays and lesbians alike were neither kept socially invisible nor stripped of legal rights so long as in most countries of the world. So, the people at the garage posed no threat of hostility if I wanted to be out, as I usually am.

But even if I wanted to be totally frank with Daniel, I couldn't give him the answers he wanted. That information was classified and sealed under a proper name: Clifford.

23

For quite a while, what I actually had was a strong friendship with benefits with Clifford. And the benefits that Clifford afforded me included offering me daily rides both to work and back to my flat, helping me with some petty difficulties, putting me to sleep most nights, and making me feel protected – considering that Clifford was an all-muscle chaperone, almost twice larger than me. I couldn't summarise that with a single word to Daniel. And if I perhaps could, Clifford certainly wouldn't feel comfortable with that because he was especially secretive about the side benefits of our friendship. Clifford kept his sexuality to himself. He never really seemed to fit into any category and, judging by his temperament, if he'd identified himself with some gay type in his younger days he'd been in one brawl after the other because he certainly wouldn't take straight jesters kindly. One of the things that made me fall so deeply under Clifford's spell – when I met him – was his account of how he made four thugs run like chickens, when he went mad after having one of his best jackets ripped open by a pocket-knife attack. If a ruined jacket proved enough to unearth such rage, imagine just what he'd do to those gobshites who always find a way to ruin one's day or one's pride with stupid comments. Let me tell you.

Being not an exemplary model of masculinity myself, from my enfant days I'd become used to comments about the quality of my voice, about my mannerisms, or any other aspect the bullies decided to pick on. Another thing that I learned soon was that the other boys of my kind were generally the most cowardly or, even worse, the most eager bullies themselves. As a mechanism of defence, consequentially, I developed a strong sense of identity and pride. Without doubt, this strong sense of identity and pride is the main mould of my behaviour towards language in a general sense and, especially, towards English.

As a child of the Eighties, growing up in a small community where the only necessary language for communication is Portuguese, I was lured by English as a natural consequence of being exposed to the Anglo-American culture both through the VHS films shown at the village pub and through the pop music played on radio and television. During adolescence, when the hormones of puberty made me more sentient to my difference from the girls, and also my difference from the boys, that English lure turned into an intense flirt, as I – stimulated by my collection of books and audio tapes, the *English at Home* – explored the forms of English and grew more attached to those forms, which seemed to encapsulate my pubescent sense of distinction. That attachment was still to foster a stronger affection as I stepped into the challenging world adulthood.

The highlight of that transition started happening from beginning of the second year of the Noughties – the time when I gave the first step to break free from the daily ten-hour confinement of the street stall.

"Do you have a background education in English that guarantee a decent level of proficiency in English?" The secretary from the Foreign Languages Department always asked that same question to all students enrolling in the Major in English Language and Literature. The process of selection, to which all applicants are submitted before being approved to this specific Major, assessed exclusively the candidates writing skills. As I started stuttering a few words, telling her about my background education in English in the publicly funded State schools and my self-instruction, she interrupted me and continued. "When the student signs to enrol in this course the student is assuming total responsibility to get through the level of English that is used during the language-specific modules of the course." Then, as I signed the enrolment form, she continued in a more casual tone. "Just make sure your English is flawless."

"I'll do my best." I said, with a sincere tone of assurance.

"I tell you this," – she continued – "because the tutors will conduct the language-specific modules in fluent English, and they don't want to have problems with basic communication, right."

"Oh, naturally. I totally agree with that." I told the secretary with sincerity, as I had enough self-confidence to believe that my English was good enough to get through the English modules.

And so, with that confidence, I started the first academic term of the undergraduate course of Letters – the first of eight half-yearly terms, aka semesters. The undergraduate course of Letters is the closest equivalent to a Bachelor of Arts with a Major in a specific language. It deals with two major areas, namely, language and literature. As for the specific language it offered Portuguese, Spanish, French and English as options within the curriculum. The choice of curriculum, English Major as an example, established the obligatory modules, which were basically the language-specific modules, *id est*, Grammar (of English), Phonetics and Phonology (of English), Applied Linguistics (to English), (English) Language Teaching Practice, and the literature modules, American Literature and British Literature. Along with these, Linguistics, Theory of Literature, Psychology of Education, and Didactic were core subjects, whilst Greek, Latin, and Roman Philology were electives.

Because a few modules, from my previous undergraduate course, had been exempted, I only had to attend a few classes during the week. I'd been exempted from *Grammar of English I*, which would be the only English-specific module of that first semester, so that gave me some extra time for working on my English skills.

Since I still had to carry on with the business in the stall, I had to make the best of those ten hours behind the counter. Blowing the dust from some old English grammar books that I borrowed from the University Central Library came first. During the quiet intervals at the stall, if I wasn't reading any compulsory text of the course I'd be revising the rules of English grammar. But when my hands were otherwise occupied, preparing sandwiches, serving a customer, or washing some plates, I pulled my most habitual trick.

"...Is that a television that you have got in there?" One of the faithful customers made that question (in Portuguese), curious about all that loud foreign babel and other noisy sounds that she could hear coming from beneath the counter.

"No, it's just a cassette tape that I recorded with the audio of *South Park*." I replied, not sure if she'd understand *South Park*, as the title of the series hadn't been translated into, or retitled in, Portuguese and she presumably hadn't even heard of that series. "I like playing it so I can practise listening to English."

"Oh, can you understand anything of what they're saying?" She asked, quite in disbelief that those alien sounds could ever mean anything actually intelligible.

"The first times I listen it's a bit hard, but the more times I listen to the same thing the more I understand." I replied, actually explaining the gradual process of understanding those audiotaped dialogues whenever I couldn't watch the full episode as I recorded its soundtrack.

"Oh, I admire anyone who knows how to speak a foreign language." She said with a glint in her eyes.

Though we lived in the capital city of the State – one of the smallest of the 26 States of the country – the great majority of the population, which ranged from lower class to lower middle class, still regarded a foreign language as a fairly distant abstraction. There, one may live an entire life – mainly in the outskirts, away from the touristic sites – without ever seeing a foreign person, and much less listening to a foreign person speaking a foreign tongue, other than on television. Just hearing the recording of a dialogue in English in a public location already caught the attention of some individuals, like that customer at the stall.

Sadly, the recurrent comments I heard, when the audio tapes played in the stall, served as a constant reminder that I was listening to a foreign language whereas I wanted to think of English as a natural tongue of my surroundings. And to maintain that thought going on I not only had to grow insensible to the customers' comments but also had to pretend that I hadn't listened to the same audio like a hundred times repeatedly. If I managed to record all episodes shown on open tv during the week, I'd have 2 new episodes of *South Park* and 2 new episodes of *The Addams Family* to listen during a week. If I missed a week I'd have to endure listening to the same episodes for 14 days.

It was either that or nothing. Listening to pop music on radio didn't work because the international hits were alternated with national ones, and the presenters would often interrupt – and they certainly didn't use English. So, if I really wanted to understand my tutor's English in the next term with the same familiarity that I understood my mother's Portuguese, I should better to continue flipping those audio tapes, and convince myself that Stan Marsh, Kyle Broflovski, Eric Cartman, and Kenny McCormick were just foul-mouthed children playing across the street, and that Gomez, Morticia, Wednesday, Pugsley, and Uncle Fester were my next door neighbours. And yet I truly am all for the biblical principle *love thy neighbour*, by the end of that semester I was sick of them all.

Thank heavens, not long from then I'd experience the first blessing of that pursuit to master English: the miracle of the seven sitcoms and the VHS tape.

24

"Hello, who is it…?" I hustled to answer the home phone before its ringing disturbed my mother's sacrosanct post-lunch siesta.

I'd begun to return home earlier from the stall that week owing to another strike of the paediatric hospital staff. By then, the semester at the university was practically over and the tutors had officially announced that they wouldn't return to their teaching activities in the coming semester; they'd join the uni staff strike. I was already envisioning long afternoons revising more English grammar books and listening to *South Park* and *The Addams Family* even more times during the breaks.

"…Hi, what's good, what's good?" I recognised the voice of my cousin Jeannie who lived in another neighbourhood. "What? Oh, no she didn't!" I could feel my heart racing lightly as she told me what a friend of hers had given to her. "Oh my God, I wanted that so, so badly… Oh, have no fear my cousin dear. I'll hop in a bus now and will be there in a jiffy."

That afternoon, my cousin Jeannie had phoned to tell me about this girlie classmate from university who just loved chatting about the American sitcoms that she watched regularly on *Sky* satellite tv. But Jeannie had no satellite at home and therefore didn't have a clue of what this girlie talked about most times. So, this girlie recorded a VHS tape with nothing less than 8 hours of American sitcoms being aired that season on satellite tv and gave that VHS tape to Jeannie, so that she could watch the sitcoms and later tell her impressions.

Unfortunately, the girlie had recorded all those sitcoms with their original English soundtrack and my cousin couldn't stand watching non-dubbed programmes and having to read subtitles. Thus, Jeannie wanted to lend me that VHS tape so that I could later make a brief description of those sitcoms to her. Naturally, I couldn't just stand there, knowing that my cousin had to go through that traumatic social obligation, and do nothing about that. So, I selflessly delivered my cousin from that unspeakable burden by taking the VHS tape with me and assuming the burden of watching all those eight hours of non-dubbed American sitcoms.

Glory glory, halleluiah! For the first time ever, I had a taste of what satellite tv felt like. For that, I had to borrow a video cassette player off my neighbour Vicky to watch that VHS tape almost every afternoon. And I wouldn't return that player without having loaded my audio tapes with new material. That material included episodes from 2 sitcoms that had aired recently on open television, *Friends* and *Popular* – this last one more like a comedy-drama –, and episodes from 5 others that I'd never heard about, *That Seventies Show*, *Third Rock from the Sun*, *Bette*! *Normal, Ohio*, and *Will & Grace*.

It was blissful to watch those sitcoms and, with a little imagination, pretend that I actually had satellite television at home. Besides, it was a relief to listen to new voices, and new theme tunes as I carried a portable audio cassette player with me around the house. Then, I listened to the soundtrack of those sitcoms in the kitchen whilst preparing a meal, in the toilet, while brushing, showering, or going number two, and in the bedroom, whilst falling asleep. And as soon as the alarm clock set off in the morning my finger slipped straight on the play key of the audio cassette player before shutting the alarm off.

During the following months I continued with that behaviour restlessly. I made an effort to pay attention to nothing else other than the sound from those audio tapes, assuming that by making English the most predominant language to my hearing sense throughout the day my brain would eventually assimilate English in its entirety – just as naturally as my brain should have assimilated my mother tongue.

Naturally, I had no knowledge of any theoretical parameter that informed me if that behaviour could produce any proficiency progress at all; but I just kept following my intuition. In any case, that behaviour should at least perfect my comprehension proficiency. And since the university tutors continued on strike and the second semester never really started, I should have plenty time at hand to become a native-like listener. Make that time even more as the paediatric hospital staff remained on strike for months and the business at the stall went so quiet that some days I wouldn't see a customer during a whole morning.

That was the definitive hint that would prompt me to think over the ultimate actions of my strategy to escape from that stall. One thing certainly was out of the question – I couldn't just leave a papier mâché dummy behind the counter and sneak out; before giving notice to the owner of the stall, I had to break the news to my father.

25

"What!?" My father raised his eyebrows as if refusing to believe what I'd just told him.

I'd chosen to tell him my plans of quitting the stall business early morning as I prepared myself to go to the stall. My father himself was also getting ready to go to his modest candy shop. Judging by the tone of his voice, I guessed, he didn't take the news well. "And how do you think you're going to support yourself?"

"Dad, I've been thinking and…" Every time that I had something vital to tell to my father it would always come out stupidly. "The stall is not taking me anywhere and this course I'm studying now offers some scholarship opportunities". I stuttered, with a totally insecure tone of voice which definitely didn't help convincing my father that I possessed enough intellectual ability to obtain the disputed scholarships offered at the university.

"And what is the problem that you cannot continue working until you get this scholarship." He challenged me under the contemptuous gaze of my older brother, who had just recently dropped out from his undergraduate course and was now helping my father in his candy shop.

"No. I can work until December, or until the strike is over, save as much as I can, and then I apply myself totally to the university." I said, making an effort to convince both my father and myself that such strategy would pay off.

But my father didn't seem quite convinced as he raised his voice and started berating me. "You know, if you don't want to work you shouldn't even bother to go anymore. Just stay home like a bum." He had that special talent to make me feel like a total incompetent – a talent that certainly inspired, judging by the smile of cynicism that my brother had smacked on his mush.

"How the hell am I going to get a scholarship working like an ass all day in that stall?" I barked angrily through bitter tears, which started erupting as I tried to control my voice.

"Listen, I have a business to run, and you're just delaying us. I have no time for this nonsense."

With that, my father simply blocked out my presence, made a nervous hand motion to my brother, and threw himself inside the car to make his away to the candy shop.

I couldn't really blame my father for not having faith in me. I'd wasted quite a good time in the previous undergraduate course and my father saw the stall business as the only thing that kept me down to earth. Yet, calling me a bum was a poor choice of words on his part. If I had any remaining doubt over quitting that stall business until there, my father's insult just left me with a steely resolve. I just wished that my father had given me a better chance to make him understand why I so much believed that my plans would work out. I even thought of throwing myself at him and saying, "Why won't you let me quit from the stall business. I must apply myself a hundred percent to this undergraduate course to master English. This is all I know. This is what I am. This is what I do."

Had I followed my heart and taken that attitude perhaps my father hadn't driven off like he did that morning; he'd have accelerated in reverse gear and tried to run over me though. Yet, I suspected that without the audience laughter of the American sitcoms that I had constantly ringing in my head that situation wouldn't look as adorable as I pictured.

With that crossed off my tick list, without any encouragement from my father, and with around £50 saved, it was time to stick to my word and follow through with my resolution to escape the stall business. That was the first piece of a puzzle that I'd start, accidentally, putting together: the puzzle on how to tap into the *principle* and trigger some form of dormant inner power to generate a desired effect on reality.

26

"I'm honey, honey, honey, honey... So honey, I'm honey, honey, honey, tonight!"

I was at the stall when that song started on the radio. I just loved singing along. Singing along was actually another technique that I'd adopted – as an alternative to the audio tape listening habit – to maintain the constant exercise of English. It didn't work well because during most of the song I just mumbled the odd word that I could understand. But when the chorus started, I simply raised my voice and sang unashamedly. "I'm honey, honey, honey, honey..." I hadn't heard that hit playing for quite some time. And that couldn't be a more special morning to hear it again, because that was my final morning at the stall.

It'd been a few more months of food serving, water fetching, and plate washing, until the university staff eventually agreed to end the strike by December. Officially the tutors also ended the strike but they decided that the pedagogical activities should be resumed in January. After that brief argument with my father I stuck to my words and so, as I'd determined, from that morning on, the stall would be under the management of another person. And whilst I waited for the owner of the stall to come and collect the keys that morning, I spend the time tidying up a little bit and, to keep my English going, singing along the radio hits.

"...Oh-oh-oh-oh! Ah want to be free-and, feel the way ah feel... Man, I feel like a woman." I was lucky no one could really understand English around there because, apart from the *oh-oh-oh-oh* and those two short lines, I basically made up most the other words of that chorus.

After returning the keys that morning, I had to stand alone by that resolution. At home, as I tried to make the best with my idle time during December, everyone seemed a little distant and remained silent whenever I mentioned my plans from then on. My mother didn't show me any support – though she didn't oppose herself to my plans either – and my brother from time to time addressed me with comments of derision.

That wasn't the first time that I'd aroused their hostility because of my attitude and stubbornness. Not long from then, things had come to a much worse state of affairs when I insisted in bringing a boyfriend home just because I wanted my parents to acknowledge that I had the same right as my brother, who could bring his girlfriend home under no censure. I never meant to bring a boyfriend home with the intention of osculating, pecking, snogging, smooching, canoodling, cuddling, clinching, clasping, playing pat-a-cake, thumb-wresting, or engaging in any other display of affection; I simply wanted my parents to acknowledge my right to bring a boyfriend home. I couldn't bring myself to understand their reluctance as I'd never made any secrecy around my romantic persuasion. Unfortunately my attitude and stubbornness blinded me to their own distress with my behaviour – a distress that wasn't a privilege of my parents exclusively.

Not long from there, my long-term partner had been through some hell because I pressed him to show that he genuinely loved me by holding hands and kissing in public locations. By some good grace of the Lord, we hadn't ever suffered any sort of violence, or even been insulted or threatened by any member of the public.

Naturally, I never meant to bring any distress neither to my family nor to my partner. Such behaviour was driven by an impulsive antagonism that I felt against any social convention that I judged retrograde and repressive. The mere thought of conformity repulsed me and I imagined myself as an activist – although intimately I had fantasies which involved a boot stamping on my face and me licking it. Still, despite being a source of distress to both my family and my partner, it was precisely that attitude and stubbornness that would prompt me to nurture a yet stronger desire to master the English language from that second semester onward.

And from that semester on, mastering English would entail more than just being perfectly able to comprehend the tutors' English – and way more than just perfecting my speaking, reading, and writing proficiency, as I'd discover. Mastering English would determine success and mediocrity in the course since, with each semester, the English-specific modules gained predominance within the curriculum of the English Major. Furthermore, mastering English not only would determine my performance in the English-specific modules, but also, as a direct consequence, determine my intellectual prestige amongst my undergraduate cohorts – and knowing well how the undergraduate students at that university usually treated each other, I certainly didn't want to become a target for their condescension.

Until here, the effort that I made during the strike had been just a preliminary step in the direction of mastering English. After revising a few English grammar books, apparently I had a grasp of all normative rules of the English grammar. But also, after listening to hours and hours of American sitcoms, I had a growing impression that the English from those sitcoms continually departed from the grammatical norms that I so much endeavoured to learn – probably the reason why I struggled to understand the English of those sitcoms before listening to each episode at least ten times. That impression was simply a glimpse of the bewildering and mind-bending facets of English that I yet had to conquer on that journey to master English. But before applying myself to conquer these facets and to garner intellectual prestige through the mastering of English, I needed first and foremost to find the means to survive within the academic environment. And that initial survival entailed obtaining a scholarship.

A scholarship would allow me to concentrate my efforts on the undergraduate course with no monetary concerns. The last months of work in the stall had allowed me to save sufficient funds to support myself for the beginning of the semester whilst I focused on finding a prospective scholarship opportunity. For such, I had to focus on finding a tutor who coordinated a research team and making sure I was well acquainted with him, or her, before other students did the same. I also had to focus on obtaining good grades because the grades average was taken into consideration when it came to selecting students to research teams. Easy as it might sound, obtaining good grades required more than just excelling in the formal written assessments. Once into a classroom with around forty classmates, a student really had to stand out from the crowd and start impressing the tutors well before getting to the exams or essays. Most students were aware of that largely unstated and unofficial rule; so they made sure that their full intellectual potential wasn't missed during classes by either the tutors or indeed their classmates. Somehow, successfulness at that scenario was to a certain degree bound to that. It could be the result of a psychic effect of social self-assertion, or perhaps, because identities aren't confidential in assessments, some students made sure their intellectual inclinations showed so the tutors would sympathise more with their subjective answers in exams or ideas in essays.

So, from that moment on, to guarantee a future to my aspirations to master English I too should subscribe to that academic rat race.

That first night of the second semester, soon as I stepped into the classroom and recognised many classmates from the previous semester, I could swear that I heard Herbert Spencer announcing, "Brothers and sisters, behold, as the survival of the intellectually fittest is about to commence".

27

ARISTOTLE

In the undergraduate course of Letters the classroom scenario – pretty much similar to all other courses around the campus in the night shift – split the students into two distinct socio-economic groups. There were the students from the city's periphery or nearby towns, who took buses to come to the university, who had come from State schools, and who were quiet, silent even, rarely expressing their ideas in class as if deliberately attempting to blend into the background. Then, there were those students from the more privileged areas of the city, who drove their own cars or whose parents dropped them off at the university, who had come from private schools, and who were invariably highly opinionated and often felt the need to share their every thought with the whole class. Members of the first group, commonly referred to as the Meekies, could be generally identified by their drowsy expressions of who came straight from work to university. Members of the second group, commonly referred to as the Richies, identified themselves by leaving their flashy mobile phones showing on the desks. Not to be so black and white, there were always a few from the first group who acted like and hang with those from the second group and a few from the second group who avoided playing the part within that social scenario. One of these few was Aristotle, who couldn't agree that his classmates allowed themselves to be labelled so bluntly into two categories.

Yet, willing or not, once inside the classroom, before the tutors and before the fellow classmates, all students end up defining themselves as part of either the Meekies or the Richies. Not even Aristotle himself with his conscious efforts to blur that stupid social boundary managed to change that. Aristotle worked by day as a cashier at a chemist, lived in a neighbour town, and made a one-hour bus ride everyday to come to the university. On the other hand, Aristotle didn't really need to work to support himself, he also had the option of coming to the university driving his father's car if he wished so, he possessed the latest model of mobile phone – though he made an effort to keep it out of sight during classes –, and although he'd had the best quality education that the finest private schools of his town could offer he didn't find it necessary to show off his knowledge during classes.

Aristotle usually challenged the social code of the classroom by making friends with the most as well as the least privileged students indiscriminately. When it came to participating in group work for some assignment he made the best to show his own example of detachment from any social clique by often joining in groups formed entirely by either Meekies or Richies.

Weeks into his second semester in the undergrad course, Aristotle joined a group formed by Meekies aiming at translating a Latin text about the legend of Romulus and Remus. Aristotle had managed to take a day off work to meet with them at the Central Library.

When he arrived there, he found the only two other members of the group who turned up already squirming in the hard seats at an antique square oak table from the ground floor of the library.

"Morning mateys. Do you think we'll manage to tackle the whole thing this morning?" Aristotle asked, with a rather discouraging tone, whilst he joined the group.

The member of the group who sat right opposite to Aristotle replied, "Well, we'll do what we got to do, and we'll do the best we can." And, throwing a look of defiance at the two mammoth hardcover Latin dictionaries that were still shut at the centre of the table, he continued. "Now, let's crack these open, and let's make it happen."

"Ok, lads, let's have this party started then." The member of the group who sat next to Aristotle said and flashed the text that they had to translate – which was printed with what looked like a zillion of different words crammed into a page-length printout – making all three classmates to draw a synchronised deep breath.

28

The tomes on the table had a yellow coloured aspect and seemed that they were about to collapse under their own weigh. As if to make up for his lack of enthusiasm, Aristotle acted fast.

"This one looks like it's been published in the Ancient Rome. It should do nicely." He said, whilst carefully dragging one of the Latin dictionaries on the table toward to him, thinking how that mouldy dictionary felt as weighty as the assignment they had ahead of them. Then, he added. "So, how can we make this quicker?"

"Well, we could write the words down and make sure we don't look up the same word twice," The member sat opposite to Aristotle suggested, not really realising that they wouldn't encounter much more than a few repeated words. "Then, I'll jot each word down, pass them one by one to your appreciation, you return them to me, so I gloss the translated word in the text and we agree on a translation at every sentence."

"Sounds alright to me." Aristotle agreed, eager to have that task finished as soon as manageable.

After having spent some time engaged in that technique, looking up the words unsuccessfully, they began to understand that the many different ending words within the text were equivalent to but a single entry in the dictionary.

The word *lŭpŭs*, meaning *wolf*, for example, could appear in the text inflected as one of its seven grammatical cases: nominative (*lŭpŭs*), vocative (*lŭpĕ*), accusative (*lŭpŭm*), genitive (*lŭpī*), dative (*lŭpō*), ablative (*lŭpō*), and locative (*lŭpī*). Also, each of these grammatical cases could appear in its plural state, which is formed by a further different ending inflection – *lŭpī lŭpī lŭpōs lŭpōrŭm lŭpīs lŭpīs* –, making up to fourteen possible forms to a single word. These different cases, including singular and plural forms, could be further indicated by the distribution of diacritics on the top of each vowel – diacritics which indicated if the vowel was either a short or unstressed one, written with as a breve (˘), or a long or stressed one, written as a macron (¯). Furthermore, these inflectional endings didn't follow the same pattern throughout all the words from the text either. Each word endings, and diacritic distributions, followed a pattern specific to one of the five declensions paradigm into which each word is categorised into.

To help one identify into which declension a word

would be categorised the dictionary entry added to the singular nominative form *lŭpŭs* the inflectional suffix of its genitive case, which is *ī*. So, where the dictionary entry showed *lŭpŭs – ī*, one might have to trace it back from its genitive plural *lŭpōrŭm*, for example. To make a long story yet longer, the group took the entire morning plus the entire afternoon to finally translate most of the damn text.

The afternoon began stretching into the evening when the translation of the text neared completion and Aristotle decided to speak for everyone. "Alright-o mateys, me don't know 'bout youse but I think we had worked hard enough and we really, really deserve a break."

"Well, it's been hard but we're so close now that I prefer to continue." The member who was still seating opposite to Aristotle argued, whilst the other member, who had started doing some squatting by the table to uncripple his legs, remained silent.

"I know but I'm really dying here." Aristotle justified and continued after a sigh. "I'll tell you what, we get a break now, just enough time for me to go home, eat, shower, and we meet earlier in the classroom to finish translating the final lines before the tutor arrive to collect the final draft. Most the words are glossed, so we just fill in the gaps, right?"

"It's alright for me." The member next to Aristotle agreed with a quick twitch on his face.

"Well, I'm not really going home, and it's not fair to keep you here. If you don't mind," The member who was the only one still seated turned to the other who was then standing by the table and continued. "We can try to advance just a little further before we have our break, right?"

"It's alright for me." He agreed, pulling another twitch on his face.

"Alright-o, I'll be at the classroom around one hour before the Latin Language class start. See youse later" Aristotle said and hurried off the library feeling relieved that he could then breathe some fresh air again after having almost suffocated under the fungi infested air of the library.

Aristotle really didn't estimate that translating that Latin text would take that long. Gladly, he'd borrowed his father's car that morning; so he was able to go home and return soon enough to finish that translation. He was a little late when he actually managed to be back at the university but the other members of the group had managed to complete the final draft of the translation. Aristotle signed that final draft, along with the two other members of the group who'd been with him that entire day and the two others who couldn't make it to the library at any time. Before the Latin Language tutor arrived, when basically all students enrolled in that module was already there, the other groups' members were all excited discussing how much effort they applied in translating the text and even comparing how they'd worded certain sentences in their versions. A particular group formed by some Richies had managed to translate only half of the text. Aristotle, who counted them among his friends, decided to show an example of camaraderie to his fellows mates by lending an earlier draft from his own group's translation so that particular group could copy and fill the gaps in their own work.

Aristotle's white chicks blushed in embarrassment as he watched one of the group members who had been so cordially with him that entire day standing up, reaching out for the draft that he'd just lent, and simply ripping it from the hands of the Richie who was copying the missing parts of the translation.

The cheery classroom background chatter reached an abrupt halt.

29

Everyone was in disbelief since the angry paper grabber had only moments before been exchanging tips with another group of Meekies. Whilst everyone knew the classmates cultivated a subtle sense of division within the classroom they never witnessed an open display of hostility as such. No one dared to break the heavy silence. Every single person in that classroom seemed to be, all of a sudden, swimming in a fish tank filled up with tension.

Aristotle had been pretty much of a friend to that study partner so he found that his classmate deserved an explanation.

"I'm sorry, I thought it wouldn't bother you if I lent out the draft we..." Aristotle gently started excusing himself, trying to calm his fellow classmate down.

But his fellow classmate, still holding the translation, turned nervously to Aristotle, and said with an uncontrolled high pitched voice, "I appreciate it if you leave me alone for tonight." And then he turned again away from Aristotle.

As if on cue even the bush crickets ceased chirping.

The other members from the same group as Aristotle pretended that no argument had just taken place and awaited quietly the arrival of the tutor who, a short time later, entered the classroom and collected all drafts for marking. Aristotle struggled to come to terms with that senseless display of bitterness, which flew in the face of his friendly and inclusive approach, but preferred to avoid further instigating his classmate's anger and maintained a dignified silence.

The only thing that calmed Aristotle was to think that amidst that earthly scenario where the students from the undergraduate course of Letters experienced the centrifugal force of social class antagonism they also experienced a more dignifying form of antagonism in which the arguments revolved around language. Aristotle remembered when he first witnessed a clash between Meekies and Richies subtly led by his friend who seemed to have a nervous disposition against the Richies. It happened during the first class of Linguistics that semester when the tutor introduced the students to the genesis of the linguistic thought.

They learned how Linguistics stemmed from the development of an old interest of intellectuals about language. They learned how the Greek thinkers, in the fifth century before the Common Era (BCE), engaged on the discussion whether the origin of words was natural or conventionalised, *id est*, whether language embodied a direct essential connection with a physical and spiritual reality or language simply embodied thought with arbitrary expression. They were introduced to Plato's *Cratylus*, a dialogue between Cratylus, who supports the *naturalist* view, and Hermogenes who supports the *conventionalist* view. They learned that in the second century BCE the same dialectic, whether nature or convention determined the origin of words, appears in the Roman scholar Marcus Terentius Varro's work *De Lingua Latina*. When the students were encouraged to support one side of the argument with examples they could think of, one of the Richies quickly came up with an example.

"Well, it's just to think of the word *table*, which in German is *tisch*, in French *table*, in Italian *tavola*, in Portuguese *mesa*, and in Chinese zhuō zǐ…" The classmate made sure to emphasise the French pronunciation of *table* and to pronounce the other words carefully, and was visibly proud to show her polyglot abilities well in the face of the rest of the class.

"...The same object is arbitrarily named differently in different languages." She concluded.

Immediately after she finished her example, one of the Meekies, precisely Aristotle's nervous friend, jumped to emphasise "And how about the similarity between *table* in English and *table* in French?"

"Well, these similarities cannot obliterate the fact that *table* and *mesa* and zhuō zǐ are obviously arbitrary ways of naming basically the same concept" The classmate added with a calm tone and a smooth expression of who was totally in control of her side of that discussion.

Aristotle's nervous friend couldn't stand that classmate's air of superiority and again, already taking that discussion very personally, jumped with his contra-argument. "Well, and how about the word *father*, which is *padre* in Italian and Spanish, *père* in French, *patéras* in Greek, and, as far as I read about it, is similar in more than a hundred languages. Obvious examples of word difference between languages cannot obliterate the fact that the origins of the word *father* very possibly may have a naturalist explanation" The nervous Meekie himself flashed a smile of smugness.

Then, another classmate came in defence of the Richie who initiated the discussion. "Well, I have to agree with that, but even so, random similarities between languages do not necessarily refute arbitrariness. Conventionalism sounds like the more reasonable base of language."

At that point another classmate interfered, pretty more calmly than the nervous one. "First, it's not a random similarity. Similarity between words across different languages is quite regular. Second, pointing out the contemporary arbitrariness of language and ignoring the *naturalist* position will not make an absolute truth of the *conventionalist* position."

That classmate finished his contribution to the argument rather happy to have confronted the Richies.

The Richies showed confidence. because they knew the Meekies wouldn't come up with more examples to support the *naturalist* position. The Meekies showed some resentment because they knew the Richies would have plenty examples to support the *conventionalist* position. It was a silly antagonism: the Richies wanted to provoke the Meekies' rage; the Meekies wanted to expose the Richies' shallowness. That discussion happened at the end of a very hot summer night inside a small stuffy room crowded with students. Everyone was clearly exhausted and before the discussion could become more heated the tutor closed the discussion.

The students heard that Varro's *De Lingua Latina* mirrored Plato's *Cratylus* as both works reach the same conclusion that the original meaning of words faithfully reproduced nature, however, this faithfulness was lost because the words were corrupted through time. The Meekies were reasonably satisfied to finally hear that Varro believed in the recuperation of the original truthful meaning through the investigation of the history of the words, *id est*, etymology.

Aristotle would never forget the radiant expression of smugness on the face of his nervous friend at the end of that night after the Linguistics class. Aristotle's friend walked to the bus stop in high spirits, confabulating with other Meekies about their triumph in the debate. Remaining friends with him felt like balancing on tightrope; however, as a good Christian, Aristotle was there to make friends not foes. So, that night after the incident involving the Latin assignment, Aristotle took the blame for his nervous friend's behaviour and secretly apologised to the classmates from both groups involved. After all, it'd all been just a misunderstanding and, all is well that ends well.

30

In the undergraduate course of Letters, all the classes of the night shift started at seven p.m. Notwithstanding, I'd determined myself to spend my day in the University Central Library reading ahead as many of the books and texts, which would form the core of the syllabus, as possible before the assignments began flooding into my academic schedule.

Staying the whole day at the library, face buried behind a book or a xeroxed text, eyes moving from the left to the right, left to right, made me feel like those Felix the Cat wall clocks marking the hours drifting slowly by. Reading and thinking and scribbling, the whole day long, left me terribly drowsy during the final hours of the afternoon. When reading and thinking was replaced by nodding off a recurrent image would flash through my mind as a sudden dream: my father calling me a bum and my brother betting I'd crawl back to the stall before the end of the semester. Then immediately, my head straightened up and my eyes pierced whatever text was in front of me. Remaining awake kept those ominous memories asleep.

That reading routine remained the same for more than two months into the semester whilst my savings slipped away. I even contemplated searching for a part-time job at some private school but committing to a job then could jeopardise my strategy to get myself into a research team and obtaining a scholarship – something that I hoped and prayed for day and night.

I continued reading and thinking, hoping and praying, but only that wouldn't get me into a research team. Besides, other students were also aiming at getting themselves into research teams and obtaining scholarships, particularly a small group of students which never missed a chance to brag about their privileged educational background.

These snooty types certainly wouldn't hesitate to trample over other contestants on the run, even more so if they noticed these other contestants came from a State School like me. They viewed themselves above the average students and ensured it transpired by dressing designer clothes, flashy accessories, and showing off their latest model of Nokia handsets. They generally arrived in small groups, showing a bright skin and a lively smile of who never had to catch a crowded public transport to reach the campus. Although these students were all smiles to mostly everyone their socialising boundaries was strictly restricted to themselves. The classroom was the temple of their boasting celebration. And right from the very first night of that second semester, I entered the classroom to find a small group of them, with their desks turned toward each other, forming an almost perfect circle, already practicing their ritualistic small talk slash brag.

"Well, I don't know about you but I wouldn't change the time I've spent in Rio this holiday for nothing in this world." One of the girls from the group said, stretching her arm and almost rubbing a bunch of colourful rubber band bracelets, which she'd probably bought there, on everyone's nose. "It couldn't be more fabulous."

"Ah, we had plans to go this holiday for the second time to Orlando, but my father is defending an important lawsuit in the City Court and we had to postpone the trip." Another girl said, sighing noisily at the end of her statement.

"Yeah, we also had to stay home because my little brother had final examinations in the Trinity Institute, and you know how strict they are over there." Another girl, with no rubber bands to show, jumped into the conversation, clearly happy to have had a chance to name drop the fanciest school of the city. "My father is a close friend of the principal of Trinity Institute and he couldn't manage to arrange an earlier exam to my brother, so we had to cancel our trip to France."

"Oh, tell me about it. I've studied there." The only lad in the circle interfered before anyone else could grab the opportunity. "I hope your brother isn't studying with Dr Arthur. I've studied with Dr Arthur there and he's totally strict." The lad continued, almost spurting a load of saliva each time he mentioned the name of Dr Arthur, who was popular on the close-knit world of academia for teaching in the most expensive private schools. "He failed an entire class when I studied there." He finally added seemingly proud of that fact.

"That's nothing. I studied with his brother Dr Milton in the Catholic School and not a single student would pass without resitting the finals." Another bare-wristed girl found her way into the conversation but couldn't manage to cause much impact since the Catholic School was known for being a philanthropic school.

"Well, no tutor from no school in this world would've made us miss this holiday in Rio." The girl waved her arm full of rubber bands to emphasise her *no*s, and continued. "My father himself cancelled many appointments with important patients at his clinic just to go this time." Then, she turned to the girl who mentioned the Catholic School. "And I don't know about you but my younger sister studied with Dr Milton for three years in the Trinity Institute and she never resat a single exam." That should caution the bare-wristed girl to keep the name-dropping in the conversation at an elevated level.

The bare-wristed girl didn't move a muscle of her face to stand up for her previous statement.

The sudden silence was interrupted by the only lad in the circle who, this time, was clutching and waving his flashy Nokia handset as he spoke. "Well, all I know is that I have no intention to travel pointlessly until I graduate because when I graduate I have made up my mind to do a postgraduate course in France."

Everyone but the bracelet girl burst in "ahs" and "ohs" of amazement.

Alas, their ritual extended into the classes and throughout the semester. During classes they were well articulated, constantly expressing observations, giving examples, and narrating personal experiences, which they judged needed to further illustrate whatever topic approached. Ordinary thoughts sounded remarkable when they expressed them. No matter how irrelevant, uninteresting, dull or commonplace the piece of information they brought to the centre of the discussions in class the whole snooty group would always agree cohesively nodding their heads in approval. The easily impressionable students they hustled with their little farce naturally didn't include me. I knew that the ultimate purpose of their theatre was to crush the other students' confidence and exclude them from the tutors' appreciation. And by attracting the tutor's appreciation to themselves they heightened their prospect of grabbing better grades and consequently being selected to research teams, and being one step to obtaining a scholarship.

Starting from that semester, however, they were met with a little surprise. And I was responsible for presenting them with that surprise well even in the introductory classes. But the best of the award was to happen when the first assessed activities began.

31

It took me just over two months to find some proper opportunities to assert my role in the intellectual pantomime that some of my academic mates staged in the classroom. *I'm behind you...*!

The thin veil of intellectualism those students had put together was successful because they sucked up to each other in perfect harmony whilst the remaining students nurtured their quiet resentment in isolation. But, being no freshman at the university, I'd had it with being pushed aside. I was willing to poke holes in their scheme. There was a potential scholarship at stake to further motivate me, thus it was time to stir those leeches apart a little and bring their scam to light. Those wearying mornings and afternoons in the library had endowed me the extra knowledge needed to highlight the superficiality of their intellect. So, whenever one of them interfered during class with commonplace comments I'd launch a careful counter-argument designed to require more than encyclopaedic knowledge to challenge. Soon, other classmates broke their silence and joined my mini crusade. The game soon turned around.

After classes finished, on the way back home, whilst the la-di-dah classmates, who drove private cars, went different ways without a chance to bond, I joined the classmates who depended on public transportation and we went the same direction, cheering our little successes during classes and boosting each other's morale.

"Tonight we nailed them, huh?" Anthony – a classmate with whom I'd formed a group assignment – kept talking as we walked to the bus stop.

"We deserved that full grade. We worked our arses off in that library all day to have that translation done." I spurted a little bit of bitterness and egotism with every word. "Alright that the tutor highlighted a few inconsistencies but he gave us that full grade because no other group managed to fully complete the translation apart from us."

"I confess I didn't think we'd make the translation with the one-day deadline that the tutor set. Good of him to propose this optional assignment instead of the written exam." Anthony sensed my bitterness and was actually trying to cheer me up. "If you hadn't insisted with us to translate that text, we wouldn't have even tried. I cannot stand Latin to be honest."

"Well, think with me Anthony – it was either presenting the translation by the following day or having two weeks to study for an individual written examination. The few ones who accepted the challenge, and succeeded, now have free time to prepare themselves to the joint presentation of Linguistics within three weeks. Mind that?"

"Phew! Yeah. About that..." Anthony made a quick twitch, thinking for a second before mentioning the inevitable subject. "Aristotle said anything about still being in the group?"

"We didn't talk since that night and I'm really not into any more nuisances right now." I replied trying to put my thoughts exclusively on the coming joint presentation of Linguistics.

"I never thought you'd have that courage, but we all liked you did it. It wasn't fair of Aristotle to lend our draft for them." Anthony again tried to cheer me up. "But yesterday he apologised with us, did you know that?" He added, this time, playing Aristotle's advocate.

"You know what," I began, giving up holding my

feelings on that matter. "I wasn't mad with him in particular. It's his sell out attitude. So, he used our hard work to pose as goodie. Why do you think he lend the draft to that particular group, huh? You know what I'm talking about." I made a brief pause trying to control my emotion uselessly whilst Anthony remained silent. "Nothing pisses me off more than someone outsmarting me. I'm honest about that. But now, don't get me wrong, up to a point we have to acknowledge their intellectual advantage. It's their right. I praise that they had a privileged education, and I judge that they had to make their own effort to explore their potentials. But, boo, don't come rubbing these advantages on my face. That's a challenge for me. They set the table, right? So, I'm just making them feast from the academic banquet more fairly. If they think they can slack off and still be on the top just because of their privileged education and because their parents are better off than ours, hear my words Anthony – that wont' happen easily. And who is not by my side on this thought is against me. So, sincerely, Aristotle may well piss off now because we nailed this translation and we'll nail the joint presentation of Linguistics. But for that we need to put our heads on this presentation from now on."

Anthony just kept twitching his face whilst I filled his poor ear with my bile during that one minute hate speech. "It's alright then. I think he'll stay with us. There we were five of us in the group and he showed up. So he made a mistake, but he's committed, right?"

Before I could say anything back to Anthony three other classmates caught up with us. "Hey, congrats to you." They had a grin on their faces. "We also had a great mark. And aren't we glad we nailed them other ones?" They basically restarted the whole Aristotle issue again, but this time I just kept listening until they hopped onto their buses one by one.

Although my personal reasons ultimately included the grade race – and an unstated dispute for a potential scholarship – I confronted the snobbish classmates essentially because of my impulsive antagonism against social conventions. Watching them so full of themselves and so conformed with their social situation was utterly revolting. By stirring the challenge a little I wanted them to learn that being really better in the classroom realm was less simple than just posing as the crème de la crème.

In the end, the challenge was essentially healthy as a motivational tonic for the academic apathy we all felt during those long nights of study. It was madness as well because I saw the classroom as a battlefield and passionately provoked some of my closest classmates in to joining my private warfare. When group coursework was assigned I'd take the command and start a campaign which sole objective was achieving the maximum grade. I immediately distributed orders as a way of sensing who was really engaged in the mission; if classmates showed any sign of dissatisfaction they'd be free to join other group from the start – a tactic that won me mortal enemies. Naturally, I was sensitive enough to identify who couldn't perform a certain manoeuvre, like earlier hours meetings for example, and I yelled my commands on the ones who could. Gladly, on the escalade to reach the best grades I always relied on a faithful platoon of allies. And so, it was imbued with that spirit of warfare that I started a new campaign, assembling a perfect coalition, for the joint presentation of Linguistics.

A new campaign was already brewing that night, and I was going to really kick all off right from the very next class.

32

"So, we have less than three weeks to get ourselves ready for this presentation." I started, having managed to assemble only five of the seven members of the group formed for the joint presentation of Linguistics before the tutor entered the classroom. "The tutor will want the names of each member of the group tonight, right? We need the names of the two non-present classmates."

"No worries mate, I know their names, but they must be coming anyway." Anthony said whilst he finished signing his full name right under mine and passed the list forward to Aristotle.

"Now, I need your names and contact numbers on a separate sheet, along with information on the time you have to prepare for this presentation. Remember that a report paper have to be produced, so please, be sincere with this – most of us work hard all day, so just let me know and I can allocate the appropriate amount of responsibility among ourselves." I waited for the classmates to finish writing their details down and proceeded with the instructions above the classroom noise. "The tutor will introduce the topics tonight, right? I pick the topic. If anyone has an objection regarding that, just join the group that select your preferred topic." I made a brief pause for reactions.

I employed a demanding attitude with the intention to bring about any hostile reaction – what would suggest a non-committed disposition. I was still feeling dejected for having fallen out with Aristotle, and embarrassed for having expressed my antagonism so blatantly with some classmates. So, the last thing I needed was forming a group with a non-committed member. I had to apply my emotions completely on that assignment because fifty percent of the final grade in the module of Linguistics would be determined by that joint presentation.

"It's alright with me." A member, with whom I hadn't yet formed a group, expressed her approval, prompting all other members to agree as well.

"Great. I have time to assume most of the responsibility for this assignment so I have to work with a topic that is comfortable to me, right? Trust me."

* * *

Joint – or individual – presentations were a traditional practice within the programme of most modules of the undergraduate course of Letters. Such presentations basically replicate the standard method of instruction of a class presentation, only with the students assuming the tutor's function. And the standard method of instruction, across all undergraduate courses around the campus, was delivered through a balanced combination of oral presentation, just like lectures, with classroom interaction and active student participation, just like seminars. Generally, joint – or individual – presentations were assessed in conjunction with a report paper or essay – however, the presentation itself is one of the main moments when a tutor could distinguish and appreciate who was who in the classroom. So, not simply for the grade, but mainly for the tutor's appreciation was that I endeavoured myself to put together a flawless joint presentation. And attracting such appreciation at that particular presentation had a further importance for me: the tutor of Linguistics coordinated a linguistics laboratory in the Sociolinguistics field known as *Linguistic Variation*.

That would be only the initial step though. The commonest route to gaining an official place in the team of the linguistics laboratory, and later applying for a scholarship, would normally involve being invited to participate in the internal reading sessions from the linguistics laboratory. Until then in the semester, no students from the night shift had been invited to take part in the reading sessions by the tutor of Linguistics. Perhaps there were too many students taking part in these sessions already, or perhaps the tutor was waiting for the students' performance during the presentations. Whatever the reason, at that point in the semester, any chance of a possible invitation would depend greatly on creating a real great impression during the joint presentations. But that wouldn't be so easy because joint presentations were usually the snobbish students' strong point, and they'd be equally organised to make their presentation stand out. That was how these students would generally guarantee their entry on to the exclusive shortlist of candidates for the opportunities of getting into any research team that should arise.

Rather than allowing this knowledge to hamper my efforts I embraced it and set out with a fierce determination to break that cycle – it was time to raise the bar on those joint presentations.

33

"Alright, that's ours." Instead of just raising my hand, when the tutor posted the choice of texts for presentations in the board, I approached the tutor's desk and continued. "Can I have a look at that for a sec, please?" When I turned around to sit, I noticed some classmates squirming and others exchanging looks – possibly because I'd just selected the tutor's postdoctoral dissertation on Variation and Dialectology, the largest text available for the presentation.

"Well, I didn't think anyone would really pick my dissertation. No one from the morning shift got it." The tutor said raising his eyebrows. "Is everyone in the group happy with that?"

I turned around and cast a look of complicity at each of the present members of the group. "Is that alright with you?" As they nodded their heads and smiled back in approval, I thought, *Bring it on*!

When it came to decide on the date of the presentations I picked the first slot – just to ensure that our presentation would be specially noticed before the tutor grew bored and distracted with other presentations. So, right after that class, I began the preparations.

First off, I stated that apart from Anthony, who lived not too far from the campus, and Aristotle, who could take a day off whenever he pleased, all remaining members of the group were rather busy during the daytime. Although they couldn't do much, they'd be willing to cooperate with my directions.

From that night on, after classes finished around 10:15 p.m., I began digesting that postdoctoral dissertation. I started reading during on the nearly fifty minutes bus ride and went on when I arrived home, making sure to master every concept and commit every piece of data and references to memory. Then, when I'd completed this process, I arranged a meeting with each group member, over the weekend or before classes, handing responsibility to them one by one for what was to be their specific part of the dissertation and ensuring they understood what they were going to present: introduction, research questions, and hypothesis, methodology, quantitative results, conclusion.

For myself and Anthony remained the responsibility of presenting the theoretical background which largely referred back to an important paper entitled *Empirical Foundations for a Theory of Language Change* – a paper considered a watershed in modern Linguistics. The authors, Uriel Weinreich, William Labov, and Marvin Herzog, had presented the first drafts of this paper in 1966, in a symposium at the University of Texas, addressing theoretical assumptions regarding language change. The subject immediately drew my interest because the authors presented a solution to a dilemma that might appear simple but which had been rather neglected for half a century since the genesis of modern Linguistics.

Linguistics emerged as science in 1916 with the formalisations proposed by the Swiss linguist Ferdinand de Saussure and his Structural Linguistics. Here, Saussure established some concepts which characterised among other things the appropriate object of study linguistics. The object of study was formalised as the *langue*, or language, and not the *parole*, or speech. The *langue* is characterised as a collective psychological phenomenon, permanent, homogeneous, systematic, and therefore feasible to describe while the *parole* is a personal physical phenomenon, ephemeral, diverse, chaotic, and therefore inadequate to description. Saussure also formalised the distinction between synchrony, which is the state of *langue* in a specific moment of time, and diachrony, which is the state of *langue* in successive moments of time. From these, in Saussure's formalisation, only the synchronic description of language is within the domain of linguistics because language change through time already implied a physical consequence and therefore wasn't compatible with the notion of *langue* as the study object.

Changes in the *langue* system could be formally represented though by comparison of synchronic states of *langue* in different points of time. These changes however were described as a discrete process because linguists lacked any theoretical basis to demonstrate how the change slash transition occurred in the *langue*. The authors of *Empirical Foundations* made a theoretical review presenting recent studies which demonstrated that alternating forms in the speech of a community (*parole*) actually revealed the surface of a deep rooted competition within the structure of the language system (*langue*). By admitting that forms co-occurred competitively within the system the authors asserted that the notion of heterogeneity was legitimate and compatible with the notion of structure (Saussure's *langue*). So, if the linguist could provide evidence of an alternating feature in a speech community he could then formally describe either that the alternating feature was in a stage of stable variation or that one of the alternating forms was becoming more predominant – in which case it evidenced a transition process, that is, a change in progression.

Naturally, the issue was a bit more complicated than that. All the references and arguments and new principles from the paper would be too much for a 20 minute presentation. It was actually a lot to fully grasp in the twenty days that I had to study the dissertation's theoretical background. And those days flew by like a flash whist I grew totally hooked on how those scholars had formalised so coherent concepts which enlightened a whole generation of linguists. I even lost my focus frequently as I fell to considering about the parallels between linguistic and spiritual assumptions – both departed from real world phenomena to speculate on the abstract issues they were concerned with, and both had preachers- and followers- ish.

With the swift approach of the D-Day, again I met each member of the group individually to go over the details of the presentation and to let them know the money we'd spend with printouts and transparencies. In the night preceding the presentation I shunned sleep almost to daybreak using those precious hours to rehearse every sentence, gestures and intonation of my part in the presentation. When tiredness struck I'd recall the stall business, the long tedious hours working under hot temperatures, and the trips to fetch water in a bucket to wash plates. That gave me enough motivation to remain awake. After a couple of hours asleep I set off early in the morning, took the bus to the university, headed to the computer cluster to finish typing everything down and printing the handouts and transparencies for the presentation. The whole day was spent on this toil. Anthony and Aristotle were with me to lend a hand; but whereas Anthony had to go home and rehearse for his part, Aristotle, who had been strategically given the shortest section in the presentation, could stay by my side into the afternoon.

After we'd ended preparing all the didactic material for the presentation, we walked to the parking lot, where his father's car was parked.

"So…" Aristotle hesitated a bit. "Please, don't mind me asking. What's with this almost masochistic behaviour? I mean, it's almost like you're choosing the most difficult way to do…"

Before Aristotle could even finish, I jumped in. "You say masochistic; I say self-challenging." I made a pause. "Listen, you're right. There's a pattern of behaviour going on. But, I can only really tell you what's with this pattern if I manage to succeed with my goals. Better still, you may figure it out by yourself, just wait and see what's going to happen after tonight."

34

"If you say so, it's alright with me." Aristotle acquiesced. "Sure you don't want a ride home?"

"Sure – I'll have something to eat around here and do a final rehearsal for later." I refused actually because if Aristotle dropped me home there wouldn't be much spear time counting with the bus journey back to the university.

"So, I think we are all set for tonight, huh." Aristotle said, after having shut the driver's seat door with a bang.

"Indeed we are. We'll put on a show in this presentation tonight." I told, making some effort to sound optimistic and disguise my exhaustion and anxiety.

"I hope you don't mind me saying," Aristotle continued, as I stood waiting for him to drive off. "But every time you mention this presentation your eyes sparkle." Then he drew a smile. "It's like you're starving and the presentation is a banquet."

"That's because I'm starving actually, and I'm thinking how I'm going to feast on those mates of yours tonight." I couldn't resist provoking Aristotle.

"Suit yourself matey-o." Aristotle said and started the car – but before he finally drove off, he added, "And, break a leg tonight – I mean it."

Later that night everyone played their part. As for me, I presented mine with the confidence and oratory skills of an actor heading for an Oscar. At the end of the presentation, the tutor told how much he'd appreciated the group's presentation of his postdoctoral dissertation.

Over the following week, after another presentation had just finished, the tutor was getting himself ready to leave the classroom when, almost casually, he called me aside and suggested that I should come to one of the afternoon reading sessions that he coordinated at the linguistics laboratory. I attended the reading sessions two afternoons, with a conviction that I already was a member of the research team.

In the third session, when I arrived at the laboratory, a student who was an official member of the research team approached me before the reading session started.

"Hey, the tutor told me that I should speak to you." She seemed a little tense. "Well, the thing is that in two months a research report has to be submitted for assessment to the National Council for Scientific and Technological Development (the governmental organization that grants funding to scientific and technological research in the country's universities). So far, I have the data collection and analysis all done but I need someone able to write a theoretical background for this report." She made brief pause. "I need someone to assume this because I have to withdraw from the research team right away. So the tutor said that if you agree I can pass the scholarship to you."

I could hear my heart beating whilst that student said those words. It was like she just knew that I'd desperately wished for that scholarship. I wanted to thank her effusively but I feared that my effusiveness could somehow interrupt the flow of that moment – like when someone awakes in the middle of a dream – and she might suddenly change her mind. So I just agreed with her quietly. In this way I became an unofficial member of the research team, as I continued the research from where the previous student researcher had stopped, and began receiving the scholarship support from her hands.

That second semester came to an end and no other classmate was invited for the reading sessions. Anthony managed to get himself into a research team of regional literature. And I, in the following semester, was officially enrolled in the research team, under the supervision of the tutor of Linguistics, and receiving a monthly scholarship straight into my bank account.

Unknowingly, I'd performed magic, and unknowingly too I'd continue doing magic to make happen every little thing that my heart desired passionately. And from that moment on, my heart's desire would again turn its focus to English.

35

"Er, how about your weekend?" I asked Aristotle, not a little bit bothered about his weekend.

"Is that correct?" Aristotle totally ignored my question. "I learned that *how about* is used to make suggestions, like when you offer something."

"I don't know. You just need to answer something in the simple past tense." It felt weird having to make up questions each time we had conversation practice in the classroom following the instructions of the exercise book. It was like we were studying English for the national census enquiry or to become police investigators.

"Alright, so, what did you do this weekend?" I asked again, following the rules to ask questions using the past simple, but hoping that Aristotle invented a fantastic story to make up for the boredom of that artificial conversation.

"Well, I went to the shopping mall with my girlfriend." As he answered I thought *puke*. "And we watched a film in the theatre." – *Double puke* – "And we ate popcorn." – *Double puke, right on his girlfriend's lap.* "And we had some ice cream. And we kissed…"

"I got the picture." I interrupted Aristotle, knowing that he was extending his mall adventure with girl-*puke*-friend on purpose to provoke me. "You know the simple past rule – And you did what all goodie snob do during the weekend in this hellhole city."

"How about we continue speaking English?" Aristotle sensibly called my attention because I'd just slipped into my mother tongue. "Complain in English, please."

"I'm sorry. You're right." In all truth, I was just jealous because whilst Aristotle had enjoyed the weekend I'd stayed home studying and saving my precious scholarship money. I guess that made me the Ebenezer Scrooge of all weekends. Such grumpiness toward Aristotle was unjustifiable, as I had no strong reason to be stressed in that new semester.

For starters, in the third semester, the English-specific modules doubled within the curriculum of the English Major and there were much less students enrolled in these modules. Consequently, in the English-specific modules, the classroom social scenario changed. The social tension lessened considerably, slowly giving place to an atmosphere of collaboration between those who could speak English impressively well, those who could hardly stutter English, and everyone in between. Everyone was encouraged to get along with each other as we were frequently paired, or grouped, during the conversational activities. The classroom dispute for the tutors' attention remained restricted to the core subjects. Besides, with my official entry into the research team, my reason to remain engaged in that dispute fell exclusively on the so coveted grades.

The mild dispute in the English-specific modules followed another path – the classmates still maintained noticeable associations based on who could speak English, which basically were those who had studied in the private schools of English. And being able to speak English for us, including the tutors, was a question of pronunciation and fluency, more than grammatical accuracy. So, as long as the student could speak fluently and with a British or American accent, grammaticality didn't stand out. But if the student stuttered or had a strong local accent, no one minded if he or she had a coherent grammar at all. As for me, amongst the night shift students, I found myself in the comfortable middle ground. All things considered, the Grammar of English classes were actually a moment for enjoyment and relaxation.

For me particular, those classes of *Grammar of English* had an extra quality: they always reminded me of a moment of enlightenment and illumination. The reason for this was the tutor. And in that very class, explaining about *how about*, the tutor was about to refresh my mind once again.

36

"Are you boys all done?" The tutor of Grammar of English, Glory – a flamboyant blonde in her late thirties – had to draw our attention, as Aristotle and I hadn't realised when all the other students went quiet. "Now I am really curious about what you were talking?"

"We were talking about the meaning of *how about*." Aristotle hurried himself to say. "I think it is used as a suggestion, like, *how about some tea*. But we have doubt if *how about* can be used to ask something that happened in the past, like, *how about your weekend*."

"Well, *how about* can be used for suggestions, but you shouldn't use it to ask about some past event. Use, *how was your weekend* instead. Or, if someone greets you saying, *how are you*, you may say *I'm fine, how about yourself.*" Glory explained with a confidence that put us all at ease to trust her judgement of correctness.

That trust was precious for me because, overcritical as I was of practically every figure of authority, usually I adopted a sceptic mind attitude toward the tutors' judgement of correctness in English. Especially in the case of that blonde tutor, it took me sometime to trust her judgement because of her jovial style of teaching. During classes, she frequently enjoyed telling her memories of the time she'd studied in England, or telling about her recent holidays abroad and her romantic adventures with the exotic men she met abroad. What really changed my overcritical mind attitude toward her was a short exchange that we had during a class in the previous semester after she casually mentioned the sitcom *Friends*.

"Sorry, what was that dear?" She overheard me sighing deeply and whinging something to Aristotle.

"Oh, it's that, listening to you talking about *Friends* reminded me that one of the things that I most fancy is satellite television so that I could watch programmes in English all the time – but I wonder if I'll ever be able to afford satellite one day." I sighed again, thinking how such idea sounded unreachable.

"Of course you will darling. In due time, you'll have satellite television and everything else you desire." She sounded earnestly positive about that.

The earnestness in her words made me instantly retract like a snail. Part of me strained to jump up and protest. "Don't joke with that." *How could that be possible*? I was desperately hoping for a monthly scholarship. *Just imagine satellite television.*

Then, as I allowed that thought to take further form, I had to conceal a silly smile with both hands, because just the mere thought of having everything I desired was an embarrassment in itself.

"Listen, bring a VHS tape and I'll record some programmes from the satellite channels for you, right." It felt like Glory could just hear my thoughts.

That classroom exchange with my blonde tutor Glory rendered my veneration and affection for her – hence, my trust in her authority as a tutor of English – and a VHS tape filled with brand new episodes of a few American sitcoms on the side.

As per usual, I audiotaped the soundtrack of the sitcoms that she'd recorded and thus maintained my ears engaged with listening to an English less conventional than that from the didactic and normative grammar books. However, into the third semester, listening to audio tapes had become more of a marginal practice to maintain myself continuously attuned to English. In addition to using English moderately during the classroom activities in the English-specific modules, as a member of the research team in the linguistics laboratory, I often had to engage in the compulsory reading of chapters and papers in their original English – an activity which kept me enthralled, not so much for the challenge of interpreting advanced technical English, but mainly for the opportunity of being introduced to a new perspective of knowledge on language, and consequently, on English.

37

The chapters and papers approached at the reading sessions of the linguistics laboratory focused predominantly on Variationist Sociolinguistics.

In a nutshell, Variationist Sociolinguistics is the descriptive study of language use in correlation to social factors – geographic region, circumstance of use, stratum, formal education, gender, age, and so forth. The texts focused specifically on fundamental notions in Sociolinguistics, amongst which *language variation* became my preferred.

The notion of *language variation* is essentially associated to the notion of *language correctness*. And the notion of correctness under the sociolinguistic perspective is different from the notion of correctness under the normative perspective. Under the normative perspective, correctness is understood as the language use that conforms to the rules and standards prescribed by canonical publications, like normative grammar books and traditional dictionaries, and imposed by institutional education. Under the sociolinguistic perspective, correctness is understood as a language ideology established and disseminated by conventional values of both expert authorities and ordinary members of a community. Whereas the normative notion of language correctness is endorsed and represented through the Standard language ideology, under the sociolinguistic perspective this normative notion of language correctness is rejected and replaced by the notion of language variation. And language variation refers to the variety of alternative forms that a language assumes – including the Standard form – when actually used by individuals.

I appreciated the notion of language variation because it felt like an authentic and honest approach to understand language use, without bias or prejudice. Naturally, I also appreciated how the normative notion of language correctness (and Standard) was authentic and valuable to the civilised humanity since language anarchy would inexorably hamper the good progress of human communication. But equally, I antagonised the blind and dim-witted support of the normative notion of correctness without an authentic and valuable purpose.

Whilst I indulged myself in both compulsory and independent reading at the linguistics laboratory, I took advantage of that practice to write down a glossary of unfamiliar words from each text and look up the meaning of such words in a bilingual dictionary. Along that indulgence, besides improving my English vocabulary and learning about fundamental notions in Sociolinguistics, I began to understand the sociolinguistic reasons behind my passion for English. But as if my introspective insights weren't enough, the mere presence of a fellow member of the research team constantly reminded me of such reasons. Margaret was her name; but, preferred to call her Peg.

And Peg became that reminder since she first approached me at the linguistics laboratory in the beginning of that third semester.

"Hey – is this the text for our next session?" Peg asked warmly, approaching the large table that occupied the centre of the laboratory where I toiled over a chapter from *The Handbook of Language Variation and Change*.

"Uh-uh," I replied her with a quite familiar tone, since we'd all been introduced to each other during previous reading sessions. "I've already translated the part I got to read this Tuesday."

"Alright, I am going to start translating my section of the text this afternoon." Peg said, leisurely taking a seat on an armless swivel chair next to a personal computer that she'd just turned on. And as she kept facing me across the table, ignoring the computer screen behind her, Peg continued. "If you don't mind, could you email me the translation so I can read ahead later at home?"

"Oh, just have a look in this computer that you're on. The translation is on a file under the name of translation-Chapter16." I said and, as Peg swivelled toward the computer, turned my attention back to the text.

All that could be heard at the laboratory was the humming of the computer because no one beside us had yet arrived. When I continued writing down the meaning of a new word from the bilingual dictionary, thinking that Peg had engaged in her affairs at the computer, again she called my attention.

"Er, do you always look up each word that you don't understand in the dictionary?" She said with a gentle smile whilst her eyes examined the sheets on which I'd written down an endless list of words.

"Yes, I like doing this." I replied with an august expression, a little smug of my endeavour. "It's my technique to improve my vocabulary in English."

"Oh, but this way you're wasting a valuable time to read a full text." Peg said, seemingly interested in the good progress of my reading skill despite her patronising tone. "The correct and most efficient manner is to try inferring the meaning of new words from the context."

"I know that, but it's just that I can learn them better by doing this. And I like really knowing the meaning of each word." I justified myself to Peg quite amiably despite beginning to feel that her unrequested suggestion was slightly getting into my nerves.

"Well, I think that in this manner you're not going to advance much in terms of vocabulary." Peg dropped that and started swivelling the chair slowly toward the computer again.

As much as I struggled not to be dominated by my anger, there was zero chance I'd let Peg go with that quietly.

Peg was a student from the English Major just like me, but her words made me infer that she somehow regarded her abilities with English superior to mine simply because she studied in the morning shift whereas I studied at night. So I put the pen down and stared straight into her overconfident eyes. "Says who? Who determined that inferring is the best way to learn vocabulary?"

"Well, I've always learned that from my teachers at the British Culture…" She made a brief pause after name-dropping the most respected private language course in the entire country, as if to let me digest the authority of her statement. "But think sensibly – the more you encounter a new word recurrently, the more chances you have to infer the meaning correctly, and that's how you get familiarised with the meaning of new words more rapidly."

Peg responded my confrontational attitude with a diplomatic manner that just gave me chills of wrath – by putting on that composed attitude she made the immaturity of my stroppiness stand out.

Still, nothing infuriated me more than knowing that she had a valid point. But I too had a valid point, and so, not to stir that little disagreement into one of my *Battlestar Galactica* scenarios, I breathed more calmly and stated my point. "That does make sense. But this is how I memorised the meaning of quite a few words without having to infer them like a hundred times before. And that cannot be argued."

But, sensing that I'd genuinely moderated my confrontational attitude, this time Peg let out a less reserved bark. "Oh well, if that works for you great. I've heard that the students from the night shift are not very advanced anyway, so that should do."

For a split second her civil manners had actually fooled me into thinking that I was being unduly judgmental of her words. But if that was her business, I too – despite not having a face all covered in slap like her – could pretend to be a shady lady.

And since the topic in question was reading, I prepared myself to read that girl for filth.

38

"What are you talking about? If students from the night shift are not really advanced how come they graduate just like the morning students? They cannot pass all modules without being really proficient in English, can they?" Actually they could – but for the sake of argument I pretended not be aware of that.

Peg then wiped the smile of superiority off her face and replaced with a mordant one. "If you want me to be sincere with that, I've heard from more that one tutor that many students from the night shift cannot even use their mother tongue right. Imagine a foreign language."

I took a long and slow breath, thinking to myself – oh no, she didn't just say that. It was time to put a gag on her mouth – and that gag would be her own words. "If it comes to that, all students from the Northern States, including us here, share similar substandard dialects which are considered incorrect by the language standards of the Southern States. So, you should know that you cannot speak your mother tongue correctly as much as mostly anyone else in this entire university." She heard all that quietly but with a light smirk. "This is basic concept in Sociolinguistics. If you look up the words instead of inferring you can actually understand these concepts from the texts we read." I said, pointing to the *Handbook* and feeling triumphant.

"Well, I don't have a strongly marked accent but I was born and raised in the Southern State of Rio de

Janeiro up to my puberty. So, I actually do speak the standard dialect. But I appreciate your point." She said, just before swivelling slowly toward the computer.

What a bee-atch! Wasn't for the foam forming in my mouth I'd have challenged her there and then to a vocabulary off. Interesting enough, although we were both aware of the Sociolinguistic theories that demystified the superiority of the normative notion of language correctness and Standard language, our behaviour toward language was certainly not consistent with these theories' principles. She supported the conservative ideology through her prejudicial attitude toward some users of the local dialect, and I, identifying myself amongst the target of her prejudice, responded with a resentment that somehow evinced a sense of shame and inferiority toward my own way of using the local dialect.

The grounds of our behaviour derived from the social values of prestige or stigma that are culturally associated to each variety of Portuguese dialect from across the States and regions of the country we dwelt.

Just as Spanish, Italian, French, and Romanian, Portuguese is derived from Vulgar Latin and was brought from Europe to the Brazilian shores during the colonial expansion of Portugal along with the explorers and settlers from the sixteen hundreds onwards. Throughout the colonial period Portuguese successfully replaced the original autochthones' language, the Tupi-Guarani, and also assimilated features of it becoming a language of its own with distinctive local features. Currently, Portuguese is both the official language of education and the colloquial throughout the 26 States of Brazil.

Portuguese, as one language, brings two nations separated by the Atlantic Ocean together.

At the same time, with its variety of accent and grammatical patterns, Portuguese creates a moat between distinct segments within the Brazilian society – between those whose dialect is marked by Standard (prestigious) features, identified as an educated variety of Portuguese, and those whose dialect is marked by local (stigmatic) features, identified as colloquial or regional variety of Portuguese.

Particularly the Portuguese varieties from the Northern States of Brazil are ideologically regarded as inferior in the Southern States and within upper or middle class segments of society. Northern varieties present accents which are fairly stigmatised and many of their distinctive grammatical features are regarded as an offence to the Portuguese language, often by those who doesn't have the minimum knowledge of what Portuguese is yet regard themselves as suitable judges of what is right or wrong in the language. Such judgements are generally based on simple, and mostly pointless, rules from normative grammar books that people can belch out at other's faces during moments of pretentiousness hysteria.

So, being born and raised in one of the Northern States, I acquired a dialect of Portuguese characterised by an accent and grammatical features which are frequently not held in high regard – that is, they are considered defective under the normative notion of correctness. Additionally, due to my strong sense of identity, pride, and stubbornness, at situations which don't require much formality, or at moments when I am caught unguarded, I tend to emphasise the marked characteristics of my dialect during speech. Under a sociolinguistic perspective this is an unconscious behaviour that individuals have to affirm their character through language. And that is what left me in a linguistic dilemma.

Being rather maniac against social conventions, I wouldn't allow anyone to have the power to influence me into conforming to a set of language standards. At the same time, I wouldn't let myself to become an easy target for individuals who, like that Southerner fellow Peg, are always on the lookout for an opportunity to exercise their sense of superiority through the explicit observation and criticism of other individuals' dialectical characteristics.

Somewhat, this dilemma must have led me to seek refuge in the English language. As I met individuals like that member of the research team I developed a thought: if I had to bend myself and my language to conform to the standard set by a segment of society, economically or geographic-ally superior, let me do it appropriately and take a shortcut by learning the language of the first world at once, the language of the former British Empire and current American Empire; let me struggle, kneel, and humble for a language which is really worth struggling, kneeling, and humbling for; let me learn the hell out of English. Such thought sowed and nurtured again and again my passion for English.

And living by the motto that actions should speak up that passion more than thoughts themselves, after having fully committed myself to an English Major, my next step to fulfil that passion was eloping. And thus, I made my mind to run away from home.

39

During that third semester, earning a scholarship afforded me to rent a place just a walking distance from the university and to move out my parents' house. That would allow me to engage more intensively in my academic goals, regarding both my writing aspirations and my English learning efforts. This step actually involved a romantic endeavour of a more ordinary kind – I'd eloped not so much with English per se but with my partner at the time.

This partner had been with me for a good while by then, and since I had this mild issue with half-commitment of any kind, I knew that by sharing a small flat with me my partner would show if he was loyally committed to or just stuck in that relationship. By the end of that third semester living together had helped us to form an idea of what we represented to each other.

"What's your problem? You're constantly making up excuse to go out with your postgraduate mates while I have to stay here guessing what time you come back." I'd initiated my habitual nagging in the middle of a conversation just because my partner kept talking about some plans for the future using the pronoun *I* instead of *us*. As I nagged he remained silent, as usual, sitting at the table with a book on his hands, patiently waiting for me to get tired. But that night I'd drunk a lot of coffee. "We're not together under a roof. We're supposed to be together as a couple. It's evident that in your head there's *you* and *me*, never *us*. What gets me is that I shouldn't bother anymore, because you obviously don't give a damn about our relationship, but I just cannot be like this. Now, ask yourself if this people you hang out with would give a damn if you really needed them. Enjoy while I still care."

"Listen." He finally reacted, perhaps because something I said touched him or just to shut me up. "I don't want to get things mixed. I told you that many of my mates from university are also my workmates and when they invite me to go out I cannot just ignore them – It's part of being there. I cannot be with you in these occasions because I don't want anyone having anything to talk behind my back. I've proven I love you many times already. I can't risk losing my job because that's how I can afford living here with you. I'm sorry you can't understand that."

"Oh, so I'm the stupid one, huh." He turned his head and lifted the palm of his hand to my face whilst I continued. "So, you have a graduation, and you're about to graduate from a Master, and you're valued as a professional by going out with the herd. Don't gimme that, please. I really cannot understand this fascination you have for these people. I just can't."

"Alright, believe what you want." He seemed ready to have the last word. "Your views on everything are always too romantic. Life in the real world is less fantastic than this one you paint. Now, please let me continue reading."

"Oh, I'm sorry for interrupting you. Sure this book is way more important. I guess it's not for work or uni, right." – I knew it wasn't – "This is the problem with us. Reading is already more interesting for you than being with me. What's interesting is that it wasn't like this before we moved together. My mistake was exactly that – moving together. The moment I became a real part of your life I became nothing to you."

"Oh, here we go," He put the book down. "Your complex. This is another thing. You have quite a reputation for not getting along with many people at the university. And you don't approve many of my mates either. I'm not going to make enemies with everyone that you consider beneath your standards of altruism and humbleness. I come from a much humbler context than you, but you don't see me hating the whole world above me. Get rid of this complex mate." He ended his speech and opened the book again.

"Ok, enjoy your reading then. I deserve this just for bothering about us." A few months with my partner and

I'd managed to go from considering myself beautiful and hot to being less interesting than a book. "I should have never left my parents' house."

He put the book down again and finally showed some real emotion. "Alright, just cut the bullshit. First, I also left my relatives', and you suggested living together first of all. Also, you left your parents' house to be near the university and not just to be with me."

"Well, I want to be close to the uni 'cos I have plans – plans that include *you* and *me* together. Not just *me*." I grew angrier but happy to see a human feeling on my partner. "This is the difference – my ambitions include us. I don't follow people around to think of myself as someone. I follow my own way to reach what I want. N' I wish you to be there, with me. This is what we should be together for – to go and to reach as a unity."

"Well, my goal is to survive for now, to pay the bills, until we don't depend of anyone's approval anymore." He replied calmer and without bringing the book back immediately after ending his sentence. "Listen, this isn't what I want, right? But if you're not happy, just move back to your parents' at once. Take what you want with you. Now, stop acting like a child. And if you leave, remember not to blame me for that. I'm just not changing who I am. It's not my fault if the world has rules you cannot accept. Now, please, enough of this non-sense. I understand you're stressed. Please, have a rest."

Indeed, I was stressed. We were together for three months and it'd been frustrating from week one. It was worse before because the first flat we moved to was terrible. We'd moved again to a more comfortable flat just two weeks before and I was enjoying the new place. All my savings were exhausted with the purchase of some basic furniture and the other inevitable expenses, and I was basically broke.

Because my partner had just got a new job and was earning reasonably well he was going out to the cinema, to a few parties – even to the nightclub once – without me. I refused to believe my luck.

My partner was just three years older, and we'd grown up in a similar social background. I couldn't understand how our life experiences truly have made our views about living as a couple so different. Well, he hadn't had any relationship with another man until three years before when I first met him – but I still couldn't admit his reserves on that issue. I trusted him so much because he'd been quite supportive on my latest decisions. But he didn't seem to mind suggesting me to return to my parents' house when he knew full well that I'd left under my mother's protests, tears, and curse. Some sort of evil eye had to be looking down upon me.

I often felt dejected since the beginning of the year but usually I had forces to fight the feeling. That night however, after talking with my partner, I just felt exhausted of everything. So, I decided to commit suicide – by starvation.

I simply stopped eating during three days. And my partner seemed perfectly content to ignore all that.

On the fourth day though, he'd already gone to work but left the breakfast table beautifully set with bread, cupcakes, biscuits, eggs, cheese, coffee, milk and even some fruit. He struggled to give voice to his love for me so I was uncertain whether to take that as an expression of love or as an insult to my suicide attempt. Either way, *chomp*! I botched my suicidal attempt.

Later that same week, something helped me forget all my misery. It struck me that the tip of white cable hanging from one of my bedroom walls looked rather unlike the ones used in residential phone extensions.

So, on my way home from University I bought two extra metres of a similar type of coaxial cable and used it to bodge an extension from the wall to my old fourteen inch television set.

Lord almighty! I could hardly believe my eyes as I flipped through channel after channel on my television and a multitude of channels blared at me, with many of the programmes being shown in their original English soundtrack!

For minutes I continued listening to that fabulous cacophony. It was madness. I then phoned my former neighbour Vicky back from my parents' house.

"Hello... Hi Vicky... It's me yes. You'll not believe it. Listen to this..." I put the phone next to the speaker all excited. "Are you listening? Yes... I have free cable!"

40

"No way!" It was the first night of our fourth semester and Aristotle became all excited when I told him that I'd found free cable during the vacations. "And how could that be?"

"Well, I reckon that because the cable company is located in an area near to the flat most buildings must have cable installed." I explained whilst Aristotle flashed a bright smile. "For some reason the reception on that flat was still on."

"And for some reason it was right in your bedroom." Aristotle began imitating the intro theme from *Night Visions*. "Oh, matey-o. I envy your luck. Cable will never reach my folks' house. And a satellite tv subscription is too expensive." Despite his exaggerated modesty, Aristotle wasn't lying about not having satellite.

I knew that because right after I moved out of my parents' house – having not yet borrowed their old tv set – Aristotle came to class one night, all thrilled, telling me about this new anthology series entitled *Night Visions* that had started showing midnight on Sunday on open television. Then, he recorded some dubbed episodes, lent me his VCR and a tv set for a weekend, and basically obliged me to watch the series.

"I guess you can watch *Night Visions* in English."

"Yes. It was showing another night on Warner Channel but I saw it just once. It doesn't seem to be on the programme anymore." I replied, noticing his disappointment.

"Oh, I was thinking that you could borrow my VCR and record some episodes in English for me." Aristotle suggested, a bit hesitantly.

"Yes, please. Bring me a tape and I'll record anything you want." Aristotle opened a smile again. "If *Night Visions* is not on anymore I'll find a series you'll like."

Indeed *Night Visions* didn't show anymore. Instead, I recorded episodes of the classic black and white *Twilight Zone* and the *Night Gallery* pilot that showed late at night on Viacom. Aristotle had never watched *Twilight Zone* until then. Just months before, when he introduced me to *Night Visions*, I narrated to him an entire episode of the classic *Twilight Zone*, which aired on television long ago. On the occasion, I couldn't imagine that I'd ever record an actual episode for Aristotle to watch. After having watched, he came to class eager to announce his impressions.

"Hey, matey-o. It was brill! *Night Visions* totally ripped *Twilight Zone* off. Even the opening sequence is identical – that nail turning in the air is just like the door turning in *Twilight*." Aristotle was euphoric. "And it's really great watching in English. Matey-o, finding this cable was really a blessing. What are the odds? Now, I see why you like *Twilight Zone*."

Aristotle kept talking about the episode that he enjoyed the most: *Valley of the Shadow*. This was an episode about a machine of high-technology that could rearrange atoms and both generate and destroy anything.

"Matey-o, if I had that machine." Aristotle kept repeating with a bright smile and dreamy eyes.

I had exactly that same thought. And I remembered the free cable. But that didn't come from any machine. Either the heavens heard my prayers, or my passion for English had been reciprocated. I'd sought for English for quite some time; perhaps this time English sought me out instead.

Still, even taking the cable incident into consideration, thinking that English could have sought me out sounded unnatural and far-fetched. All in all, in a global scale, English gradually gained presence in the daily context of non-English-speaking free countries throughout the last decades – a consequence of the technological development and availability of the mass media like radio, television, cinema, video cassette players, video games, and internet, all of which carries along chiefly American products. In the beginning of the twenty-first century, it is mainly the internet availability that makes English present to many individuals wherever they turn to. In previous decades, English also marked its incidence on individuals' reality – though on a lesser scale – through diverse media.

The incident with that cable made me recall the extent of the incidence of English on my own reality back in the Eighties and Nineties.

41

In the Eighties, English appeared to a generation who witnessed and embraced all the rage of the American cultural influence of the time. The amplitude of my exposure, growing up in Brazil, must reflect that. Great swathes of my childhood were spent in front of the TV, hooked on the Universal, Warner Bros., and Hanna-Barbera cartoons, the ABC, CBS and NBC network series and sitcoms, and the cinema productions which aired on tv long after their theatres' release. Although all of these were dubbed, here and there, English words from titles or signs that clearly related to images on screen still filtered through the viewers' cognition.

The most direct contact with English sounds came from the pop songs – most from the soundtracks of Brazilian soap operas – that became instant hits on radio. This had an odd side effect: thousands from the younger generation by then would happily sing hits by artists like Freddie Mercury, Madonna, Michael Jackson, Oingo Boingo, and Pink Floyd without understanding a single word of what they were singing.

Yet a more conscious use of English in speech came through loanwords. In the Eighties, English named everything that was supposed to be cool among the youths. Loanwords like *yes*, *boy*, *man*, *brother*, *cap*, *bike*, *hang-loose*, *popstar*, *night club*, *show*, *MC*, meaning DJ, *drink*, meaning spirits, *look*, meaning appearance, and all dance and music styles names, like *break-dance*, *rock*, *funk*, *rap*, *soul*, *house*, and many more, were part of the youth colloquial. Furthermore, English was carried along imported brands and products, like *Jeans*, *Walkman*, *diet Coke*, *Coca-Cola light*, *Care free*, an intimate absorbent, *Glade sun*, an air freshener, *Sun Down*, a sun screen, and countless more. Also, certain areas naturally attracted English terms, like sports, with *surf*, *kite surf*, *body board*, *paraglide*, *skate*, *motor cross*, *mountain bike*, and *cooper*, meaning jogging. Hard core terms of Social Communication and Commerce also used loanwords like *business*, *marketing*, *lobby*, *ombudsman*, *VIP*, *slogan*, *know-how*, *ticket*, *self-service*, *outdoor*, meaning billboard, *data show*, meaning overhead projector, and *shopping centre*, under American spelling. All these were words actually used and spelled under English conventions, along others that were adapted to fit Portuguese spelling conventions.

In the Nineties, before the internet revolution reached the particular regions where I dwelt, English was still distant to many like me. Lyrics of popular hits were sacred possessions shared only among friends. A friend of mine, named Helen, kept relics like *Black & White*, *Like a Virgin*, *Express Yourself*, *Erotica*, and others neatly handwritten in a hard cover folder. Her great project was to transfer all those handwritten lyrics into a computer archive – none of us had a computer. At times, we seriously engaged in cracking the lyrics of impossible songs like *Guilty*, by the Bee Gees and Barbary Streisand, *Wuthering Heights*, by Kate Bush, and *I Will Survive*, by Gloria Gaynor. The second stanza became the forbidden unexplored zone. Radio shows devoted to translations of English songs produced hilarious non-sense lyrics. Hard core English was still so alien to everyone that in the middle Nineties, in a children's tv show called *Xuxa Hits*, the group Twenty Fingers performed *Short Dick Man*, a hit that includes words like *get the fuck out of here*, with no censorship in front of a bunch of dancing and cheering youngsters.

This innocence and alienness over English was brushed away with the Noughties.

By then, on national radio stations, taboo words in *Eminen*'s hits started being beeped out. And with the new technology, whilst the world shrunk English became larger than life. Vocabulary dealing with computers reached people's language as fast as the high-tech novelties. Once a new product reached the market there was no time for renaming it. Increasingly, Hollywood films, mainly from the superhero genre, were released with their untranslated titles. English was taking over billboards, baptising shops, and replacing brand names. English went from an extra feature on the curriculum vitae to a compulsory requirement for jobs and became an asset worthy of monetary investment. English became big business as language courses occupied expensive properties in fancy avenues. Being skilled in English became a coveted power, a symbol of success and class distinction.

Within this picture, thinking that English reciprocated my passion because I'd stumbled on free cable indeed sounded like a stretch of imagination.

But I desperately needed to believe that something in this world loved me in return, because in that apartment where I was living my pleas for attention continued to be completely ignored by my partner.

Since persistence had always been part of my nature, after much complaint, and a lot of rejection, it was time to appeal to my lowest trick in an attempt to at least attract my partner back to my room.

42

"Lovey, your favourite cartoon is showing. Aren't you coming to watch *Aquaman* with me?"

It was late at night and *Aquaman* was about to start on *Cartoon Network*. Since the flat had two bedrooms my partner slept in a separate one when he wanted quiet and peace – which was basically all nights as I liked to fall asleep watching TV.

"I don't want to stay up late tonight." He answered from his bedroom.

"But tomorrow is Saturday." I wanted to go there and drag him by force. But he was 22 pounds (10 kilos) heavier than me – and not an ounce of body fat.

"Yes, but is the only time I got to meet and discuss an assignment with a mate." Though that was an utter excuse, he was telling the truth.

"Please, come and watch with me." In other nights that would be an argument starter, but I was too happy with the cable to spoil that moment. I always wanted to watch cartoons late night, and open television never showed cartoons at that time. "Just a little, please."

Perhaps because I insisted almost purring, he decided to come and tuck himself under the covers behind me. He remained silence for a moment and eventually talked. "I won't stay long."

"Ah, they'll show *Saturday Night Live*." – Reruns of *SNL* showed every night at midnight and I'd only heard of *SNL* before those days. – "Please. It's so good watching together. You don't care for the things I like anymore."

"I'm here right. So, don't start." He paused for a moment. "Listen. How long do you think this'll go on? We're not paying for it."

"Well. Whether we use or not, it's there." I said calmly, not willing to think about that.

"But the cable was clipped when we arrived." He insisted in spoiling the mood, although he clearly enjoyed watching as well. "The flat lease is in my name and I want no trouble with the owner."

"I know. But you know what I think about this." I turned to face him but he kept staring at the TV. I put on a solemn tone and said. "I think this is a gift." He rolled his eyes; yet he didn't seem pleased, he couldn't hold a straight face.

"Listen." He started with a mild smile. "It's alright. But you know how I feel about these ideas of yours. It's that you fantasise too much sometimes. Don't be angry, ok." He paused, pondering the consequences of what he was about to say, and let it out. "But you'll end up hurting yourself with these ideas."

We'd already had that discussion. He usually was considerate but rather sceptical about such ideas. I usually strived to make him understand that our main problem was that our beliefs diverged and that would ultimately lead us to different paths. But I didn't want to go down that road again. At least his honesty about that made me happy somehow. "It's alright. But we should enjoy while we can, huh?"

"Yes – there's no harm there. Let's watch amoretto." When he called me by that word I knew all would be sweet between us.

In the following morning my partner was back to his pragmatic mood. He disappeared for the morning, sent a phone message informing me that he'd stay away through the afternoon, and would be back late in the evening, if not later. My own obligations were much; but at least then, when I found myself alone, I had cable and tv in English to keep me company. And I'd desired for that so much that I didn't dare to be miserable then.

So I decided to stop bothering my partner with whinges and kept minding myself that no matter the explanation on what had brought cable to my bedroom, I should accept that English was there for me, and I should better enjoy it.

I then bought a small cart to drag the tv set around the flat and began watching, and watching, to sheer exhaustion.

I was watching in my bedroom whilst falling asleep, whilst waking up, whilst getting dressed to university, in the bathroom while brushing the teeth and showering, in the living room during breakfast, in the kitchenette whilst washing dishes, in the tiny laundry area whilst washing clothes. I was watching programmes in English in ways I'd never watched before. I was watching all I could fit in between reading sessions, research activities, and university course work. I was watching shows long forgotten by the open television channels – *The Simpsons*, *Futurama*, *Family Guy*, *King of the Hill*, *Married with Children*, *The Nanny*, *The Twilight Zone*, *Night Gallery*, *Goosebumps* –, I was watching shows I knew only by name and others I never heard of before – *SNL*, *Larry King Live*, *Titus*, *Malcolm in the Middle* –, I was watching shows I didn't give a damn about – *Caroline in the City*, *Coach*, *Home Improvement*, *Reba*, *Wings* –, I was watching simply because they were shown in English. And I was watching my favourite, *Will & Grace*, and loads of cartoons.

I felt like the world's happiest and luckiest man. Then, one morning, I heard the door buzzer.

When I opened the door, it was the cable installer.

43

"Morning. I represent the company supplier of cable and I'm here to disconnect the main cable." The installer made no fuss about that.

"Ok, go ahead." I answered, a bit uncomfortably. "You need to enter?"

"No. I'm just notifying. The main wire is in the hall." Without saying no more, the installer walked to the hall, pulled a pair of clippers from his pocket, and with a swift single snip severed my source of joy.

I mourned throughout the entire day at the university.

Later, when I met my partner back home he didn't mention anything. I waited for a minute and eventually expressed my feelings. "Well, better to have had cable and lost than never to have had cable at all."

My partner opened a smile.

"Listen – let's do one thing. Tomorrow we'll find out how much a NET satellite contract costs and if it's affordable we can share a six-month contract." He surprised me. That was the partner I'd fallen for.

The next day we found a common free time and met at the NET satellite shop. A six-month contract would cost almost half of a minimum wage monthly, but as we agreed to share, we could afford it. And to think that the entire previous day I'd thought that English – and my good fortune – had suddenly abandoned me. I even felt guilt. Perhaps, I should be a little more patient with my partner. I embraced him. "Oh, I love you."

As usual, my partner looked a little uncomfortable with that public display of affection. But who really knows if there would be other opportunities to show how much I appreciated him? *Carpe Diem*. I ceased the moment and I was proud of that. And that gesture of love was blessed. The sales assistant, a pretty young lady, felt so touched to see a committed couple like us that she arranged to offer us a one-year contract which would cost one third of a minimum wage monthly.

"Oh luvvy. Shall we go for a full year contract?" I beamed at him; but then I noticed he had a look on his face that decidedly didn't share of the same excitement.

"What...?!"

44

"...So after they pull him from inside the wall, the other man says they were holding on to half of his body all the time. And he thought he'd been there inside the other dimension wholly. But it was just his mind playing tricks on his senses you see. Then..."

"The staff confirmed the strike." Aristotle interrupted me, sounding disappointed.

We were in the classroom waiting for the tutor to arrive and I'd engaged so intensely in narrating a *Twilight Zone* episode that had shown in the night before that Aristotle's aloofness passed me by.

As I didn't say anything back, Aristotle added: "They start this week; and I guess the tutors won't take long to follow."

"I cannot find that all bad." It was almost the middle of the fourth semester and the main assignments had been already set. Though only two of the four modules were English-specific, the predominance of literature modules demanded strenuous hours of reading. I tried to cheer Aristotle up by making him see how we could take advantage of the imminent strike. "Let's say the tutors follow the strike. We can always get together to read the texts for *American Literature I*, and discuss ideas for the assignments."

"We'll see about that later." Aristotle responded to that suggestion with a disinterested tone. He started fiddling with his mobile – presumably texting his girl. I knew Aristotle wanted to graduate fast, so he could get a stable job in some State school and wed his girlfriend.

"Hmm, your enthusiasm tells I won't see even half of you during the strike." With his eyes on the phone, Aristotle didn't bother responding to my comment.

"Yep – I already lost you to another dimension." I said, not loud enough for him to hear.

And I was absolutely right about that.

Aristotle vanished soon as the tutors joined the staff strike – something they agreed to do immediately on the grounds that the students would struggle to continue attending classes and completing assignments without having access to the university facilities like the computer clusters and the Central Library.

The strike lasted months. The activities at the linguistics laboratory continued through the strike though, keeping me busy during the morning only. I used all the free time left to read ahead all the compulsory texts and, naturally, to watch the satellite channels until my eyes pop out.

When classes resumed, I'd been watching programmes in English so much, that being back to a classroom crammed with people using their mother tongue made me feel like I'd been on holidays in some English-speaking country. Those months of intense watching and listening to American television had benefitted my listening proficiency noticeably. I could understand the *CNN* channel, which had no captions, quite confidently – though *CNN*' formal English didn't pose half the challenge of the rule-breaking English of sitcoms, that was a start.

By the end of the semester, I could also brag about my hard won ability to read difficult texts in English honed mainly by attending, and excelling in, the module *American Literature I* which covered the literature produced during the European exploration of the New World as well as early American Literature until 1820.

The syllabus included texts from the volume one of *The Norton Anthology of American Literature*. Among others, the following texts were included: extracts from the 3rd book of John Smith's *General History Of Virginia, New England and the Summer Isles*, entitled *The Proceedings and Accidents of the English Colony in* Virginia; extracts from *The Complete Works of Captain John Smith*, specifically *A Description of New England* and *New England's Trials*; extracts from William Bradford's *Of Plymouth Plantation*; two excerpts from Thomas Morton's *The New English Canaan*, namely *The General Survey of the Country* and *The Incident at Merry Mount*; some of the Anne Bradstreet's poetry, like *A Dialogue between Old England and New*, *In Honour of that High and Mighty Princess Queen Elizabeth of Happy Memory*, and *The Flesh and the Spirit*; one of Cotton Mather's accounts of the trials against witchcraft held in Salem, Massachusetts; extracts of Jonathan Edwards' *Personal Narrative*, from *The Life and Character of the Late Rev. Mr. Jonathan Edwards*, and two of his sermons named *A Divine Supernatural Light*, and *Sinners in the Hands of an Angry God*; a Benjamin Franklin's essay for the twenty-fifth anniversary issue of *Poor Richard's Almanack* entitled *The Way to Wealth*; and Thomas Jefferson's *The Declaration of Independence*.

I'd had plenty time to read them all thoroughly and to produce numerous vocabulary-enhancing glossaries during the strike.

Those indigestible texts became food for the mind thanks to the tutor, Dr Luna, whose presentations contextualised some obscure accounts of American history, not explicitly expressed in the texts, on the difficulties of settlement of the first English settlers and on how these first settlers were determined to remain in the wild America and to mould those savage lands into a home which they could be proud of.

In her classes, Dr Luna breathed American culture into the students' intellect and guided us to make sense of America's place in the world. Through Dr Luna's presentations we came to realise how pivotal religion and pragmatism had been in building the foundations of intellectual thinking that made the United States the economic empire it is today.

In the very last class of *American Literature I*, when Dr Luna began to return our essays with the corrections and marks, I had goose bumps all over my skin. That was the moment to confirm if my commitment and effort upon those texts had paid off.

45

"I saw that." Aristotle whispered, referring to the mark on my essay. Since Dr Luna was still talking about some of the essays with us, I pretended not to have heard him. But, Aristotle insisted in passing a note (in English) to my desk.

Well done. You deserve that full grade.

"Quiet." I mouthed with a frown, and ignored him until the end the class.

When Dr Luna left the classroom, Aristotle jumped out of his desk and began with his overemphasised Dale Carnegie's *How to Win Friends and Influence People*-style flattering. "I am so – so much – proud of you."

"Oh please… The tutor was generous." That humble attitude hardly camouflaged my smugness, as I could tell, judging by Aristotle's sneer. So I tried to beat Aristotle on his own game. "Well, your speaking assessment mark in *Grammar of English* was way better than mine."

"Hmm, which means you do compare, which means you do mind, which means that my compliment is appreciated. So, I'm proud of you, matey-o."

Aristotle flashed his front teeth, twitching his nose. He knew he was right about me. I did compare marks when the tutors placed them at the departmental notice board. Aristotle also knew this specific grade meant a great deal to me. That was the first assessed essay in English from the course and I'd commented with him that the grade would measure the level of my writing proficiency.

The tutor had highlighted inconsistencies on grammar, but a full grade meant that my writing proficiency – which includes ability in terms of coherence and cohesion – reached a reasonable level.

"Well, thank you. I'm happy really. But I have to say: with my mark in the oral assessment lower than yours, my spoken English must be in shambles."

Aristotle narrowed his eyes to slits and said, "I'll take that as a self-deprecation."

Sadly, for both of us, it was not self-deprecation. All the tape listening, telly watching, and text glossing, had virtually no effect on my spoken proficiency and my English still sounded pretty much the same. But after a prolonged semester of virtual brainwashing from *American Literature I*, more than ever, I was determined to mould my barbaric English into a full-fledged American English which I could be proud of.

If my wildest ambitions had never before threatened to take me beyond the borders of my State, the desire to improve my English knew no such boundaries turning to the United States as an idée fixe as a new hope for it. And the solution would be the exchange programme agreement which the International Affairs Office maintained with some overseas institutions.

Students who had been overseas all seemed to speak English more fluently than the unfortunates who never had a chance, or couldn't be bothered, to go. America was the extra mile my English needed to progress.

But, taking part in the exchange programme, if I could gain a place on the scheme, involved paying an airline ticket and gathering funds for lodging and food, most of these to be paid for in the mighty American currency, the Dollar, which was nearly three times the Brazilian currency. Ironically, after my scholarship had delayed owing to the staff strike, I had to borrow money to afford public transport for some time. If some of my classmates knew of my considerations in taking a chance on the exchange programme I'd become the laughing stock of classroom.

No. This was a luxury for the wealthy. I'd crossed the line this time – another pretentious fantasy, more pretentious even than having satellite months ago. Yet, the memory of that fantasy, satellite tv – once a dream, then mine for some precious months – gave me strength and set my mind. After all where there's a will there's a way. Besides, in that fourth semester I'd realised that *Will & Grace* weren't simply words that give title to a sitcom but that they summarised the underlying ideas of those texts of American Literature *I*.

If I learned something in *American Literature I* it was that many American intellectuals had in their writings bequeathed more than just classical texts. Their literary work presented testaments of faith and commitment which would serve to improve themselves as Americans and consequently the country throughout time.

Driven by hopes of a better life for all Captain John Smith and his men crossed the ocean to reach a savage land; he tells of the weakness and sickness induced by a diet of biscuits while enduring the rigours of life at sea for over five months, then the hardships endured by those that survived throughout their settlement in the Virginia Colony; yet he still remarks that "everything of worth is found full of difficulties." William Bradford tells how the Pilgrims relied chiefly on faith in search of a place where they could practice their religion in freedom; he tells of the diseases the Pilgrims faced in their journey from England along the Mayflower and of the self-sacrifice endemic during the settlement of Plymouth, Massachusetts. Jonathan Edwards recounts making a solemn dedication of himself to his faith and vowing to spend his lifetime in search of self-improvement and self-perfection. Benjamin Franklyn's main message with his poor Richard's maxims goes along the lines that it's always wise to save time and money because these are the most precious values on earth, and being diligent to your industry is a sure way to wealth. And finally, Thomas Jefferson makes it clear in *The Declaration of Independence* that among the precious rights endowed by the Creator to men is the pursuit of happiness.

As it seemed to me, it is the American's depth of belief in this right which has made them so determined to challenge all obstacles in their pursuit of land, religious freedom, faith, self-improvement, wealth and whatever constituted happiness for them. Compared to these accounts of faith and commitment my plans of going to the USA to improve my English seemed a small, almost insignificant challenge. All in all, if my aim was to copy their language well perhaps I should also make an effort to emulate their very ethos.

Yes. I was determined. *I was going to America*!

46

WILLIAM

The exchange programme of the International Affairs Office opens as many doors to overseas universities as possible to local students. Yet each year, as more students become aware of the advantages that this programme offers, the competition for specific overseas universities increases. The places at overseas university are awarded to each student considering their choice of university and their grades in a language proficiency test organised by the I.A. Office team. So, if ten students apply for an overseas institution that offers five places then the five students with the highest scores in the proficiency test succeed whilst the others may be offered a place at other language equivalent institution by the I.A. Office team. The places available are confirmed yearly just over a month before the process of selection starts. The exchange programme kept an exchange agreement with educational institutions in countries where Japanese, German, Spanish, French, or English, were used as first languages. The United States of America and United Kingdom were generally the destination for students whose choice of language is English. For the academic year of two thousand and three the choices were Central Connecticut State University or Mississippi College in the USA and University of Manchester or University of Leeds in the UK. Taking part in the exchange programme offered during that year was perhaps the greatest risk William had chosen to take in his young life.

William remembered how reluctant he was when his lady friend Ana insisted with him.

"C'mon, let's apply together for the selection process of the exchange programme." Ana almost pleaded. "At least to test our English proficiency; no commitments whatsoever."

"There lies the problem. You have studied years at the British Culture and I never been to any private course. I don't stand a chance." William knew his English was good but not enough for a formal proficiency test.

"Is that what you're afraid of? That's no excuse. Besides, when we pass, there's this ex-girlfriend of mine who lives in Leeds now and she can perfectly help us to find a job over there."

William ended up accepting the invitation.

Initially, coming from such humble origins as his, William could hardly bring himself to imagine being in a foreign land. He'd been born and raised in a small village situated thousands of kilometres away from the capital city of the State. Living in such place, his contact with English came basically from the grammar lessons that he had at the State school. Yet, he improved his English mostly by exchanging song lyrics with friends and translating them using a pocket bilingual dictionary. He enjoyed doing that because he liked singing songs in English, but most importantly, he liked actually knowing what he was singing about. His most intense experience with English happened during his adolescence with the event of his conversion to Protestantism when he joined the Regular Baptist Church of his village which was run by Baptist American missionaries.

William had left his small village and moved in with his uncle's family at the capital city in order to continue his educational path. Despite his uncle's family support and fair treatment, life under a roof that wasn't his parents' always had its constraints and downsides.

Life gave him a break when he started teaching Portuguese Language and Regional Literature in a fancy private high school; that allowed him to afford moving out from his uncle's house.

William had just finished his Master's degree on Regional Literature, and was enrolled on his second Major in the undergraduate course of Letters when he let himself be persuaded to apply to the selection process.

The exchange programme demanded heavy investment and William had to weigh that decision cautiously. Having lived a life devoid of luxuries, he knew well the value of money. In his job at the high school he battled daily to keep up with the demands of the principal, the coordinator, the students and the students' parents. They kept him on his toes constantly. On top of this, years of distance from his immediate relatives, combined with the murder of his father during his first undergraduate course, had left him emotionally insular and unable to share his workday anxieties with anyone.

A long period of pain had made him grow dry and given him an inner strength which allowed him to cope with the ceaseless pressures of an unforgiving world. He loathed having been born in a remote corner of the planet, far from real civilization, and never accepted this as his lot in life. That had driven him to fight fiercely for a better place in the world. After so many life shortcomings, he was finally taking the place in the world he'd so much fought for with his job in the high school. Because the high school was located in the fanciest area of the capital city, that job brought with it, besides a reasonable salary, some element of prestige.

Going on an exchange programme was a dream that he'd kept censured in the back of his mind. He was too self-conscious of his reality and socio-economic place.

But then, the savings from his job, and the scholarship that William received from the postgrad programme during his Master's degree, enabled him to pursue an exchange experience at a British university.

And a British university would be just perfect for his English!

William always aimed for the British standards of pronunciation and was proud of speaking with a marked British accent amid undergrad students of English who usually made efforts to mimic the American pronunciation. Naturally, having had a poor language experience, his efforts to mimic the British pronunciation focused on the more marked and stereotypical features of distinction between the British and American English.

When uttering words like *Peter* or *butter* he always ensured that he used all the breath of his lungs and strength of his jaw combined with his tongue muscles to squeeze the 't' sound just to make it sound distinctive from the American flap 't' in the same words. He considered the forms *going to* or *want to* sacred whilst *gonna* or *wanna* were aberrations of English. Also, whenever he heard a learner of English dragging the postvocalic rhotic 'r' sound in words like *car* or *door* just to sound more American, William's face would twitch in disgust.

Taking into consideration William's conceptions regarding the distinctions in pronunciation between American and British English, he had one certainty: two semesters at the University of Leeds surely would boost his perception of these distinctions.

Gladly, that year, a good few places were available at the University of Leeds – ten precisely. Still, for each place offered there was a horde of eager candidates.

When the result of the language proficiency test was posted online, William and Ana were waiting together.

47

"That has to be wrong. I can't have failed in the speaking test. I've already presented a class seminar in English. How come they failed me based on a simple interview?" Ana couldn't shake the feeling that she'd been cheated. She, however, also failed in the written test and that couldn't be contested.

"I'm sorry – don't know what to say." William was surprised to realise that Ana, who had so insisted on that enterprise, had failed in the proficiency test whilst he, on the other hand, had passed.

"Oh God, it can't be true, they must've made a mistake." Feeling disappointed, and unavoidably embarrassed, she barely heard William's apologies. But after calming down a little she managed to say to William. "I'm sorry you didn't pass too."

William was surprised. "What are you talking about? I did pass."

"Nuh-uh. Here." – She pointed to the scores in the screen. – "Only these ones were selected. Your total score was just above seven, but it wasn't sufficiently high to get you a place in Leeds."

William squint his eyes towards the computer screen and realised, more disappointed than in disbelieve, that Ana was indeed right.

Later in that same day, however, William was contacted by a member of the International Affairs Office team who offered him another option: one of the two places available at the Mississippi College!

Despite his disappointment at being offered an American destination, William couldn't refuse the offer as it could be his only chance to go abroad. Still, it'd prove to be a much better option than his first choice.

The Mississippi College was administered by a Board of Trustees elected by the Mississippi Baptist Convention. William knew this was a considerable stroke of luck because he'd be going to an institution run by members of the same religion he professed commitment to. To tell the truth, he'd been a little distant from the Church and from his religious obligations for some time but that didn't mean he considered himself disconnected from the Baptist persuasion. Particularly in a moment like that – when his faith seemed to have called out to him – William couldn't allow anything to hold him back from that unique opportunity. And so, when September came, off to America he went to attend the largest private university in the state of Mississippi.

Despite having taken all the money he'd saved from his scholarship, plus his last three months wages, William still didn't buy enough Dollars to pay for the accommodation and catering expenses. And his student visa prohibited him from working in the USA. William felt less uneasy though, when he found out that the other student who also came to the Mississippi College faced a similar financial situation.

The Mississippi College, however, knowing the situation of the newly arrived students offered to help wholeheartedly with their academic expenses. William particularly, received some of the most costly books of the course. Both students received excellent treatment, being constantly invited for meals in the house of the Language Department coordinator and for days out at cultural events around Clinton. William attracted a special sympathy and regard from the two ladies who worked in the Language Department. That gave him the certainty that he'd made the right choice in coming to Mississippi. Besides, owing to that experience, he was closer to the Baptist Church than he'd been for a while.

Indeed, William had been distant from the Church lately to avoid conflicts between his moral commitment as a member of the Baptist Church and the fact that he'd enjoyed a long term relationship with another homosexual male – with whom he'd lived beneath the same roof for over a year before embarking on the exchange experience. So, despite all the blessing of being drawn closer to his faith and being so well regarded by the Language Department staff, William had to exercise discretion regarding his homosexual inclinations to avoid offending those who treated him with kindness. He didn't want to run the risk of losing their affection. All in all, that was a strict aspect of his intimate life and no one's business but his.

However, William never hid the fact that he'd left someone he loved back home. On that note, William was quite clever, because it saved him the need to explain why he was never interested in dating any girls around from the Mississippi College.

And to ensure the authenticity of that story, William usually let others know that he maintained contact with his loved one back home. Naturally, he used scrupulous caution around that subject and, whenever he mentioned it, he always made sure to refer to lady friend's name: Ana.

Occasionally, one of the ladies at the Language Department would ask, "And how are things going with this young heart?" Or even comment on William's state of mind. "It seems like you've been missing your sweetheart these days."

William had to be quick and astute when responding. "Yes, I didn't manage to get in touch with Ana lately." He usually exercised sincerity. Yet, he had to be careful not to let his speech be carried away by his feelings and end up revealing too many details about this or fall foul of contradictions.

"Please, don't let yourself feel heavy-hearted. If you ever need, come and use the office's phone. It's good to say a quick hello to your mom, girl, friend, whatever."

William was reminded of that quite often at the beginning. Once he even asked Ana to play along, and actually phoned her from the Language Department office so that she could speak to the ladies at the office.

William also had to be diligent with the contents of the movies he borrowed from the library; they could check his records, or his roommate might see and comment with others. The nearest video rental shop outside the campus was far off; except by car, there was no easy way to reach the nearest off-campus facilities in Clinton. Once he'd decided to walk there and someone stopped by the road to give him a ride and tell him of the dangers of making that way on foot.

Once, during Easter, near the end of the exchange programme term, when his roommate was out for the weekend, he took the risk of renting a movie outside the campus called *Burnt Money* – a Spanish movie about a bank robbery with a strong explicit male homosexual theme. Though William knew he could always say he failed to read the synopsis on the cover, to avoid any awkward situation, he kept the video well mixed among a bunch of books he brought in a shopping bag. Just two days later, William hardly believed it when he read an e-mail from his partner telling that he'd watched *Plata Quemada*, the same movie, that very same weekend. William felt deeply moved as he read about that coincidence. He couldn't stop thinking about the emotional connection he had with his partner and being slightly remorseful for having left him behind to embrace that exchange experience. He felt an unusual strong need to share his intimate thoughts about that coincidence but wouldn't dare to share it with anyone.

When the classes restarted after the Easter holidays, one the ladies at the Department came to William soon as she saw him. "Are you feeling alright this morning sweetie?" Her tone sounded more like she wanted him to know that she actually noticed that he was feeling heavy-hearted.

"I'm fine – just a little headache." William had to find an alibi to what should be obvious on his expression. "But I had a good rest these days."

Then, like she could feel that William really needed to unburden himself, she put it more carefully. "Is there anything you want to open up with us? Just come to mama, sweetie."

"I'm alright, for real." William answered, putting a smile on the top of an expression of who didn't have a hint about what she was talking. And as he followed his way, for a very brief moment, William pondered the worthiness of having gone so far at the price of denying his emotional identity. It was like being there but not being himself.

William brushed those thoughts away immediately because his intellectual accomplishments had always been detached from his emotions. He always dealt very cautiously with emotions for fear of falling trap of his heart feelings. Had he followed his heart in the first place he'd probably never have had that experience at the Mississippi College. Now those two semesters in an American institution were adding greatly to his already brilliant academic curriculum.

Also, his English proficiency improvements showed like never before. Nearly a year surrounded by native speakers from the State of Mississippi had had an amazing effect on William's spoken English, which now sounded distinctively marked by stereotypical features of the Southern American English.

48

When the six-month satellite tv contract neared its end I bought a second-hand VHS player for a bargain and began to record a veritable library of T-90 tapes on SLP speed. Once the contract ended I always left a tape playing on the player to make believe that the satellite tv had never abandoned me.

These tapes became an addictive lifeline as only the soundtrack of American Sitcoms or the wacky noises of Warner Bros cartoons on the background could induce me to fall asleep. Night after night, I found myself waking in the early hours to rewind the tape back to specific episodes of *Will & Grace* or *South Park* which would allow me to drift off again.

After a few months of heavy use, the VHS player was in a dire state, tangling the magnetic tape around its head drum, and filling its carcass with a mess of film so regularly that I'd stopped bothering to put its top cover back on. One night I awoke around 2 a.m. to see that a tape not only had coiled around the mechanisms of the player but spilled liberally on to the floor around it. I couldn't fall sleep again with the sight of my favourite sleep inducing episodes strewn around my bedroom floor. So I rose from bed, sat cross-legged on the floor, opened the tape case, and started to reel the tape back in.

When I came to myself it was 3 a.m. and, instead of having reeled the tape back into its case, I was half buried in seemingly endless coils of wayward black VHS tape. For one second I looked at that image and wondered where the hell from came that obsession to fix that particular tape when it could easily have been chucked away and another one could be played instead.

But I simply couldn't accept that one of my tapes was lost, and I didn't stop until the last inch of tape was safely wound back inside its case. Then, I placed the tape back into VHS player praying to fall asleep fast before it entangled once more.

Hardly had my beautiful eyes shut, I heard, over the sound of the canned laughter from tv, a distant rapping at my bedroom door. "Half past five. Will you get up?"

"Yes mom, just a sec." I inspired deeply, feeling like most mornings lately: with an endless hangover.

I stumbled across the living room to the toilet, leaving the VHS tape on, loud, so I could listen to English from there. I had to shower, get dressed, catch a bus, and be t the university around 7 a.m.

"Have something for breakfast before you leave." My mother reminded me of that every morning then – maybe because I had a look of malnutrition on my face.

"I will mom." I replied agreeably from the toilet. Yet, I didn't really felt like having anything. I just felt depressed; so depressed that the canned laughter of the sitcoms on tv sounded muffled and ominous. And at that time in the morning, I already wished for the end of the day, so I could crawl back into bed again. That wish though, just made each day longer and sadder.

Yet my little world had crumbled throughout the fourth semester, into the beginning of the fifth semester I still felt very much crushed under the rubble of its fallen debris.

The foreshock of the catastrophe happened when my partner informed me – just after signing the satellite tv contract – of his decision to take a chance on the exchange programme offered at the university. Though I could've applied to the exchange programme that same year too, having spent most of my scholarship sharing the costs of the flat with my partner, I couldn't even afford dreaming with that.

So, when September approached, without further ado my partner cancelled the lease on the flat, and wished me goodbye and good luck.

By that time, the university staff had already ended the strike, but because my scholarship had been delayed for months, I found myself penniless.

And just like that, I was compelled to return to my parents' house.

49

Initially, I relied on my mother even for bus tickets – and as if being back and broke didn't seem humiliating enough for my mother, during many nights she made me listen to her "I told you so" sermons.

But I really hit the jackpot that semester at the linguistics laboratory. As if sensing a need for sympathy, my research advisor started threatening to throw me out of the research team and revoke my scholarship because he considered that my performance at the laboratory meetings weren't up to his standards. Worse still, some fellow lab mates – possibly to score points with my advisor – took a visible delight in agreeing with any observation over my incompetence.

During that period, my partner often phoned me, but that didn't make me feel much less dumped – and someway forsaken. Melancholy took over every single inch of my body. My stomach, my heart, and my brain all ached harmonically. A constant nausea wouldn't let me eat, feel, or think. Desperate, I'd started resorting to the only thing that lessened that pain: sleeping.

Only sleeping by the sound of tv shows in English could soothe my tattered nerves. It was like being in an inverted version of *A Nightmare in Elm Street* – I feared waking up.

Thus, no matter how gently my mother woke me, each morning felt like the beginning of a long nightmare.

She usually would say, "It's past the time you get up. Why are you still in bed?"

Because my life is pathetic, mom – I wanted to reply. But instead I'd say, "I lost the time, mom." My mother wouldn't allow me to snooze any longer. Her morning calls inspired me to muster up some courage and go to the university. But, that steam cooled down quickly and so, at any free time between the laboratory hours and the classes at night, I'd come home and have a lie down, trying to escape from the pain of existing – even if no matter how long I slumbered that pain was the same when I awakened.

That morning particularly, after staying good part of the night awake repairing that tape, I had an extra reason to be drained. So, at lunch time, I came home for a shut-eye.

After sometime tossing and turning in bed, a thought crossed my mind: sleeping didn't make me any more comfortable, and even if it could, why in the world I wanted to feel comfortable anyway. Being tired could hardly add to my misery. And since I felt so miserable, I decided to attempt suicide again – this time, by tiredness.

"Mom, I'm off to university now. I won't be back for dinner." I told to my mother who was already languidly lying on bed for her siesta.

"But it's scorching outside. Why don't you have some rest now? I'll prepare some coffee before you leave later." She slurred, her tone sounding a little concerned.

"It's alright. I'll have something to eat over there." I couldn't let myself be tempted to the comfort that my mother offered.

"Get more money before you leave, and please..." She paused as if she was about to sob. "Have something healthy." She almost implored that, leaving me to guess how much my appearance revealed my wretchedness.

After a bumpy ride to university, on a bus with a loud roaring engine that helped to keep me wide awake, I arrived at the linguistics laboratory to find my research advisor walking frantically around the room, checking printed forms, shouting commands, as if conducting a tornado drill.

"C'mon people, let's make this thing work!" He hollered repeatedly when not engaged himself in some activity.

A few good months before, my advisor had been elected the head of the *Circle of Linguistics Studies of the Northeast*, and consequently the linguistics laboratory became the main headquarters of the CLSN. As the head of the CLSN, my advisor was responsible for the realisation of an annual meeting, and for such he needed a healthy number of volunteer students to help with contacting, by email or phone, old members of the Circle to remind them of paying the annual membership fee and updating their personal data, and inviting students and academics of linguistics and literature to register as new members.

Thus, whilst the research activities continued in the morning, during most afternoons the laboratory was crammed with volunteers of the CLSN. I also volunteered regularly, but since I'd decided to remain awake as much as possible I began volunteering all afternoons. From that afternoon, I threw myself wholeheartedly at any task available. No task was beyond me, no list of members' names and data was too long to type, and no hour was ever inconvenient – at least by my admittance.

I carried on with my research during the morning, ate peanuts or a sandwich for lunch, and stayed through the afternoon till seven p.m., when classes started. The laboratory mates and the volunteers would come and I'd already be there, and when they left I remained. Within the second week that I'd engaged in that routine, my advisor called me aside.

"I have something to talk to you." He sounded queerly diffident.

As I faced him, I began to wonder: *what I had done wrong this time*.

50

Before I had a chance to say anything, my advisor continued. "So, here is the thing – you spend the day here basically, so what do you say of being part of the official team of organisers of the Circle and being put down to receive a monthly allowance?"

I found it strange that, after promising to have me disconnect from the research team not a month from then, my advisor came with that proposition.

Whatever had made him change his mind about me, I didn't have much to think about. I instantly thought of my plans to apply for the selection process of the exchange programme and, bearing in mind that every penny counted from then on, I saw that proposition as the first positive sign for those plans. "Oh, that's great. Count me in then."

"So, welcome to the official team." He smiled with satisfaction and, without saying any more, carried on with his affairs.

So, bang went another suicide attempt.

Though I stayed the entire day awake, the adrenaline of getting my part of that mammoth undertaking done washed away even the remotest sign of tiredness.

With the constant activity at the linguistics laboratory my thoughts started shifting from the heartbreaks of the past semester and settling on the approaching selection process of the exchange programme, which should happen towards the end of that fifth semester – when the places available at the overseas universities were confirmed.

It was actually past the time to focus my thoughts and efforts completely on the selection process of the exchange programme, since I was well aware of how competitive it was.

To be awarded an overseas placement the primary requirement was to achieve a minimum score of seven in an English proficiency test graded from nought to ten. The minimum score had to be achieved across the four proficiencies: reading, writing, listening, and speaking. I had never taken part in a language proficiency test as such and I knew from start that I should work on my speaking proficiency urgently, with all the energy and at all opportunities.

My speaking proficiency had been honed essentially in artificial and sparsely frequent classroom routines. It'd been some time, also, that I had been taking part of a group meeting called *English Club*.

The *English Club* happened in a building that belonged to the Regular Baptist Church and lasted about an hour on most Saturdays. I'd been invited to join the group about a year ago, along with my partner who was a faithful member of the Baptist religion. Who organized the meetings of the *English Club* was an American-born preacher – name Timothy – along with his family. The weekly meetings consisted of the following routine: reading an adapted Bible text in English – with breaks in each paragraph for any questions about the meaning of words or phrases – a brief lecture on the text led by Timothy, and, at the end, the distribution of cookies with drinks and a free chat among participants.

The advent of the *English Club* could be regarded as a blessing of divine inspiration, to say the least. Outside the classroom, the *English Club* gave me an opportunity to experience a non-artificial situation of interaction in English, even if only for a few measly minutes a week, and even if the conversation had to remain in an extremely formal level because I was acquainted with most of the participants in that environment restrictively. Meetings of the *English Club* allowed me to exercise my spoken English, which at my age was semi-stunted compared the development of my other skills.

Sadly, at the beautiful age of twenty-four, whilst I thought that my pronunciation had been refined to an acceptable standard, I strongly suspected that my grammar was appalling – even if I couldn't realise that myself. Besides, I usually struggled to express myself efficiently without a scripted speech. Quite often I couldn't get the simplest idea across without Pythonesque circumlocutions – any attempt at engaging in a casual conversation in English would make an emergency sign shine brightly on my clammy forehead, obfuscating my interlocutor and making me feel like being crushed by a giant foot.

Speaking hadn't been the centre of my concerns until that fifth semester. If a joint – or individual – presentation was assigned, in English or otherwise, I invariably relied on a script, which I either learned by heart or simply read parrot fashion.

American Literature I had been the first English-specific module on literature of the course and Dr Luna had wisely conducted the classes using the students' mother tongue to ensure that all students fully comprehended the ideas of the texts. And because Dr Luna made no fuss about using English during American Literature classes, the students felt no pressure to express themselves in English either.

The fifth semester, however, posed a new challenge with the module *English Literature I*. The tutor of this module, Dr Austen, conducted classes using exclusively English and demanded students to craft their comments and responses likewise. Naturally, conducting literature modules in English was optional; however, by that stage in an English Major there was a tacit expectation that students should be able to both understand and express themselves in English. Therefore, Dr Austen rather expected than demanded a positive attitude towards English during her classes.

If that wasn't enough to encourage me to make a concerted effort to express myself well in Dr Austen's classes, two extra pressing factors came in to play for me personally: Firstly, the grades from the English-specific modules would also be taken into consideration by the I.A. Office team through the selection process to certain overseas universities. Secondly, Dr Austen and her husband were both members of the assessment team of the I.A. Office, and would be judging the English proficiency test.

Bearing these facts in mind I knew from start that during *English Literature I* classes I'd have to do the impossible to use English to express myself, and more importantly, to impress Dr Austen.

Inadvertently, I was about to start, once again, executing the elements of behaviour that served as a combination to gain access to, and to tap into, the *principle* and make it all happen almost magically.

51

To start putting a strategy together I had first and foremost to make up for a lifetime without using English in genuine casual speech, and concentrate on improving my speaking proficiency urgently.

The initial action toward that goal began from the moment my mother called me in the morning. "It's time get up morning bird."

"I'm going mom." That was one of the few non-English sentences I normally used through the day – after that I'd engage in thoughts and speech using primarily English.

Since the fresh memory of having been exchanged for two academic terms abroad still inflicted me with terrible feelings of rejection and regret that early in the morning, I developed a ritual to exorcise those feelings and soothe my resentful spirit: I recited the *Our Father* in English before getting up, and then went on praying silently for my day, and for my future. Hell, if nothing else, it meant the first thoughts of the day were in English – what should hold benefits in its own right because it meant a positive mind attitude with a side effect on my targeted proficiency.

Throughout the day, if I wasn't reciting *Our Father* repeatedly or praying, I'd softly sing an American pop song. My favourite song, however, was from the European group *Eiffel 65*; *Too much of heaven... a life and soul hell bound...* And when I didn't know the right words of the song, I just made them up, trying to fit the rhythm of the melody, to keep it going. *Heaven... Yeah... I just don't know what now...* The trick was not to give up, and don't allow the English to be silent within me.

Other times, when my repertoire of songs exhausted, I'd carry on describing silently my ongoing actions. *I walk to the bus stop, walk, walk. I'm walking. I see live people. I wait for the bus, wait, wait. I'm so bored. Oh, the bus is coming. Thank God. How do I say get up in the bus?* In order to evoke a wider vocabulary variety, I described anything that I saw around. *A house, another house, the house is yellow, there is a man getting out of the house. Someone is crossing the street. Oh, what a handsome boy. Look at those arms – yummy! That tree is so tall. There is a bird flying in the sky, the sky is cloudy this morning.*

That technique helped me to avoid engaging in verbal thoughts – otherwise known as *internal monologue* or *inner voice* – that weren't in English. It sounded strange, naturally. But at that point, I wouldn't mind if I suddenly started hearing voices in my head, as long as they spoke English.

And if that technique to control my *internal monologue* to narrate all that was going on around me felt somewhat strange even to myself, I really needed to step up my determination to improve my speaking proficiency when I had to get off the bus and start verbally interacting with others. It was at this point that things would turn out to sound even more bizarre.

52

I was still to try out the most tangible technique to improve my speaking proficiency: to actually articulate English in as much conversational situations as possible.

And since no family member, neighbour, or friend could understand English, my strategy to converse was compulsorily restricted to verbal contacts with some classroom and lab mates. But even around language aware mates, trying to engage in casual conversation in English still felt pretty awkward. And I only realised how much when I first tried that approach with a fellow member at the linguistics laboratory.

"Sylvia, would you mind if I speak with you in English?"

After keeping myself busy and quiet most of the afternoon – when many student researchers or volunteers of the CLSN were at the lab – I finally gathered courage to approach the only lab mate who remained there.

"Oh, are you speaking English now?" Sylvia was the most mature fellow member of the research team and she generally made me feel more comfortable. She studied the Major in Spanish but I knew she could understand English. Though she responded using her mother tongue and drew a slight smirk on her face, I still trusted that she'd make no objection.

"Yes. It's that I need to practise English because I'm studying with this tutor – Austen, you must know – and she also evaluates the students' participation in class. She likes us to use English in class and I need to practise conversation to sound more natural." I'd learnt that justifying preamble by heart to introduce the new code into the conversation stream. I also used that excuse to maintain my plans about the exchange programme secret.

"Well, I'm particularly alright with that." Sylvia continued with her amused smirk. "But I won't answer in English."

"That's alright. Please, be a little patient. I still have difficulty to speak." I said, already feeling a bit uneasy.

Sylvia continued looking at me, but I simply didn't know what to say anymore. So I made a little shrug, as if to say *that's all*, and stopped interrupting her.

I used that same introductory disclaimer with others mates, both from the laboratory and classroom, and henceforth, from daily greetings, through gossip and discussion of current affairs, to banter and academic conversation, English was officially declared the tongue of the academic realm.

How do you say and *please be patient* became sentences used constantly as a mean to gain time, and to organise my thoughts in English. Many times *sorry, I am lost now* would close the conversation because silence was preferable to resorting to my mother tongue. Some mates were patient with my struggles, others less so, some answered in their mother tongue, and others, unleashed from their own inhibitions, followed my lead and started practicing along with me to varying degrees.

Continuing with an attitude like that to language was extremely difficult initially. Using English for actual communication was generally viewed as a practice strictly restricted to classroom environment, and exceeding that boundary felt extremely bizarre. I found resistance to that practice even among some classmates from English-specific modules.

The first one to object was Renata – a classmate from the morning shift – when I continued speaking English after a class of *Grammar of English V*.

"Er... we can speak normally now." Renata said, switching her English off. "We're not in the classroom anymore." She held a smile of embarrassment and kept looking to the sides.

"What's the problem? I need to practise English." I made an effort to remain focused, finding unnecessary to go about further reasons.

"Isn't that a little..." Renata paused before using the word in English, and finally spit it out. "A little of show-off?"

Renata used that word, which I honestly regarded as the most offensive word with respect to the practice of conversation in English; *show-off* in that context, meant a public exhibitionism for attention seeking and ostentation; it was this feeling regarding the use of the English language that had an incredible power to repress and inhibit the simple practice of a second language like English.

I wanted to go for a complex discussion on that matter. I actually understood that Renata's attitude.

Because of its immediate association to economically developed countries like the USA and the UK, and its local prestige as a language learned mainly by upper class individuals, English was viewed as an object of adornment rather than just a language. Speaking English in a public place in an essentially monolingual community like ours was indeed viewed as showing off. But putting that idea together in English would take me an awful long time, so I went for the gist of my purpose with that conversation.

"Show-off or not, I do need to improve my English. There is nothing wrong with that. It's actually legal."

"Well, I don't feel much comfortable with that." Renata threw a spooked look to me and began staring desperately to another classmate who was coming in the opposite direction, as if seeking for sympathy.

I restrained myself not to lose my temper and end up switching to our mother tongue to express my view on that yokel and provincial attitude of hers. So, to carry on in English, I took a deep breath and let out a sentence that I repeated to inspire myself all the time.

"There's nothing wrong with using English outside classroom. It's just a language for Chrissake." I felt smug for using *Chrissake* – it sounded very casual. But before I could draw a smile, Renata found her escape and ditched me.

Dagnabbit! I wanted to scream that exclamation I'd listened Grampa Simpson shouting in a moment of anger in *The Simpsons*. But there was no one close to hear my rage.

Happily, other mates were willing to converse in English, because I simply avoided talking at all to the ones who did not. By any means I'd allow anyone to dissuade me from my conversation practice. More than language behaviour, that attitude was an intellectual assertion. Weird as it felt sometimes, I had to persist with all my techniques. I believed that just listening and reading wouldn't make my speaking proficiency advance anymore. I had to get used to producing random utterances, without thinking too much during that process, to try and reach automaticity.

Furthermore, the language proficiency test would happen soon, and the judges wouldn't be evaluating how much I fitted socially, but how much my English fitted to their standards.

And it was especially considering the judges that I had to take action on my English also during Dr Austen's classes – I couldn't simply rely on preparing myself to excel at the speaking proficiency test and let Dr Austen have an impression that my English wasn't actually up to her standards during the classes of *English Literature I*.

So, my endeavour on that setting reached a further stage: there, I should better use English not only well, but also impressively.

To do so, I had an ace up my sleeve. It was time to pull that ace out, and put my strategy into action.

53

The first procedure was to fully read and understand each text prior to class – skipping this stage was actually common among students.

The second procedure was to use the margins of the text to annotate of any thoughts or interpretations that might have a chance of being verbalised in class.

The third procedure was to make a perfect choice of a short story for the compulsory individual presentation and production of a complementary essay.

The *English Literature I* programme covered short stories from the end of the Victorian period to the early twentieth century, by authors like Oscar Wilde, Dorothy Richardson, James Joyce, D. H. Lawrence, Katherine Mansfield, and Dylan Thomas. I knew that Dr Austen's doctorate thesis approached screen adaptations of the novel *Emma*, so to cause an impression my presentation should address a short story that had been adapted to screen. Only the longest short story in the programme would fill the bill: James Joyce's *The Dead* was adapted in 1987 by John Huston. I couldn't imagine how that choice would be related to my decisions in the near future. So, during the end of the year recess, I began the preparations.

Step one was to get hold of a xerox copy of *The Dead*, start reading it and make a glossary with every single word I wasn't familiar with or not sure about – my trusted technique. *The Dead* occupied the last fifty-seven pages of the Penguin Popular Classics edition of *Dubliners*. Certain paragraphs took me over an hour to read and scribble down a list of words with their meanings garnered from an old bilingual dictionary.

One specific paragraph presented a description of the Christmas supper table with words like *creased, strewn, sprigs, parsley, ham, crust, crumbs, frill, shin, side-dishes, minsters, shallow, blancmange, stalk-shaped, raisins, almonds, Smyrna figs, custard, grated, nutmeg, upheld, bowl, wrapped, celery, sentries, squat, decanters, port, dark sherry, squads, stout, ale, sashes.* All those words, which comprised one fourth of all the lexical words in that paragraph, were absolutely strange to my English world thus far.

Step two was to get hold of complementary texts on *The Dead*, especially on its adaptation to screen. For that, my departed partner came pretty handy because he had access to the electronic virtual library of the Mississippi College. He e-mailed me some relevant papers published by the *Literature Film Quarterly*, among which two, by Pederson Ann and Pilipp Frank, had interesting insights on the narrative and aesthetic devices used both by James Joyce and John Huston to depict the epiphany of the main characters – Gretta and Gabriel Conroy – towards the end of *The Dead*. To be honest, at that moment the topic and contents of the complementary essay were actually of secondary importance. My project entailed showmanship time because a great show had to be put on to wow Dr Austen and ensure that she noticed that I could use English magically. That challenge was the essential ingredient, the real McCoy, the step three.

After long nights awake doing all the necessary readings, the presentation was ready to be prepared. All was well and good except for one small thing: I had no idea how to transform all the information from a sheaf of notes into a cohesive and interesting presentation. I was really focused during those days yet no interesting ideas would come to mind. So, I thought that a change of scenery could get the creative juices flowing.

I then loaded a folder bag with all the relevant texts plus a bunch of film OSTs and set off to spend the weekend at the house of my lyrics fanatic friend Helen.

After a whole afternoon chewing the fat with Helen, when the night came, she went out with her girlfriend to watch the last instalment of *Lord of the Rings*.

Before leaving me alone with my thoughts, never tired of bossing me around, Helen said her parting words. "When I return you'd better have the whole presentation ready, mister." She used an exaggerated half humorous half patronising tone.

"Have no doubt. The genius will be in action tonight." I used an overconfident tone to disguise a fear of reaching the end of that night with no real directions on the paper.

But rather than dwelling on this prospect, to cast the fear aside, I made a prayer, put the OST of M. Night Shyamalan's film *Signs* on the stereo, pumped the volume up to the last decibel, and wandered off for a shower.

54

I had programmed the *Main Titles* and the penultimate track *The Hand of Fate* – my favourite – to play. When the latter started playing out loud whilst the water washed over me, it just brought a flood of ideas for the presentation in flash. As I felt an amazing excitement, I leapt off the shower, walked naked to the kitchen, still dripping with water, and threw myself at the papers on the kitchen table to scribble that flood of ideas down in full before it lost its sense.

At that right moment, it made all sense in the world.

So, I had read *The Dead* by James Joyce and some academic papers about its screen adaptation. I was still trying to find an essential aspect common to both the short story and the film adaptation that could be genuinely explored in an academic presentation about literature. In the *Signs* OST, scored by James Newton Howard, that specific track, *The Hand of Fate*, is incidental to the climax which involves a moment of epiphany of the main character, played by Mel Gibson. In the short story *The Dead* the character Gretta also experiences an epiphany when she listens to the Irish folk song *Lass of Aughrim* – the song *Lass of Aughrim* in the film became the incidental leitmotif to both Gretta's and Gabriel's epiphany. *Signs* is a film directed by M. Night Shyamalan, who also directed *The Sixth Sense* and whose known trademark is to make the viewers experience epiphany along with the main characters. In *Signs* as in *The Sixth Sense* James Newton Howard's musical portrayal of these epiphanic climaxes also reaches the soul of the viewers.

Epiphany was a word basically new to me. I was still digesting its meaning, having just learned it with the help of the complementary texts on *The Dead*. *Epiphany* entered English during the Middle English via Greek *epiphainein*, meaning *reveal*. *Epiphany* refers to a moment of sudden and big revelation. There's a religious meaning of *epiphany* which refers to the manifestation of Christ to the Gentiles as it's in the Bible in Matthew 2; this sense comes from Old French *epiphanie* and ecclesiastical Latin *epiphania*. Overall, *epiphany* has religious connotations, as the revelation of a truth of divine proportions that comes to change the meaning of one's life and reality. The concept of epiphany couldn't be clearer to me, though, than in the minutes I jotted down the ideas for my presentation of *The Dead* – when I had my own soul touched by the film music of James Newton Howard.

Exactly whilst *The Hand of Fate* was playing, all those thoughts and half thoughts flooded through my mind suddenly to form a cohesive whole, just like a revelation. My own epiphany.

The presentation I put together focused on a comparison of how music was used as an aesthetic device to depict the characters' epiphany both in the short story and the film *The Dead*. I scripted my speech, prepared transparencies, handouts with extracts from the short story, prepared Huston's film adaptation sequences to play on the VHS – the DVD would be released only 2 years later –, prepared the *Signs* OST to play, and prepared myself for a theatrical presentation. Delivered with vigour, certainty, and a little flair, that presentation was my masterpiece performance, one that even my jaded tutor would take some time to forget.

The presentation naturally would garner no credit toward the language proficiency test but would at least get me a high grade in the module and make sure Dr Austen had a good impression of my English.

When the language proficiency test drew closer I began talking in English even with my image in the mirror – hopefully a sign of nerves, not madness. Even to my mother I addressed myself in English, and though she couldn't understand she replied with humorous comments; she knew just how important practicing English was for me during those days. By the time the language proficiency test happened I'd prepared myself to speak in so many ways that on the interview, under an expert watchful gaze and without a script at hand, I hardly recognised my own English.

All the nail biting paid off. I passed all the four proficiency assessments. And the final score of the selection process, which weighed the proficiency test result and the grades from the English-specific modules, was sufficiently high to classify me to any overseas university. That was fortunate because at the beginning of the selection process when it came to opt for the choice of overseas university I'd had a change of heart.

Hearing from my departed partner about his exchange experience during that period served as a warning to me: as an out gay man I would likely be a misfit if I opted to study in an American university like Mississippi College.

So I changed my mind about going to the USA and opted instead for the hotly disputed University of Leeds.

55

"Congratulations matey-o! I'm really glad you passed. But it doesn't surprise me." Aristotle always found a way to overemphasise his compliments. "I wish I had that courage."

"Thanks." I thanked in English. "I wished you hadn't quit applying along. We could be going together." I said, this time, not using English with him for the first time in three months.

"I wouldn't have passed anyway. The competition was tough, and I didn't prepare myself like you did." Aristotle never seemed tired of exaggerating his modesty.

"Well, let's agree and disagree on that." I switched back to English, preparing myself to begin a pointless discussion that we had other times before when practicing our English.

I'd met Aristotle half an hour after confirming the official online result with the students classified to a place at the University of Leeds. He was actually the fourth person who I told about my success. I'd phoned my mother, my neighbour Vicky, and my friend Helen first. They'd all shared my apprehension until then, knowing that the outcome of that selection would have a profound effect both on my life and on my reputation as a student from the English Major. It was known among some classmates that a classmate, who was also competing for a place in Leeds, was heard commenting that my English would hardly match the minimum standards required to pass the language proficiency test.

This veiled insult played on my mind whilst I checked the laboratory computer for the online results. And as it played, I tried to suppress my anger and control the hammering in my chest by silently repeating the verses 5 and 6 of Judges 12: about the capture of the Ephraimites by the men of Gilead and the word *Shibboleth*.

At that moment, feeling as one of those disguised Ephraimites fugitives seized by the men of Gilead as they sought to cross the fords of the Jordan, I pleaded "let me go." Before allowing the Ephraimites to pass, the men of Gilead demanded them to pronounce the word *Shibboleth*, because that word contained a specific sound – *sh* – which the Ephraimites couldn't pronounce without revealing their true identity. "Shibboleth" I repeated, imagining how an Ephraimite must have felt staring into the eyes of their seizers, waiting to be sentenced after pronouncing *Shibboleth*. 42 thousand Ephraimites were slaughtered for failing to pronounce the word password according expectations.

Had I failed to pronounce my English right, my fate would've been less dreadful, naturally. Still, English sure functioned to me a bit like the biblical *Shibboleth*. And just like then, English would prove on some later occasions to be a lifesaver – and a password to success.

Winning a place at the University of Leeds strengthened my faith on that journey to conquer English. I felt like a hero and an explorer, like Christopher Columbus, Charles Darwin, or Peter Pan. That summer, my foreign exchange adventure was about to begin.

All I had to worry about then was money. If the American Dollar cost three times the value of the local currency, the British Pound cost five times. So, from that night on I started concentrating on the acquisition of capital. And since there wasn't much to do, apart from saving the scholarship and the monthly allowance of the CLSN for the next months, I should speak to my father and, hopefully, count upon his partial support.

"What!?" My father lifted his eyes from the crossword he had on his hands, raising his eyebrows. That was the first chance I had to talk about my success in the selection process of the exchange programme.

"Mom didn't tell you?" I started stuttering, sounding stupid. "By this coming September I should travel to England."

Judging by his expression it seemed like I'd just told him that I was preparing myself to travel to Mars. After breathing deeply, he seemed to restrain his shock.

"I think you should worry about finishing your course and getting a job first." He sounded less cheerful than I'd pictured. "How will you support yourself there? Is that free?"

"The university is free, but we got to pay the flight, accommodation, and food. But…"

"And how the hell you'll get money for that? We cannot afford this you know." He flatly informed me.

"I can find a partial job there. That can make up for the expenses." I said, seeing on my father's expression that he sensed that I was making serious effort to convince myself of that.

"Well, at your age you should know what you're doing. I'm not telling anything anymore." He went silent, turning his attention to the crossword again.

At least he didn't berate this time. Still, I couldn't avoid feeling angry with the pessimism that my father so naturally injected me with.

Gladly, the struggles and little triumphs I lived along the latest leg of that journey learning English had made me more fearless. And my determination to go on that exchange programme just grew stronger after my father's words of discouragement.

I'd actually grown calloused to deal with people who had that gift to undermine my self-esteem, people who sought to forge their opinions as facts concerning the possibilities of what my future could or couldn't hold. Some challenged me openly; others offered advices loaded with good intentions. Challengers and advisers sincerely believed they could feed me with their own fears disguised as insults or suggestions. Both types usually developed utterance templates in their approach. "Oh, you should be careful with that because of this or that..." Or, "Why are you doing this, you should be doing something else?" Or better yet, "Snap out of your *Bobby's World*, you ought to be more realistic over matters."

I mentally shielded myself from all types and certainly didn't encourage them to come to me. Yet, they came anyway. It should be something they sensed on me, like dogs sense fear. Perhaps it was my appearance. Of medium stature, slim, innocent stare, well shaved, and after a good night's sleep, I could pass for a 16 year-old then. Perhaps it was my behaviour. Usually inventing new techniques to accomplish tasks, expressing unusual ideas – generally in a broad local accent –, seldom too serious, often dreamy and absent-minded, and always in love and with a silly grin, I'd normally have a childlike demeanour. Such features probably made me an irresistible target for intimidators and patronisers. Had I bitten back when others barked at me, life would have been one long brawl.

However, if by then I still had the serenity to avoid expressing my anger against my father's attitude and stay focused on my goal to study overseas, midway through the following semester, as no sign of promise toward that goal surfaced, I let weariness and worry get the best of me.

If I had any ability to do magic – a non-conscious way of tapping into the *principle* –, in those days this ability had apparently vanished. And I'd need a bigger dose of magic to go through with that. Since the necessity motivates us into action, I would learn how to reach the *principle* through a different route.

56

After a two-week recess between semesters, which coincided with the Easter holiday, again I started the hectic routine that saw me running from the linguistics laboratory to the classroom from morning until night. Only at the end of the day, following a bumpy and noisy bus ride, when I returned to the comfort of my parents' house, I was finally free. Free to work into the small hours on the daily assignments for the next classes.

Many nights, I resorted to stabbing myself with a pen, both to maintain myself awake and chase away the dreams that distracted me despite my wakeful state – the stabbing technique was quite clever because it wasn't the pain that worked but the element of surprise; I used my writing hand, which was the last part of my body still awake, to suddenly assault any other part of the body, thus startling me.

After dropping asleep nearly 2 a.m., I had to rise and shine four hours later to catch the bus and begin all over. I did that because I swore to myself never to allow anything to disturb my focus, which consisted in having all the modules' routine assignments done, to continue practicing English in conversation, and to board on a plane to the UK and become a full-blown exchange student at the University of Leeds. That mix of focus and stress made me develop a stronger mental and physical discipline; alas, with a side effect: it made me less tolerant to anyone who dared to undermine my self-esteem with suggestion or challenge.

My hardening attitude caught my advisor a little off guard. Since he'd made me a member of the official team of organisers of the CLSN he ceased complaining about my performance at the laboratory meetings and threatening to throw me out of the research. Instead, my advisor saved his energy for the times when something went wrong with the dealings of the CLSN. Naturally, whenever he had a hissy fit, I was the one he sought to discharge his frustrations on. And my advisor decided to perform one of his thespian acts right in the middle of that semester, on a Friday evening of what had been a busy week for me.

"What's this? Please, may I ask what exactly this means." My advisor had entered the laboratory around 6 p.m. – right as I prepared myself to leave.

He'd brought with him the secretary of the laboratory – who was also his sexagenarian semi-senile Stepford hag, and who sometimes was herself the target of his outbursts. Besides her, there was only another student researcher, who was waiting for her boyfriend there. What gave me a hint that he'd come to throw a tantrum was the way he lifted and dropped on the table a cardboard box filled with around a thousand forms containing personal data of old and new members of the CLSN.

"Was I supposed to have done something with this again?" I'd been through most of those forms, and none of the other organisers above me had given me any more directions.

"Were you supposed...?" He mocked my tone.

Oh dear, was he playing the questions-only game?

"...Have you contacted these members yet?

"Yes, most of them, including the others in the computer list." I knew that he was angry because he'd been away that week and no other organiser or volunteer had showed up to keep the annual meeting proceedings progressing.

"Listen, I checked the inbox of the CLSN and there are hundreds of emails of members asking for confirmation of their annual membership fee payment." He began a bit edgy already. "We need to confirm all of them."

He then started distributing the forms around the table so that we all could check who had paid the fee, following a list in a catalogue with all the members' name. What he was really doing was shuffling the forms I'd confirmed throughout that week with the newly arrived forms still to be checked and updated.

"The internet is down for three days now. And I don't have a computer at home." I said controlling my nerves, knowing that all would be solved.

"And you did not let anyone know! This is serious. There are teachers and doctors paying. They need the confirmation letter to organise themselves. We are only three months from the meeting." He became vociferous, almost convulsive. "You think you are here for your pleasure? You're not here to listen to music."

At least I learned that someone had grassed my habit of listening to *The Simpsons* songs in English all day whilst I worked on those forms and emails.

"Alright, just tell me what to do and let's do it because no one else will." I was ready for a long day's journey into that Friday night.

"I don't know why I have to put up with this incompetence. Look at this!" My advisor continued emptying the forms and passing them around to the secretary and to the other student as they continued silent, organising the forms, stapling some loose sheets together, and checking the catalogue. "It's been a whole week to do this. A monkey would know better."

He seemed determined to cause me as much embarrassment as possible with his belittling diatribe.

I continued silent, checking the forms and catalogue. I repeated to myself that all would be right, that we'd have the work done, and he'd recognise that he and I and the secretary were really the only ones who actually had things done regarding the annual meeting. Yet, in minutes of rant he managed to usurp me of my hard earned confidence. Still, I met his onslaught with a calm gaze giving not an inch to his mounting fury or dignifying it with a response.

Perhaps sensing the self defeating turn his chosen path had taken, my advisor grabbed a sheaf of around a hundred forms and, after a nervous shuffling and checking, threw them at me and yapped, "It's unbelievable! These forms are all out of order. We're not going to spend the whole night checking at random. Hear me, tonight you are not leaving until all these forms are neatly classified in alphabetical order."

Oh for the love of Judy Garland! She had totally lost it now, I thought. I'd show him that I'd do things calmly. So, I got all the forms he threw at me, sit down cross-legged on the floor, and began spreading them in bundles sorted by each letter.

I could feel him watching me, with an expression that accentuated his resemblance to Bob Flag from Michael Radford's *1984*.

As if he seemed to think that sitting on the floor didn't put me in position enough low for him, he decided to continue. "You cannot even put something in alphabetical order!"

To what I stood up, picked up my folder bag, said "Good weekend everyone," and I made my way toward the door – my every footfall echoing in the silence that my action had created.

57

Rather than my insubordination what must have left my advisor speechless was that after months of unchallenged tyranny he'd utterly failed to crush my soul. Whilst I fully respected his authority, knowledge, and experience I also knew he was a renowned bully who often reduced his student researchers to tears during his often public dominance rituals. He was expecting that from me but that evening he was cut short midsentence, because I'd promised myself not to allow anyone to talk down to me like that anymore.

I made sure not to think about that incident during the weekend, knowing that I'd be thrown out of the research and all but that I'd never accept that anymore. On Monday morning, when I arrived at the laboratory, after attending a class, my advisor already had summoned a university clerical worker to take over my responsibility in the CLSN.

"Oh, there he is..." My advisor greeted me, noticeably calmer than the last time I saw him.

At that moment, I felt utterly ashamed of my insubordination. So I, feeling shy and embarrassed, replied. "Good morning. What do we have to do this morning?"

"This is Ms Miles, maybe you're already acquainted with her." He introduced the clerical worker to me.

I did know her, but not well. "Hi Ms, you alright?"

"I'm alright, how are you?" Ms Miles had a very friendly approach, and put me at ease right from start.

"So, here is the thing – for the meantime you can brief Ms Miles regarding all our contact work and files that needs sorting here. You have the following two weeks and henceforth dedicate yourself to the research only.

"Sounds right to me. I'll do whatever we got to do."

"I leave it to you then, 'cos the world weighs upon my shoulder right now." He said it whilst hitching his bag on his shoulder and already making his way out of the laboratory quite dramatically.

Completely unaware of the coordinator's leaving performance, Ms Miles was already rattling furiously on the keyboard; she looked noticeably focused and diligent with her work.

From then on, the clerical worker became a second secretary of the laboratory, and official secrety of CLSN. She and I worked together but still hardly kept up with the flood of mail, emailing, phone calls, and payment confirmation with the members of the CLSN. The two week deadline came and went but it'd become obvious that the job was simply too much for one person. They needed me to stay on. From that moment on my advisor employed subtler techniques to attempt bringing me down, drawing attention to my every little mistake without really shouting them at my face. More than once, just to tease me, he derisively remarked in front of others at the laboratory, "You barely have IQ to put anything in alphabetical order…" But I was ready to tolerate that for the sake of funding the precious trip to the UK. Besides, my advisor's senseless criticism was no more than a masquerade, because he evidently trusted and respected my work but sought to hide this from others. Naturally, as I was only half convinced of that, just to be on the safe side, in any work I undertook on his behalf I never settled for anything less than excellence to prove him my value.

Until the end of that sixth semester it felt like I was caught in the middle of a tornado. My scholarship contract ended in June and I continued running errands and printing certificates to the CLSN.

The seventh semester started in August and I enrolled in three core subjects only; the tutors of these subjects agreed to receive the final compulsory assignments by mail from Leeds. The annual meeting happened in the initial days of September – just over a week from the time that I should be in Leeds.

I waited for the end of the annual meeting to receive my last allowance. By then, I'd managed to buy only a hundred pound because Pound Sterling banknotes had vanished from all banks and exchange shops. On top of that – given that I needed all the money I had to start paying my initial expenses in Leeds – I hadn't bought a flight ticket to go to the UK. For that issue, I was expecting that my father sold his 90's Volkswagen Gol.

That car had been rusting quietly on the entrance of the house because my father could no longer drive due to his nerves and my brother, who had a driving license, was unemployed and couldn't afford the fuel. Unbelievably, even though we'd spent over a year squeezing past it to get into the house my father was set against selling the car to pay for the flight ticket and sulked whenever the subject surfaced. I knew it wasn't fair to demand that from my father – he worked morning to night and that car, rusty or not, had cost him his sweat. But I had to board a plane to Leeds, and had no time to dwell on feelings of guilt.

Gladly, on that first Sunday of September, my mother's sister's husband heard about the situation and offered to buy the flight ticket using his cheque book to pay for it in instalments. He then asked my father to repay him whenever he could. We managed to find a cheap flight for the eleventh of September.

On the day we left to the airport my father told my brother to get the car out to valet and put a *for sale* sign on the windscreen.

At the airport, despite the excitement, I was feeling bad for my father. He had no real obligation to sell his most valuable possession. But that wasn't all. With the Pound Sterling at the rate of almost 6 times the value of the local currency, my mother also had offered to help. She'd emptied her bank account funds and made full use of the loan she was entitled to as a State employee – a loan that should be repaid over the next 5 years straight from her salary. Still, there was in truth little room for guilt or shame when my travel to England hung in the balance. Besides, just that week a coincidence reassured me that I should be following the right path of that journey to conquer English. I accidentally met a student, who had just been to Leeds, willing to sell Pound Sterling. Thanks to that – and my mother's money naturally – I'd start my overseas adventure with a total sum of £1.005.

And I do believe that it wasn't because I carried with me part of my mother's future salaries that she was on the verge of tears at the departure gate.

"May God cover you with His blessing and…" My mother gulped, keeping her promise of not crying at the airport. "…Mom loves you."

As to my father, when he gave me a hug and said, "Have a nice journey and God bless you." I could tell that he was no longer thinking about his Gol.

It was my first time on a plane; first take off, first flight, first landing, Guarulhos Sao Paulo; first time in an international airport, *Barajas* Spain; first time in a foreign land, *Heathrow* in England. The first time I ever spoke English with a person that couldn't really understand Portuguese. My first time in an English line

– *Queue here*. First time on a subway; first *mind the gap between the platform and the train*; first time at *Victoria Station*; first time in a *Cross Country Express* train; first time ever observing a sunset after 8 p.m. First time at *Leeds Railway Station*. First experience of temperatures under 10 degrees Celsius, my first time in a traditional Victorian small residence – 20 North Grange Mews. And, finally, my first night and first *Our Father* in England before going to bed.

The first time, since my initial move to come to England, that I surrendered to fear, doubt, regret, and remorse for having gone so far, for putting my father and my mother through so much, for interrupting my life back home for a dream. I thought on how far from home that was. Only an inexplicable force, a blind faith of a religious type could have brought me that far. I shut my eyes. *To hell with those thoughts*! Tomorrow would be another day. The first full morning in the Old World, in the United Kingdom, on real English soil, surrounded by real natural English without having to press play or stare at a tv set. Real, untainted, unfettered, unfiltered, unabridged, fresh clear bright beautiful English!

58

The cold bright morning sunlight filtered through the window and on its travels gave light and muted colour to a beautiful English morning. The temperature was just below ten degrees around Yorkshire. The radio forecaster announced "a fine but chilly start with sunny spells across the county."

I was there in England. I was still there. And there I should remain to keep my ideals of glory alive. A morning such as that meant glory itself.

I rose from bed, brushed, showered, had a cuppa watching *The Basil Brush Show*, and walked to Leeds train station ready to enjoy another day. Short queue, train ticket, free *Metro*, electronic gates, escalators, platform ten, seven fifty-one Northern Rail train to Blackpool North, one stop at Outwood, and Wakefield Westgate. Clifford remained in his car at the short-stay parking waiting for me.

As usual, I brought a medium white filter coffee and a bag of double chocolate cookies. On the way to Doncaster we made another habitual stop for coffee at Jay-Jay's café in South Elmsall, where the beautiful young Sonia politely prepared a mouth-watering egg butty and her mother Sue enlightened our day with her bright loud laugh and a frank local accent.

The *Metro* had finally given up printing headlines warning England about a new wave of snow and the ominous return of the Big Freeze. It was a Wednesday, but not a usual one.

At Whittington Street, it was same old same old. Hoovering, wet cleaning, finishing, hosing, shampooing, blade over, waxing, stretching, flexing, dancing, listening to Mr Robbins, thinking about English and my purpose of being there and now and again stifling the odd yawn. In the afternoon I tried to keep myself warm inside Unit twenty while organising the tools and recycling the masking materials scattered around the floor. A few tradesmen were still hanging around waiting for the last customers to make a decision on the cars they'd been test-driving – or in Ewan's words, *taking for a spin*. In the meantime, Dan had joined me for an idle chit-chat as per usual.

"I guess you do not know what *mo* means." I challenged Dan.

"*Mo, mo…*" Dan repeated, obviously not knowing the answer.

"A gay man. A homosexual." I said triumphantly with a smug expression of an English learner who had successfully challenged a thirty year old native speaker.

"Oh… As in ho-*mo*…" Dan said, making me realise where the word *mo* came from.

No matter how much English I thought I'd learned, natives always showed a greater intuition about the language. I knew the word *mo* from *Will & Grace* – same place I first learned words like *fag*, *queer*, *dike*, *gaydar*, and *straight*, meaning heterosexual. It was always the same: when I had a chance to show off a few new words to Dan, he'd know other ways the words were normally used, or where they were more commonly used, or why the words forms were like that.

Then I'd know what linguistic process underlay those uses, or why certain words were used in a determined manner or in determined occasions, and how the words could be categorised in English. I could say that *mo* resulted from a process of word formation named *clipping*, that the process of clipping was very common and productive in English, that words such as *ad*, *bro*, *sis*, *ho*, *pub*, *fridge*, *telly*, all resulted from the same process, and even that such process somehow reflected human language tendency to be economic, i.e. to convey maximum meaning using minimum effort.

I could still say that *mo* is one among several other alternative words used to avoid the word *homosexual* because the word *homosexual* conveys meaning to a sensitive subject, and the same happened to other words associated to issues regarding sexuality, intimacy, or bodily functions. Phew! So much I could say about that single word, yet my crippled intuition couldn't realise that *mo* was a word clipped from *homosexual*. Furthermore, the variety of words for *homosexual* that I knew could be trampled, trodden, and crushed by the massive inventory of words Dan himself knew.

"What other words do you know for gay man?" I asked eagerly, trying to restrain my excitation because I knew I was about to open Pandora's Box.

And if Pandora's Box contained all the evils of the world, then the contents of Daniel's chatter box should not be much behind.

59

"*Woolie Woofter*." Daniel started in a casual, serious tone, which prompted me to emulate his tone. "*Woolie Woofter*. Why?" To what Daniel replied "Rhyming for *poofter*. A *poof*."

Poofter was a more common term to me.

Clifford, who was nearby the unit, entered and started untangling the blow liner as a blatant excuse to listen to our conversation. Daniel turned straight away to him and loudly said: "Words for gay man..."

Clifford thought for a second. "*Bender*."

Dan opened a naughty smile and shot "*Shirt lifter*."

I looked puzzled and asked, "Why *shirt lifter*."

Daniel searched for support looking at Clifford, who remained serious, so I intervened. "Dan. It's just English to me. It's important for me to know. Go on..."

So Daniel swallowed his embarrassment, positioned himself in front of me and adopted a professorial tone. "If you bend this way, you pull your pants down, then you have to lift your shirt, huh."

I smiled encouragingly towards Daniel and looked at Clifford as if asking him to fuel the conversation.

"*Fudge packer*," Clifford saved me.

"*Fudge nudger*," Daniel complemented opening another naughty smile. "*Arse bandit!*" Clifford said over a chuckle towards Daniel who cracked laughing and very proudly launched "*Pooh stabber*."

"And *dykes on bikes*, have you ever heard?" I challenged Daniel with a new topic.

"Big *lezzo. Carpet muncher. Muff diver*," Daniel totally showed off with a haughty giggle.

"Yeah but, what *dykes on bikes* means specifically?" I addressed the question to both Daniel and Clifford.

"Dykes riding bikes? 'aving sex." Dan replied, putting his hands forward, as if holding the handlebars of a motorcycle, and wiggling them.

"No," I said, smirking at Dan's gesture. "It's a group of lesbian motorcyclists – from San Francisco, I think – that participates in pride parades"

"Didn't know tha' one… 'ow 'bout *one eyed bed fairy*?" Dan asked, grinning and looking a Clifford.

What the hell was that now? "A *queen* again?"

"No." Daniel replied and, not satisfied enough, shot back: "*Humpton, shaft, tally wacker, bald avenger.*"

I looked at Clifford for support and he saved me with a more American one: "*Wiener.*"

I showed Dan that I finally got that saying a few words I knew myself – "*Willy, ding dong, knob*" –, as I thought of a new way to harvest more words. Then I remembered a *South Park* episode called *A million little fibers* where they used the word… "*Mingie.*"

Daniel then showed confidence saying, "Easy one. Get that. *Snatch. Beaver. Fanny. Pussy. Cunt…*"

I pretended to ignore them all just to see his smug smile – but I actually ignored the first two only – then I proposed another. "What about *the twins*?" Dan made a puzzled expression so I continued. "*Hooters, boobies, jugs.*"

Dan protested. "Too American, they are. Proper English ones are *knockers. Baps. Tats.*"

Then, it was my time to protest. "No, no, no, no… *hooters* and *boobies* may be more American but all these others have no nationality."

Then, Dan gave a sardonic "Huh!"

I pretended to enjoy the naughtiness of the exchange to keep Daniel talking. I also restrained my will to dash and scribble those precious words down not to break the spontaneity of the chat. Between spoiling the mood and forgetting the words I chose to keep repeating the words mentally. Then, I thought of another word to keep the challenge up. "*Heinie*, do you know *heinie*?"

But then, Dan cut me short. "Is tha' why y'r 'ere fur? T' learn bad English?"

Oh Gawd, Daniel was about to start his scrutiny all over again. *Damn it*.

60

"That's not bad English. That's just English to me." I tried to explain and excuse myself at the same time.

"That's really bad English, mate." Dan insisted, emphasising the two noun modifiers, *really* and *bad*, and using a reprimanding tone of voice.

Then, I put on a serious face and started in an exaggerated savant tone. "Well, my interest is purely linguistic. Observing naughty language to me is the equivalent to a physiologist observing a human body. These words are… let's say, like a wild orchid that you only find if you get in touch with the wild nature."

"I told y're dodgy. Y' 'av a Master's Degree in English bu' ye trying t' learn bad English. If ye teach your pupils these words y'll be sacked." Dan continued teasing, as he did now and then.

I felt obliged to explain myself more seriously.

"It's not the taboo words that interest me, Dan. I enjoy learning them, clearly. But it's to see… how can I explain? It's the variety of words that's interesting to me. It's the associations between these words and their meanings... Ah, that is it! Also, because I'd never learn these words in a formal institution, because no teacher want to be sacked, huh. So I'm here to learn from you." I said the last part with a half sarcastic half serious expression to confuse Daniel about my sincerity.

In that moment, Ewan entered the unit wearing a happy smile of who had just made a sale. "An' wha's Jonesy so 'appy about. Been learning slang from Dan?"

"I am learning language not slang." I protested a little sarcastically.

"I could 'ear it. Y' two couldn't possibly be talking about knockers." Ewan used a more than ironic tone.

So, I used an even more ironic tone, to confuse him on what was really my reaction to his comment. "Sure. We know my interest in knockers is purely linguistic."

"So, y' were learning slang then." Ewan insisted.

"I know nothing about *knockers* being slang. The OED probably classifies it as informal. That I know."

"Informal. Colloquial. That's all slang. We 'ere speak slang English." Ewan said it, already a bit edgy whilst deviating his gaze away from me and searching for something that even he should be not sure what.

I noticed Clifford looking at me askance.

Dan instantly broke that oppressing silent with a cheerful comment. "Our slang is way be'er than t' Queen's English. So, learning with us is good for you."

I tried to complement Daniel's mood. "You betcha!"

But Dan seemed seriously determined to make a point. "So ye see... In t' Queen's English we learn we 'ave t' say *I am going to the market*. Bu' we say *I'm off t' t' market* or *I'll nip t' t' market*. We can say t' same in fewer words."

It was interesting to see how Dan truly felt strong about his choices of words, about his very own English. How he was ready to stand for his dialect in the face of Standard English, which he called the Queen's English.

Dan hadn't gone through Higher Education so I supposed that English language teachers from lower levels in England must teach their students about the social value attributed to language use, about linguistic differences between local English and Standard English, and perhaps that was how Dan learned to be proud of his own English.

Ewan was from a different generation, when concepts of language variation, language prestige, and language stigmatisation were probably not well-accepted in schools yet. Ewan's poorly informed knowledge regarding English wasn't much different from most people's ignorance about language in general – an ignorance that generates so much bigotry.

When I awkwardly objected to Ewan's concepts about colloquial English being simply slang language, he appeared obviously offended. I wanted to explain Ewan right there and then but I doubted he'd have cared, and in fact I bet he'd have felt even worse. My strong desire to make Ewan aware about some notions on correctness (and wrongness) in English was misplaced in setting and occasion: we were all in a garage, not in a lecture hall, and I was a valet man, not a lecturer. All in all, although I'd just finished a Master in Linguistics, without a proper script in hands, I'd just leave Ewan even more befuddled.

So, thinking how large the world's need for linguistic awareness was and how small was my power to rectify it, I restrained my impulses and left Ewan alone.

Still, I continued thinking what would I say if only I had a proper chance to enlighten Ewan.

61

LABOV

"Excuse me. Where are the women's shoes, please?" A man, looking in his early thirties, politely enquired as he carefully approached a floorwalker on the ground floor of *Saks Fifth Avenue*, located near the centre of the high fashion shopping district of Manhattan.

"On the fourth floor." The floorwalker replied hurriedly, as any good New Yorker would do.

But before the floorwalker had a chance to proceed with the busy affairs of a New York dweller, the enquirer leaned forward and insisted. "Excuse me?"

To make sure the insistent enquirer would let go, the New Yorker replied more emphatically – this time making sure those two simple words could be clearly heard. "Forrrth floorrr."

"Thank you, ma'am." The polite enquirer said to the floorwalker and they both went their separate ways. The man kept murmuring those two simple words – "Forrrth floorrr, Forrrth floorrr…" – over and over, imitating the way the floorwalker had just spoken.

"Next!" A cashier from the ground floor of *Saks Fifth Avenue*, despite being extremely busy behind the counter trying to keep pace with the Manhattans' shopping frenzy, continued paying attention to that enquiring man. *That the man probably must be dyslexic or has some type of amnesia*, the cashier thought.

Earlier on, the cashier himself had been approached and asked where the women's shoes were by that same funny man. Although the cashier informed the man that the women's shoe store was at the 4rth floor twice, the man still hung around that same floor for a considerable while approaching other floorwalkers.

The cashier saw when the funny man finally seemed to have given up relying on memory only and picked up a little notebook from his pocket to note the directions down. Still, that man took ages to jot down such a simple direction.

"Next!" When the cashier called the next shopper in the queue, a large lady holding several shop bags stepped forward, completely blocking the cashier's view of the floor. When the lady shifted, the cashier saw that the inquiry man seemed to have finally found his way to the lift and disappeared.

That man reminds me of Marsha White, the cashier thought to himself, referring to a character in a *Twilight Zone* episode called *The After Hours*. He'd watched that episode 2 years ago. In this episode, a shopper named Marsha White insists with a few staff members at a department store that she'd purchased a gold thimble on the 9th floor; after they inform her that the store has no 9th floor she eventually remembers that she is actually a mannequin who lives at the store.

Well, the man was slim but not cute enough to be a mannequin like Ms White, the cashier thought before shouting, "Next!"

The enquiry man's cognitive problem was however more serious than the cashier supposed. After spending a good few seconds taking note of the direction to the women's shoe store, the man stepped out of the lift on the second floor and started again. "Excuse me. Where are the women's shoes, please?"

On the 2nd floor, he continued approaching a few more people at Sacks: stock boys, cashiers, sales persons, and floorwalkers; always taking notes of their answers. When he eventually entered the lift again, soon as the doors opened on the 3rd floor, he stepped out seeming to have forgotten about the notes and all.

And yet that man's hippocampus seemed to be in an utter mess, the man's sense of purpose had certainly not been affected because he continued asking, "Excuse me. Where are the women's shoes?"

At least, after interrupting a few more hurried individuals, the enquiry man made his way to the lift again and reached the 4rth floor. Then, as if still not sure where he was, he continued approaching other floorwalkers: "Excuse me, what floor is this?"

"Hey…! Haven't I just met you, like, minutes ago downstairs?" One of the floorwalkers who the man approached on that floor said, with an expression of surprise and impatience on his face.

"Oh, I'm sorry. I didn't realise it." The man felt awkward. He didn't want to attract attention to him and, unlike the ground floor, that floor was much less crowded and far more spacious. Though the stunning models at that floor were pretty busy displaying the high fashion garments to individual shoppers, there were receptionists stationed at strategic points specially to screen out non-buyers like him. But, as he started making his way out of that situation, he noticed that the floorwalker started looking around, quite paranoically.

"Hey, wait a minute. I know you what you're doing. You're from *Candid Camera*, aren't you?" The floorwalker asked loudly and turned around all excited. "Where are them cameras?"

But when the floorwalker turned again he only managed to see enquiry man disappearing behind the closing doors of the lift. "What the…? Weirdo…"

62

In post-9/11 days, a suspicious acting person like that enquiry man probably wouldn't go far like that.

However that happened in the early 60's, when paranoia still was more of a delusion than a real sense a danger. So, by then, the enquiry man managed to approach and ask the same question to 68 persons at *Saks Fifth Avenue*, 125 at *Macy's Herald Square*, and 71 at *S.Klein On The Square*. And after approaching this many people, managing to make them utter "fourth floor" at least twice, the enquiry man still managed to discreetly keep register on his notebook of the occupation, sex, race, estimated age, and the accent of each person that he approached in those stores.

The man's investigation methodology at the New York City department stores became famous as one of the groundbreaking pioneer works of William Labov – a man who, after a 12-year career as an industrial chemist, became the founder of the Variationist Sociolinguistics.

Until then, standard theory in the mainstream Linguistics hadn't been equipped to deal with the great deal of variation in the every-day life language.

Subsequent to the Structural Linguistics influence in America, from the second half of the 20th century onwards the dominant approach to linguistics followed the formalisations proposed by the American linguist Noam Chomsky and his Generative Theory. In his theory, Chomsky basically renamed the Saussurean dichotomy *langue* vs. *parole* as *competence* vs. *performance*, competence being more precisely the individuals' unconscious knowledge of the systematic rules (abstract grammar of language) that underlie their performance (actual utterances). Under the formalisations proposed by Chomsky, the proper object of linguistics is the competence, and the main concern of linguistics is to present a description of this competence – videlicet, a description of the underlying systematic rules in the individuals' mind.

Thus, linguistic investigations should in principle disregard the language variation that appears in actual utterances because such variation was regarded as a phenomenon restricted to performance – a result of the speakers' intelligence, memory, attention, and so forth. It didn't matter to linguistics if people said *to.may.toes* or *to.mah.toes* because in everyone's mind the word had only one form and one meaning – the same goes for constructions like *I'm going to* or *I'm off to*, etc. All these expressions represent the same thing, and so the variety of forms do not matter do the linguistic description under Chomsky's formalizations.

This is when Labov enters the world of linguistic investigation to propose both a methodology to deal with actual every-day utterances and a formal theory to explain language variation.

Labov addressed first the belief in the mainstream Linguistics that language variations were completely random from person to person in speech (performance). Labov wanted to show formal evidence that language variation actually followed a mathematical regularity when correlated to individuals' social characteristics like gender, race, age, social class, and also the formality of the conversational situation. If variations in speech could be formally evidenced to follow a mathematical regularity across a range of speakers, then it would be proven that those variations didn't simply happen randomly but started taking place systematically in the mind.

So, to reach such formalisation Labov started interviewing and recording people, collecting actual speech data (speakers' utterances) that evidenced language variation. Besides observing speakers' utterances, Labov kept a record of their social attributes (gender, race, age, social class, etc.) so he could track these attributes later.

Then, Labov focused on a specific feature of English that is known to be variable in speech – in the case of the department stores study was the pronunciation of the postvocalic 'r' in the words *fourth* and *floor*. In this linguistic context 'r' would be pronounced as a rhotic, as it commonly is in American English, or not pronounced, as it commonly is in British English. Labov then selected *Saks*, *Macy's* and *S.Klein* as a sample of the speakers' social class because each department store would correspond to a different social stratum of shoppers and staff. The other social characteristics like occupation, gender, race, estimated age were controlled or observed whilst Labov himself enquired about the fourth floor.

Labov knew that to elicit the full spectrum of the speakers' language variability the linguist had to find means to lessen the *observer's paradox*. The *observer's paradox* is the effect caused in the speakers' way of speaking by the presence of a formal observer; in other words, when the speaker knows that he/ she is being analysed by a linguist researcher this speaker may feel embarrassed, shy, etc., and may tend to speak more artificially. Thus, Labov's methodology involved either lessening the formality of the interview somehow or simply acting surreptitiously, as he did in the *Saks Fifth Avenue* pretending to be looking for women's shoes.

The New York department store survey showed that the variability of 'r' in *fourth floor* depended on the combination of social contexts. First Labov showed that the rhotic variable of 'r' was more prominently pronounced when the speakers repeated the two words more carefully a second time – when Labov insisted in asking "Excuse me?" –, thus showing the rhotic to be probably the most prestigious form. This was further confirmed because the rhotic variable was also more favoured by the speakers at *Saks*, from upper middle class, followed by the speakers at *Macy's*, from lower middle class, and less favoured by the speakers at *S.Klein*, from working class.

That meant that the other variable – when the pronunciation of 'r' is omitted, as in / fɔ: θ / and / flɔ: / – was the stigmatised form, appearing more in the careless utterances and increasing its occurrence on the reverse order of the social class scale. Labov showed all these data in raw numbers and percentage, thus proving mathematically that the variability in the pronunciation of 'r' in *fourth* and *floor* was stratified socially. With Labov's works like these he set the cornerstone for further sociolinguistic investigations relying on numbers and correlations.

But Labov's contribution was not restricted to a modern approach to linguistic survey method. The work of Labov established a social truth about English which importance transcended the scope of the academic scientific method. And it happened when Labov decided to use his method to investigate the black English vernacular in the inner city of New York and to demonstrate scientifically that this vernacular English had features of a dialect with some rules which were unique and distinctive from those of Standard English. This dialect, after Labov's work, was formally recognized by academics and is now widely referred to by the name of *Ebonics*.

63

Ebonics is a blend formed by *ebony* and *phonics*. The term Ebonics itself originated in the 70's according to the Concise *OED*. Currently, it's also equivalent to a more formal term: *African American Vernacular English* – also *African American English*.

The term Ebonics itself was originally coined by the American and social psychologist Robert Williams; more precisely in 1973. *Ebonics* is also the title of a book by Robert Williams published in 1975, subtitled: *The True Language of Black Folks*. This book presents the African roots of Ebonics and refutes the popular conception that Ebonics was merely a slang English or a wrong or poor English. Nevertheless, the merit of advocating for Ebonics isn't entirely Robert Williams'.

William Labov in the late 60's already applied his innovative method of sociolinguistic survey and analysis to formally show a set of grammatical rules – coherent and relatively distinct from those of the Standard English – which characterise the dialect of English that is now colloquially called Ebonics.

The methodological procedures of survey and sociolinguistic analysis of Labov concerning Ebonics are documented in his work published in 1972: *Language in the Inner City*. Here, Labov presents a description of the Black English Vernacular, or BEV – as he preferred to call. Labov identifies BEV as an English that has a relatively uniform grammar, that is found in its most consistent form in the speech of black youth between the ages of 8 and 19 who fully participate in the street culture of the inners cities of urban centres like New York, Boston, Detroit, Philadelphia, Washington, Cleveland, Chicago, San Francisco, Los Angeles, and others.

To get to the linguistic formalization regarding BEV, Labov collected samples of actual individuals' utterances using a methodology like that of the NY department stores – to reduce the *Observer's paradox*. Particularly here, Labov, with help of fellow linguists Clarence Robbins, John Lewis, and Paul Cohen, conducted individual interviews in various locations, amongst which is South-Central Harlem in New York.

Labov took part in activities of recreational social interaction with teens and pre-teens of the community (South-Central Harlem) who were members of groups with names like *Thunderbirds*, *Aces*, *Jets*, and *Cobras*. Labov watched the interaction of members of these groups, often recording their speech with a central microphone for the group and lavaliere microphones in each member individually. Labov also conducted individual interviews with adults of these areas.

With his method of collecting and analysing speech data, Labov – in *Language in the Inner City* – formally documented, among others, a frequent and consistent grammatical feature of BEV: the omission of the copula *be*. Copula is a linking word, particularly a form of *be* (*am*, *is*, *are*) linking subject to complement; like in *My name is Bond*, the verb *is* functions as copula to link *My name* (subject) to *Bond* (complement).

The utterances of speech that Labov collected and analysed showed that the use of the copula *be* in BEV is a variant feature – i.e. sometimes occurs, sometimes doesn't. But Labov pointed out that the omission of the copula *be* occurs much more frequently and more consistently in BEV. Roughly speaking, this means that it's much more common to hear a black young person from the inner city of large urban centres in America saying *I beautiful* rather than *I am beautiful*.

The sociolinguistic methodology of survey and analysis that Labov proposed did provide the scientific tools for the formal description of a set of grammatical rules of African American Vernacular English. Thus, Labov reinforced the foundations in the conception of distinction and authenticity of this dialect of English, which Labov called Black English Vernacular, and that is now generally called Ebonics. The scientific legacy of Labov, however, reached far beyond the academic circle, as it triggered an important social effect.

Prior to works such as Labov's, teachers weren't aware of the features of Ebonics that systematically differed from those of the Standard English – as regards to grammatical structure, vocabulary, and phonetics. So, at school, when students used their English with typical features of Ebonics that deviated from the Standard English, teachers believed that these students did this because they were lazy, sloppy, or just inclined to bad behaviour. The sociolinguistic work of Labov offered a systematic description of the features of Ebonics, and along with it, helped to lessen the misunderstanding and prejudice of teachers towards students, black or Puerto Rican, who spoke and wrote English with the marked features of Ebonics.

The most important aftermath of Labov's linguistic enterprise was that by formalising a theory of language variation, he established that the variability is inherent to language and not only an inconsistency of speech. And variability occurred at all levels: from pronunciation, through vocabulary, to syntax as later studies confirmed. Labov sowed the seeds to question the conventional notions – essentially bourgeois – that language has just one most functional and correct form.

In his scientific approach to language variation, Labov formally showed that the conventional notions of language correctness reflected fundamentally the association between variant forms of language and the social status of its users. Variants frequently used by upper class individuals hold status of prestige and are considered to be correct. Variants frequently used by lower class individuals hold status of stigma and are considered to be wrong.

These notions elucidate, for example, the reasons why local dialects – along with their distinctiveness of vocabulary, grammar, and pronunciation – are usually branded as improper or slang and often misrepresented as a symptom of ignorance and incompetence. This happens because the most upper class factions of society – which generally wield political power and control mass media – dwell in the wealthiest urban centres of a country. Notions of linguistic prestige also clarify how the associations between language correctness and education ultimately reflect the social status of speakers, since the access to most prestigious centres of higher education is usually granted to upper class individuals.

Undeniably, after Labov and his undercover mission in the department stores of New York, along with his field work in the inner city, the general ignorance about language variation and correctness which perpetuates so much prejudice gradually would lose its force within the intellectual circles of either linguistics or education. And although he had to challenge some of the fundaments of the dominant linguistics approach of his time, Labov knew that his Variationist or Quantitative Sociolinguistic was there, fair and square, and the linguists had better to get used to it.

64

Daniel had just brought a new round beer to the table: a can of *Foster's* for himself, a bottle of *Stella Artois* for Clifford, a pint of *Carling* for Dave, half a *Guinness* for Ewan, and a *Früli* strawberry beer for me.

"Wha' kind o' democracy do we live in? T' other day a bloke from Sheffield told me 'e queued fur more than two hours an' still couldn't vote. Thousands were denied voting. We cloned Dolly, why couldn't we clone polling stations on t' sixth o' May?" Ewan said that after downing half a pint of *Guinness* in one gulp.

"You askin' me? We vote Labour. It's no' my faul' we 'ad a hung parliament – an' now, a fine coalition between Tories and Lib Dems. Our parliament is now split. 'ow abou' that eh, chuck?" Dave teased, knowing Ewan wasn't happy that the Tories had failed to obtain majority.

"Did you read *The Sun* on Sa'urday?" Ewan carried on with the banter, knowing Dave had a subscription. "They said Mr Brown was holed up in number ten. They called 'im a squatter. 'ow abou' tha'?"

"Gordon Brown should 'ave stayed." Daniel corroborated his father's position, without getting involved in the bantering mood.

"Well, now our merry man resigned, innit! 'twas like end o' season in *Coronation Street*. Mr Brown 'olding 'ands wi' wife Sarah n' 'is two li'l ones, leaving number ten behind." Ewan used a tone of satisfaction that didn't convince. Everyone knew he wasn't happy with the coalition.

"Three years as PM was enough." Clifford interfered whilst Ewan kept humming *Coronation Street* tune. "At the end of the day, a Lib-Lab coalition would mean a coalition of losers. You're with me?"

"A' the end o' t' day Tory won, tha's all it ma'er." Ewan added restlessly. Then turning to me, he put on a serious tone and started imitating a BBC News anchorman reading the headline with an exaggerated Received Pronunciation accent. "At eight-ten p.m. the Queen Elizabeth the second officially invited David Cameron to become her twelfth Prime Minister." Ewan killed two birds, rubbing the fact in Dave's face and teasing me about English. "Is tha' proper fur Jonesy?"

As if suddenly realising I'd been cornered by that conversation over parties and coalitions long enough, they all turned their attention to me and remained stone-faced waiting for my answer.

65

After Ewan had a brush with my language remarks, the evening became quiet at the garage. Dave shut Unit fifteen earlier than usual and came to yack with Ewan about the last 5 days after the election. They argued on whom was the right man to take over number ten, until they finally reached a mutual conclusion: we should all nip to local pub and have some pints before Clifford went to the auction in Leeds.

Clifford noticed my expression begging for his approval. "Ok, go on then."

We were all off to the pub. I felt an excitement built up along the day: surrounded by so many enthusiastic natives, listening to their accents, absorbing the way they expressed their ideas toward each other, being included in the centre of the conversation. Bliss!

I'd ever been so close to live native English like that. Not even when my previous English bosses talked among them at the manager's office and I remained listening quietly to avoid spoiling their mood. Whenever they noticed me they'd fall back into the usual distant and formal talk, speaking pragmatic denotative English. And then I was right there at the heart of the banter, as Ewan teased me over English again.

I thought this time I could be a bit less controversial on the topic language. If my Master in Linguistics didn't entitle me as a proper lecturer so far, at least it should've enabled me to deliver a decent speech about English.

"Have you ever heard *Fry's English Delight* on BBC Radio 4?"

Except from Clifford they all shook their heads.

"It's a series with thirty minutes episodes broadcast between two thousand and seven and two thousand and nine. A specific episode approached the discussion about what was actually right or wrong in English. Another one discussed what proper English really was. So in total it is one hour of hard-core discussion with professors, elocution teachers, newspaper editors, lexicographers, communication skills adviser, voice coaches, speech therapists, and other experts talking about the subject you proposed me to have an opinion on. It is not a simple issue to talk about as you might think. So, I don't believe whatever I say will really have an effect on the way you think about proper English."

"Come on Jonesy, tell us. We trust you." Ewan insisted while everyone else kept quiet staring at me.

"For one, I work in a garage under your orders and, normally, people only respect ideas in general from those above them in the social hierarchy. In the same way people are more inclined to accept views on English from someone in a position of social prestige. So, normally people from the highest ranks of society have the final word on what is right, or correct, or proper in English. It is not by accident that Standard English is mostly referred to as the BBC English, or the Queen's English, and that Northern English might be regarded to second importance. However, Standard English is not organically right, correct, or proper. It is conventionalised right, correct, or proper following normative grammar regulations, which may even defy logic. One example is the norm that disapproves split infinitives even though they appear often in speech and they don't interfere with syntax or meaning. The non-split infinitive norm was conventionalised in English mirroring Latin: infinitives in English shouldn't be split 'cause infinitives in Latin are made up of just a word."

I took a quick breath to muster some energy. "This conventionalisation is good to a certain extent because it sets a common standard to communication. If everyone started writing with irregular spellings, for example, it would cause confusion. Convention, regulation, norm, must be observed to the point it benefits communication. People do speak with different accents and different grammatical choices though. But, there are places and situations where the standard must be followed for the sake of communication." I noticed my audience squirming with impatience. "I can finish saying that Standard English is right, correct, and proper when there is a purpose to use it. If the audience is diverse the Standard English enables a wider reach. In this case it feels right, correct, and proper. When the audience is small, familiar with local English, the local English is sufficient to communicate. In such familiar context Standard English and big words might just bore the audience. So, in this case, Standard is wrong, incorrect, and improper. And that is why when Ewan impersonated BBC English in this table it sounded comic, because it was obviously inappropriate to a conversation between Yorkshire workmates in a pub."

Phew. I felt my heart racing in excitement, feeling blissful to have them goggling at me. I finished the last sentence addressing everyone at the table in an affected manner, as if they were attending a lecture of mine. I hoped that they'd understood my sarcasm towards Ewan. Initially, it felt like I wasn't going to find my away back to Ewan's remark but, gladly, I managed to choose the words carefully and conclude my brief speech without stumbling. So I thought. Or perhaps the *Früli* had found its way into my cerebral cortex.

There was a brief moment of silence afterwards whilst they seemed to avoid facing each other.

Clifford glanced quickly at the clock.

But before he could say anything Daniel asked, "Ye know wha' people call me?" Before I could say anything he carried on. "Gobby. People say I'm loud n' I say wha' I think. Y' know wha' people call ye?"

I remained silent.

The only thing I could think was, *Why my Lord, why*? And I braced myself like for the hundredth time that year.

66

"People say y're dodgy"

"Why people say I'm dodgy, Dan?" I emphasised the word *people*, since Daniel himself called me *dodgy* all the time.

"Y' don' say y'r age, y' don' say wher' ye from, an' why y' working in a garage instead o' teaching. Y' 'av a diploma. If I 'ad a diploma, I'd be in a school teaching, meking sixty grand a year."

"We talked 'bout that b'fore. Bu' just so you know, I'm still learning, Dan. How am I supposed to teach?"

"Y'r English is already excellent. An' I'm no' jus' saying. Other foreigners 'ere can barely speak t' essential wi' us." Daniel looked at the others at the table, expecting for a sign of agreement.

"I have a purpose to be in the garage. It can make a difference between me and my old uni mates. Also it makes me happy to be close to English as I am now."

"English is everywhere in England." Daniel insisted.

"Not the same English as in the garage." I restrained myself from talking about language variety.

"Y're learning bad English from us. Slang" Ewan interfered, completely ignoring my speech from before. He simply never missed chance to have the last word.

Then, I lost control over my tongue again.

"We discussed about slang. Northern English isn't slang. Doncaster English isn't slang. Whittington Street English isn't slang. There's more to English than that."

Ewan smirked; aware he'd made me lose it again.

"I'm not going over the same discussion again. It is too much risky for me to say anything about slang specifically. The boundaries between slang, jargon, regionalism, do not sound completely clear to me. It must be easier to identify each category than to actually identify words within each category."

"Yer thing. Long as y' keep jonesing t' cars, I don't care." Ewan again made sure to have the last word.

"Jhonsing?" That was a new word for me.

"*Jon.es.ing* – Our word fur wha' ye do at t' garage. Valeting cars wi' t' special touch o' Jonesy. *Jonesing.*"

"Oh, alright." Suddenly, I felt pretty happy to let Ewan have that last word. "Come again!"

"Cheers." Ewan lifted his empty half-pint glass, prompting Clifford to go and get the last round in.

67

Foster's, *Stella*, *Carling*, *Guinness*, and… *Strongbow* – this time, Clifford returned bringing a replacement for my *Früli*. "Oh, thanks. Wh… what kind of beer is this *Strongbow*, Clifford?"

Daniel answered instead. "Tha's no beer. It's cider."

"Isn't *cider* a specific type of beer?" I challenged Daniel, assuming that he was splitting hairs just to show off.

"No." Clifford replied. "Cider's made from fermented apple juice. Beer's made from fermented barley an' flavoured with hops."

"Oh, right, I believe in you." I said, under a blurry impression that Ewan and Dave sniggered at me.

Paranoia perhaps. In any case, I thought better to shut up not to get carried away going on about English again – what would unavoidably happen because, with inebriation kicking in, everything within my field of vision that wasn't shrouded in haziness gained colours and contours which highlighted English.

Clifford, *Daniel*, *Dave*, *Ewan* – neighbours from Whittington Street, native speakers from South and East Yorkshire. English gentlemen in a pub, at the table, holding drinking containers – aluminium can, brown bottle, tulip-shaped pint and half-pint glasses. They could distinguish the content of their drinking containers using specific words since that was just a detail of a scenario that had been part of their ordinary routine for years. For them, the words *cider* and *beer* referred to different realities, different kinds of fermented alcoholic beverages. For me, judging from my experience in England, cider and beer had comparable colour, came in comparable containers, and were sold side by side – hence, the difference between them was a fuzzy concept. The same fuzziness applied to different kinds of beer – apart from *Früli* which, as I'd learned, was a fruit flavoured beer.

Ale, *bitter*, *draught*, *lager*, *porter*, *stout*, *barley wine* were words which I knew but struggled to identify what they actually referred to. The names of those alcoholic beverages were just details in the myriad of words for drinks and dishes within the cosmos of public houses which I either vaguely understood or completely ignored. And just like the garage, pubs had their own inventory of vocabulary. Even the action of having a drinking tour around several pubs gained a specific verb: pub-crawl. As I thought of that, a wave of loudness brought in a group of pub-crawlers.

By then, everyone had sipped their last round and exchanged their last teasing remarks.

I remained absorbed in my little universe searching every empty niche of my mind to accommodate words, phrases, banters, and discussions that had transpired throughout that Wednesday and that lingered floating around me in bright fluorescent colours.

Then, that floating English froze midair and faded.

"Wake up Jonesy. We're off now." Clifford awoke me from that trance.

68

On the way to Leeds Clifford and I went through the customary routine. *Morrisons*, muffins, cookies, chocolate éclairs, *reduced to clear* pies, a *reduced to clear* roasted chicken, a 2 litre bottle of diet grapefruit pop – our basic provision for the following day.

Clifford decided to drop me off at my flat before heading to the auction in Rothwell. He informed me that he couldn't stay later that night with me.

On the road, I remained unusually quiet. And since Clifford wasn't much of a talker himself, *BBC Radio 4* filled the silence. I felt terrible whenever Clifford left me alone at night but nothing would make him change his mind.

Smashed, I crashed in bed. Hardly had I hit the mattress, all that evening enthusiasm turned into misery as I started thinking about my still unsolved visa status. That triggered a familiar nausea: stomach, heart, and brain pang. The duvet offered me some feeble solace.

With all lights off, my *Matsui HD Ready* tv threw dim flickering flashes on the walls. A rerun of *The Sarah Jane Adventures* was on *BBC Three*. I thought on how delayed I was in my plans to write. Almost 4 months and I'd managed to produce only drafts and scribbled pages. And there was a world still to read.

I worked Monday to Saturday the whole day – sometimes through the small hours, helping Clifford – and the sight of blank pages waiting for the last drop of my forces at night or on free Sundays offered me a discouraging prospective. *Oh, to hell with doubts.*

One thing was beyond doubt: no matter how hard I tried to achieve something, life always excelled in bringing me down. Sometimes, all I had to cling to was faith. That night though, even faith had forsaken me. As falling asleep in that gloomy mood would do me no good, I held the pillow tightly and prayed to wake up inspired and with a more positive mindset in the morning. *Psalm 91* from King James Bible. *He that dwelleth in the secret place of the most High shall abide under the shadow of the Almighty.*

I began to feel a fire reassuring me that writing was the right thing to do. The more it burned, the more I believed that my salvation depended on filling those blank pages. My thoughts then wandered to reminiscences that strengthened that belief. Two weeks ago, on St George's Day, Ewan came to give my weekly wage and, unusually for him, had done so with a broad smile. Noticing my expression and the latent question therein, Ewan then explained the reason to his good humour: Ewan had sold more cars during that first financial quarter than in any comparable period during the history of the company.

That information stirred a genuine curiosity in me, and I couldn't resist asking. "Are you practicing some sort of *secret* ritual?"

I only realized it was too late to go back with that question when I saw Ewan's expression: his face was bright red, as if he was ready to burst.

69

Ewan then burst into laughter: "Ye can't be right, Jonesy. *Secret ritual*? 'ard wo'k, I tell ye. 'ard wo'k. Y're crackers in t' 'head. Y' foocking are." Ewan said whilst already walking away, as if he wanted others to listen to that.

If I had a penny… Hard work was enough of an answer to me, and it did make a lot of sense.

I'd noticed a spark of obsessive determination in Ewan's look when I saw him that week pulling some old bangers from inside Unit eighteen to make space for the increasing number of newer cars he'd bought at auctions. That very night after we left the pub, Ewan had commented to Clifford that, thus far, in everything he'd put his mind into for that year he'd achieved success – and despite the coalition, even the political party he supported, the Tory, had returned to power.

That reminded me of my former resolution to pursue my passion for English and how that led me to the MA at the University of Leeds and to the graduation ceremony in the Great Hall.

That also reminded me of a former classmate who'd shown me a film called *The Secret* which supported the affirmation that anything a person thinks persistently – mainly under a state of strong desire, emotion, and faith – would frequently be manifested into its physical equivalent. Suchlike concepts didn't astonish me. Being born into a Catholic family, and being quite curious about the weirdness, oddness, and bizarreness around religion and spiritual matters, I grew up trying to understand the principles behind miracles and misfortunes. Although I understood that thought (an idea, a plan, etc.) is the natural starter of any enterprise, I also appreciated concepts about a mystical connection between thought and physical reality.

While non-mystical views sound reasonable and uncontroversial, mystical views usually offered explanation to how some people managed to achieve success under difficult and unpromising circumstances. Apparently, I'd experienced that mystical connection during my journey learning English – yet each success on that journey resulted from hard endeavour, they'd equally been impelled and favoured by situations outside my control. Still, what that experience led me to realise particularly was that just like thought and physical reality, language and physical reality seemed to share a mystical connection as well. And the genesis of that realisation happened one night, just after I started the Major in English, when I dreamt with a lecture in which the tutor talked on the creating power certain words enclosed because they'd been preserved since its origins.

I had further glimpses of that mystical connection between language and physical reality when I read Plato's *Cratylus* and his *naturalist* view of language, and when I learned about other theories on the nature of language – chiefly Labov's approach to variation, which showed mathematically how variant forms of a language stemmed from and mirrored social situation (status, setting, circumstance) of individuals, that is, the physical realities to which individuals are connected to.

Recently, at Ewan's garage, I had an insight on such connection. Before then, I not only ignored the word *valeting* but also failed to notice the valet service often offered in petrol stations. After I truly learned the meaning of *valeting*, by living its meaning as part of my ordinary struggle, every valet service caught my eye, from the signs describing the options of valet – mini, full, external, internal, and all ranges – to the lads toiling over the cars with soap and water; the area where they plied their trade seemed to spring to view.

It was as if truly learning a word revealed a part of the world to which that word is connected to. A world revealed by a word.

70

Half asleep, I remained reminiscing on those beliefs with nostalgia, going back to when I started learning English, reading and revising the twelve books of the *English at Home*. Each volume showed on the cover a picture of cultural icons of Britain.

Book one showed a bowler hat with the Union Jack flag printed on its side, book two showed the bowler hung on an antique rack, book three showed the bowler hung on the antique rack behind a tea table, book four brought the image of a Grenadier guard wearing a bearskin hat, book five showed Buckingham Palace, book six showed a double-decker bus in front of a Town Hall, and all others followed the same pattern – with exception of book twelve, which showed a skyline of Manhattan.

All those images, so distant from my world then, had now become somewhat a part of my reality. This was just a development of my journey learning English. Or perhaps, more mystically, a change from within my mind which now observed a reality filtered through the light of English.

All that reminiscence faded when a strong nervous stomach cramp awakened me.

The tv had changed to ITV Three. *On the Buses* was showing. Cockney. In 4 hours my work routine would start. I should make an effort to rise and do some writing. The duvet was so comfy. *But nothing good comes without sacrifice*, I thought. I should write those words down on a piece of paper.

I reached for a sheet which rested on the little table next to my bed. One small gesture, a giant token of my commitment to write. The sheet of paper kept slipping off my fingers. Was I dreaming? A glance around the blurry room and, at least it still felt like England. Again I shut my eyes.

A slide show of images, me on a hammock, reading aloud the sentences printed in the *English at Home*, and listening to the affirmative and interrogative sentences from audio tape, flooded my memory. *Listen and repeat*: *the book is on the table… the dog is under the chair… I am here… you are there… is the book on the table?* Another glance. No, not yet.

Part Two

1

A hazy beam of sunlight squeezed through the still closed curtains coming to rest right on my sleeping visage, its gentle caress calling me from sleep. A strong scent of fresh paint filled the room. The chilling air cut straight through three layers of blanket that I'd pulled over my shivering body during the night. A stream of steam spiralled above me along with my breath as if produced from a long cigarette puff. I wondered how anyone could survive in these arctic climes. It felt far too early to rise, but remaining in bed under those useless blankets held little appeal. Besides, a friendly sunbeam seemed to promise a warmer world outside.

So I flung back the covers, with only a slight gasp, and hobbled over to the window to discover what daylight had beckoned me to see. The window overlooked a grassy backyard from the halls of residence known as North Hill Court. After I threw the curtains completely open the radiance which filled the outside world with golden colour tones also inundated my room, making me attempt to some details within it which I'd overlooked on my arrival at that student accommodation of the University of Leeds.

Room 6, from 20 North Grange Rd., was a spacious shared room, fully carpeted, furnished with wardrobes, beds, desks, chest of drawers, and small racks; two of each item. There was also a wash basin in the room. Sheer luxury!

I approached the wash basin to brush my teeth and wash my face on it. Two metallic taps. I ignored the little letters h and c imprinted on each tap. I turned the left hand corner tap on. A humming noise from the water pipes and... presto! Hot water started pumping.

In the bedroom, vocabulary review from book seven: *he turns on the hot water tap...* So, hot water taps were real. Naturally, lessons from *English at Home* portrayed British culture. Until that morning those had been mere words for me. Back home, sinks were single tapped and had tepid water only – with a 24 degree average temperature throughout the year water was naturally tepid. As the warm water filled my hands, those words acquired a true meaning to me.

I felt like a new self had been awakened to that truth. A sudden emotion brought tear to my eyes. What an amazing feeling. Oh, if my classmates back home could see me now. How fortunate! I'd asked for the cheapest accommodation available and they still arranged me a palace. Another flow of tears followed a concern: how much would it cost? It was really time to start worrying about that myself, because since my arrival in Leeds others had done that for me.

The international students who arrived in Leeds between the 11th and the 15th of September could book the *Meet and Greet* service that the International Office offered free of charge. The *Meet and Greet* team were a group of more experienced students who waited at the Bradford International Airport, at Leeds Train Station, and at Leeds Coach Station to welcome the newcomers. They assisted the international students with their luggage, placed them in a van, drove them to the accommodation office to collect their keys and again to their respective accommodations, dropped them safely, and wished them good luck.

Before the Meet and Greet team dropped me at North Grange Road no one at the accommodation office mentioned anything about accommodation expenses. Their greatest concern apparently was allocating all students to a safe dwelling. I couldn't be more thankful for that.

At the time of my arrival at Leeds, despite being 25, internally I was no more than a child begging for a human gesture that could make me feel safe. At the University of Leeds, under all the conspicuous pressure of hundreds of new coming international students, the Meet and Greet team and other staff members transmitted a sheltering sensation. Well, it was time to find out if that first impression given by the Meet and Greet team and accommodation office staff would stand because the university awaited me to deal with the cold bureaucracy of the registration proceedings – which included signing the accommodation contract.

Thus, beneath a sunshine that tinged the hazy air with a bright orange-hued shimmer I set forth.

2

At the entrance I saw Martin – a German housemate who I'd met in the previous night just after entering the accommodation. Martin, even if visibly young, had manners of a middle-aged gentleman.

"Gut Morning. Are you walking to the uni now?"

"Yes, I hev to get there quick. It's late already." I replied, hoping that Martin wanted to come along.

"Oh, I'm waiting for Jackob, from room two." Martin said with a formal tone.

"Ok. I'm cool." I meant to say *alright* but used *cool* as a joke, making a reference to the low temperature.

"So, I see you later." Martin said, without moving a muscle of his face – though he'd probably understood my intention to be funny.

"Cool... I see you." I tried a rhyme. Flatlined again.

Watching too many American comedies before coming to Leeds left me thinking that every sentence I uttered should sound witty. I wanted my English to sound ultra-advanced and make a clever impression. Instead, I made Martin squint at me puzzled. That made me rush off before Martin thought I had a screw loose.

Off the top of North Grange Road, I began what would become a routine for the coming months.

I followed downwards from there, passing by North Grange Mews, all the way to the bottom of the road where it meets Headingley Lane. Then, hanging a left towards the city centre and keeping to the left hand side of the road, I passed by a bust stop, Johnsons Drive-in Dry Cleaning, North Hill Road, traffic lights, Leeds Girls' High School, which stands on the opposite side, Ashwood Villas, Ashwood Hall, which is the City Church Leeds' site, Cumberland and Grosvenor Road. To my right hand side a string of shops – including Hyde Park Barber Shop, PC Consumables, The Final Curtain, and Budget Booze – lead away to the corner where Victoria Road spurs off from Headingley Lane. At this standpoint, in the beginning of Victoria Road, I caught sight of what appeared to be a vacant food shop and off-licence which curiously preserved two signs on: *Sam Widges* and *Cellar Vie* – puns I'd grasp only years later. Next to me on the left, stood S.J.Moran Properties and R.P.M. Properties at the corner where Regent Park Avenue took off from Headingley Lane. Another string of commercial houses, namely drink føød, Clock Café, Sugar Shack, Fish and Chips, Retro Boutique, and The Hyde Park Pub, led to the end of Headingley Lane – from here Headingley Lane became Woodhouse Lane.

Just a bit further, I reached a junction: to my left, Woodhouse Street; to my right, Hyde Park Road. I still passed by The Hungry Caterpillar, Aladdin Newsagent, La Cafetíere, Atticus, Robovideo – a 24/7 DVD store –, Michel's bakery, and L'Oranaise Café Restaurant.

From here I already descried Parkinson Building's Clock Tower looming majestically in the distance.

Then, as the brash commercial buildings petered out, I suddenly caught myself breathlessly goggling at the most beautiful park I'd ever seen in my entire life.

Hyde Park stood just metres from me across Woodhouse Lane, capturing the brightness of the air and transforming it into sheer green. A splendid landscape as green and clean as that, which I thought existed in films only, now projected itself like a slice of heaven on earth in the middle of a city. Tall leafy trees formed a ring around the park broken only to follow the sides of a pathway which bisected this grassy Arcadia. While I stood there for a moment to look at the people walking along the pathway, Martin caught me up.

"Hey, Jackob went through the park." Martin awakened me from my trance.

"Is it free of charge to walk around that place?" I assumed Martin knew that information, since he'd been in Leeds longer than me.

"Eh…" Martin squint at me again, but then started smiling. "Oh. You're joking, right?!"

I didn't have a clue how Martin mistook that for a funny remark. "No, I'm serious."

"Ah, verry funny." Martin beamed at me, prompting me to shut up for the remainder of the promenade.

I'd check that on the way back. First, I had to know what the accommodation expenses would be, and then see if I could afford a walk there. Meanwhile, I'd enjoy the free view. And the landscape on the left side was no less stunning: right beyond a gravelled area, where cars were parked, stood hundreds of Victorian buildings, all similar in shape and colour, composing the most beautiful panorama I'd ever seen. That panoramic view was under the constant gaze of a vigilant statue of Queen Victoria who sat on a pedestal at Hyde Park's entrance at the top of Woodhouse Lane. Here pizzerias, takeaways, off licences, and pubs multiplied in number.

On the right hand side, at the corner where Clarendon Rd. finds its beginning from Woodhouse Lane, was the site of The Library – popular among students, I judged, since many of them came out of it with wide smiles pasted on. Only later it came to my knowledge that The Library was actually a boozer, former place of a genuine library. Despite this false start, the first of the University of Leeds' buildings really sits across the road: Houldsworth Building and the School of Mechanical Engineering.

Martin and I continued along the pavement on the left side of the road, passing by Pizza Milano, The Ale Shop, Fortune Cookie, Luckys, Punjab, The Pack Horse, The Cellar Café Caldo, The Eldon, and the Quakers Meeting House at the junction with St Mark's Street, before we crossed at the traffic lights to the right hand pavement. A few more steady steps and finally, there I was, at the steps of the Parkinson Building, gawking at its colossal Clock Tower. It was 11 a.m.

Suddenly, I caught myself shaking; not because of the cold air, but because I knew that soon I'd learn how much I'd have to fork out for the accommodation.

3

I looked around, enthralled. The Parkinson Building steps were crowded with students, sitting, eating, smiling, talking, and englishing. At the ground there were a few luxurious galvanised steel litter bins emblazoned with *your litter please*.

I threw an impressed look at Martin pointing at one of the litter bins. "Is that a garbage can?"

Martin raised his eyebrows. "Yes. You see, even the bins here justify the international reputation of politeness that British people have."

I searched for something clever to complement his words. But was all that came out was, "Wow!"

"I'll stay here for now. We catch up later, yeah?"

"See ya." I said, and completed quietly with a "Smell you later," staring stupidly as Martin climbed the steps.

Alone, I continued on towards Cavendish Road, slightly to the right from Woodhouse Lane, where the university main entrance was.

There was a hustle and bustle of students, coming, going, forwards, backwards, sideways, alone, accompanied, walking, skipping, dancing, and playing. Beautiful, young, lively, fancy, those students didn't seem apprehensive or anxious like me. I had the impression that mine was the only frown to be seen in the milling crowds. So, reminding myself that there should be really nothing to fear and much to accomplish I looked ahead, inspired, gulping down the fresh air, and advanced firmly towards the main entrance, determined to strike cleanly on my first registration day.

Before the academic registration itself a few other compulsory tasks needed completion: signing the accommodation contract, opening a bank account, registering with a local doctor and getting a few vaccination shots, and registering with the police. I couldn't consider issues, like surviving for example, before these tasks were completed. There should be a few targets, a dozen obstacles, and a hundred pitfalls on the way. I felt the same adrenaline rush from my London mini-odyssey commuting from Heathrow to Victoria Station via underground, during which I was bearing a rucksack, porting a hand luggage, dragging a huge suitcase, and balancing on the top of platform shoes – the only available footwear that I considered fancy enough to wear in an European setting.

So, there went I to complete each task, wearing my platform shoes, wobbling fancily from place to place, as if competing on an *It's a Knockout* tournament around the University of Leeds.

In between one task and the next we students could unwind in the Christian tent, pitched opposite the Leeds University Union building, enjoying the social activities other students had prepared for us, whilst trying free orange squash, blackcurrant juice, coffee, tea with milk, and biscuits. Then, there were also the International Welcome activities at the International Student Office at the 18 Blenheim Terrace, just across Woodhouse Lane, opposite to the Parkinson Building. There they offered talks on the easy steps to complete some of the compulsory tasks, and also guidance on saving money. In between talks we were encouraged to sit and meet other international students while trying a few free sweets and drinks.

Everywhere I turned to there were students with different skin complexions, eccentric faces, peculiar manners and gestures, speaking English in all accents. These other international students smiled warmly to each other, moved slowly as if afraid to knock something down or collide with another student, spoke carefully, and listened even more carefully tilting their heads to understand what everyone else was saying.

At the International Student Office I realised that, like me, other students were trying to save money by looking out for any chance to eat for free. As wherever we turned to around the campus we were being given biscuits, cakes, sweets, and squash, the international students' sugar levels should be high during that welcome week. No wonder we all looked so happy.

The academic registration process itself was another marathon: collecting the registration document from the Parent School – the School of English in my case –, enrolling for the appropriate modules at the Academic Fair, getting the Parent School stamp on the registration document to verify the chosen modules, and confirming my status as exchange student to the Accounts Receivable staff so they could stamp the registration document stating a financial authorisation to register.

Finally – after almost a week walking to and fro, eating at the Christian tent, attending guidance talks at the School of English, queuing after every stamp, spending the nights reading all the "how to" leaflets and the Taught Student Handbook – I was standing firmly at the Sports Hall Two entrance holding my fully stamped registration document and enrolment forms, ready to go through the completing stage of my academic registration process. It only took a few good minutes standing on my platform boots on a queue into a white tent. Then, inside the tent the queue went on for around 2 hours until I could leave from inside the tent and gaze upon what seemed another hour of queuing until I was inside a big hall in front of a digital camera and someone behind that camera suggesting me to put on a happy face for the picture of the student ID card.

"Cheers..." I heard before a click. That picture depicted the summary of what existence brings to all human souls: hope and glory with a hint of tiredness.

Dozend of activities went on around the campus that week, combining hard-core bureaucracy – which coordinated a multitude of individual processes dealing with each student – and light entertainment, which helped the first-timers who were away from their home to assimilate the new cultural environment osmotically.

My cultural shock didn't really begin until I held my student ID card. From then on the Christian tent was dismounted, the free food vanished, the entertainment ceased, and the excitement of the new gave way to the obligation of the real.

4

By that time I'd already phoned and emailed home. And I'd learned that the accommodation would cost £1.400 to be paid in three instalments, the first one due only in November – that'd give me a little time to organise myself financially.

I'd also met Laura – the only exchange student from our home university who'd chosen Leeds and with whom I'd keep a close contact through that experience. I'd met Laura only after the exchange applicants were classified to Leeds. She'd travelled a week ahead of me and arranged to stay with an English gentleman before her student accommodation became available. When I run into her amidst the rush of the registration process we sat down in a café to have a cappuccino.

"Oh, let me tell you. Second day, I was at the Christian tent and I met this all smiles and charity English girl who invited me to have a meal at the cafeteria of the Student Union Lounge. I was a little reluctant to accept because, you know, prices here aren't for the faint-hearted and I felt embarrassed that she might want to pay for me. So, from a selection of these exotic mouth-watering sandwiches displayed at the counter, while I went for the cheapest option, the girl went for a three-and-a-half pound sandwich…" I waited for Laura to sip her cappuccino. "Guess what, when we finished eating, the girl was all smiles and excuses telling me she had no money with her. Then I ended up having to pay for us. Honest to God, I had my eyes all misty whilst she promised she'd pay me back."

Laura bit her bottom lip to suppress a laugh. "Dear, consider yourself lucky. Remember I told you I stayed a week in this English guy's house…?"

I nodded in affirmation as Laura went on. "So, this guy told me his cousin needed cash and he asked if he could borrow some off me. I stupidly told him sixty pounds was all I had left, and I still needed to purchase food, thinking that he'd excuse me. Guess what he said? He told there was a place at the station where he could get food for free and borrowed my sixty anyway. So far, he never even mentioned paying me back."

Laura ended her story and started eating the residual froth of the cappuccino. My jaw was hanging open.

"The cappuccino is my treat." I was so touched that I felt compelled to offer that as a token of solidarity.

"Thank dear. Listen, come around to my house later; so we can all go along to the station with this English."

Caught up in Laura's enthusiasm, I nodded at once.

And so, that evening, after the completion of the registration, I set off to Laura's, 47 Clarendon Rd.

"Good evening my young lad." The English gentleman himself attended the door. He spoke with a clear diction and a deep voice. "Pleased to meet you."

"Pleased to meet you too." Before I could introduce myself he interrupted me.

"Laura told me you're coming along with us. We'll wait in the kitchen before we go." The English gentleman, different from what I'd imagined, fell more into the hippie type. He dressed layers of coloured jumpers, had long hair, and lively grey eyes. "I'm Craig by the way." Craig held the door ajar, until I entered.

With gentle manners and a simply beautiful English, Craig captivated me during the time we waited to go to the train station. After an hour chatting, Craig, Laura, and I went from Clarendon Rd. through a short cut.

From near the bottom of Clarendon Rd., we turned left at Hyde Street, crossed to Clarendon Way and followed downwards, passing in front of Leeds Dental Institute, by the Centre for Bioscience, under the

Worsley Building, and bearing right to Calverley St. after the General Infirmary. We reached the end of Calverley St., passing by the Leeds City Council on the left, the Brotherton Wing and Portland St. on the right, and crossing Great George St. Here, at our left, stood Leeds Central Library, and at our right, stood Leeds Town Hall, that was being refurbished. These buildings faced the main avenue cutting across Leeds city centre: The Headrow. After crossing it, we followed through East Parade, turned left at Quebec St., finally reaching the back entrance of Leeds Station at Wellington St.

Inside the station Craig guided us to Upper Crust, a café and takeaway food shop, where a lady friend of his worked as sales assistant. When we arrived there, the girl Craig knew was about to close the shutters. All tables and chairs were already piled up and there was a large transparent bag resting on the floor – a bag loaded with sandwiches which were going to be thrown away.

I couldn't quite understand what we were doing there, until Craig eagerly squatted near the large transparent bag. "Hurry up, let's help ourselves."

5

More than quickly Laura produced carrier bags and extended one to me. "Get this one and fill it up, quick."

In less than a minute we filled up those carrier bags. It was utterly weird. The sandwiches were all sealed in plastic wedges packaging, but these were smeared with grinded coffee powder, bits of food, and ragged tissue. All we minded was that the sandwiches were fresh and free. They were 24 hour sell-by date sandwiches, so they couldn't be sold anymore.

Soon as we stuffed our carrier bags we rushed away to the Station main entrance, at New Station Street.

Once we reached the bus stop just after Gateway Yorkshire, we beat the coffee powder off the plastic cases and dig in those exotic sandwiches. I had no idea what they were, but my mouth was watering.

Laura started explaining to me what those sandwiches were: *cheese and tomato*, *egg and tomato*, *egg salad*, *egg mayo*, *ham and cheese*, *tuna cucumber*, *tuna mayo*, *BLT*, *prawn cocktail*, *chicken salad*, *chicken and ham*, *chicken corn*.

"Do you like prawn?" Laura extended a prawn cocktail sandwich to me.

"Prom? What's prom?" I asked, chewing a cheese and tomato sandwich.

"Shrimp; let's change for a BLT." Laura grabbed a BLT from my bag before I replied anything.

The light was hazy and steam came out of our mouths when we chewed. It looked like I'd been caught in a weird dream, as if I was drunk, not noticing what was around me much. I could smell the coffee powder and then I felt a little nausea and stopped chewing. Two or three ladies at the bus stop seemed to pay no heed to that bizarre scene. Craig was holding his own full carrier bag, acting very normally, smiling at us.

I wondered Craig was a hypnotist having a laugh, making us eat off a rubbish bag. Laura didn't seem to mind as she kept asking me to exchange sandwiches.

We carried on through the foggy night led by Craig. From New Station St. upwards, through Park Row, until we reached The Headrow again, more to the east from where we crossed earlier. We entered the southern entrance of a mall called The Light, took the escalators up to its main entrance at Albion St., and continued upwards until the end of Albion St. – the point where it turns into Woodhouse Lane. We turned right at Merrion Street as Craig decided we should go inside the Merrion Centre.

We arrived there just in time to see *The Flying Machine* in motion. This moving sculpture was protected inside a glass dome right in front of *Morrisons* – a supermarket where food could be bought at ridiculously cheap prices according to Craig. I promised myself to return there soon but at that moment, after a whole week trudging around after stamps and free food, tiredness finally had won me.

I headed all the way upwards through Woodhouse Lane, passing in front of Parkinson steps, and through Headingley Lane again. Back at 20 North Grange Rd., I devoured another sandwich, prayed, and crashed in bed, thinking about the many names of food, street, place, and verbs that I'd learned just that week. It thrilled me to think how much more there was yet to learn until I could speak English flawlessly.

Then, a daunting thought crossed my mind: £1.400! I already had less than the £1.005 I'd brought. But before I could worry, an eerily hissing sound followed by a rattle of bangs passed right beside me through the wall. *A haunting*? I should better pray. *"Our Father…"*

6

Barely had the ghastly sounds faded away at night, a thump of footsteps started echoing beside my room. They were from the other housemates who went about their day, trotting up and down the stairs. Particularly, the room 5 housemates had a loud tv on and the hinges of their door made a high pitched squeak whenever they came in or out of the room. In bed, I half slept, half listened. It felt early for so much hustle and bustle. The feeble daylight showing through a chink in the curtains gave the impression it was just dawning. Yet, it was nearly 12 p.m. of a cold, very dark, Saturday.

It was the first day after registration. Sleep still called to me courtesy of a broken night's sleep, constantly interrupted by the banging and groaning of the pipes which snaked through the walls feeding the antiquated heating system. Still, whatever my body might say, Greenwich said noon. That morning, rising from bed involved good measures of yawning, stretching, and sighs. A sense of anticipation began to clear my thoughts; after days of compulsory tasks, for the first time, there was no urgent direction to follow.

As I shuffled from my room to the communal shower I bumped into Emanuelle – an Italian housemate, hot like hell – who greeted me, as usual, with a frank merry smile and a stare into my eyes.

"Ciao Johnny. How are you this morning?"

"I'm a bit lazy. And you?" I replied, embarrassed to be seen before my beauty shower.

"Super! You coming with the house to Hyde Park pub later?"

I thought for a second, wondering how much that would cost me. "Yes, yes. What time?"

"Not sure. Not before six. We knock at your door after that." Because he smiled widely as he spoke, or because of his accent, everything Emmanuelle uttered sounded like he was joking.

"I'll be here. Thanks for inviting."

"Not at all Johnny." He said, touching the side of my face, as if he was about to kiss me. "See ya. Ciao."

With a few hours to spare I set off on my first trip to *Morrisons* to stock up on essentials – my budget would stretch to nothing more actually. With an eye on price alone *Bettabuy*, the supermarket's budget brand, soon filled the basket. 20 pence cans of beans and 5 pence noodles were to be the staples of my diet. Since one can't live on beans and noodles alone, I filled my basket with soap powder, paper towel, a box of tea bags, a bottle of skimmed milk, sliced bread, *Buttery* margarine, apricot jam, banana flavoured milk, a box of cereals, and double choc chip cookies; most of these proudly bore their *Bettabuy* banners.

I left *Morrisons* studying the till receipt and realised that a full basket had cost less than £10! I was surprised and relieved. Starvation had seemed to be looming but those prices would give me time before my funds run out. I couldn't rely on hunting for free sandwiches.

I was still settling down with a life outside the walls of the University of Leeds. Out in the street I was very much a stranger on foreign soil constantly surprised by the world around me. Earlier that week, near Hyde Park, I'd thought that the beautiful floral bouquets exposed on the pavement were for sale. It took me time to realise these displays were just part of a flowerbed. Also, even if white people were common in American films, seeing so many Caucasians together in the flesh felt rather strange; the cloudy sky cast a light on them that made them look like beings from another planet, with translucent complexion, motionless expressions, large bright eyes, blond or ginger hair, and some frankly eccentric hairdos. Folks in the street looked cold and distant, as if they couldn't express emotions or feel empathy. They walked fast too. No one sauntered or wandered; they strode steady and hard. I couldn't keep up with their steps, no matter how fast and large were my own steps. Perhaps the law of gravity was more rigorous in England and my muscles were still adjusting. The air itself was punishing me: my muscles ached, my lips were chapped, and the bones in my hand didn't move without cracking anymore.

During that year I'd thought of myself as a strong human being, who had all under control, including emotions. I'd ignored my fears and pains since I'd arrived in Leeds. I could recognise some essence of my behaviour in the attitude of those flight attendants from TAM Airlines who dressed impeccably, spoke, smiled, and moved with robotic gestures. Yet, that cold grey Saturday afternoon was really getting into my nerves. There was a lump in my throat, a crush in my heart, and butterflies in my stomach. On top of that, chilly winds were cutting right through my soul.

On the way back from *Morrisons*, dragging heavy carrier bags, I repeated, "Keep it together. Be brave."

But my heart came to my mouth when, out of nowhere, a black piece of something passed fluttering next to me. Shocked at the sight of what I mistook for a giant crow, I turned to watch its departure; this second look revealed a rather less frightening truth: it was a flying umbrella, broken, distorted, being dragged by what felt like a twist, certainly driven by the same howling gale that had ripped it from its owner's grasp.

I hastened my steps home, afraid that I might end up meeting Mary Poppins bruised and battered across the road searching for her umbrella.

7

Back at 20 North Grange Rd. most housemates gathered in the 3rd floor kitchen, drinking Robinsons Barley water and cooking pasta. They were the Italians, Marco and Emanuelle, the Germans, Jakob and Martin, the Spanish, Javier, the Mexican, Ricardo, and the Romanian couple, Alina and Victor. Missing this roll call were the American girl who shared a room with an African girl on the ground floor and used the kitchen downstairs, the English lad on my floor who never joined us, and the girls of room 5, Nicola and Vanessa, from Poland and Czech Republic in that order. We formed the crew from North Grange Rd.

I joined them upstairs, after preparing my own meal in the 2nd floor kitchen.

"Ciao Johnny. Come have pasta with us." Emmanuelle had both hands extended in my direction.

"I have instant noodles here. Thanks." I excused myself while Emmanuelle went on saying a few things I didn't understand.

Javier pulled a chair for me next to him. "I heard from Martin that you're looking for a job. Did you manage to apply yet?"

"No. I passed by the Joblink in the Student Union, but there's nothing for me."

"I am planning to apply for a job too." Javier sounded a little unsure of that. Like all the other students from Europe, Javier was there under the Erasmus scheme, so he received a monthly scholarship.

"Well, I really need to get a job. It's not an option for me." I said, a little concerned that the others might discriminate against me for that.

"Well, I have intention to marry after Leeds. Some extra money is welcome."

"Cool. I tell you if I find anything and you do the same, right?" I told Javier, feeling a comfort of sorts to learn that I wasn't the only member of the household with financial concerns.

Nights before, I'd calculated the amount of money I had left and how far it'd stretch. I'd paid around £80 for the train from London and the Young Persons railway card. Another £100 went for the house deposit. A charge of £530 of the first instalment of the house due in November would leave me with just over £200 – though with no other urgent bills to pay until January. Thinking back to the effort and sacrifice it'd taken for both me and my mother to amass £1.005, I compared the ease and speed with which it was disappearing. At least, £200 would see me through 20 trips to *Morrisons*.

Hopefully I'd find a job placement before that. These concerns ran to the back of my mind as I went with the North Grange crew to The Hyde Park pub.

The pub was so vibrant, full happiness, and packed with students who seemed to have not a care in the world. There were two large tv screens, one showing a game of darts and the other showing *Around the World* from Daft Punk. Behind the counter the hard pushed staff seemed happy wearing cheery smiles under the incessant shouts for drinks and packet of crisps. *Were they students making some extra cash?* I wondered. I couldn't imagine myself working there. Behind us, a group of men suddenly jumped up from their seats, waving their glasses aloft and shouting, aggressively, supposedly because someone on tv had hit the bullseye.

I wanted to share of their enthusiasm but again my thoughts were a bit more sombre, and maybe a bit too sober, on what would be of my experience in the city of Leeds. I was there to perfect my English and make myself worthy of my parent's sacrifice. But it'd been a tough week and I felt homesick. So, there, in that superb pub surrounded by carefree students, perhaps a break in my obsession on keeping all under control would make no harm. I, then, shouted at the girl behind the counter. "Can I hev a glass of beer, please?"

8

VALERY

"Education is the most valuable asset humble parents can bequest to their offspring." Had Valery ever been a guest on *Quote... Unquote* she'd immediately have identified the author of that quotation as her father.

That was actually Valery's often cited quotation, recurring whenever the opportunity arose as a token of wisdom for her children and of reverence to her late father slash formal teacher – from whom she'd inherited not only an education but also the vocation.

As a good daughter who learned her father's lessons well and a caring mother who was aware of her family's economical prospects, Valery made sure that her children attended school regularly and followed the standard educational path provided by the State with a religious commitment. Although she'd been through regular periods of financial hardship Valery had always ensured, even in the tightest of times, that her children never went hungry for food or thirsty for knowledge.

Valery had a professional degree in pedagogy which, whilst not as advanced as a university degree, adequately qualified her to teach pupils up to their 4rth year in the initial levels of education in a State School. Since the State job offered her a stable income, she'd become the main provider for her family as her husband struggled to hold down a permanent job.

Perhaps because of this, she usually had the final word over most issues affecting the household. Not that her husband offered much by way of dispute, since his interests revolved mainly around the worlds of sports or politics. Valery wasn't a harridan however. She only resorted to her financial authority when whinging failed to achieve her goals – and rarely did her whinging fail. Someway she was used to be in control; the choice on what her family ate, or how they dressed was hers. Her spouse never cared to choose clothes even for himself.

The bank account was in her name. So, when money problems surfaced it was Valery who'd apply for credit. She decided when the house needed refurbishment; she prayed for the miracles that delivered her older son from violent bouts of bronchitis; and, when her younger one was diagnosed with leukaemia, she organised a novena in the Catholic chapel which apparently converted the disease into a profound anaemia.

Sceptics believed the younger one was only wrongly diagnosed; Valery attributed the miracle to the prayers. She decided the religion that her family should follow and what charitable acts they should undertake. And with the stories she often used to tell at meal times Valery instilled in her family what she saw as an appropriate code of moral conduct.

During her late thirties Valerie experienced a series of traumatic events that culminated in a miscarriage. That left her suffering anxiety, depression, and finally led her to a nervous breakdown. She was admitted to hospital for inpatient treatment and returned home after a week, outwardly improved but reliant on powerful prescription sedatives which left her drowsy. The pills phase lasted long enough to make Valerie gain some weight until a lady friend, who'd been through a similar situation and seemed to have beaten her demons, came to offer help and support. Valerie's friend confided in her that she'd replaced the drowse inducing drugs for alcohol. Desperate to escape from the zombie-like state which her medication damned her to, Valery followed her friend's lead.

A carefully controlled intake of alcohol allowed her to control her nerves and cope with her depression whilst still remaining alert for most of the day. Over the years the amount of alcohol needed to keep the desired effect gradually increased and it also became a relief to other frustrations. For most of the day Valery stayed wide awake, and then following her after lunch sips and usual afternoon siesta she was simply booze awake.

Valery's dependency on alcohol improved lightly when she had to deal with her younger son's issues on homosexuality.

After her child bluntly informed that he preferred the company of boys and was in a relationship with a person of the same sex, she wept, made him sit on her lap, and rocked him like a baby saying, "You're a child yet, my son. You have to realise that at fourteen you're not yet mature enough to make such judgment."

Valery went from whinging at her younger son to begging her older son to talk some sense into the boy.

Her older son discussed the matter with his younger brother in harsh raw terms. "So you fucking a faggot up the arse. It's normal. A friend of mine had a regular roger with a battyman in high school. That didn't make him batty. But, look, that's no good. He ended up in the batty's hand. He couldn't keep a regular girl. Once we were hanging at the city with our birds and this friend of mine had to let go of his quick 'cause one of these benders approached and made a sign meaning he wanted to see him. Look bro, I have one thing to say: let go of this man before he get obsessed with you."

That incident occurred as Christmas was descending upon the household and other family members were coming over for the holidays. And so the subject was dropped for the sake of discretion. Not for long though.

Sometime after the holidays, with the house free of guests, Valery took the matters in her own hands again and had a little argument with her errant boy. No one knew how it started but those who heard the argument figured out Valery had had it with trying to talk the boy round and switched to beating the homo out of him.

The first the rest of the house knew of the mother-son argument was when the boy loudly stated his point. "I am gay yes!"

Valery's counter argument was "No, you're not." Yet, acutely aware that her speech part in the argument was short, Valery needed to reinforce her point with a persuasive slap across the boy's face.

9

The discussion continued in a polite and organised turn taking argument and counter argument. "I'm gay." "You're not." Slap. "I am too." "No, you're not." Slap.

The argument became more heated as the boy's turns became shorter and more assertive. "Gay!" And Valery resorted to more persuasive body language techniques throwing punches and kicks into the mix.

Valery's sister-in-law, who lived with them, pleaded for the boy to stop challenging his mother. The argument raged on for some time, with neither party giving so much as an inch and abated only when mother and son finally found something they could agree on: they were too tired to go on.

Later, with a cooler mind, Valery admitted that trying to solve the problem with an argument like that was madness. The school year had started and that stressful situation could end up disrupting the boy's education. If she really wanted to help her son she had to be more reasonable. So, she decided, it was time to seek professional help.

To this end Valery took her youngster to see an urologist. Surely a doctor specialised in the male sexual area would be an authority on such matters and should be able to give an informed opinion on the normality of her child's maleness. She wouldn't waste time with psychologists; a physical examination would determine it quickly and precisely. She took the boy to the doctor where he was stripped naked, examined, and positively diagnosed as hundred percent male – or what Valery interpreted, heterosexual.

"There's nothing wrong with the boy. A specialist attested her son had no homosexual disease." Valery repeated that verbal diagnosis, from then on, when the subject surfaced or before they started any argument.

That way, and with the help of her faith and prayers, Valery re-established control over the matter and overcame that complicated phase, allowing everyone in her house to go on with their normal daily affairs and the young one to concentrate on his education unimpeded by any unnatural thoughts.

10

At The Hyde Park pub, the North Grange Rd. crew met with other students from the accommodation of North Hill Rd. Amongst these were some students from my home university who'd become quite popular within the international students' circle by organising parties in their house since they'd first arrived. They all proceeded from The Hyde Park to The Eldon. I went back to North Grange Rd. with Javier and the Germans.

Inside my room the silence was broken only by the boiler pipes vibrating against the walls. Well, at least all that noise would cover up my imminent weeping.

After a whole week holding back the tears, the little alcohol I'd drunk at the pub, helped them to roll freely.

I thought of my family, our struggles with money, how much everyone had sacrificed for me to be there, their expectations of me, of my father selling his car, of my mother signing away part of her wages, of her alcohol dependence, and how everyone in our house disliked it, of my stupid anxiety over the little money I had left, on how dull I was compared to other students, and of my obsession and pretentiousness over English.

Deep inside I knew there should be a reason why I had to go through all that. So, I calmed down, grabbed a leaflet on *how to apply for a job* and read it through again, determined to go and get a job after my first lecture on Monday.

11

No seminars were scheduled for that first week. Still, lectures started Monday at the Roger Stevens building, which sits at the centre of the University of Leeds.

Once the lectures started, at every hour from 9 p.m. a flood of students rushed through the internal wide staircases searching for the right lecture venue in the different levels of the building. Those who had lecture at the lower level theatres reached Roger Stevens building from the level 7, which is a middle level from outside. Those who had lecture at the higher levels theatres traversed the Red Route walkway which is a lengthy network of corridors at the 10th level connecting different buildings on the campus.

The Red Route is suspended in the air between Edward Boyle Library and Roger Stevens lecture block offering a breathtaking perspective of the reflective watery landscape at the Roger Stevens' east side. It was mesmerised by this view that I made my first trip to the theatre 22 to attend the opening lecture of *Victorian Literature* delivered by Professor Francis O'Gorman.

A lecture like that, I'd only seen in American films. In that lecture, I sat along more than a hundred students on a large tiered auditorium facing Prof. O'Gorman who stood in front of us in a lower level. Behind him, projected at the huge white board, was a photograph of Queen Victoria with a wide grin on her face.

"Pay attention to this portrait of Queen Victoria." Prof. O'Gorman started, with an English accent that sent shivers down my spine. "She is amused indeed. Her smile highlights and symbolises the prosperity of the British Empire during her monarchy from eighteen thirty-seven to nineteen and one: a period known as the

Victorian. The Victorian period witnessed England's expansion and zenith of imperial power overseas, as well as the astonishing progress of the industrialisation to seize the opportunity of a growing international market. A modern urban economy based on mechanised large scale production and commerce gradually replaced farming and landholding as the country's main economical foundation. Consequently, a migration process was triggered. The masses, looking for commercial success and work opportunities, gradually shift from the countryside to urban areas…"

While Dr O'Gorman proceeded I thought on how that Victorian social scenario of yonder seemed to have reached out for me in those modern days. I'd come from an underdeveloped corner of the world to a modern British city on a quest to improve my English. To me, Leeds – which gained city status during Victorian days – stood as a promise to personal success and future career opportunities. Furthermore, since I was in Leeds looking for work to guarantee essential dwelling and provision I felt almost a Victorian myself.

Hopefully, I wouldn't have to face the struggles the Victorians endured. Back then, if one side of the coin showed a smiley Queen Victoria the other side showed weeping proletarian children enduring the new social situation. The progress of Victorian times showed on the reverse overcrowded cities, slums, poverty, appalling working conditions, exploitation of child labour, homelessness, starvation, diseases, prostitution, crime, and things of the sort. I struggled to imagine people in England, a land of dreams, being struck with such difficulties. Those social difficulties of Victorian days were portrayed in Charles Dickens' *Oliver Twist*, or, *The Parish Boy's Progress*. Yet, despite having seen a few cartoon versions of it, I knew little about that period in the history of England.

Actually I was to find out that, apart from what I knew about the modern authors, I knew very little about England as a whole, and the little I knew about England was mostly filtered through American cinema. I was familiar with authors like Arthur Conan Doyle, Wilkie Collins, Bram Stoker, Robert Louis Stevenson, and Oscar Wilde, mostly because their work had been adapted to cinema. Now, things were about to become more serious since those authors were supposed to be read and I'd have to read also about the Victorian social context to understand where they were coming from.

And to make things easy right from start, the opening compulsory reading, to be discussed in the following week's seminar, was George Eliot's novel *The Mill on the Floss*; 534 pages (Penguin Books ed.) of hardcore English for whom had read only short stories. Hopefully, finding a job would be less difficult.

"...And so now, at the beginning of the twenty-first century, we have an opportune moment to think again about what constitutes the Victorian period. Good morning." As soon as Dr O'Gorman bade that *good morning*, everyone in the theatre 22 dashed off making room to a new wave of students who were already waiting, standing by the lateral doors that led straight into the rows of seating within that theatre.

From one moment to the next the corridors and staircases of the Roger Stevens building were crowded; and in a blink of eyes, deserted again.

After having understood barely half of the lecture my head was spinning amid that hubbub. I wanted to embark on a plane right back home and forget all that. But I'd started digging that hole around me and it was too late to escalate its walls off. Again it was time to pay for my pride and continue digging until I'd either reach rock bottom or find a light on the other side.

The job hunting season was about to begin for me.

12

From the Roger Stevens building, I followed east, down the ramp, reached Willow Terrace Road, crossed by the entrance of the Sports Hall, and went straight to Calverley St. towards the train station. From there, I was ready to observe the second commandment of the jobseeker: go to the Jobcentre.

The first commandment was to buy of a phone – the mean through which employers could reach applicants.

I'd read those commandments several times in the *how to apply for a job* leaflet until I fell asleep on Saturday night. Then, next morning, as I readied myself to go to the city centre to purchase a mobile phone, Javier knocked at my door inviting me to come along to Arndale Centre, at the other end of Headingley Lane.

Earlier that Sunday, Martin had been to Wilkinson supermarket over there, and he'd seen LG mobiles on promotion for £20. So, Martin, knowing that Javier wanted to purchase a mobile phone, told him about that. When Javier and I arrived at the Arndale Centre we realised the LG promo actually was at Somerfield.

I tried my best to focus on the words of the beefy, blond, baby-faced salesman who spoke with short syllables and an educated local accent. "You have two options of purchase: our basic monthly contract costs only fifteen pound a month and gives you two hundred cross-network minutes and two hundred free texts every month, plus this free flip handset with a built-in one megapixel cam, a headset, and free email. Or, if you want a more flexible plan without a set monthly bill, you can simply choose one of our pay as you go phones from as little as twenty pounds, plus a fifteen quid top-up voucher, and still get free email access."

Oh happy Sunday. All I ever had until that day was a second-hand tacky Siemens A Fifty, with monophonic ringtones, that my mother had given me after I moved out. And then I had in my hands a brand new flashy LG mobile phone NEC 'c' three thirteen, with coloured animated icons on the screen, and a camera!

I was rich. Not even the wealthiest of my classmates back home had one like that.

If on Sunday my new toy made all my troubles seem so far away, that Monday morning it brought me back to a less coloured mood on the way to the Jobcentre.

Once in the train station, I asked at the information point where the Jobcentre was and how to get there. I started following directions from New Station St. reciting King James Version of the *Lord's Prayer* – the only I knew by heart. *Our Father which art in heaven.*

I crossed the traffic lights at Bishopgate St., followed left through Boar Lane, and turned left at Lower Briggate. 3rd building, just after a furniture shop and a fancy restaurant, was the Jobcentre Plus office.

Inside, the office was ultramodern with a dozen touch screen kiosks where applicants could browse through job options by area, salary, and types. Once the options were narrowed down, a summary description of the jobs selected were displayed on the screen. Then, at the light touch of a sensor in the screen, a machine printed those details in thermal paper. The screen then showed a message informing those printouts should be taken to an available desk assistant who'd supply the application forms to the chosen jobs.

Before going to the assistant I skimmed through a few alternatives around Hyde Park and the City Centre. -*Bar staff*, carries out general bar duties, cash handling, customer service, maintaining cleanliness of the work area; need to be honest, reliable, and hard working; shifts to be discussed further.

-*Café assistant*, main duties: operating coffee machine, cash handling, and waiting slash clearing tables; shifts can be flexible; full training is given to the applicant.
-*Kitchen staff*, expected to perform cleaning duties mainly, help with food preparation, and close down the sink area at the end of the day; the position involves working evenings; if needed full training is provided.

"Please, have a seat. How can I help?" The Jobcentre assistant – a sophisticatedly dressed beautiful woman with a warm smile and an absolutely helping tone of voice – made me feel quite comfortable. She began explaining the most efficient way to apply as she browsed through the options in the printouts I handed her. Then, she simply interrupted her speech and said, "Oh... this one is just next door to us. Why don't you call in now and speak to the manager."

Assuming she meant close, I thanked, took the application forms that she'd given me and legged to find the address she'd just indicated.

Minutes later I was back to the Jobcentre, explaining to the same lady I couldn't find the address. To what she stood up, and took me by the hand.

"Would you come with me, please."

I had completely ignored the meaning of *next door* in her directions. The place was simply in the neighbour building, a Malaysian restaurant called Georgetown Restaurant.

She entered the restaurant, which wasn't serving yet, and addressed the man behind the counter. "This young man is interested in the vacancy in the kitchen. May I leave him to your care?"

"Certainly madam." The man replied in polite and accented Malaysian English.

"I leave it to you now." The lady bade me goodbye.

The badge pinned at the man's chest level read *Manager - Mr Thillay*. "Just follow me."

13

Mr Thillay took me downstairs and showed me the kitchen. "Have you ever worked in a kitchen before?"

I smiled and replied with a confident tone of voice. "No sir, but there's no secret. I washed dishes many times in my house."

Mr Thillay cut me short. "This is nothing like your house. This is a professional kitchen." The muscles on my face paralysed as I tried to keep a smile slapped on, while he continued in a serious tone. "The work here is done at a professional level."

I acquiesced insincerely – "I understand, sir." – not really knowing what difference could make washing the dishes in a house or in a restaurant, except for the amount of plates and pans.

Mr Thillay then took me upstairs again. "I'll take your details to give to the main manager. Thank you."

From there I went back to the university to attend the introductory lecture of *Language, Text and Context*.

After the lecture, at 5 p.m., I returned to my room.

So, I had a job prospect and application forms to deal with – though filling them in made no sense to me. I had no faith in getting a reply to any application. Regardless, making sense or not, I knew those forms needed to be filled, sealed in envelopes, and mailed to prospective employers. A few blank slots needed to be filled with experience. I listed *research on linguistics, working as secretary for a linguistic group, 6 months teaching English for children*. Again, it made no sense; café staff had nothing to gain from that kind of experience. *Working as a stall waiter*? It didn't sound professional. The forms required references too. Would they call abroad? How would they check that?

Filling in those forms was rather draining. I sealed the last envelope, prayed, and jumped into bed.

In the following morning I woke up in a wonderful mood; a mood mirrored by the weather, that had a beautiful sunshine, and not a cloud in the sky. The first lecture wouldn't start until 1 p.m., so I planned to go through Hyde Park first, take photos of the flowerbeds, and after that post the application forms at the post office. Right in the middle of my photography session my mobile phone rang.

The handset screen flashed: *No caller ID.*

14

The night was about to begin when we were formally introduced and then left to ourselves to be more closely acquainted with each other in that 2 metre square room. In one corner was I, 55 kilos or 121 pounds, with a firm stare that said "bring it on, all is under control," and a dripping forehead that said "wish I had a nappy on."

I made the first move to prove my valour, firmly grabbing the bar at my head level, and pulling it down.

Slam, steam, screech, and swoosh.

That officially launched my career as a dishwasher.

The lever I pulled served to slide down and close the steel doors of the industrial dishwasher located at front right corner of the kitchen's dishwashing station of the Georgetown Restaurant. Once the dishwasher was properly shut a twister of boiling water and steam, along with a deafening cacophony, would break loose like hell inside it. The used crockery was brought by the waiters and slid through a steel counter at the left side of the sink. Then, I'd dispose the leftovers into a rubbish bin, stack the plates well onto a plastic rack, press the hose's nozzle over the sink to rinse them off, slide the rack into the dishwasher, pull the lever down, fill another rack whilst the washing cycle finished, slide the first load of plates off the machine, slide the next rack into the dishwasher, and pull the lever down again.

I kept the cleaned utensils back in the cupboard in their places, and went on repeating that process non-stop from 7 to 11 p.m. Then, the large pots and pans had to be manually washed up before I cleaned and sanitised the sink's drain and the dishwasher's filters. The final step was to wipe up the dishwashing area.

In that first week the sink outflow pipe was broke, so all the water went straight from the sink into a large bucket which, once full, had to be lifted, carried, and the dirty water thrown into a drain inside the kitchen. Although my working routine reminded me of one of the nine circles of punishment from *Dante's Inferno*, I felt simply in heaven. I had a job baby!

That work solved at least three of my most urgent concerns. One, it'd provide financial relief, allowing me to afford the accommodation fees, buy books, pay for photocopies and printouts, and eat in the campus. Two, there was a meal at the end of the every shift; so, one less meal to worry about. Three, it'd provide me with a social experience beyond the university sphere. Another perk of being hired, naturally, was that the new social set brought along with it a new universe of English words and accents. That new universe started gaining shape when my mobile phone rang that Tuesday morning and, on the other side, I heard a male voice with a slightly accented South Asian English.

"Good morning, this is Mr Dharmendra from the Georgetown restaurant. Are you happy with the kind of work Mr Tillay showed you yesterday?"

"Yes. I am, sir."

"Are you able to come this morning and bring your passport along?"

"Yes. I am, sir." I tried not to sound too thrilled.

Mr Dharmendra had belled and interviewed me that very Tuesday. He wasn't an English native but despite having a slight accent he spoke fluent and creative English. His approach, as we he sat facing me across a small table for the interview, was very easy going.

When I asked if I'd have to be trained first, Mr Dharmendra said: "Here we do like the mobile phone plans: you learn as you go. Just be ready for tonight." Then he assumed a more formal tone. "You can start working with a provisional National Insurance Number, but you have to go to the Inland Revenue, behind Merrion Centre, to arrange an appointment and get a permanent Insurance Number. Is that clear?"

"Yes, sir."

Mr Dharmendra slipped a piece of paper across the table scribbled with the letters TN followed by my date of birth and the letter M, which stood for my gender. "This is your Temporary National Insurance number. See that you make it here just after six o'clock."

With this, Mr Dharmendra slipped my passport back to me across the table and escorted me to the door.

I almost skipped my way up Briggate.

There was still some free time before the lecture started that morning, so, instead of taking pictures of flowers, I approached people sitting in the benches at Briggate and asked to photograph them. They reacted quite naturally, allowing me to do so with smiles. First, two lads and two ladies who seemed delighted with my request. Then, a fancy mature couple who suggested it'd be amusing if they posed with serious faces and their legs crossed toward each other. White, blond, beautiful, and well dressed people like that I'd never seen just sitting around in the street back home. I also approached the elegant gentleman who stands in front of *Harvey Nichols* and whose work is to smile and open the glass doors for the shoppers; a mounted police officer; and a gentleman smoking in a rather fancy suit. I still approached a lad selling *The Big Issue* newspaper who made no fuss about the snapshot, but didn't seem amused – I was clueless on why he looked so serious.

In those naive approaches my eyes saw England simply as a dreamland and all English people as celebrity-like, sophisticated, ultra-civilised, polite, and above all, wealthy people.

After another *Victorian Literature* lecture, I hang around Edward Boyle Library until nearly 6 p.m., making some effort to read on *The Mill on the Floss*. My mind lacked focus though, and George Elliot had made no effort to go easy on a foreign clientele.

Thanks heaven for *SparkNotes.com*. Until here, I'd thought that internet summaries were a resource for the academically-challenged and intellectually-impaired only; and, frankly, I still felt it was shameful but, needs must. I'd feel that need after botching the first seminar preparation activity for *Victorian Literature* and being the one silent student in a room full of British students. Printed summaries soon became documentary proof of my scholarly incompetence at the School of English.

Yet, that evening, whilst I assumed my function in the kitchen of the Georgetown Restaurant and danced with the dishwasher, the excitement and stamina made me disregard the imminent problems those working hours would bring to my academic commitment.

15

On the half-hour journey back to North Grange Rd. – up Briggate, left at Headrow, then up Albion St., Woodhouse and Headingley Lane – those thoughts on academic commitment had plenty time to surface.

In the first nights, though, I was still quite charmed, observing the partiers in the clubs and pubs lining Woodhouse Lane. Often, I dodged drunken denizens who wobbled along the pavement; twice I was stopped by merry lads who played and joked with me, inviting me to come along to Baja Club. Particularly, on the 2nd night a fancily clad lady addressed me and mentioned something about *business opportunity*; thinking that she might need me to hand flyers out for cash, I followed her at Boar Lane. I found it a little strange; but I wasn't afraid that she might mug me because we were in a crowded street – and indeed she wasn't a mugger; she meant *business* as in *"are you interested in business?"* When I realised what she actually meant I apologised generously, flushed with embarrassment. This was a new use of the word *business* – not one I'd ever forget.

Despite that little incident, everyone who ever approached me was always cheerful and I've never so much as seen a real mugger, or felt threatened, on my way back from work to the accommodation.

Although non-European students were only allowed to work 'half-time,' the workload in the kitchen required way more than 20 hours per week. So, in those first few weeks time was pretty tight. Balancing the demands of my course, the compulsory reading, the seminar preparations, and the assessed assignments, against my need to work and earn money became impossible. Sleep became a luxury I simply couldn't fit into my schedule. I had two options: drop a module or drop dead. I made a huge effort just to remain awake during long centrally heated lectures. More and more often, at the Edward Boyle Library, rather than reading I simply dozed until it was time to set off for work.

In order to finish writing some essays I went from work straight to the 24-hour cluster in the Irene Manton building and burnt the midnight oil.

The most frustrating thing was that it didn't matter how strong I felt, how much effort I put into reading, how much sacrifice I made, my success was laughable. I simply wasn't good by the standards of an English university. At some point, I had to surrender and think of the best way to benefit from that experience without compromising my responsibility as an exchange student at the University of Leeds. I was miles from excelling academically in England, so I reluctantly lowered my academic goals, committing myself only to the compulsory preparations and assignments. I would still manage to pass the *Language, Text and Context* assignments; but would fail in *Victorian Literature*.

If nothing else, crossing the Atlantic Ocean to take a place at an English university should ultimately benefit my English skills. So, to compensate for my academic shortfall, I promised myself to make the best use of time to take full advantage of the English language.

This decision would again strengthen the influence English had on my life, generating amazing events right around me and bringing me closer to the *principle*.

16

Things got to a smoother rhythm after a month working as a dishwasher. The sink outflow pipe had been repaired, a new fellow had been hired to assist me with the dishes in the busiest days, and I'd been assigned to other tasks around the kitchen helping in the pre-preparation of food and making desserts. The hardest tasks were also given to my care. On Fridays, all tiles in the kitchen had to be sprayed with D-10 sanitiser and wiped out, the walk-in refrigerator had to be cleaned and restocked, and the grease and grime accumulated in the trolleys, cupboards, and stove had to be scraped.

The hardest of the hard tasks, though, was a one-off: the dried grease accumulated in the grease duct system had to be scraped; for that, I had to climb and stand on the stove – whilst one of the burners remained on!

During the hardest tasks, other staff members in the kitchen would often come and say how hard a worker I was and that I should take pride in my skills. Perhaps they noticed a hint of dissatisfaction all over my face, or they just knew those were the least flattering tasks within the kitchen routine. Frankly, I'd retire doing that happily. It'd still be England – top of the world –, and they'd still pay better than many English teachers earn at my home State. Still, even if my visa allowed me that, I hadn't come to England to settle down. I thought of the hard work in the kitchen, and all the burdens of that whole experience as part of some spiritual process that had, ultimately, English as a catalytic element.

Either for spiritual or earthly bound reasons moving around through the kitchen stations helped me to be acquainted with some English varieties. Standing alone in the dishwashing station only gave me a chance to hear English in quite limited occasions:

-When the waiters came down bringing dirty crockery and greeted me, over the screeching noise of the industrial dishwasher – "Evening Johnny lad. Looking good tonight! Take care of these ones, will you?"

-When the chef shouted the name of the dishes – "Table five. Chicken Tikka Masala, ready!"

"Nasi Goreng, to table seven!"

-When the shift manager came down to praise the kitchen team's work – "Fantastic!"

"Magic…! Smashing service tonight!"

Apart from that meagre English what filled my ears, seven to eleven, was the dishwasher pandemonium, the kitchen appliances being banged around, the food in the saucepan sizzling, and the microwave oven humming.

Georgetown Restaurant staff would communicate and shout instructions among themselves using Hindi. Some of them would also speak with a specific regional dialect original from the Indian State they came from. I learned that information with the apprentice chef Rajaram, who – perhaps because we were both students at the same age level – became closer to me.

Rajaram explained me where they all had come from and clarified their positions within the restaurant hierarchy: Mr Dharmendra (senior manager) came from India, Mr Thillay (general manager) from Malaysia, Sukumar (executive chef) from Thailand, Ajesh (supervisor), Aju, and Kannan (waiters), came from different States of India. Rajaram himself also came from India. Aside from chef Sukumar, who'd learned English as a kid from the tourists in the streets of Bangkok before he moved to Singapore, all of them had formal secondary education in English, since English is an associate official language in India and the medium of instruction for Maths and Sciences in public schools in Malaysia.

Thus, when I fulfilled functions in other stations or waited on tables a few nights, I listened to instructions in South Asian English or Malaysian English. I soon grew accustomed to their accents and could perceive some minor grammatical differences.

Maybe because those dialectical varieties of English had come from a distant world, a world which I haven't experienced myself, they only had an effect on my recognition skills without affecting my own English. Yet, the world within the kitchen, a world to which I'd been directly connected to, bestowed me with a variety of vocabulary that was fast assimilated to my English.

And, following the long English learning tradition, there was plenty hard work involved on this process of assimilation.

17

While operating the dishwasher, by the sink without a chance to use English, as the tableware multiplied and gained diverse shapes, I focused on how each shape was identified with a specific word. I began washing superordinates – cutleries, bowls, plates, pans, utensils; then, moved on to stack and organise hyponyms – knives, fish knives, fruit knives, forks, cake forks, toasting forks, spoons, tablespoons, teaspoons, mixing bowls, pasta bowls, rice bowls, salad bowls, soup bowls, appetizer plates, butter plates, salad plates, entrée plates, dessert plates, saucers, sauce boats, sauté pans, saucepans, broiler pan, chestnut pan, frying pan, stir-fry pan, grill pan, square griddle pan, wok, ladles, tongs, spatulas, whisks, scoops. A few items that ended up in the sink belonged to categories I failed to identify.

Whenever chef Sukumar summoned me to a new assignment, he introduced me further to little universes within the kitchen's cosmos. Once a space within the kitchen was used to a specific function or to the preparation of a type of food, and observed specific regulations, it had likewise a specific designation – sauté station, fry station, grill station, broiler station, salad/ meat station, window station, and dessert station.

Each station was like a planet with all the necessary material floating around it like satellites and a variety of terms to name each material. At the salad slash meat station, vegetables and meat were prepared for stock or immediate consumption. It was placed next to the walk-in freezer and had two counters to separate veggies and meat preparation areas. To prevent cross-contamination from one type of food to another they used colour-coded chopping boards: red for raw meat, blue for raw fish, green for salad and fruit, brown for vegetable, and white for bread and dairy.

Veggies cutting and chopping was assigned to me. Bean sprout, beetroot, carrot, cauliflower, cucumber, garlic, lady's finger, leek, lettuce, onion, purple cabbage, sweet corn, sweet chilly. Loads. Cleanse, peel, chop, slice, crosscut; then, pickle, or keep them in a vacuum sealed bag. Chef also enlisted me to the dessert station where there was a cooler filled with ice-cream, double cream, evaporated milk, squirty cream, syrup, sauce, bananas, pineapple, cherry, and large ice blocks. There I prepared *pisang emas* – boat dish, half lengthwise cut banana, pistachio and coconut ice cream scoops, chocolate sauce, almonds, coconut flakes, mint, two cherries; *nanas JB* – square dish, four pineapple halves, dark rum, maple syrup, vanilla ice cream scoop; and *fruit tartled* – boat dish, crumbled ice, hot blackcurrant tartlet, double cream, strawberry sauce. I still went around other stations, gutting prawns, stirring pots, scrapping the grill, cleaning the sauté area, sweeping, and mopping a few stations.

The nightshifts in the kitchen were hard at times. But, it gratified me in financial terms and English-wise. Each drop of sweat amounted to a word or verb to my English; and unlike money, that is spent, each item of the kitchen's English would be forever saved in my language bank. The kitchen made me rich, but just. Outside its routine, a lavish world of English beckoned, offering me chances to hit the jackpot. And like Faust, I'd not think twice to pawn my soul for each chance.

18

Almost faithfully, my routine through the Semester 1 of my exchange programme in Leeds can be summarised like so: start early at the University of Leeds, attend lectures at Roger Stevens building, attend seminars at the School of English, read at Edward Boyle Library, do the seminar preparations and draft the essays at the Irene Manton Cluster, borrow books from the Parkinson Building Library, rush to Lower Briggate most evenings and drudge through the shifts at Georgetown Restaurant, and do a late night schlep amid the merry partygoers back to North Grange Road.

This routine stayed the same as the scenery around me transformed. The leaves on the trees gradually went from green to light yellow, blazing orange, or burnt red. Autumn slowly gave place to winter. The leaves kept changing colour shades to a homogeneous sheer brown and started falling to the ground. Stripped maples, beeches, and birches mourned their fallen leaves which were raked in heaps and removed by the collectors. The green of the trees, the blue of the sky, and the light of the day were carried away. Shortened daylight hours were a minor seasonal nuisance matched only by the greyness of the clouds that condensed the atmosphere, and the wetness of the weather that dampened my spirit. At least, all lectures and seminars from Semester 1 reached the end. Relief, thy name is vacation – Not!

December arrived. All housemates went to their home country across the ocean; some travelled to enjoy a holiday in some European resort. As for me, it was an opportune time to earn extra and learn extra English: the Christmas festivities at Georgetown Restaurant attracted many guests, so, there were plenty working hours available and diverse functions to be filled there.

In the days leading to Christmas, I washed dishes with my dishwasher mate from 11 a.m. to 11 p.m., with breaks, naturally. On Christmas Eve, as I closed down the sink area, Mr Dharmendra approached me.

"Er… would you feel comfortable about waiting at tables tomorrow and on Boxing Day?"

"I'm… Do I have time to be trained?" I asked.

"You know our motto: learn as you go." Mr Dharmendra bobbled his head. "It'll be quiet, don't worry. Just make sure you're here before ten, right?"

"Yes, sir." I said, shaking in my boxers.

That night, I returned to the accommodation with nose, cheeks, and ears entirely numb. The temperature should've dropped below zero. Brrr humbug!

The accommodation was deserted. Each footstep echoed in the house. I crashed in bed listening to the radio Javier had left with me. *BBC Radio 4* was airing the Midnight Mass from St Chad's Cathedral in Birmingham. I changed the dial. *Classic FM* was playing *Sugar Plum Fairy* from *The Nutcracker*. Again, I changed. *Radio Aire* was playing *Do They Know It's Christmas* by Band Aid – this song had been playing non-stop all over Leeds, including at the restaurant; this was followed by Slade's *Merry Christmas Everybody* and Mariah Carey's *All I Want for Christmas is You*.

As I nearly dozed off, *Happy Xmas* (*war is over*) by John Lennon and Yoko Ono started. It was my mom's Christmas favourite, even if she only knew a version to Portuguese of that song – a version that she insisted on playing again and again every Christmas season after the year I came out at home.

That reminded me: I should call her in the morning.

The calming tune of *Happy Xmas* put me into a deep slumber, until alarm ringtone of the phone went off.

I lingered on bed listening to the radio presenters' chat; I couldn't fully understand their English. As they became more intelligible to me, I could discern terms like Father Christmas, Rudolph, chimney, presents, London Weather Centre, white Christmas, sledge, snowman, snow balls, snow fight, snow… I jumped from bed, heart racing, and withdrew the curtains with a jerk. I goggled through the windowpane at the most beautiful image I'd ever caught sight of.

19

A thick layer of white snow coated the entire backyard view, reflecting the mild royal blue light that glowed upon its milky surface. The room was filled with all the splendour of a winter dawn. Amid that blue glow, bright white snowflakes descended circling, swaying, like millions min-comets hitting the ground.

Watching the snow fall, I got dressed: white collared shirt with a black jumper over it and *George* black trousers. A little afraid to slip and fall in the snow, I walked to the city centre equipped with the mobile phone camera, taking pictures of the streets, my footprints in the snow, and myself. I'd left early to buy an international phone card and call home but all shops were closed. With half-hour to get to work I popped in at Clarendon Rd. to Laura's accommodation.

Laura's housemates had gone home too but she hadn't been by any means alone. Laura's sister, Claudia, came with her husband and daughter from the Netherlands to make her company until Boxing Day.

When I rang the doorbell, it was Claudia who answered the door. "Merry Christmas Mr. We waited for you last night. What happened?"

"The manager asked me to work as a waiter this morning, so I had to go home to get the right clothes."

"Oh, working as a waiter. You fancy pants!" Claudia continued with that kindness during the time I waited there, chatting with her, her husband, and Laura, over tea and toasts. As I left she minded me. "Don't you dare not to come over tonight. I got a surprise. If you need to go home, call us, and we'll pick you up."

"Alright, I will. Thanks." I said, glad that I would not have to be all alone on Christmas night.

When I arrived at the Georgetown Restaurant, wearing a black jumper over a white collared shirt, well shaven, and neatly groomed, the managers and waiters kept saying, "You look very smart!"

I was glad that I'd have a chance to strut around the tables showing my elegance that Christmas morning. But first, as part of that new function, I had to hoover the floor, tidy the toilets up, and learn to set the table.

All ran smoothly. The guests arrived around 11 a.m. and they were truthfully kind. Mr Thillay taught me to address the guests, smile, offer them wine, and ask them if they were enjoying Christmas. The pianist they hired performed at dinners only. So, that morning, they had Christmas hits and a few carols playing in loop. *White Christmas* by Bing Crosby and *Let it Snow* by Vaughn Monroe were the classics. Among the popular ones was *Simply Having a Wonderful Christmas Time* by Paul McCartney. *Last Christmas* by Wham had an effect on Kannan who waited at tables singing along with a whispery voice. *Christmas Wrapping* by The Waitresses had an effect on me since it made me lose focus trying to understand its words. Then, the carols: *We Wish you a Merry Christmas*, *Deck the Halls*, *Jingle Bells*, and others I knew in Portuguese versions.

At some point *Rudolph, the Red-Nosed Reindeer* started playing. And all guests joined in a merry unison. It amazed me how naturally they started singing along as if they didn't have a care in the world. I thought such scene happened only in American feel-good flicks. Yet, it happened live, in 3D, and I was in the middle of it.

At night, the 3D cinema session showed a different genre: a dishwashing drama starring a smart-dressed former waiter as the main protagonist. More of a buddy flick actually; action revolving around two dishwashers – I as the good-looker. The soundtrack was rather incidental as well, as the Christmas songs and carols came from upstairs and could only be heard between the dishwashing cycles. Still a Christmas themed film.

At the end of the shift we had our meal and wished each other merry Christmas. We even pulled a few Christmas crackers apart, put the hats and crowns on, exchanged the toys, and read to each other the riddles that came on small strips inside the crackers.

"*What do you call a blind dinosaur?*" I started, but no one tried a guess. "*Do-you-think-he-saw-us!*"

Rajaram jumped in. "*Why jelly babys go to school?*"

Kannan then replied, "Not to be thick like you."

Rajaram shot back. "*To become smarties* you idiot!"

"*Who can't you trust in an orchestra?*" Aju read his.

"Your mother, that flatulist!" Kannan teased him, prompting a general laughter.

"Bugger off Kannan. I won't tell the answer now." Aju responded. But since we all protested, wanting to hear the answer, Aju read the solution. "*The fiddler!*"

"*Why can't you play joke on snakes?*" I tried another one. "*Because you can't pull their legs!*"

After each answer, we looked at each other a bit puzzled as we didn't quite get the play on words. I kept all the paper strips to look the meaning of some words up later. Finally, I closed the sink, the kitchen's lights were turned off, each of us grabbed two heavy plastic bags full of rubbish, and we left the building to dispose them in a backstreet just a few metres further down Lower Briggate, right in front of Queen's Court.

Out of nowhere Kannan approached me from behind and whispered with a malicious tone, "I know what you thinking... You got quite a heavy load there, I see."

Kannan surely caught me gaping at a fit blond lad on a tight t-shirt who was smoking in front of Queen's Court. Because the restaurant staffs were Hindus and Muslims, and I didn't know if being openly gay clashed with their religious code of morals, I'd kept discretion on that issue to shun any trouble. Until that moment.

"C'mon," Kannan insisted. "Am I right or not?"

20

Georgetown Restaurant branch in Leeds was the first business set up in the Dyson's Clock Building after the *John Dyson & Son Ltd. Jewellery and Watchmakers* closed in 1990. The facade of Dyson's Clock Building displays two beautifully designed large clocks. The one on the left is a two-sided clock, framed on iron work spandrels topped with the letters *D* and *S* on both sides and engraved with the motto *Tempus Fugit* under them. It still has *1965* designed in gold lettering on its side and a sculpture of a surmounting, scythe holding, Father Time. The other clock sits on the main entrance, within a grand pedimented architectural case that shows the name *John Dyson* and the house numbers *25* and *26* imprinted on its face. Under the clock's frame the inscription *founded 1865* marks the company's foundation date, although John Dyson set up business in these premises only in 1872. The most historically significant feature of the facade rests above this clock: a time-marking gilded mechanism, consisting of a metal ball that dropped daily punctually at 1 p.m, known as *time ball* – hence, these premises display, sculptured in bold letters right underneath the cresting of the facade, their status of *Time Ball Buildings*.

These time ball buildings remount a time when cities and towns in England were administered on a local mean time. And Leeds Time was 6 min 10 sec behind Greenwich Time. By the middle of the 19th century local mean time became a major inconvenience because country-wide services of transportation and communication, which had become then considerably developed, had to operate on multiple time zones. These country-wide services resorted to the Greenwich Observatory to send them daily telegraph signals and keep them synchronised with London Time.

Because Dyson's Clock Building had a time ball synchronised with the Greenwich Mean Time it became a well-known assembly location where people gathered every day to set their watches to the time ball at 1 p.m.

Whereas in the days of John Dyson and Son Ltd. the Dyson's Clock Building attracted Leodensians concerned with adjusting their wrist or pocket watches, in the days of the Georgetown Restaurant the gathering epicentre of Lower Briggate had shifted to the courtyard of Queens Court which had become by the end of the 20th century the heart of Leeds gay scene.

And right there, night after night, I found myself, walking from the Dyson's Clock Building, carrying a heavy bag of rubbish to the skip in the backstreet that faced the entrance of Queen's Court. And each night when I crossed that backstreet, the hurly-burly of the Queens Court always made me wonder: why in the world from all jobs available in Leeds the one offered to me had to be right next to a gay village where I could see a million gorgeous merry lads having a good time while I myself only had a hard one.

On a daily basis, I disposed the rubbish in the skip at the gates of heaven where hundreds of angels sought for company, and went on to enjoy a lonely half-hour walk back to the accommodation at North Grange Rd. Then, I'd sleep without the angles, or even a roommate to whom I could talk. It wasn't all doom and gloom though; a few good nights, I was kept up by an Irish born gentleman named David Crystal.

David Crystal is a legendary linguist and academic, author of famous books like *Rediscover Grammar* and *The Cambridge Encyclopedia of the English Language* – both of which were essential reading material to most seminar preparations of *Language, Text and Context*.

So, from September to December, I'd only enjoyed the nocturnal company of David Crystal and myself.

By the middle of December though, I'd earned enough to afford a portable DVD player which proved to be a powerful aid for the lonely nights. On my away back from work, nearly midnight, I'd often stop at the 24/7 DVD store in Woodhouse Lane and check out a film from one of the self-service touch screen kiosks: insert membership card; press 4-digit code on screen; browse back-catalogue by genre – *erotic*, *gay*; touch picture on screen to select movie; press *select* button; press *exit* to complete the session; check out rented items in the dispenser; remove membership card.

There were exactly 3 options of gay erotic films to rent, none of them explicit or with a decent storyline. It felt like I was going through puberty again, discovering the secrets of gay eroticism in the ultra censored Quantum Leap films from 1999.

Indeed, a life as an out and proud gay person amid a mainstream conservative society awarded me with miles on the solitude airlines. I seldom enjoyed gay clubs and often fell for straight acting lads. The rare gay partners who I had a relationship with were more like mates with disappointing views about commitment, and the few straight partners who I often met were more like primates with a vague notion of commitment. Solitude was my faithful companionship, matched only by endless hours obsessing over English. Another minor hassle of being out and proud, more frustrating by far, was going through events which required careful wording regarding my sexual identity.

After coming out at the age of 14, I'd faced mother, father, brother, mates, classmates, and even strangers. In time, I grew tired of defying others, of discussing my view on the subject, of my in-your-face attitude. I myself got used to it. Keeping a low profile became vital to avoid embarrassing the straight lads who enjoyed my company.

And I'd made use of the same low profile vigilance to avoid potential problems at Georgetown Restaurant. Much like in any typical straight-oriented workplace, the staff had found ways of slipping prying questions into conversations during the end of the shift meals. They often asked the classic "do you have a girl?" They also insisted on teasing remarks as to sexual matters. Aware of the cultural gap between mine and the staffs' I kept out of harm's way by keeping discretion. I was especially cautious with Kannan, who had this itch on teasing me about that. And that Christmas night, as we passed in front of Queen's Court, Kannan again found his way around the gay issue.

"I bet ten quid I'm on to what you up to with your heavy load." Kannan displayed a nasty expression.

He'd crossed the line a bit this time, so I confronted him. "I bet ten quid I'm on to what *you* up to with my heavy load. You want it."

Kannan replaced his nasty expression with a smirk. "I'm talking 'bout your heavy load of *rubbish*. I want nil with it. But *you* want to get rid of it. Giv's a tenner."

I couldn't believe it; Kannan played me along and I'd failed to see it coming. Defeated, I tried to call it even by saying something witty – "I'll give you…" – But it came out rude, "…Fuck all."

I dropped the bag of rubbish in the skip and trod off. Kannan stayed behind, laughing harder and louder.

Upset, I tried to lighten up as I headed to Clarendon Rd. recalling that Claudia had mentioned a surprise.

21

"…So fancy pants, this is what I had to tell you." – When I got to Clarendon Rd., Claudia was ready to join her husband and daughter who'd already gone to bed.

Laura had had guests that Christmas, but they've been gone too. She and Claudia stayed in the kitchen tidying up and waiting for me, as they wanted to announce the surprise Claudia mentioned earlier on. – "Would you consider coming with Laura to spend New Year's Eve with us in the Netherlands?"

Claudia's invitation made me equally thrilled and disappointed. "Oh! Thanks for considering it, but the restaurant schedule this week won't allow me to."

"I knew fancy pants wouldn't go." Laura interfered a little impatient. "Can't you just talk to the manager?"

Claudia was more composed. "Ok, listen, tomorrow you're working aren't you?" – I nodded confirming. – "What if I come and talk to the manager personally?"

Still hesitant, I agreed, "Alright. If they excuse me from work this week, I'm willing to go, off course."

"All settled then." Claudia winked at Laura.

Laura and Claudia didn't wait much longer after that, leaving me alone in the kitchen's sofa bed to catch up on some sleep. I needed to be up and about early on Boxing Day; the city centre shops would be open, and I should buy an international call card to phone home.

As the Boxing Day came, all flowed according to Claudia's plan. She came to the Georgetown Restaurant with her husband, daughter, and Laura as guests; then, at the end of all courses, Claudia approached Mr Dharmendra and Chef Sukumar and asked if they could release me from work in that last week of the year.

They made no fuss about that.

By the end of that Boxing Day shift, Claudia already had booked an extra ferry ticket to Amsterdam for me, and was ready waiting to drive me to North Grange Rd. to pick up some clothes.

When I finally managed to phone home, my mother was pleased to hear such great news; she wished me a late happy Christmas and a safe trip to the Netherlands.

22

FREDDIE

What a wonderful first world. The bird's-eye view from the airplane window offered an awe-inspiring impression of the ground below, where neat square red rooftops orderly arranged in symmetrical blocks demarked residential areas. At the arrival, the airport was a world, encompassing a massive duty-free shopping area, terminal after terminal, kilometres apart, all housing countless gates; floor upon floor of restaurants, pizzerias, cafés, pubs, convenience stores, bakeries, stands filled up with brightly wrapped intriguing sweets and chocolates, vintners, newsagents, game stations, a shopping paradise. Then, the coach station: science fiction made fact; it had talking touch screen information kiosks, cosy cafés served by smiley baristas, a multitude of stands and shops jostling for attention in this scaled down version of the massive airport. On the way, the roads ran smoothly beneath the coach's wheels as it passed by stylishly designed milestones, endless tunnels, enormous bridges and flyovers that seemed to reach the sky. The carefully laid out towns were filled with beautifully designed two and three storey dwellings, each group of which shared one colour and individually displayed its shades, separated one from the next by clipped green hedges and close cropped lawns. The office buildings preserved their old-fashioned facades combining history and fashion in precise measures. The enthralling sight of those wonders of the first world heightened the satisfaction Freddie felt at having left behind the capital of his home State where everything always had felt to him so hideously shoddy.

Back there, the bird's-eye view from the airplane window shed tears over an uh-oh-inspiring view of the ground below, where a haphazard mix of cardboard, aluminium, tiling and other materials hardly distinguished mangrove and slum-like areas. The airport was a bungalow, sheltering (not enclosing) a small number of stands selling snacks and local handicrafts, a newsagent, one gate, one terminal, one storey above the ground – themed if you like. Then, the coach station: an ongoing retrograde nightmare, with touchy-feely beggars pleading for spear change, smutted stands, small facilities, smelly toilets, smoggy atmosphere, slummy surroundings – much like the local airport, a lot larger though. The roads weren't very modern, no tunnels, no flyovers, just short bridges, and rusty milestones; yet, unlike the other States of the country, most roads of his home State were smooth and spacious. The towns were filled with simply designed dwellings, mostly refurbished to all shapes and dimensions, generally hidden from sight by surrounding walls painted in carnivalesque colours. The office buildings' historic architecture was blighted by modern facades which combined tackiness and tawdriness in disproportional amounts.

"Ha-ha, you get me?" Whenever Freddie made comparisons between the capital of his home State and New York City, a wave of sarcasm would reverberate through the walls. His diatribe would vary between acerbic and sarcastic as he embellished the shortcomings of his hometown and highlighted his observations with belly laughs so contagious that everyone in earshot choked along. Now, living in the first world, immersed in American civilisation, Freddie felt especially delighted in bitching about his former compatriots too. "Picture this: you walk down the streets of New York City and the passing crowds are full of beautiful people. The enthusiastic atmosphere endows them with lively eyes, sparkly look, friendly expression, and pretty faces." His tone changed from excitement to mockery. "Now, walk down the streets of my hometown, and the wandering crowds are full of people who cannot look beautiful because the high temperature leaves them with bleary eyes, weary look, dreary expression, and sweaty faces."

Amid the laughter of Freddie's housemates, one of them spoke. "Such a shady queen you are. Careful hunny, all of us here come from the same country. You might end up pissing someone off."

"Hell to the no!" Another housemate intervened – one who specially appreciated the way Freddie used his words. "First of all, you need to learn to tell shit from Shinola. Second, I come from Rio, sweetie. That's Southeast, not Northeast – a thousand miles south at least. And I came to shine. If the bitch like reading the hell out of her folks from the North, let she yell Fidel."

The other housemates started yelling "damn right," "fierce," "amen," prompting the former housemate to complete his criticism. "Chinese, Japanese, dirty knees... We're all the same, darling. But, that's not my business. Go on, I like a comedy queen."

Encouraged by a general heckle from the other housemates, Freddie continued. "Dear, clearly you underestimate my point. It's not so much the place itself – it's the people who make the place. People here in New York have a mind sharp like the edges of a diamond, whereas in my hometown people have a mind shaped like a half-pint carton of milk: square. Square like everything there."

Under a wave of cheer, the housemate argued again. "I'm sorry, hunny, but a place like the North is backward because the government is crooked, not because the people are square."

"Well, let me say just this – the people live under a democratic regime. So, the government do represent their voice." Freddie asserted.

Another housemate interrupted, speaking louder. "Girls, girls… Hollywood is desperate for the script of *The Bitches Go to Washington*, but here, you get all political, and we're dozing off. Snap out it." The housemate mimed a bitch slap followed by a pimp slap, vocally faking the sharp sound effect. "P'shh, p'shh!"

Again, Freddie spoke. "Sincerely… no matter whose fault it is, I couldn't live forever in a place where the nearest thing to a pub is something like a dull bodega serving greasy appetisers, beer in bottles, and cheap imitation spirits. I'd prefer being buried alive than to continue in a city where the only gay clubs are no more than naff mousetraps crawling with kitschy dressed snobs and obnoxious bartenders."

After all housemates started laughing again, one of Freddie's fondest mates said. "Ciccone darling, a drop of your saliva in the water supply of this city, and the entire population of New York is doomed."

Freddie enjoyed when the housemates joined in the basement to throw shade. Actually, Freddie enjoyed everything about that place because he was where his heart belonged to: New York City – the world's fourth most densely inhabited city; the place which dictated trends of culture, art, fashion, and entertainment to the rest of the world. Though there were yet steps to climb – Freddie shared a shabby brick apartment building with other compatriots in Astoria, Queens – he already felt on the top of the world, a place he was well worthy of because he never stinted in his efforts to reach for the things he desired.

And Freddie knew full well how to get there; he'd learned the secret art of turning his will into reality. Freddie just needed some time and the right tools.

23

One of Freddie's strongest yearns, for instance, had been to escape from the outskirts of his hometown.

Certain things in this world were just wrong and he certainly didn't belong to that forsaken corner of the world. Happening to be born in a community with such conventional ideas must've been an accident; actually, a disaster, a catastrophe, a Greek tragedy. Some days Freddie really felt like gouging out his eyes with so much aversion to local values; he'd rather permanent blindness than visualising himself sharing in the ignorance of the local folks.

In his younger days Freddie struggled to understand why the other children seemed to have no imagination like he did. They'd pick on Freddie for his ideas and for other futile reasons: the bright colourful clothing he liked to wear, the overly polite tone of his voice and girlie choice of words, the theatrical games he proposed to play with the other boys, his enthusiasm over the Independence Day parade. There seemed to be little about him the other children wouldn't try to ridicule.

In time, Freddie's alienation for the locals evolved into hatred, then into loathe, then constant nausea. As Freddie reached puberty his tolerance reached its limit and he started suffering from something like a morning sickness that lasted from morning to the early hours until sleep released him from the day. Deep in his guts Freddie knew the cure for his malady was to run away and place roots in a more fertile land.

By growing up among traditional folks but having an eccentric personality, Freddie ended up cultivating the willpower and knowledge to manipulate destiny. And well into the genesis of his apprenticeship in matters of controlling destiny Freddie envisioned the most certain escape route: emigration to America.

The original revelation happened when Freddie, still aged 10, was caught in the heart of a cattle stampede.

The outlaying district where Freddie lived was made up of a few blocks of newly built houses surrounded by wild pastures, private owned ranches, and cut through a main road. A routine could be observed in the district: each morning a herd of cattle was driven from a nearby ranch to a fenced off grazing land then returned to the security of the ranch in the early evening. Driving the cattle demanded great skill and caution because the course the cattle were driven through crossed the main road and skirted along the town.

The person in charge of the cattle was a muscular man on horseback who through strength of will as well as arm seemed to have a strong command over the will of those beasts and herded them flawlessly along the course he chose. Strictly speaking, the man was a *vaquero* – the Spanish word which originated *cowboy* – but Freddie associated the man's features with the cowboy image that he knew from American westerns.

Indeed the cowboy could have slipped out of those celluloid fantasies as he dressed for the part in high heeled boots with pointed steel toes and spurs, tight thick jeans hugging his legs and leaving a sweet bulging contour, a worn out leather jacket over a thin white full-length opening shirt, which being half buttoned exposed most of his swarthy chest, a red bandanna around his neck, and a wide-brimmed fedora casting a shade over his bright brown eyes.

Freddie was mesmerised not only by the cowboy's appearance but also by how he could, with just the help of one assistant on foot, so completely dominate around three dozen cows and oxen, keeping them calm and orderly together throughout their course.

One odd afternoon, when being driven back to the ranch, the cattle were startled by the noisy engine of a passing vehicle. The cattle dashed back to the pasture in the wrong direction and turned down a street where Freddie was playing with a bunch of other kids. Instead of running wild, like the other kids did, Freddie stepped onto the pavement, pressed his back against the wall and remained quiet, eyes riveted to how the cowboy dealt with the stampede.

The cowboy's expression remained calm as he firmly spurred the horse and galloped after the ox leading the stampede. Freddie's heart raced along with the hoofs of the cowboy's horse. All in a flash, Freddie saw the cowboy grab the ox's tail, roll it around his arms, make the ox lose its balance and tumble down on the asphalt. Then the cowboy started a piercing cattle call that calmed the herd, assembled them back, and led them through the usual route like a western Pied Piper.

The incident deeply impressed the young Freddie who, from then on, ardently remembered the intense feeling he experienced when he watched the cowboy's control over the stampede. That incident made Freddie recognise a mechanism the cowboy employed to exert control over the events: controlling the cattle, or the right one amongst them, equals to controlling the whole situation. His passion rested on the power the cowboy seemed to possess without being fully aware of it.

Afterwards, Freddie became ever more conscious of how most people were very much similar to those cows and oxen, always in need of someone to give them direction and make them feel safe. As Freddie grew older he learnt how to deal with people around him in a similar fashion, making sure none of them would run wild, and if they did, ruthlessly dragging them down.

Freddie also promised himself to find a genuine cowboy who could make him feel that same thrill every day. So, Freddie grew hooked on the idea that a genuine cowboy would be waiting for him in America.

24

"Make it to America, and you're a hero by your own merit. Make it to America and you become an X-man, a Superman, you become a self-made man. In America you can become a superstar. If you can make it there, you can make it anywhere." Freddie loved reciting that during meetings with friends through his adolescence.

The trouble for Freddie was to make it to there to begin with. If he wanted to go, then he needed to grow. In a flat square world Columbus visualised a globe before embarking in his adventure across the Atlantic. Thus, changing to America meant for Freddie changing his views of the world and himself in the first place. That entailed exerting control over events to make them happen. His chief act of control was to change his dull Christian name to one with a more international vibe. So, he unofficially named himself after the lead vocalist from the 70's rock band *Queen*: Freddie Mercury.

Mercury was how everyone came to know him. Studying was off the agenda. It'd take too long to graduate and longer still to earn enough money to live up to his aspirations. All in all, he couldn't wait for time to steal his beauty and youth and reach America as a decrepit Methuselah. Once Mercury turned 17 he started his own business cutting hair and soon became the most successful hairstylist in the district. Then, Mercury became locally famous for his flamboyant, overly self-confident, charismatic, light, and agile style; but most of all, for his venomous tongue. Mercury's metamorphosis was complete when he bleached his hair and began performing as a cross-dresser.

Mercury's athletic body type, white skin, sharp facial features and short bleached hair served him well as he morphed from Mercury during daytime into his second alter ego, characterised as Madonna, at night.

On the gay scene, Mercury performed in the few clubs and bars of the city taking advantage of Madonna's newest look for the *Girlie Show Tour*. His performance routine consisted in lip-synching *Erotica* and *Fever* wearing a dominatrix costume, complete with a velour catsuit, latex thigh-length boots, a latex mask, and a braided leather whip he simply loved to crack. He felt great delight in scandalising the audience as he introduced to the stage two muscular submissive males and, with them, boldly enacted a ritual of bondage and discipline to the best of his knowledge and passion.

The audience always reacted deliriously to that part of Mercury's performance, sensing the amount of effort and affection he poured into his modest show. They could feel Mercury's love, especially at the end of each presentation, when he addressed the audience with the same words: "Love is sacred my dearests. Allow love penetrate deep into thy hearts and feel its power shifting the mountains that cast shadows over your realm." After that, followed by the two submissives, Mercury would throw rubbers to the audience dancing and lip-synching to *Bye Bye Baby*.

The presentation itself didn't merit the investment. Yet impersonating Madonna on stage gave Mercury great satisfaction; the applause and adulation were satisfying in themselves but for Freddie the real accomplishment was what he added to the humdrum little lives of his fans.

Mercury's real economic pillar was his hair salon. Besides basic hair cutting, Mercury also offered services such as brushing, blow-drying, straightening, relaxing, lengthening, curling, weaving, colouring, perming, and general cosmetic treatment for damaged hair. He was skilled in straight razor shaving too and was licensed to trim and shave beard – a service offered only to a limited male clientele as he intentionally used imported creams and lotions to increase the price of the service and restrict it to a few wealthy customers.

The salon was busy from opening time to the moment customers were informed the appointments were all booked up. Although two other hairstylists also worked there, the customers really came because of Mercury. The ambiance in the salon was established by the eloquent narratives Mercury shared with customers. He just loved retelling the incredible life stories from American talk shows he watched on satellite like Oprah or Geraldo. The excellent service, usually heard of by word of mouth, would bring customers; but, what really kept customers coming was Mercury's ability to add a little taste of thrill to their dull lives. Satellite tv was a dear commodity and nobody ever heard of those stories in the open channels. Customers were quickly hooked on the tales of amazing events staged in the distant land of America. Mercury made sure the customers, mostly women, had a spacious waiting area with good acoustics, so they could hang around the whole afternoon and evening inebriated by hair chemicals' vapours while marvelling at his eloquence.

Mercury felt exhilarated whenever he found a chance to include one of his personal accounts among the repertoire of stories from those American talk shows. He liked to give the impression that the life of those Americans living in America wasn't much different from his own, as if he truly belonged there. One impressive story he saw in Geraldo concerned a series of grisly murders around America involving a network of Satanists. When talking to customers in the salon, Mercury subtly linked that story to the time two thieves broke into his studio flat.

"…Ah, it was late one night, and woke up with them threatening me, demanding the hard cash in the safe. I was still groggy from sleep but I made a dash through an open window. One of them had a knife, and all I felt was a slash in the back, and then again in the thigh before I managed to jump." Mercury sighed momentarily whilst delighting in the female customers' horrified "ohs" and "ahs" before carrying on. "I recall that night vividly. It was a full moon night and, as I only sleep in the nude, I remember that under the moonlight the red colour of my gushing blood contrasted brightly against my pale skin." Another ovation of "ohs" and "ahs" delighted Mercury.

After watching Oprah hosting guests considered to be workaholics, Mercury couldn't wait to share with his costumers more of his accounts. "Yes, so they're called *workaholics*, it's a new thing now. Not as much as a new thing, but a new word. We don't even have a translation for it; it's *workaholic*, same as in English, like we say *topless*, *sexy*, *strip tease*, *fashion*, *Vogue*…" Mercury said the last word making a dramatic pose with both hands miming the frame-like gesture that Madonna made worldly famous in her *Vogue* video. After that, Mercury gave his costumers a moment to breathe and absorb his knowledge of English as he mentioned that so casually and confidently; then he continued. "I just *love* to work. Come shine come rain, on workdays and on holidays, I just love this. Just last year, on the New Year's Eve, I had to rush through the last appointment at nearly midnight; I put the final touches on a perm just in time to pop open a bottle of Moët Chandon right there and then at the salon with the assistants and our friends."

These accounts were roughly 15-rated and therefore, under Mercury's censure restriction code, appropriate for the salon's clientele. The X-rated accounts were shared exclusively with Mercury's companions whilst drinking beers or sipping spirits in the after-hours.

25

By the day, at his salon, the conversation topics that Mercury offered were often a little risqué, but even he knew to draw a line in front of his clients; his accounts were enough to titillate and amuse but rarely to offend. By night however, at the local bar, such self-censure quickly waned and adult themes held sway soon as Mercury met with the gang – as he called his mates.

As a rule, Mercury controlled the gang's chatter. Topics ranged far and wide but sex was often the key element. "…So, what's the maximum number of times that you managed in the shortest period of time?" Or, "What is the weirdest place that you did it?" Or yet, "C'mon, tell mama which objects you've used as toys?" And more than once, lifting a bottle of Cola, someone proposed, "And the Lovelace award goes to… let's see how far can you deep throat this bottle."

With the gang, Mercury never missed a chance to bitch about people's affairs; he elected who they should bitch about, who they should praise. He too set the mood, which was lively and gleeful usually, but turned a bit gloomy, when he downed a few Jasmine cocktails.

Jasmine cocktail had a special effect on Mercury. The cocktail's sophisticated visual along with its red pinkish colour was a trademark that Mercury claimed as his. The exotic Jasmine cocktail served to bolster his self-awareness of uniqueness. He'd introduced the gin cocktail to the local bar's staff after having watched Paul Harrington mix it on an American tv show. Jasmine cocktail was exclusively prepared for Mercury as the owner of the local bar couldn't afford *Cointreau* – an orange flavoured sweet liqueur used in its preparation. When Mercury went for a drink, in the local bar, he'd bring *Cointreau* with him and ask the bartender to kindly mix the ingredients.

The gang always knew when Mercury's mood was about to turn sour by the way he carved his teeth into the lemon slice used to garnish the border of the glass. So, slowly, they'd fall into a deep silence, mesmerised as Mercury narrated some personal romantic tales.

Mercury would never grow tired of telling everyone about when he was just 15 and had his first long term affair with a man, 20 years older than him. "…He was a heroin addict and one night he died of an overdose right in front of me, just after we'd made love." Death was simply the introduction of that story. "Ah, he used to bring little gifs every day for me. He knew just how to make me feel loved, cared for, truly especial. And no man ever treated me well in bed like he did." He'd often say staring blankly. "Oh, the way we made love was beautiful. Our pleasure came from the intimacy we shared. I will never forget him."

The gang that normally hung out with Mercury included his two assistants, the assistant's friends, the assistant's friend's friend and so forth – as long as Mercury approved them in the group. They were mostly adolescents, fully dependent on Mercury's irresistible leadership. Being part of the gang meant popularity and distinction. It also meant free ordinary drinks, salted peanuts, and roasted cashews. When bars owners invited Mercury to impersonate Madonna they knew beforehand they'd have a full house. They knew Mercury would advertise the show and invite the gang members, who would then invite their friends, who would invite other friends too, and this gathered crowd would inevitably come along to the show.

The gang members greatly admired Mercury's sharp wit and the way he made them feel special about being who they were and what they were. They'd normally meet during weekdays in their local bar, greet, sit, engage in conversation, consume alcoholic beverages despite their little age, sometimes leave for casual sex, then return to see if anyone was still hanging around. At the weekends they often went to a beach hut where they'd practice the standard ritual: gossiping, bitching, swearing, bad-mouthing, back-stabbing, and laughing their arses off at everyone else's expenses.

Whenever or wherever the gang assembled, they'd run their mouths fast and wild and would spare not a soul. Even Mercury ended up as the butt of their jokes after he left to America. "She was a true chameleon: she impersonated Freddie Mercury by day, Madonna by night, and Michael Jackson after midnight…" One member of the gang enjoyed repeating this in a very sarcastic tone. "Girl… honest to God, his impersonated celebs started eclipsing one another just after she began a love story with a fourteen year old. She got in trouble big time 'cause of that boy; and guess what; the boy even had a celeb name: Boy George if my memory isn't playing tricks. Ha-ha! Just too many celebs to a single love story." – That member laughed hard. "Mercury didn't see it coming; but that boy caused her celeb personas to meet their demise."

26

All started when Mercury spotted Joy hanging around with her own gang. Amongst Joy's gang was a young and innocent looking lad. Mercury consulted with the gang and found out a member who knew Joy. "Why don't you invite her to join us for drinks later tonight?" Mercury suggested, quickly managing to befriend Joy. He paid her special attention and plied her with drinks, corn chips, potato chips, and other snacks. His next move was to invite Joy to a night out. "Oh, and bring that cherub friend of yours along."

Joy was enough sharp to grasp why Mercury approached her, and from then on she ensured that the young lad fully learned the advantages of befriending Mercury and walking the line with him. Quicker than a lightning bolt the young lad fell under Mercury's spell. Joy kept her little luxuries; Mercury kept his little treat.

From the first time they met, Mercury learned that his new young friend loved telling tales from the few American shows on open tv, that he was also fond of the Southern American cowboy stereotype, and that he enjoyed running his gentle fingers through Mercury's bleached hair. Before he could say "oops," Mercury had fallen for the young lad hook line and sinker.

The young lad was out, loud, and proud but not effeminate, as one might expect. He had open-minded views on sexual preferences too; sadly, this open-mindedness clashed with the feelings Mercury nurtured for him. The young lad couldn't think of two men having an affair that wasn't strictly justified by sexual impulses. This meant one thing: Mercury wouldn't wait long to see the young lad slip through his fingers or fall prey of one of the gang's smart asses.

Initially Mercury captured the young lad's interest with little luxuries: new clothes, nights out to gay bars with friends, days out on the beach with friends, VCR film sessions with friends, and satellite tv watching… with friends. "I'm tired of sharing his company with everyone," Mercury confided to the closest members of the gang. "And I'm struggling to make him understand we needed time together alone now and then."

Mercury knew just what to do to engender peer pressure, pleading help from within the gang and telling each one what they should say to persuade the young lad about the importance of staying faithful to a person. The gang delighted themselves, noticing Mercury's desperate effort to avoid defeat in his oldest game.

Mercury then appealed to heartfelt declarations to the slippery object of his affection. "I love you. Do you love me?" Mercury asked in front of everyone.

All that conversation about love just sounded bizarre to the young lad. Eventually, Mercury changed strategy again: better than having the young lad's will tamed was having the young lad's heart tamed. Mercury had in their time together enough time to know the young lad's preferences. So, he disposed of his flamboyant style, boycotted his camp wardrobe, ceased his Madonna impersonations, and shook the dust off his long forgotten combination of jeans, denim jacket, and raw leather boots.

"Next thing we knew, the doll was dressed up cowboy-like, wearing a straight face, and then ditched us after work." One former salon assistant recalled. "Apparently, the strategy paid off. The boy stopped hanging out with his friends and became more willingly opened Mercury's sway, if you know what I mean."

Mercury knew the risks involved in keeping a relation with someone of that age. It was against the law to engage in intimate relations with someone below the legal age of consent. The gang grew bored with Mercury's frequent complaints. "It's so unfair that the law brand me with a disgraceful scarlet P when society should be obliged to me. It's hard to grow up as a homosexual in this poor dead end neighbourhood. For a minor like him it sure is better to engage in a serious relationship with someone older like myself than sleep around with other less experienced boys. Besides, it's not the first case in the world, and I'm not the only one in this world to feel this way."

Mercury often referred to a text that he read back at upper school on how in ancient Greece it was an institutionalised practice of aristocracy for a pre-adolescent boy to be trusted to an adult male who would be the boy's teacher and protector. The words used to identify the boy, *eromenos* (beloved), and the man, *erastes* (lover), make obvious how their social roles went beyond pedagogical purposes. Mercury used to mention a show that he saw on satellite tv about a man dash boy love association called NAMbLA. Unfortunately it was a North American organisation in a galaxy far, far away from the primitive society in which he was trapped. Anyway, nobody would dare to mess with him in the neighbourhood if the young lad's parents themselves weren't bothered about the matter.

Within that situation, most members of the gang had their social strings cut off from Mercury; he gradually distanced himself from everyone who wasn't linked to his work at the hair salon. And, after that, the last the gang heard from Mercury was that he'd gone to the US. Some said he'd more like fled to America after his fling with the young lad had taken a scandalous turn.

Mercury and the young lad had started kissing overtly a few times in the local bar – which wasn't gay until the whole gang arrived. On the Christmas Eve after they met, Mercury and the young lad had dared to dance together in the local club, where the majority of the patrons were straight. The gang often recalled the joy they'd felt when *Into the Groove* started booming across the dance floor and Mercury and the young lad went from dancing apart to getting closer and closer until their bodies were wound together. They were free from threats because the club was crowded with gang members and because most straights over there knew and respected Mercury. Though no one else was drunk enough to follow Mercury's lead they formed a circle around the couple and celebrated that moment whistling and clapping to the rhythm of the music.

"That Christmas Eve she made magic." One of the mature members of the gang often repeated, recalling how Mercury made the gang members feel for a brief moment the taste of being themselves in the face of their mainstream straight community.

Sometime later, Mercury's influences over the young lad came to a halt. The gang members heard bits and pieces about that from a former assistant of the salon who witnessed the events to the bitter end: "When the boy's mom found out of Mercury friendship with him she didn't take the news well. I was at the salon the day she came and discreetly advised Mercury to stay away from her son or she'd be forced to press charges against him for sexual abuse. The jig was up."

It was known that, after this, the two lovers still met a few times but the lad's mother knew how to impose her will and the romantic fantasy Mercury had fostered drifted away like so much smoke. Not far from there, Mercury was heard complaining more and more about the petty small-minded views of the backward society around him; embittered, Mercury made his move. He terminated the lease of the salon, gathered his savings and added to them by selling personal assets, cast one last glance at the salon building, and went ahead with his aspirations of migrating to America.

27

The colours of the flowers with which the spring had patched the fields along the A-one were being brushed away. The heat wave made the weather hotter and hotter on a daily basis. A giant halo around the sun gave to that hazy summer day a particular charm which Clifford and I admired on our away to Doncaster.

"I guess you don't know the name for this phenomenon." I challenged Clifford as I tried to find an angle to take a picture from inside the car.

"*Sun halo* I'm guessing…" As I shook the head, Clifford said. "Go on clever clogs, tell us."

"It's listed in the OED as sun dog or mock sun. And there's another name I can't remember now."

"Never 'eard of it – it's beautiful. Ah'll find a spot t' stop so you can ge' a proper photo."

Clifford stopped by the A-one at a coffee trailer that had the Union Jack and the St. George's Cross flapping on its side. I took photos of the sun dog whilst Clifford smoked a *ciggie* – as he called. Then, we queued for a coffee and as we waited to be served I distracted myself reading the list of breakfasts served there:

large breakfast, small breakfast, bacon breakfast, sausage breakfast, spam breakfast.

I was awaken from my spell by the voice of a man next to me who'd been served a large breakfast complete with 4 bacon rashes, 2 eggs, a portion of sweet beans, sliced tomatoes, bread and butter, and a white coffee.

"That's a proper breaky, that be!" The way the man pronounced the word *proper* with a rhotic pos-vocalic *r* sound instantly made my ears perk.

I'd developed my perception skills enough to know he wasn't American. If the man was Irish I'd recognise that – I'd watched the full *Father Ted* series. And that man's intonation wasn't Scottish either. So, either I'd misheard the rhotic pos-vocalic *r* or he came from a region other than Ireland or Scotland where the *r* sound is pronounced before consonants and at words' end.

I cast a begging look upon Clifford, hoping he'd notice my interest. Yet, he was about to order a hot drink to both of us and seemed to have ignored me. "Can ah 'av two coffees, please?"

"With or without?" The man behind the counter asked, already filling the cups with coffee.

"Just a slash, please." Clifford said looking at me as I firmly tried to get his attention with a cheeky smile.

"Where's his accent from?" I asked in a low tone.

"South," Clifford replied quickly.

"Exactly, please." I insisted, smiling as if just making a comment on something else.

Clifford was always helpful in these situations. Whenever he noticed my interest in knowing where a certain person came from he'd engage in a casual chat with that person. He seemed to have clicked why I was interested in the man's way of speaking. So, he addressed to the man behind the counter in an audible voice so the other man would be able to hear.

"Y' know, just t' other day a chap from Cornwall bet wi' me that the summer in t' South is much 'otter than 'ere up North. I don't believe the's a difference."

The man looked at Clifford over that large portion of bangers and said. "Not much all the time but beginning of this week was more."

I was all ears to the way he pronounced *more*. I prayed to Clifford find something else to say.

"Y' know, if 'e said summer in Lisbon was 'otter alright, but we're a small country. Then again, I don't travel much to t' South."

"T'is hotter sometimes I tell you. I be actually from South Hams and I go to and fro every week. It's slightly hotter there most times."

"The Cornwall chap wasn't far from t' truth then." Clifford said to close the conversation.

The man agreed with a sonorous "Arrr."

Clifford then looked at me a little smug.

I couldn't get right where he was from but Clifford would tell me. Clifford had an ability to engage in talks proper of who was in the used car trade for a good time.

Before we returned to the car I thanked, smiled, and I said "Have a nice day" to the man behind the counter. That thank, that smile, and that *have a nice day* was an old trademark that I'd learned during my exchange programme in Leeds when I myself worked behind a counter serving hot drinks to hurried customers at the Upper Crust in the train station – my 2nd job in Leeds.

28

On those trailers along the road the options of hot drinks were generally limited to tea, coffee, and hot chocolate. At the train station in Leeds, tea, coffee, and chocolate options multiplied in varieties and sizes; and, to follow the language protocol, these varieties and sizes were specified with a particular name.

At Upper Crust the options were *PG Tips tea*, *Earl Grey tea*, *filter coffee*, *caffè Americano*, aka *Americano*, *caffè latte*, aka *latte*, *cappuccino*, *mocha*, *espresso*, *double espresso*, *espresso macchiato*, *standard hot chocolate*, and *mint hot chocolate*. The drinks which weren't strictly made with milk could be either *white* or *black*, like a *black filter coffee* or *white filter coffee*. If the drinks were prepared with either skimmed milk or semi-skimmed milk these drinks had another word added to their denominations. In the case of teas it'd just be *tea with skimmed milk*. In the case of coffees it'd be *skinny*, just as in *skinny Americano*, *skinny latte*, *skinny cappuccino*, and the like. All drinks were served in three sizes, named *small*, *medium*, and *large*.

So, when a customer asked, "Can I have a medium skinny latte with two sugars, please?" I rushed to transform that combination of words into a nice cuppa.

And that was just the basic vocabulary. In the Upper Crust I still had to learn a lot of word combinations, as well as the natural burden they implied. I learned to use the coffee machine, to load the fresh coffee beans into the grinder, to keep the steam arms of the coffee machine clean, to press the precise buttons for each shot of coffee, to heat the milk, to froth the milk, to remove the froth off the milk, to serve each customer ahead of the queue, to use the touch screen till, to issue the receipt properly, to say "How can I help," to up-sell – by suggesting large size drinks –, to say "Thanks, have a nice day," and most of all, to smile beautifully and brightly whilst performing all these actions.

To keep that smile on the face, I was smile coached by a Portuguese manager of Upper Crust: Mr Antonio.

For the first time, throughout a life with a few frustrating events, my face had a smile slapped on for longer than a few minutes: from 6 a.m. to 2 p.m., it was smile, smile, and put on a happy face. And boy, oh boy, that wasn't difficult because until then I'd never been obliged to speak English that much. In the first shift that I worked at the train station, serving native English speakers who talked to me directly, my face was smiling, my tongue was rolling and twisting, and although my English was burring and drawling, I felt greatly fulfilled. The formal English of the lectures and seminars, the short chats with classmates, or with European accented housemates, or with South Asian English speakers in the kitchen, all these hadn't yet quenched my thirst for English like that first shift did.

And for all that, I had to thank Laura.

After Laura and I returned from the Netherlands I told Laura that the job at the Georgetown rewarded me financially and offered me some experience in English but most of the time I had little opportunity to articulate my own English in the kitchen and that frustrated me. Since Laura herself had found a position at Pumpkin Café train station in the month she arrived in Leeds, she told me that the Upper Crust often had a staff shortage on weekends. So, I went along with her to the station and she introduced me to Mr Antonio, who put me on the roster for the weekend shift.

Since my arrival in Leeds, I'd been missing a proper chance to exchange utterances with native speakers of English. Upper Crust gave me the nearest thing to that.

In the Upper Crust only a few sales persons didn't speak English as a first language. All supervisors and kitchen staff were native speakers of English too. One of them, a Leodensian from birth named Aggie, always snapped me out from my slumberous state in the morning when giving orders with her energetic high pitched voice. "…put t' chairs n' t' tables outside, and wipe t' top of t' tables wi' D-ten, chop chop."

I just loved listening to her perfectly aspirated *t*'s and those full blown sibilant consonantal sounds. It sounded like she had tiny cymbals glued to the tip of her tongue and behind her front upper teeth. Another one was Louise, a natural-born Scouser who'd recently moved from Liverpool. She worked in the kitchen preparing baguettes and was a reserved 24 year old girl.

The few times I had a chance to listen to Louise talking in the kitchen it simply sounded unintelligible – something like German! One morning, she was by herself in the kitchen and told me something I couldn't quite understand.

"Pardon me." I said, prompting her to utter the same in fewer words. "Pardon me." I repeated, embarrassed.

Then, Louise uttered a single word loudly, with a light expression of amusement on her face. "Melhh!"

I thought on the endless hours of sacrifice I'd been through trying to improve my English. How could I be defeated by a single word? Louise probably thought I had no competence in English whatsoever.

"I'm so sorry; can you spell that, please?"

With a patient smile, she grabbed an empty half-pint bottle of milk and repeated with a rising tone. "Gwan n' fetch soum melhh. N' t' kitchen." Then, she pointed to the empty bottle, "Melhh!"

"Oh, thanks." Relieved that Louise sounded more amused than annoyed, I excused myself and went to get milk at the stock fridge on the other platform.

From that day I learned that Louise pronounced the final consonant sound in *milk* as a heavily aspirated 'h' sound, as the first sound in *hot*, produced at the back of the throat. When I returned all the other staff began speaking to me imitating Louise's rising intonation and her aspirated 'h'. Through the rest of the shift they kept repeating *mealhh*, *loohh*, *bahh*, at any chance they had.

Working at the train station gave me a sense of closeness to natural and real English – the vernacular. I heard staff members saying *me* in places I'd learned to use *my*, and *us* in places I'd learned to use *me*, and saying *youse* as a plural of *you*. I heard customers and staff thanking me with "thanks, thank you, thaaank you, thanking you, tanks, fanks, ta, ta luv, cheers, cheers mate, cheer hun, beautiful, lovely, brilliant, fantastic, magic, superb, you're a star, great." I heard customers specifying the quantity of milk in their coffee as "just a little, just a bit, a drop, a droplet, a dribble, a dash, a tiny dash, a slash, a splash, a touch, a jot."

Upper Crust was my English heaven. There, I found myself surrounded by a variety of pronunciation and vocabulary that I was ignorant of and could never think it could be considered real English. At the train station, the concepts of preciseness and correctness regarding pronunciation, vocabulary, and grammar that I'd learned from my experience with English back home, started to give place to a more inclusive notion of its dynamicity. The English at the train station embodied the dynamicity of those commuters coming and going from place to place constantly in touch with the many varieties of English within and without the United Kingdom. Those were the people who could speak English and no one could tell them otherwise.

Coincidentally, at the dawn of that experience with English vernacular, my hotmail inbox flashed an email that reminded me of how my experience with English back home was constrained by the orthodox views on English that my undergraduate course endorsed.

– Sender: *Aristotle*. Subject: *News from your friend* –

29

After having abandoned our plans to apply for the exchange programme together with an excuse that he couldn't stay a long time away from his girl, Aristotle promised to stay in touch and use English in his emails.

Dear friend, at the beginning of this year a private school offered me a work as teacher. I turned it down. The salary offered was quite disappointing. Compared to the money you make per hour washing dishes in Leeds the salary was a joke. Remember I told about my project of a personal computer. It's complete. I finally assembled all the parts as I had in mind. It now has a keyboard goldship that triggers all programs and even Internet with just a touch of a button, a 17 inch Samsung monitor, a Sony DVD recorder, a HD chassis with a transparent side cover and with a blue neon light inside the coolers, which are also transparent with neon, and an Intel-Pentium 4 clocked at 3.6 GHz – currently the fastest in the world. A cousin of mine helped me to import a few parts from the USA through the internet. Now I plan to import the newest release: Pentium 43.8 GHz! You're really lucky because you now have access to the most advanced technological devices in Europe. Mate, I have to confess, I really miss our conversations about film and cinema. By the way, you should check some of the internet news on the new Superman movie. I leave you with a hug.

I read Aristotle's email while lying in bed from my mobile phone that had access to Internet; so I replied telling how I read his email and that probably the latest generation of mobile phones in the UK were miniature versions of his ultra potent PC. As usual, I had this little problem with Aristotle; he had an amazing patience with my views on the world and my intransigent academic demands, but I couldn't keep from teasing him about his own views and personal ambitions. I also disliked this technology fever Aristotle nurtured.

Though our shared interest in English language and American series brought us together, I often clashed with Aristotle's conventional and conformist attitudes. At times, when we talked, he sounded so proud to mention that he was acquainted with someone who he considered important or that he shared a common interest with a social circle he considered important.

In my short-tempered days, I usually confronted Aristotle with the same speech: "I care little about being acquainted with some hotshot; I care greatly about making people willing to get acquainted with me. I loathe thinking of myself as a guest and I love thinking of myself as a host. I don't enjoy being part of other's world, joining a social circle, following a trend, or accepting standards."

Our conflict was no different when the topic was English. Aristotle once came to tell me with great admiration about a tutor who I hadn't met yet. "Yes, the tutor's very strict! He says he can't admit a student talking with a British accent and using American words like *subtitles*, or *windshield*, or *line*. It's unacceptable. If a student speaks with a British accent, he or she should use *caption*, or *windscreen*, or *queue*."

I hadn't enough knowledge on English to have an informed judgment on the rightness or wrongness over such views on English. But that just sounded pathetic.

Aristotle naive enthusiasm for suchlike ideas just threw my tongue into convulsion. "How can a tutor demand this from a student of English? Just consider our proficiency level; we still struggle to speak fluently. How the hell are we to determine what's British or American? It can't be just me…" A violent cough cut me short. "Fu…" – Cough, cough.

I choked in my own words, knowing that I wouldn't go much further with any argument; I had no formal ground to dispute against an idea supported by a tutor of English. Aristotle knew that, and didn't want to hurt me by supporting an idea that he visibly approved. So, I breathed deeply and silently swallowed my resentment.

I resented Aristotle, resented the tutor, and resented myself for neither conforming nor knowing any better.

Reminiscing on that, I had a mild suspicion that so much dissent and resentment wasn't normal at all. And I guessed such disposition had been transmitted down to me from a man who I knew during my youth – a man who seemed to possess the power to bend the world to his will. Essentially, this man had been an old flame.

30

This man and I had nurtured a short relationship. Though his dressing style and camp behaviour didn't charm me from start, I offered no resistance to his will. When we first met he seemed to have the world turning around him; yet, not long passed for him to start acting more the way I liked – just to show me how truthfully committed he was. I loved watching American shows on tv with him and especially admired the way he had to make of the world our world. In his company, I lived my most impressing experience as a gay person.

It happened on Christmas night, little after we met.

We went clubbing on a straight venue in the suburb we dwelt. We had a group of friends with us. He and I were familiar with the words of Madonna's most popular songs and could understand their literal sense.
When *Into the Groove* started playing, we felt that the words *I'm tired of dancing here all by myself, tonight I wanna dance with someone else* spoke to us. So, we slowly approached each other's boogieing bodies, and we danced together to everyone's dumbfounded gaze.

That Christmas night I felt what's to have a longing truly quenched. I had a taste of being myself and not being afraid or ashamed of that. I felt the happiness of coming off the shadows for a moment and sensing the light of social recognition. And I refused going back to those shadows or being ashamed of my true self again. From then on I grew a sense of cautious rejection to people who came telling me how to look, behave, think, or speak. I grew particularly cautious of people telling me the limits of my potentials as if they could determine the limits of my future itself – what naturally included the limits of my language ability.

Recalling Aristotle and how he often conformed to some uninformed notions on English that we were indoctrinated with at our undergraduate course, I felt that my dissent and resentment had been vindicated. For that and other reasons, on that summer morning as Clifford drove me to Doncaster, where a few cars awaited me, I smiled. Just like when I started working as a dish washer and as a barista I still had a sense of purpose pulsing strongly within my heart. If nothing else, that passion to learn, and pursue knowledge on, English had at least freed me from the chains that possibly still held others like Aristotle bound to old and misconceived notions regarding English.

"Wha' ye thinking?" Clifford snapped me out of my stillness.

"Of where that man in the café said he was from."

"South Hams; South West of England. It's on t' South coast of Devon."

"Did you notice how that man pronounced the words *proper*, *more*, and *hotter*?"

"Think so, yes. Tell us what's special 'bout that?"

"According to an old tutor of mine that man cannot speak English…"

31

The level of progress of a society possibly mirrors the level of that society's linguistic awareness. Back at my undergraduate course of Letters such levels were high regarding Portuguese. Most tutors of the Classic Languages Department had just been awarded their Doctorates at other Universities in more developed regions of the country. Meanwhile, up to the time of my exchange programme, most tutors from the Foreign Languages Department didn't have a Master's degree in some linguistics, or language-specific, area. The English Major was more literature-based and the few tutors who had Doctorate degrees had done them in English Literature. So, whilst the syllabus of the English-specific modules on literature was brilliant, the syllabus of the language modules followed the lessons of the same book series used in private English courses.

I recall a tutor, who'd just graduated from her Doctorate in English Literature, spending 10 minutes telling the story of *Odysseus and the Sirens* to illustrate how the simple past tense – the topic of the class – was used in narratives to describe imagined past states and events. Then, her class followed a pattern: presentation of grammatical rules in the use of simple past tense, presentation of simple past tense in negative and interrogative sentences, and filling out book activities.

The level of linguistic awareness regarding English that we students were supposed to have stopped here; we should master those grammatical rules so we could teach them forward to our own students in the future. That was the general concern with English language.

There was a particular tutor, though, whose greater interest fell on English language rather than literature, and whose approach to English was a bit less plain.

Mr Harrison was a chubby little middle-aged man who walked and talked fast. The multimedia classroom of the Foreign Languages Department was reserved weekly for the 3-hours lecture of Phonetics and Phonology of English that he delivered with sparks of satisfaction in his eyes. He carried an atmosphere of Britain, or perhaps America, around him, which he matched by turning the room air conditioning to its lowest temperature: 17°. For that reason, students would come to class wearing thick wool jumpers to avoid the clattering of teeth to death.

The contents of Mr Harrison's lecture consisted of a mix of hardcore technical information on phonetics and phonology, personal history of his education in English, and language information on why, apart from him and the British aristocracy, nobody else could really speak English. His favourite classroom mottos were "that's totally wrong" and "that's ridiculous English."

Mr Harrison was proud of his English, and rightly so; after a former English teacher discouraged him, by his own effort he claimed to have attained perfect skills in RP English. He'd promised himself to learn proper English just as had promised to visit Disney in Orlando, and he did so. Disney, a propos, seemed to have been his most significant experience with English abroad.

The didactic material put together by Mr Harrison proudly bore the stamp of the most expensive English course of the city, where he also taught. With such material, he introduced to the students invaluable information on phonetic and phonology of English – the International Phonetic Alphabet, the consonantal and vowel sounds of American and British English, the grammar of syllables and the phonotactic constraints, stress and intonation, and a little more. Alas, with Mr Harrison there was a catch: he taught these topics in phonetic and phonology under the premise that only by consciously learning all those topics a student would be able to attain full proficiency in English – an idea that he frankly stated using another of his favourite mottos: "If you don't know that, *you cannot speak English.*"

A remarkable characteristic of Mr Harrison was his ability to assert myths about speaking proper English with an air of authority that made such myths stick to students' mind as the ultimate fact on learning English. Such myths spread like an outbreak among students of the English Major who eagerly repeated them further.

Mr Harrison's most popular myth was "*you cannot speak English* if you mix sounds that belong exclusively to American and British accents." His argument was that learners should make a conscious decision on each sound of English they used when speaking; if they spoke with a British accent and used a rhotic pos-vocalic *r* sound they couldn't speak English because rhotic pos-vocalic *r* is a feature exclusive of American English. Another trendy myth was "if you don't learn each intonation curve of English along with its matching speech pattern *you cannot speak English.*" This entailed that learners had to make a conscious decision on which specific intonation pattern they should use when uttering sentences; if they used a rising intonation in a declarative sentence – just like Scousers and Australians do – they couldn't speak English because rising intonation in English occurred exclusively in declarative interrogative sentences.

Summing up, in addition to the natural difficulties of learning English Mr Harrison simply loved to specify rules of proficiency that made English the unattainable language of Xanadu.

Most students were delighted with Mr Harrison's premises on speaking English. They rejoiced having the privilege of learning new complicated information on phonetics and phonology and they rejoiced preaching them forward because all that, and the difficulty in learning all that, distinguished them from the average Joe learning English.

Because my skills English were hopelessly beneath the prerequisite standards preached by Mr Harrison, when I attended his classes I naturally antagonised his premises and tried to find information that justified a different view on learning English – a quest doomed to fail as most of the tutors from the English Major shared similar judgment on the complexities of English.

But all was not lost. During the exchange experience at the University of Leeds, I started to see the light of those complexities.

32

The light started flickering at the opening lecture of *Language, Text and Context* when two fundamental questions were projected at the huge white board behind the theatrically eloquent Dr Fiona Douglas:

What is language? What is English?

Dr Douglas introduced her audience with an array of concepts evoked by the words *language* and *English*.

Some definitions transmitted sense of honesty in the first place: 'Language is a dialect promoted by élites,' or 'Language is a dialect with an army and navy".

The lecturer, Dr Douglas, reinforced that honesty.

"I'm not here to forge any linguistic criteria to praise language over dialect, i.e., the official standard over the regional vernacular. The concept of language, as we may consider, is merely a socio-political one." Dr Douglas stressed, keeping an eye on a script in her hands and other on the audience. "In the same way, submitted to pure linguistic criteria, Standard English and other dialects of English, be them regional or international, are no more correct than the other."

The presented definitions of English didn't simply tell apart what's right English or what's wrong English.

Dr Douglas still read a definition authored by the British Lexicographer Sir James Murray. "English is not a square with definite sides containing its area; it's a circle… nowhere bounded by any line."

"Naturally," – Dr Douglas emphasised – "English is distinguished from German, French, and Spanish by an exclusive set of grammatical features and pronunciation. Still, English itself, under synchronic perspective, can be authentically identified with a variety of grammatical features and vocabulary which characterises, and distinguishes too, its many dialects. Once these dialects are identified, they may be tagged with distinctive names. British English, for instance, identified as the English as used in Britain, has dialects named as English English, Scottish English, Irish English, and Welsh English. English English, for example, identified as the English as used in England, has dialects named as Southwest English, Northern English, Central English, East English. Northern English, for instance, identified as the English as used in the North of England, has dialects named as Northeast English, Lower North English."

In that order, as I could understand, as more geographically specific dialects are characterised they are identified with further names.

English English, for example, still has local dialects named as London English, Yorkshire English or Tyke, Liverpudlian English or Scouse, ad infinitum. The same specifications may be, following this logic, extended to American English, Canadian English, Australian English, New Zealand English, Caribbean English, South African English, and South Asian English.

These varieties are characterised under geographical criteria. A variety of English could also be categorised under social criteria. BBC English is an example.

Another distinction clarified in Dr Douglas' lecture was the difference between dialect and accent. Dialect refers to distinctive grammatical/ lexical characteristics; and accent, to distinctive pronunciation characteristics. Generally a dialect has also a characteristic accent; yet, an accent may be used to speak any dialectical variety. A person can speak with the grammar and vocabulary of BBC English and still sound as a Scouse.

The instant that truly thrilled me in Dr Douglas' lecture happened when she presented some cross influences between American and British English, and talked on features of a London regional speech, known as Estuary English, that in the last decades has spread to the counties adjoining the river Thames and beyond.

In summary, in that opening lecture, English was, in no moment, pinned down to a single permanent set of grammatical, lexical, or phonetic features. Another interesting thing about that lecture was to realise that Dr Douglas – native of Scotland, proficient speaker of Standard English, a Dr with expertise in English – could use her academic authority in English to define normative boundaries, to state what English is or isn't, to state who can and who cannot speak English, and to resort to important names to support such views. Still, she seemed to let that chance escape and presented an impartial non-normative perspective of English.

At the end of that lecture, I thought of some mates preaching about the boundaries of English by the light of misconceived normative notions of grammar and pronunciation that they learned from Mr Harrison. And I wished they had a chance to be seating in that lecture theatre – so I'd look them in the face and say "Boo!"

Despite all my silly rebellious thoughts, I somewhat understood the position some tutors of my home university assumed – including Mr Harrison. For them, English was a precious language that belonged to other nations, and therefore, that the students should show respect for by properly learning and using normative standards of grammar, vocabulary, and pronunciation as presented in grammar books. The tutors had learned English in that way; they passed those views and attitudes on to us students, who, either for selfish or for selfless reasons, reverenced those principles.

The increasing availability of English in the media was still insufficient to make tutors and students effectively aware of the dimension of its linguistic complexities. The lack of a more appropriate linguistic awareness made tutors and students learn to accept and reverence concepts of an unrealistic English standard. And to the best of our knowledge English conformed uniquely to either an 'American' or a 'British' standard.

The tutors' and students' perspective of English reminded me of the prisoners' perspective of shadows in Plato's *Myth of the Cave*.

33

Plato's myth goes about these prisoners who'd lived from birth restrained by chains at the bottom of an underground den. In front of these prisoners there's a wall where moving shadows are projected in the same fashion of a theatre screen. Those moving shadows in the wall come from real moving things behind these prisoners. The prisoners can see the moving shadows in the wall but they can't see the real things behind them. If the prisoners can't see the real moving things behind them logically they can't see the blaze which throws those shadows on the wall in front of them. As far as these prisoners are concerned, those shadows are the only real things that exist. They know nothing about the real things or the blaze, or anything outside the cave. Plato explains that humans in the world as we know are like these prisoners and that all the things the human eyes see are nothing more than shadows from real things of a spiritual world.

Comparably, back home what we acknowledged as the real English wasn't the diversity of English dialects spoken by actual English speakers of England, Ireland, Scotland, Wales, United States, Canada, Australia, New Zealand, etc.; the English we acknowledged as the real English came from artificial material produced for pedagogic purposes. The little English we had access to from tv or radio was the closest thing to real English we knew. Still, we certainly filtered it through our artificial normative understanding of English. So, as we learned that only Americans pronounced rhotic pos-vocalic *r* sounds we'd thoroughly ignore if we ever heard such sound in the English of a British person speaking on tv. And the English we read from literary works weren't less artificial than the English of lessons and grammar books – ultimately, all written forms of language are artificial because they are no more than shadows of the human speech.

In Plato's myth some prisoners have a chance to escape from the cave and become aware of the real things and the blaze behind them, and even aware of a world of light beyond the cave.

To me, the lectures of *Language, Text and Context* represented the onset of the journey outwards my English linguistic cave, a journey which culminated with the working shifts at Leeds station when I could have a clearer glimpse of the English I'd once known as a shadow. Alas, not much my eyes grew accustomed to the light coming from outside the cave, it was nearly time for me to return home and get used again to the feeble light which illuminated English over there.

Gladly, before my return, there was still a few more exploring to do in the realm outside the linguistic cave.

34

The postman delivered the mail at North Grange Road just after 7 a.m. He generally slipped letters and parcels through the letter box. But when these were larger than the mail slot, or when a signature was required, he'd leave a red form notifying the addressee to come in person with an ID document to collect the mail at the Headingley local office located nearly 2 miles from the accommodation. So, a few mornings at 7 a.m. on time, if I expected large parcels with DVDs, CDs, or books from Amazon, I'd come downstairs, park myself at the vestibule, and wait for the postman.

The first morning when the postman came, he greeted me with a familiar name. "Oh Pelé."

It made no sense. Why he'd mention a footballer who had the same nationality as me? "Pardon me."

"Y'oh Pelé." The postman basically repeated.

I had to have misheard it and he couldn't be let go without telling the meaning of that. So, after getting my mail, a bit timidly, I asked. "What does *oh Pelé* mean?"

Noticing my struggle, the postman courteously rephrased. "It's ea'ly mo'ning and ye' already off bed."

"Oh, thank you, yes. Early riser, I am"

He then bade "Good day t' ye." And left.

Well, not enough time had passed for me to get used to how "up early" sounded in Yorkshire. Yet, it felt like ages as I'd been constantly on the go from my arrival in September to the beginning of the second semester.

At least working full-time on holidays had paid off. I earned enough to afford purchasing the books and audiobooks I needed: *The Norton Anthology of American Literature*, and *of British Literature*, *The Complete Works of Shakespeare*, and Melvin Bragg's *The Adventure of English*, among others. These could cost up to a full month's grant back home. I could afford my favourite American cartoons and sitcoms released on DVD to date. That material could serve as teaching resource and for future academic enterprises. That was a way of carrying the English language with me when the time to return home arrived. The English I'd pack in suitcases should compensate for the low marks of semester one exams. And to make sure those marks were properly compensated, as much as it could possibly be, it was time to revamp some old habits.

Weeks into semester two at the University of Leeds the weather turned miserable. On the bright side, it snowed a lot. It hadn't snowed after my return from the Netherlands and snow was still a novelty for me. I loved taking photos in the snow at Hyde Park, watching the snowflakes falling on the way to university, to the restaurant, to the train station, and on the way back.

Halfway through semester two my enthusiasm for snow snuffed. I'd dropped a module and carried on with *English in Time & Space* and *Shakespeare on Film* at the School of English. I'd adapted myself better to the university's routine. No exams were scheduled for semester two, and, apart from when I worked full-time on the Easter break, my work hours dropped radically.

Under that lighter rhythm, my plans to take full advantage of my contact with English picked up steam. Part of that endeavour was to be on the lookout for free newspaper DVDs.

One Sunday morning, as I worked at Upper Crust, Louise showed me an issue of the *Daily Mirror* that a customer left on a table. "Loohh. That's good fu' ye."

"Oh, thanks Louise." I said, whilst reading in the front page: *Free classic British comedy series inside.*

"Y' welcome kidder. Y' got to 'urry oop." Louise pointed to the small prints. *DVDs are limited and must be collected from Woolworths.*

"Woolworths? Is there one around here?"

"Ye 'av t' go up to Merrion Centre." Louise replied and called my attention. "You go' a customer, luv."

I waited for my 30 minutes break and, during that time, dashed to the Merrion Centre before the DVDs run out. Coincidently, I'd been scheduled to work during mornings that week, so I had to make the same run every day before 9 p.m. to collect the DVDs.

Like this, I became acquainted with *Tony Hancock*, *Porridge*, *The Likely Lads*, *The Good Life*, *Only Fools and Horses*, *Keeping Up Appearances*, *One Foot in the Grave*, *Fawlty Towers* and *'Allo 'Allo*!

I also was back to basics. Most housemates from semester one had completed their Erasmus programme and returned to Europe. Javier was back to Spain but left his portable radio slash tape recorder to me. Naturally, I made full use of it: if I wasn't reading or watching DVDs, on went the radio; my listening skill, after years of American English, should get better adapted to the local English dialects. For this, I tuned to *BBC Radio Leeds*, *Radio Aire*, *Real Radio*, or *Galaxy*, whilst getting dressed, putting the kettle on, having tea, munching cookies, eating crisps, showering, or going to bed. But that wasn't enough.

To feed my listening frenzy, I went to a pound shop underneath Leeds Shopping Plaza at Albion Street to stock on packs of tapetronix audio tapes. I decided to audiotape as much radio shows as possible. This is how I did: when I left to the university or to Georgetown I'd leave a tape being recorded but I never listened to them because they'd supply me with fresh material to listen to in the near future back home.

All that radio listening got me quickly hooked on the *BBC Radio 4* half-hour comedy shows aired on weekdays at half-past 6 p.m; recording them became compulsory. I had to record all shows, no matter where I had to be at half-past 6 p.m. So – bearing in mind this was before podcast became popular –, I had to be near the recorder if I wanted to record a radio show. As business at the restaurant had slowed down, I had many nights off. But if I had to be at work, or anywhere else, there were two options. One, I'd carry the recorder with me, preset on *Radio 4*, find a socket and plug it in wherever I was, keep an eye on time, stay alert to press the rec button when the show started, and go on with my affairs. Two, I'd knock at one of the housemate's door – generally the girls of room 5.

"Evening Vanessa, hi Nicola. Sorry to interrupt." I started, with the tape recorder in hand.

"Hi Jones, come in." Vanessa answered with a frank smile. "You want us to record again?"

"Yes, I need this favour tonight. Is that ok?"

"It's ok. Same time?"

"Yes, half-past six – you just need to press rec."

"Alright, we'll do."

"There's another thing." I said, a bit awkwardly for abusing of her kindness. "There's other show at eight. But what I want to record doesn't start at eight."

"Yeah, what is it?" Vanessa sounded curious.

"It's an interview… with a monkey that can talk."

"Wha…?" Vanessa looked at Nicola, who started rolling on the bed covering her face with a pillow. "A monkey what?" She said, tittering as if about to lose it.

35

"Yes, monkey that can talk. They announced it. I don't want to miss that."

Vanessa started laughing and saying something in Czech to Nicola – "Chce nahrávání z rádia opice, kteří mohou mluvit." – whilst Nicola kept rolling in bed.

They reacted like that because I had a reputation in the house of talking about strange things and ideas. Finally, after calming down, Vanessa answered. "It's all right… I'll record it for you."

That night, I looked right stupid: after the show with the talking monkey wasn't aired, the girls laughed at me even harder. They also had the half-past 6 comedy show on tape – what balanced the night's events.

With diligence and the housemates' help, I recorded a rebroadcast of *That Reminds Me* (with Keith Barron), a few rebroadcasts of *The Right Time*, and of series one of *Clare in the Community* created by Harry Venning, of series one of *15 Minute Musical*, new *The Now Show* presented by Hugh Dennis and Steve Punt, one *Laurence and Gus Untold Stories*, the opening show of *Armando Iannucci's Charm Offensive*, and new shows of *The Hitchhiker's Guide to the Galaxy*.

That recording and listening madness was yet to be topped by brand new modalities of English practice.

The English in the Upper Crust had become a routine. I'd learned new words and did little more than repeating greetings and the occasional neutral remarks. So I contrived a mean to exploit my speaking routine in the Upper Crust so as to improve my pronunciation.

I've always had the impression that English native speakers had some difficulty breathing through their nose when speaking, so they avoided producing sounds that needed full closure of their mouth. It was perhaps because of this that English speakers uttered the sounds *p*, *t*, and *k* – as in *pick*, *tick*, and *kick* – followed by a sudden release of air, producing them with aspiration rather than with a full closure. Also, speakers in Leeds gave me the impression they used the back of their throat – the more posterior part of the vocal apparatus, in phonetics-speak – to produce sound constraints quite frequently and naturally. This idea was reinforced by way some speakers often shunned using the tip of the tongue and the upper teeth to pronounce the *t* sound as in *bottle* and *better* and used a glottal stop instead.

So, during my Upper Crust shifts, to avoid making full closures with the front part of my mouth whilst speaking with customers, I stuck a soft mint on the roof of my mouth and tried to restrain my tongue from taping it. It felt weird at the beginning but I believe I achieved the desired effect in many sounds.

Still, when routine is limited, vocabulary is limited, and the vocabulary progress at the train station slowed down after the second month. I needed a new setting to practise English. That's when, one morning after a lecture, as I crossed in front of Parkinson steps on the way back to North Grange Rd., I realised what the new setting could be.

"Morning. We're representatives from the Church of Jesus Christ of Latter-Day Saints. I'm elder David and this is elder Joshua." This dashing Mormon missionary, who sounded like Philip J. Fry from *Futurama*, approached me. "May we talk to you for a sec?"

"Yes, my pleasure." David's American accent had me nodding with a silly smile at *Morning*.

36

"We go around preaching about Jesus Christ..." – The other missionary, who sounded British, spoke. – "His teachings and how they can improve people's lives. Are you interested in learning about our mission and the Book of Mormon?"

"Yes, I enjoy talking about religion actually. Does it have to be now?"

"No, no." The American Mormon spoke. "You can take this card with you, if you will – here. There's the address of our ward building, just down the road. And there's a number so that you can let us know what time is convenient for you to attend one of our meetings."

How could I refuse? It isn't every day that a handsome native English speaker like that approached and gave me a number. "Of course – I'll send a text."

"That's awesome. I'll wait for your text eh... What did you say your name was...?" David asked whilst the British elder seemed ready to jot my answer.

A week later, I met the elders at the former Blenheim Baptist Church building at the end of Woodhouse Lane. I thought of that as a chance to learn on the Mormons' faith and Church. Plus, there should be plenty new words to go around with them. In the first meeting the elders' smooth accents and angelical appearance easily lured me to further meetings. And since I'd been trusted to the care of an American and an English elder, the meetings were the equivalent of having English classes with fitter versions of Brad Pit and Hugh Grant. If still on earth it was like that, imagine what their heaven should be like. *Oh my*!

The elders gave me *The Book of Mormon*, generous attention, and a choice to join their religion. After a few meetings at the ward building they invited me to come with them to attend the dominical service at the Vesper Road Chapel and to other social activities promoted by the church members. As I wasn't scheduled to work on Sunday shifts anymore, I accepted the invitation.

In the first morning at the Chapel, before the service started, I spotted a man who was the spitting image of Mel Gibson. He probably caught me gawking at him because he shifted from his seat and came to greet me. That same morning an English lady, who had talked to me at the entrance of the Chapel, sang a beautiful song during the service. In the same way Mel Gibson lookalike's handsomeness made my pupils expand, that lady's seraphic voice made my heart accelerate. A flood burst through my eyes. All that water must have been still within my soul, on a pond which calm surface reflected overdue dreams and frustrated passions. Thinking that perhaps those waters could be better channelled with the use of religious engineering, that morning, I considered being baptised.

Ironically, my search for new words in the setting of the Church of Jesus Christ of Latter-Day Saints led me to get acquainted with a single, yet powerful, word: the 'word of wisdom.' And since through my English learning journey no new word was ever learned without sacrifice, that 'word of wisdom' was no exception.

The 'word of wisdom' is a healthy code which those who wish to be immersed in baptismal waters must observe. To follow the 'word' I had to abstain myself from any alcoholic drink, coffee, or tea. The elders introduced me to the *law of chastity* which forbade relations. *Easy*. I'd been celibate since my arrival in Leeds – I could turn a lamp bulb on just but touching it. The last thing to do was to agree with the tithe: a 10% voluntary contribution from our income to the church. All ready and set. I just needed to answer the baptismal interview questions that elder David had to ask.

"Do you believe that God is our eternal Father?" Check. "Do you believe that Jesus Christ is the Son of God, the Savior and Redeemer of the world?" Check. "Do you believe the Church and gospel of Jesus Christ have been restored through the Prophet Joseph Smith?" *Why not*? Check. "Have you ever committed a serious crime?" Check. "Have you ever participated in an abortion?" Check. "Have you ever had a homosexual relationship?"

I didn't think they levelled criminals, abortionists, and homosexuals together. "Eh, I am a gay, actually."

"Oh..." Elder David squirmed on his seat for a mo.

37

Elder David managed to be diplomatic about that. "I'm afraid you can't be baptised right now."

"I'm really sorry. It's that, people normally realise it and... I thought you knew and never talked about it."

Despite that the baptism still happened: on Sunday at the Vesper Road Chapel in a blue pool with warm water. Only instead of me they baptised a Nigerian girl.

Well, being gay isn't all about having fun. It is also about being denied a faith. What really made me sad was that after 8 months of hard work and no sex, I still was looking for the fun side of being gay. I continued attending a few meetings at Woodhouse Lane and the elders were considerate to me all the same. Though I'd already gone through some minor conflicts for living as an out gay, being officially denied something because of that still hurt. Just another day in the life of a gay.

By this time, lectures and seminar had ended at the School of English. I passed *Shakespeare on Film* whilst *English in Time and Space* was a flop. Catholics still mourned Pope John Paul II, the new Pope, Benedict VI, had been elected, and news about the general elections was on BBC radio all day. The sunny days started, and more people were gathering and barbequing at Hyde Park. I had a little more than a month to go back home.

Mr Dharmendra had stopped scheduling me to work at the restaurant and at the train station, I only worked weekends. Time enough at last. I tried to take full advantage of each second still left of English in Leeds.

I'd basically moved to 47 Clarendon Rd. as well. Laura had been through a difficult time because of her father's passing just before the Easter break, so I'd kept her company after that. Generally, after she fell asleep in her room I'd go downstairs to the kitchen in the basement to practise English, i.e. talk, and play games with the other housemates. Besides me, another almost permanent guest in the house was Shay – an Asian descendant native English speaker who enjoyed watching American flicks in his laptop until late night.

Around midnight, after everyone retreated to their rooms I stayed with him, watching the trashiest horror flicks ever just to have a chance to speak to him. We shared the sofa bed and film watched until half 3 a.m., fuelled by the gin and Red Bull he mixed to keep us awake. After that I'd let him go through the back door that led straight to a backstreet between Clarendon Rd. and Kendal Lane, where Shay dwelt.

After five hours sleep I'd rise and shine, have tea with toasts, butter and jam, press the rec button of my recorder, and head straight off to the Language Centre for a 2-hour practice of British intonation and rhythm. Afterwards, I'd go to the level 7 of Edward Boyle, pick a classic horror and watch on an available VCR. Then, I'd go back to Clarendon Rd. near 1 p.m., just in time to munch something and chat with Laura as she readied herself for her 2 p.m. shift at Pumpkin Café. Then, I'd repeat the Language Centre and Edward Boyle routine.

In the frenzy of one of these routes Valeria, the Italian housemate, stopped me by the door.

"Where are you going Jonesy?" Veleria smiled.

"Edward Boyle, are you coming too?"

"Nuh-uh, we're going to Hyde Park this afternoon. Benji didn't tell you? I'll kill him." Valeria said, all smiles, referring to her German boyfriend, Benjamin.

"No. Who's coming?"

"Aida, Maja, Nicola, Svatia, all of us. They're still at Morrisons buying stuff for the barbecue. Wait for me in the kitchen. I'm coming down in a jiffy."

After everyone arrived, we followed to Hyde Park.

The firmament was absolutely blue, the sunny atmosphere was pure gold, the grass was intense green, and everyone was dressed in multicoloured fashion. All those bright colours and all those people at Hyde Park made me wonder: why the hell I spent most of my days alone listening to English recorded that came from dark magnetic reels and watching black and white films. A strong longing for some colour and romance came upon me. So, I took a decision.

In the following days I stopped watching classic horror films and started watching all the modern films with a male gay thematic available at shelves of level 7. I watched around four films a day and I still borrowed DVDs to watch back at the accommodation when Shay wasn't there. Among many rubbish films I was lucky to watch pearls like *Querelle*, *My Beautiful Laundrette*, *Longtime Companion*, *My Own Private Idaho*, *Beefcake*, *Hedwig and the Angry Inch*, and *The Fluffer*.

One afternoon, when it seemed there were no good films left, I stumbled across the only available VHS copy of Nigel Finch's film *Stonewall*. It was the first time I learned about the Stonewall riots.

38

STONEWALL

The western world is familiar with the Village People – the disco group that features a police officer, a cowboy, a Native American, a biker, a construction worker, and a G.I. – and with how their songs and visual style are referential to the pop gay culture. Far less people, however, know that their name refers to NYC's Greenwich Village, a neighbourhood popular among the gay community in the 60's. Greenwich Village is also the place of the famous Stonewall Inn – a gay bar around which the riots that sparked the American gay revolution, known as the Stonewall riots, took place.

If in the 21st Century the western world may often feel lonely and unfair for a homosexual person, the history of pre-Stonewall America tells of worse days. In the post-World War II America, for example, homosexual sex was reported to as sexual perversion and there were Antihomosexual laws to penalise and criminalise whoever transgressed heterosexual conduct. Consensual sex between two adults of the same sex was legally a crime; depending on the State where the law applied, punishment varied from revoking or denial of professional licenses, job dismissal, to imprisonment in a mental institution, shock therapy, castration, or lobotomisation. In NY, individuals would be subject to arrest if caught wearing fewer than 3 items of clothing appropriate to their gender. Psychology classified homosexuality as mental illness, and deviance. Finally, when it comes to religious views over the matter it's easy to complete the picture. In a society as so, saying that homosexuality is natural would be the equivalent to saying that the earth is round in the Middle Ages.

Worse than being condemned by law, science, and religion was living under society's endorsement of these views. Assumed or closeted, homosexuals endured social discrimination and exclusion; some young ones experienced family rejection and were thrown out in the street; others suffered official and unofficial harassment, as police and mafia alike saw gays and lesbians as easy targets for blackmailing and extortion. Pushed down the path of marginality, homosexuals lived in the shadows of society.

Within such murky scenario, the Stonewall Inn days came to bring some light of hope and put men against men, in both the good and the bad way.

39

Much before the Stonewall riots, at the turn of the 20th Century, the section of Greenwich Village where the Stonewall Inn is located already had a history of strong of social identity and a long tradition of bohemian life. A popular gathering place among actors, writers, composers, artists, and other intellectuals, its atmosphere of social open-mindedness appealed to gay men and lesbians who sensed in the Village a non-threatening environment where they could socialise.

The genesis of Stonewall Inn happened amid the Prohibition, when bars weren't allowed to serve alcohol and very modest restaurants, known as *tearooms*, multiplied as an alternative vicinity to socialisation. Among these, one of the more notorious was Bonnie's Stone Wall, a tearoom named after the autobiography of Mary Casal, *The Stone Wall* – a rare example of American literature that depict lesbian love, from 1930. As this tearoom expanded into a full restaurant by the 40's it was renamed as Bonnie's Stonewall Inn and then again Stonewall Inn Restaurant by the 60's, when it already had lost its first characterisation and former notoriety. It was in 1967, after having its interior burnt in a fire incident and remaining sometime empty, that the building of the former Stonewall Inn Restaurant was refurbished by the son of a Mafioso, known as Fat Tony, who transformed it into a gay club that's still famous today as the Stonewall Inn.

In the middle of an oppressive atmosphere against homosexual freedom, the mafia tricked the law and made of the Stonewall Inn a homo-friendly environment. Its clientele mixed the conventional masculine type, businessmen, young camp males, hustlers, transvestites, scare queens or flame queens – specific types of drags from the 60's –, some hippie straight women accompanying their male gay friends – derogatorily named *fag hags* –, and a few lesbians.

At the Stonewall Inn the homosexual community could socialise with the same liberty enjoyed by the conventional hetero folks. What distinguished the Stonewall Inn from the odd gay clubs that remained open at the time was its reasonably large dimension, the jukebox that could be played at the drop of 10c per song, and specially the fact that in there a man could dance with another man without being gruffly threatened to stop or leave the place. The club managed to promote such friendly mood only because the staff maintained a high level of admittance discretion. The Stonewall Inn only admitted customers after they'd been screened in by the doormen through a peephole to avoid the entrance of heteros or undercover police.

In the Stonewall Inn days, police raids on gay bars were frequent. In these raids the police officers would intimidate and harass customers at will, as well as wreck the place if they pleased. Whenever police raids were about to take place bright white lights would be switched on to warn patrons, so they had time to stop dancing together or remove any fashion adornment which could give the police excuse for verbal abuse. The police would also take inducement from the owners to keep the bar off raids or to tell in advance when they were going to strike so the mafia and the customers would be ready to keep a low profile.

The police weren't the only ones to give the Stonewall patrons hell. The owners of the club themselves weren't as considerate to the gay community as one may take them for. After the State Liquor Authority (SLA) controlled the law in a way to make illegal for homosexuals to be served alcohol in bars, private owners were forced to desist their business resulting in the closure of almost the totality of NY gay bars during the 50's. Organized crime then stepped in to take advantage of the situation. Stonewall Inn regulars were constantly pressured to order drinks which were overly priced and watered-down. The main bar staff worked with no running water so before serving the next customer they simply swilled the glasses in a tub filled with the same water for the whole shift. Overflowing toilet pipes, constantly damp bathroom floor, no fire escape exits, and a narrow lobby as the only way out may complete the picture of how the Stonewall Inn meant to the mafia simply a mean of making easy profit from its desperate clientele.

Though all this doom and gloom happened right under the nose of Miss Liberty, her oppressed gay children weren't completely abandoned. Since the 1950's, amid such dreadful atmosphere of ignorance and isolation, resistance started with the initiative of Harry Hay who founded the Mattachine Society in LA. An organisation such as Mattachine offered social recognition to incognito homosexuals and therefore a sense that these individuals weren't alone in the world.

The activities of the Mattachine Society comprised social education, through the means of talking sessions, research group on homosexuality, and strategic political action against legal oppression. The political and intellectual engagement of the founders of Mattachine Society is represented on how they coined the term *homophile* both to characterise the movement and as a noun; replacing *sexual* with the morpheme from the Greek *philos* 'loving' de-emphasised the stigmatised view of sexual obsession that the word *homosexual* incidentally implied. Extra branches of the Mattachine Society were established in Washington and NY.

Following Mattachine example other organisations were founded, including a lesbian organization named Daughters of Bilitis, and the Homophile Youth Movement in Neighbourhoods, which was founded by Mattachine's dissident member Craig Rodwell. Organisations multiplied as new branches were opened and former leaders started their own organisations. Their main actions almost invariably included handing flyers, publishing newsletters and organizing picket lines, and other social activities to attract new members and bring the community together.

In the West Coast, militancy among homosexuals increased considerably more than in the East, mainly in San Francisco, where just the Society for Individual Rights, founded in 1966, had 7 times more members than Mattachine–NY. Over 50 homophile organisations were established in America by the time the Stonewall riots occurred. And the repercussion that the riots had is represented by the number of organizations established 2 years afterwards: 25.000.

When the Stonewall riots broke, other violent reactions had already occurred in the Tenderloin, San Francisco. In a branch of the Compton's, a local chain of restaurant, gay street youths, hustlers, and transvestites were disliked because of their social stigma and dependency on the venue as a hang out. When the new manager discouraged their patronage they resisted the security guards and police coercion with violence and promoted general mayhem.

Stonewall riots development was much more significant historically, however. Rather than an outburst of violent reaction, the Stonewall riots started as a spontaneous demonstration. The first spark was ignited after a police raid at a peak time on a summer Friday late night; the ejected patrons refused to disperse and started forming a crowd outside the Stonewall Inn. Patrons from other bars, nearby residents, tourists, passers, and others keen on the sudden hullabaloo joined the frustrated crowd at Christopher St. where Stonewall was located. Once patrons were liberated from inside the Stonewall Inn some paraded flamboyantly catwalk style, some bowed graciously to the crowd, some gave vogue, and others opened their arms to receive the crowd's warm cheers as if they were famous cinema stars walking over the red carpet.

The police started loading the detainees inside the paddy wagon with growing violence – Mafia members, followed by non-mafia employees, then some regulars. After police clubbed a transvestite and a smashed bull dyke who resisted being shoved into the paddy wagon the crowd's frustration grew into anger and bam!

All hell broke loose.

40

Outside Stonewall Inn, the crowd went from hailing, cheering, clapping, and quipping at police officers, to booing, yelling, catcalling, swishing, shrieking, jeering, swearing, flipping coins at the police officers, and going berserk.

Cornered, the police officers were forced to retreat and barricade themselves inside Stonewall.

From the top of their lungs, the crowd repeatedly shouted 'gay power!' They also called the police 'pigs' and 'dirty coppers' and tried to break through the Stonewall Inn doors. The mobsters rocked the paddy wagon, slashed the tires from police cars, and targeted Stonewall Inn with cobblestones, bricks, bottles, rubbish cans, litter, anything imaginable. Even a parking meter became a battering ram.

After most of the detainees escaped the paddy wagon, when the rage had already taken off to the streets, to the civilian's cars, and other establishments' windows, the Tactical Patrol Force (TPF) came to rescue the officers entrapped inside the Stonewall Inn. The crowd, not cowed by police reinforcement arrival, never dispersed until dawn brought a fresh morning to Christopher St.

The most surreal and sublime event of the Stonewall riots happened when the line formation of TPF faced off a dancing Rocket line of queens; the TPF advanced marching towards them as the queens advanced back, with arms around each other, kicking their legs up, Rockette style, and singing to the *Howdy Doody* tune: *We are the Stonewall Girls! We wear our hair in curls. We wear no underwear. We show our pubic hair. We wear our dungarees. Above our nelly knees...*

The police raid actually had a positive aftermath to a new generation of homosexuals: once forced off the ghetto to Christopher St. they realised the outside world could be as gay as the inside of Stonewall. So, the demonstrations gained a less heated tone throughout the weekend and Wednesday from the following week with the young ones affirming themselves, writing slogans, singing, holding hands, celebrating freedom. At some point, Christopher St. was blocked.

When drivers insisted crossing Christopher St. the protesters targeted their vehicles. The police again used violence, and protesters again used irreverence.

For all their bravery, spontaneity, legitimacy, and campiness, the protesters of Christopher St. made of the Stonewall riots a symbol of homosexuals' resistance. The riots brought the gay community together making the police force to realise they were ready to come out of the shadows in mass and stand up for themselves. The riots also drew attention of the press to the ongoing state of social intolerance and repression in the heart of civilised America.

After Stonewall, the homophile movement celebrated the riots in annual demonstrations called Christopher St. Liberation Day. These demonstrations became the genesis of the modern pride parades. The bravery of those queers, nellies, queens, butches, dykes, gays, lesbians, men, women, Americans who dared to challenge society's ignorance and prejudice carved the way for homosexuals to be proud of themselves.

41

As a 25 year old gay man, with a history of love frustrations and yet to affirm a stable social place in the world, watching Nigel Finch's *Stonewall* gave me a cathartic relief that brought to my lonely heart hope and to my feeble mind strength. I could identify within my heart a similar kind of passion that took gay people to affirm themselves during the Stonewall riots. The pride of affirming myself as a gay person and trying to have a dignified life honoured the pain and the rage of those who fought for their rights before, during, and after the Stonewall riots. Nigel Finch's *Stonewall* also stirred a mix of strong emotions inside of me.

The end of the semester at the University of Leeds, the approaching time to return home, and all that sense of living a colourless life had left me feeling moody, glum, and cranky.

After watching Nigel Finch's *Stonewall*, I borrowed a volume from the history section of Edward Boyle: *Stonewall* by David Carter. I then, went to spend 3 days secluded at the accommodation in North Grange Rd. At the end of that time, after reading most of David Carter's historic account of the Stonewall riots, I waved my closing good-bye to North Grange Rd. and headed to 47 Clarendon Rd. where my remaining days in Leeds should be spend at.

Though I was no longer working in those remaining days, I'd slept very little and was feeling exhausted and emotional.

When I arrived at Clarendon Rd., I met Laura in the kitchen. "What happened fancy pants? I tried to reach you a hundred times. I was going to your house today."

"I'm alright. Just wanted to be by myself. Didn't you get my text message?"

"Of course I did. But how you dared to ignore my calls? Don't do that anymore." Laura sounded upset.

"I wish I had time to do that. I have no more time left in Leeds."

"Oh dear, I know how sad you must be. You clearly love this place." Laura assumed a motherly tone. "But you have a life waiting for you there; and a career."

"That's what I'm sad about. My life here is a bit depressing; but there, all is just so utterly unbearable."

"Don't be so dramatic. Gee." Laura poked fun.

"You say that 'cause when your time here ends, you go straight to the Netherlands."

"Ah, about that: guess who's in the Netherlands?" Laura paused. "Shay! He went there for two weeks just to smoke weed with friends. How fancy is that?"

"Oh, just shoot me." I felt gutted. "My life's already stupid as it is. Now, my English speaking mate's gone."

"Don't be sad. 'Cause you got me baby."

"But you don't speak English with me. Shay does."

"Well, we have our own mother tongue. But forget about that. Listen. I'm off today. Since we're all leaving the house within two weeks, we could get together tonight and go to the Dry Dock to celebrate." – Laura knew just what could cheer me up. She knew I loved the Dry Dock pub because of its picturesque setting: it's situated inside of a canal boat which stands on dry land on a traffic island in Woodhouse Lane. – "So, what do you say…?"

That night was fantastic!

It seemed like the DJ just read my mind. He played the hits I'd fallen in love for throughout that season in Leeds – *What You're Waiting For* by Gwen Stefany, *The Weekend* by Michael Gray, and *Filthy Gorgeous* by Scissor Sisters. I drunk pints of *Früli* and danced my frustrations off. After all the crew from Clarendon Rd. returned to the accommodation, Laura went to bed and so did everyone else.

I decided to stay in the kitchen watching a gay flick in my portable DVD. Around 3 a.m., the Italian housemate, who had dated quite a few girls from the nearby student houses, came down to join me. Pretty much like in those gay films I'd been watching lately, the kitchen gained an erotic atmosphere as the Italian slouched sleazily on the couch and pigmented the opaqueness of my world with all the colours of romance one can think of. After having longed so much in those days, I finally had my romantic adventure.

Around 5 a.m., after dodging a kiss, the Italian basically threatened me to keep my mouth shut about what happened before he left the kitchen.

In the following day, the Italian kept some distance and I, a bit used to that type of gay-straight situation, simply ignored all that. Then, all the following nights, I'd remain watching films in the kitchen and he'd come again until my last night at Clarendon Rd.

When the day to go back home dawned I had my suitcases packed with English language: DVDs, CDs, audio tapes, dictionaries, Cristal's *Encyclopaedia*, Victorian novels, language books, paper selections, magazines, calendars, flyers, leaflets, mini guides, and all the lectures and seminar handouts. I parked those English packed suitcases in the vestibule, as I waited for the private cab to take me to the coach station.

When I least expected the Italian pulled me inside his room, and, behind closed doors, he kissed me passionately. That, I knew, was the kiss of death of that love affair. *Just another day*, I thought.

I'd been very happy with the success of my exchange experience in Leeds, and, pretty much like all my previous experiences, all that happiness seemed to have reached its expiry date. I boarded the coach and left my heart behind in Leeds. Victorian houses, Hyde Park, University of Leeds, Church of Jesus Christ of the Latter-Day Saints, Merrion Centre, Georgetown Restaurant, Railway Station, Upper Crust, clean streets, modern roads, green hills, drunken partygoers, friendly leodensians, supportive tykes, polite Britishers, and English language; I carried all these within my mind.

42

Blimey! The weather must have had decided to inflict the world with some extra burden that morning. Papers gave the population two words: *scorching* and *blazing*. England had become a giant tanning booth.

Official forecast services registered temperatures of 26 degrees. Yes, may be indoors, for those who work in offices and drive air-conditioned cars. In the outside, in the real world, in the streets, in the markets, below the bright mighty sun, that number should round up to 30.

At least the weather services announced that the sea mists would cool down the temperatures in coastal areas. That solved all... for people living in Whitby, Scarborough, Bempton & Flamborough Head, Burton Constable, Holderness & Spurn Head, Grimsby, and other coastal locations. I prayed for the wind to blow that coolness inwards the land because Doncaster was miles from the coast and it was Saturday: day to wash all cars parked outside Unit twenty at Whittington St.

"Aye oop!" Ewan arrived dragging the hosepipe and showing a winner smile on his glowing red sun-kissed face. He'd just been showing off to Clifford, under that piping hot weather, a convertible he'd bought in the auction at Bawtry. "An' 'ow's Jonesy today?"

"I'm alright." I replied, not really much cheerful.

"Good. Let's crack on wi' these ones outside. I hose them down n' y' sponge."

I couldn't share Ewan's enthusiasm that morning. On the way to work I asked Clifford to check my hotmail on his mobile phone and the inbox had an email from my old pal Aristotle.

Jones, I have some news to you! I'm going to be a father, my wife's pregnant about 3 months. I'm thinking on names: if a boy, I want am wondering to call him David Kalel, which means 'David from the Hebrew beloved' and Kalel is based on the Kryptonian name of Superman (Kal-El) which resembles the sound of vessel of God or sent by God. Please, *tell me your opinion. Do you prefer a simple Portuguese name like Jose or Paulo? Anyway, how are you my friend? Any good movies. I found in the internet the complete series of the*

'Twilight Zone' to download in xvid. I'm downloading it to remember those beautiful moments you talked about this astounding anthology tv show series, during our graduation! I'm missing your messages that help me so much, my dear friend. I hope you're O.K. there in U.K. God bless you, and make all your beautiful dreams to come true! From your everlasting friend from the South, Dio!"

Hardly had I finished reading Aristotle's email a lump in my throat strangled me. That email buzzed in my head all morning. I kept thinking on the different turns our life had taken: Aristotle was lawfully married to a partner, had a stable work as a teacher of English, lived in his own house, was about to father a baby, and would download from the internet the entire series of *Twilight Zone*. I was awfully related to a closeted partner, had a clandestine work as a valet, lived in a rented studio flat, wasn't even allowed to own a puppy, and couldn't afford internet connection.

I thought on how, despite all my efforts towards self accomplishment, I'd come to that. No matter how much I tried to control the route of my fortune, once I reached a specific point, it just seemed to execute a mechanical U-turn and bring all my aspirations to a halt.

I'd experienced that torment times before, having to consider how pretentiousness generally lay at the root of my struggles. Although I somewhat developed an awareness that I'd always have to go through burdensome for each goal I set myself to reach, it'd always been impossible to restrain fears and doubts from devouring me from inside until I was left gutless.

Under that scorching summer morning the old record was playing the same melody again and I, again, stubbornly refused to bend my knees. Perhaps the latest incidents tricked me down the garden path entrapping me in an illusory fantasy of success and glory.

That being the case, if Mr M, the masked magician, had a chance to expose the highly guarded secret behind the fast ones that those latest incidents pulled on me he'd reveal, behind some camouflaging curtain, that at the heart of each trick was English. Such tricks however hadn't a remote chance to appear on *Magic's Biggest Secrets Finally Revealed*. So, I had to continue valeting at Whittington Street to discover, once and for all, if there was actually a secret behind those latest incidents and what exactly English language had to do with it. Then, besides the natural qualms that already troubled that quest, there was still Aristotle, who seemed to possess a special talent to bring me down, repeating with that email a feat similar to when we'd just graduated from our English Major.

43

It'd been months after the end of the exchange programme at the University of Leeds, and two weeks I'd had attended the graduation ceremony of Letters. I'd been living in a rented a room at my friend Helen's, a walking distance from the university. It was early evening and I was studying to the entrance exam of a Master's programme in Linguistics offered at the local State University. I'd been reading a copy of part 1 of *The Handbook of Sociolinguistics* for a while, trying to keep my eyelids open, when my mobile rang. *Aristotle*.

"Hi matey-o, I'm calling to tell that the State started recruiting teachers. We should apply together." – Like most recent graduates, Aristotle had been expecting a chance of employment in the State schools. The State seldom recruited teachers for permanent positions and, despite the ludicrous salaries offered, working in a State school meant a stable career for life, health insurance, and a guaranteed pension scheme. The process of recruitment to permanent job is made through the means of a written exam, a curriculum assessment, and then, over a period of 2 years, the successful candidates are officially appointed to their posts. – "The State doesn't pay much, but it's a secure job and we can prepare ourselves together."

For a moment I hesitated. "Oh, eh... Listen, I told you I have something planned. Actually, I'm working on this idea since the exchange programme."

"I know, but that can be just to guarantee. You have a monthly income, economical stability; nothing will stop you to keep working on your idea."

"I know but... I really need to focus. I can't put my thoughts in nothing else other than my idea now."

"Come on matey-o. That's an opportunity. It's a permanent position. You'll have time and peace of mind to try whatever you want later."

"Aristotle, you have to understand one thing – after all the endurance of the exchange programme, the hard work, what I learned in Leeds, the investment, and after all I've gone through to improve my English, I'm not settling for less. I have to follow my path."

Indeed, with two academic terms at the University of Leeds under my belt I had to try something further. Over 10 months of constant touch with English, hadn't endowed me with the native skill that I yearned for – actually, having observed the natural irregularities and peculiarities of native speakers' English led me to a conclusion: native-like proficiency seemed impossible to someone over 20 like me; still, my proficiency advanced light years as to spontaneity and confidence. Not to mention the knowledge on English I'd acquired at the School of English.

After my return from England, just a semester left to graduate, I took advantage of a 3-month strike in the middle of the term to study hard and get good grades. It paid off – my final average score added to 93% of the maximum grade. Everything was set for the next move: apply for a substitute teacher position at the Foreign Languages Department where I'd just graduated from.

Every other term they needed temporary staff to teach *English for Specific Purposes* – a compulsory module across other courses around the campus. The number of permanent teachers was beneath the demand so the head of the department would conduct a selection process consisting of a presentation of a class on a specific topic of English to be assessed by a board of three permanent tutors, and an assessment of the candidates' academic CV. Substitute teacher wasn't my goal exactly but it added greatly to the curriculum of a graduate and generally would be a step to getting a permanent place in a University department. Usually, 2 or 3 places would be available for applicants. As that was my turn to try, that term they only needed one.

And Aristotle knew the competition would be tough. "Well. I wish I had that courage matey-o." He switched to his standard overemphasised compliment – though his tone sounded as he meant, *If you're stupid enough, go for it matey-o.* – And not happy to sow the seeds of discouragement, he added. "But think of this: you're trying for a short-term job. If you change your mind..."

"Ok, but you know me. I'm not changing my mind." I said, certain that all Aristotle could hear was *hee-haw*.

We stretched the talk a little further, and ended up wishing to each other a genuine "Good luck!"

Aristotle's call minded me that failing to classify as a substitute teacher would leave me on a £30 a month wage of my current position as an apprentice English teacher. Until then I'd been financially relieved because my former advisor renewed my research grant for that final semester only. So, that'd better work.

44

I had no option other than stuck to my idea, even with my faith slightly undermined by Aristotle's call. Besides, the entrance examination of the Master's programme in Linguistics would happen a week before the selection to classify a new substitute teacher. So, I had to focus on the entrance examination too because being enrolled as a Master student would count points in the assessment of the candidates' CV during the selection process for the substitute teacher. I couldn't hesitate between two paths.

With that in my mind, I intensified my caffeine intake and followed reading the suggested texts for the entrance examination of the Master.

Success! With that out of the way, I waited for the selection to classify a substitute teacher to be officially launched at the Foreign Languages Department. When it finally happened the topics on English for the class presentation were informed: one of which would be drawn 24hs before the candidates' class presentation.

When the time to draw the topic came, candidates gathered with the judging board. There were 5 of us, amongst whom I only knew 2; one of them particularly had been in the exchange programme in Leeds with me.

We all remained silent as one of judging members spoke. "...We will show that the five topics are being put inside the bag." Each topic was printed on separate strips of paper. "And now, would one candidate come and draw one of the strips...? Thank you."

Another judging member held the strip of paper, so that we could see it: *The cultural implications in the teaching of English language.*

That same member proceeded with the protocol. "In twenty-four hours the first candidate must be here to start the presentation. The number in the application form stands for the order of the presentation. Remember that each presentation must last between forty and fifty minutes and that a formal class plan has to be submitted along with the presentation. So, feel free to go and start equipping yourselves for your class presentation tomorrow. Have a good day."

That instant, my marathon started.

First, I skedaddled to the Central Library to borrow a book that could shed some light on that topic. Once there, breathless, I saw the candidate who'd been to Leeds already coming off the library, loading a dozen books on the backseat of her car. *Fair play*... I just needed to scamper faster. Once in possession of the books, I dashed to meet Mary Ann, a former substitute teacher who was then working at the International Affairs Office – she'd promised to help me with some tips on how to present a class to the judging board. Mary Ann told me to pass later at her apartment and borrow *The How to Be British Collection* that had some comic insights on English use and on British cultural stereotypes. Then I raced to catch a bus to my parents' to get *The Simpsons Around The World in 80 D'Oh's* DVD which featured *The Regina Monologues* episode; in this one, the Simpsons go on holiday to England. From my parents' I caught a bus to Mary Ann's and then another one to my friend Helen's to start working on the presentation and on the formal class plan.

I had no computer but Helen let me to use hers to type things down. It was all set when Helen's house turned into hell house. Helen decided to have a brutal argument with her partner that night and as a sign of protest her partner decided to target me ripping all the power cords of the computer off the plug. I wondered if the other candidates were being as lucky.

It was 12 a.m. I wanted to break down in distress.

Sadly, there was no time to weep about my fortune or to wonder on the absurdity of all that. So, I phoned my former partner William.

"Come over." William was absolutely supportive.

Since he lived on the other side of the city, I called a taxi and went to finish typing everything on his laptop.

Dawn was breaking when I managed to have all prepared. After 2 hours of sleep I went to have the material printed, to get dressed at Helen's, and to put on a pretty face in front of the judging board at 11 a.m.

The core of the presentation consisted in presenting how modal verbs like *can*, *may*, *must*, *will*, and *shall* carried an important function to convey politeness – a feature largely associated to British people. Initially, I presented a general concept of *culture* and how vocabulary in general can be strictly connected to culturally bound topics (like *football*, for instance). After these formalities I started narrowing down the focus and setting up the mood to a lighter tone. I illustrated an awkward situation presenting an email I'd exchanged with an American in which I started with '*cheers mate*' and the American replied '*never call me 'mate' again. I don't like that British gobbely-gook.*' The jocose observation in the American's email drew emphasis to the choice of greetings available to two distinct cultural referents. Then I used lesson 25 of *The How to Be British Collection* to illustrate, with humour, how politeness can make a difference when speakers phrase requests. Lesson 25 has a caricature of a similar situation with 2 different outcomes: 1, a British passer-by is totally oblivious to a man who's drowning and shouting '*Help*'; 2, the same passer-by gently throws a life belt to the drowning man who has rephrased his sentence to "*Excuse me, Sir. I'm terribly sorry to bother you, but I wonder if you would mind helping me a moment, as long as it's no trouble, of course.*"

With the mood set I went on showing specific sequences of *The Simpsons*' *The Regina Monologues*, comparing how modal verbs appeared more frequently in the speech of the British characters when these met with the Simpsons' family members. To conclude the presentation I assigned a preparation: students should form groups, choose one of the British sitcoms I'd brought on DVD to class, and do a similar analysis highlighting features of politeness in the characters' speech so we could discuss them in the next class. The preparation was justified in the fact that, as future teachers, the students should be familiar with observing English in that manner; I still clarified that they'd still have a chance to analyse other sources like emails, news articles, texts, and so on.

With that, I addressed the judging board directly – "May I leave?"

"Yes, please." One of the judges replied in a neutral tone. "Results will be posted within twenty-four hours."

45

In the following morning, barely had I crossed the doors of the Foreign Languages Department, the secretary came and greeted me. "Congratulations! You're the new substitute."

"Thanks." I replied the secretary with a long sigh.

Those words brought me a sense of relief. Being a substitute in the Foreign Languages Department was a major step to a promising career. And it provided me a reasonable wage of nearly £300 a month. From then on, I should complete the Master in Linguistics and later try for a permanent job at any university in the country.

The story of how English shaped my fortune should end here. Weirdly, my inner voice spoke: *Not so soon.*

46

The prospective of getting a permanent teaching job in a university sounded comfortable enough. I'd set aside my ever-present aspirations to write. The risks, struggles, and stresses that I'd gone through until then drained all my heart and focus. And I craved to enjoy life a little whilst still young.

But, rather than calm, the language of the American empire, of merry England, of the promise, English came to my life to bring storm. I realised this during that first term that I assumed the position of substitute, when I introduced my students to the story of English.

As substitute, I was trusted to three groups of *English for Specific Purposes*, aka ESP, and a group of *Basic English Grammar*, aka *English I*. There were 5 meetings with each group per week, combining 20 hs of class instruction – officially, substitute teachers still had to work 20 extra hours outside the classroom. Each ESP group had nearly 50 students and the *English I* group around 25. The ESP students came from varied undergraduate courses and the *English I* students came from the Portuguese Major.

In all groups, the students' English proficiency level was insanely asymmetrical; a few ones had basically no proficiency at all and were hardly familiar with written cognate words, some students were familiar with the Basic English they'd learned from obligatory school subjects of previous levels of education, and other students had had some formal instruction in English in language courses. The teacher, aka I, stayed in the middle toss juggling between the formal basic lessons of the syllabus and trying to maintain the advanced students motivated. Naturally, I more struggled than juggled through the formalities.

As to *English I*, things run fairly smooth. English wasn't the *English I* students' priority, but I managed to guide the contents according to their interest in the topics of linguistics related to English. When it came to ESP, though, the road became a little bumpier.

Specifically in ESP, after applying a questionnaire to survey the students' English educational background, it was my obligation to balance the students' needs and the syllabus. The syllabus was organised in a spiral-bound brochure that students had to purchase. Copies of that brochure were made to match the number of enrolled students and were sold at one of the several kiosks around the campus. If these copies remained unsold, the kiosks' owners would inform the coordinator of the subject (ESP), and the coordinator would talk to the teacher to ensure students purchased the brochure and teacher followed the syllabus. In fact, owners of the kiosks pressured the coordinator since they made copies of the brochure available beforehand to ease students getting them, otherwise students would form long queues whilst waiting for copies to be made. Unsold copies meant loss.

Still, the more proficient students could easily reach good grades in the assessments without purchasing the brochure or even attending classes. Then, the less proficient students saw no real reason why they needed the brochure or to attend classes when they could also reach good grades just by cheating during assessments as they knew that no teacher could have nearly 50 students crammed in a small classroom under effective surveillance. The more honest and interested students didn't take long to follow that lead. On top of this, most students agreed: English offered no real contribution to their course curriculum.

Whilst piles of brochures stacked in the kiosks, students' attendance dropped with each class.

I frankly explained to the students about my obligation to demand compulsory attendance and about the coordinator's pressure regarding the brochure. The students frankly agreed that they could purchase the brochure if attendance was excused. It felt like teaching inside of a huge whistling pressure cooker and still trying to keep the noise down.

Rather than learning English the students needed to learn how English actually related to them both as intellectuals and laypersons. So, after weeks going through the syllabus with little success I set the second assessed assignment so all the students came to class – I used the same approach to all groups of ESP.

Before actually handing the assignment I asked, "Are you aware of why English is a compulsory subject in their course programme?"

Some answered, "English was made compulsory in the course programme by a law." Others answered, "English skills added in all professionals' curriculum." We'd actually already discussed that. Others still reminded, "Second language proficiency is a prerequisite for students at postgraduate programmes." Something also mentioned in previous classes.

Then I insisted. "Does anyone agree that even if removing English from the course curriculum the competitive job market still will exert some pressure on a graduated person to be familiar with some English?" And since the students didn't offer much argument to contest that, I proceeded. "So, I propose that you rate a percentage of the amount of English that you naturally find around you, through your daily affairs; and rate the amount of English that you currently speak actively."

Invariably, the students came to a general agreement: Up to 2%, English was found naturally. And some students could speak English, but generally no one spoke English actively.

So I reminded them: "Think of all the words linked to technology such as *DVD*, *cd*, *PlayStation*, *windows software*, *Word*, the processor, *hard drive*, *pendrive*, *laptop*, *email*, *online*, *chat*, *mouse*, *click*, *X-box*..." After reading a long list from a script, I asked, "Now, consider how many times a day you actively use, or hear someone using, these words." Following a script, I also reminded them of the American pop culture from radio and tv, and of the trendy culture of naming every shop, magazine, product, or brand with English words. Then, I asked, "Could you rate those values again?"

The students came to a new agreement: 4% to 5%, English appeared in their daily affairs. And they really used many English words in their active vocabulary.

Finally I asked, "Can you think of the reason why English exert so much presence in your language?"

Most agreed on the economic influence of the USA.

Following from their answers, I informed them. "Now, you should take careful note of my words, especially proper names and dates, because this class is a preparation for the assessed assignment. This is a presentation of a perspective on why English is present in your course programme and how English may affect you as future graduates."

Then, gripping the script with shaky hands I began.

47

"First, you're right to associate the English influence in the language around us with the American economical power – or influence as you prefer. This English influence is indeed a symptom of an effective process of social dominance that happened in different circumstances to other people throughout history. Just like English is a foreign language to students as you here, English was a foreign language to Native Americans when the Pilgrims fathers landed at Plymouth Rock in New England in sixteen twenty. You should indeed be aware that English itself wasn't the native language of contemporary England until little after the five hundreds."

As I managed to grab the students' attention I went on more confidently. "The origin of English is narrated by a Northumbrian Monk, known as Venerable Bede, in his *Ecclesiastical History of the English Nation* – written in Latin. Bede tells that the Celtic people, the ones who were early inhabitants of Great Britain, suffered constant invasions and attacks in the early decades of the fifth century by the Northern nations, the Scots and Picts. These Celts pleaded aid to the Germanic nations, the Angles, Saxons, and Jutes, who instead of helping decided to dominate Britain. These Germanic invaders established their power and opened a route to bands of immigrants who came and settled bringing along their language. These invaders were indistinctively referred to as Saxons and later as Angles. Thus, the name of the invaders' language was referred to as *Englisc – Angle + isc*. The English of this period is commonly referred to as either *Anglo-Saxon* or *Old English*. In the same way that in the present a profusion of English words entered our language through technology, in the past Latin words entered Old English through religion. The Christian missionaries exerted influence on English through literacy, through the vocabulary related to the Church and its services, theology, learning, and a few others specific subjects linked to the missionaries' universe. Another strong influence came from the Norse language which was pushed into the realm of English along violent Viking raids on Britain from the eighth century and regular settlement of the Danish and Scandinavians."

The students had time to jot down some of that information, whilst I paused to breathe. "However, the English that reaches us through scientific and academic texts isn't exactly the English of this period but an English that had a fierce influence of Norman French."

I interrupted the flow of information for a challenge. "Can any of you think of a reason why French could have exerted a fierce influence on English?"

Some said, "Invasion." Others, "Settlement." And others repeated yet, "Economical influence."

So, I confirmed, "There are elements of all these aspects, following from a battle between England and Normandy for the throne." Then, I continued. "Many authors affirm that at least two thirds of the English vocabulary comes from French. This flow of French into English couldn't have happened smoothly. It followed the ascension of the Duke of Normandy, William the conqueror, to the throne of England. The former king of England was Edward the confessor and had named William the successor to the throne; but when Edward died it was his brother-in-law, Harold Godwineson, Earl of East Anglia, who was crowned. William then came to claim his right to the throne. William has done that in the Battle of Hastings, in one thousand and sixty-six, when he defeated King Harold. After this, England had to wait three hundred years to another English-speaking king ascend the throne. England became a state of Normandy and all the positions of power were occupied by French-speaking nobles. Other historian monk, William of Malmesbury, wrote that no Englishman had remained an Earl or Bishop or Abbot. French became a porter of power and authority. French was the language of government, law, and church. Latin also was used on administration and education. Still, English wasn't swept off England; it remained the language of the people."

"Further, in the very begging of the twelve hundreds, a rivalry between the ruler of Normandy and England, King John, and the king of France, Philip the second, interrupted the harmonic unit shared by these two ocean-split kingdoms. The sense of identity of the English as distinct from the French would reflect on the language. Long story short, English slowly regained status and reaffirmed itself as the language in power."

I paused briefly to allow the students to digest that information. "The English of this period of French dominance is known as Middle English and is strongly marked by French vocabulary. Such strong French influence in the Middle English was bequeathed to the Modern English that reaches the world today. The status of French still shows today as French rooted words are more used in formal situations than Anglo-Saxon ones, which are more frequent in colloquial language. A former tutor of mine presented a quite meaningful image: an animal created and slaughtered by the English living outside the castle would be referred to as *pig*; but in the process of being prepared by the Norman cook, more appropriately the *chef*, and served for the Norman nobles inside the castle, this same animal would be referred to as *pork*. English versus French word pairs like this are abundant in Modern English such as *king* and *royal*, *begin* and *commence*, *doom* and *judgement*, *happiness* and *felicity*, *friendly* and *amicably* and the list goes on. Thus, because French and Portuguese are sister languages, Portuguese speakers like us are able to encounter the amount of cognate words that we so much rely on to understand English. This is even more common in the English that you students are likely to read in your specific area of knowledge because academic texts are written with a more formal and technical language."

To calm down a few students who looked impatient already, I flagged the closing statements. "I will conclude highlighting that such a language influence phenomenon is a symptom of social dominance and imposition that happened in much the same way with your mother tongue. Remember two things: one, the tongue you speak has been brought from a long distance as a result of the European colonial expansion; two, the way you speak is somewhat imposed to each of you by means of standardisation and through formal education. So, whenever you open your mouth, you echo the Portuguese overtaking on the autochthones' dialects that once formed the local language. Therefore, simply by rejecting the formal English instruction in the classroom won't stop English from being part of the local reality. We admitted that up to five percent of English vocabulary already was naturally associated to the tongue you use actively. You here in the classroom are no less in the middle of this ongoing process of English takeover than the Celts were almost two thousand years ago. And as your teacher I am here to make this process, which I hope to have made you aware of, as much pleasurable and beneficial as possible. We're in the middle of an inevitable process of language assimilation, so let's make the best of it."

The students' reaction to that short lecture showed that they'd never thought of English through that angle. I justified that lecture as an essential part of the second assessment. The syllabus of ESP focused on techniques to exploit readers' recognition of information in texts; this involved, among other skills, prediction of word meaning through context and cognates, skimming of texts for instant information retrieval, and being rather familiarised with texts' content – this last one worked well with ESP students since they supposedly knew the background of academic texts from their specific area.

That lecture provided the students with background knowledge for a 2-page complex text in English on the history of Old and Middle English; they had to read this text and answer a 5-question quiz in the next class. To eliminate the chance of cheating there were 20 questions randomly mixed across each quiz. The questions focused on dates and names and students had to highlight the answers in the text. I wanted to show to the students them that they could to locate information in that way; I also wanted to show them that English wasn't as linguistically distant from their own tongue as they thought. More than anything, that lecture hopefully enlightened the students regarding their role as more than formal second language learners but as living individuals in a contemporary story of English.

That appealing lecture should be enough to have the students rushing to purchase the brochure and willing to attend classes. But just to make sure, I informed that every week there'd be a preparatory class, an assessed activity on a subsequent class, and a feedback class. I followed the brochure but ensured that the activities related to students in a more personal level asking them to bring a paragraph of a text from their area of knowledge and applying the activity to their text. I half convinced and half obliged the students to attend classes. They all got the brochure and didn't mention attendance exemption anymore. They made through the assignments without complaining or cheating.

That reminded me of how students wanted meaning and motivation to endure their academic obligations. I'd been there too. And I did what I could to provide them with meaning and motivation with their classroom experience with English. That semester for example, an ESP group of the night course had been allocated to a very small classroom. During hot summer nights, quite a few times, whilst they answered exercises I went outside to the corridor and used a folder as a fan to pump some air into the classroom. Some passers commented on how amusing that was. I thought that was just part of every English learners' challenge. If I'd learned one thing reading on the earlier stories of English, it was that English always ensued from battles and struggles. It hadn't been much different to me since when I seemed to have entered into that story.

Until then, I wasn't fully aware that I'd been caught in the eye of hurricane English. But I was just about to find that out.

48

That early in the morning, the only refreshing tonic at hand was a shower. It hardly purged my fatigue though. It'd been another night awake after a long week of lectures, reading, and working. As usual, I had the radio on, very loud by the way, whilst I showered.

"And now, the news at six: a new report on the Potters Bar train crash suggested it'd been caused by bad maintenance practices dating back from the days of British rail; concern rises as more Polish soldiers are killed in Iraq; scientists stated that a vaccine against cervical cancer will be available in two years; Michael Jackson's defence team gathers to work in Santa Maria and plan to call a list of celebrity witnesses to help back up the singer's denial of sex abuse charges; the crypt of St Peter's in Rome is open to the public so that people are allowed to visit the tomb of the Pope; the UK general elections campaign is running at full steam…"

For a split second, under the water, as my eyes shut, I minded to hurry up to go to work at Leeds station.

Next thing I heard was the sound of magnetic tape tangling around the mechanisms of the cassette player.

"Oh, no," I moaned. "Not the one with *Clare in the Community*."

The morning was complete. As if it wasn't enough that I had to resort to audio tapes and make a mental effort to pretend that I still had a life in England, in the hope that all that role play had an effect on my English, then the audio cassette player refused to play along.

I could always resort to cursing in English. Yet, that morning I'd reached the end of my tether.

It was the end of my first semester as a substitute teacher and as a Master's student. I'd just ended marking the final assignments of *English I*; I'd spent the weekend writing down the marks and attendance frequency of all 4 groups in the official school records. That morning I planned to hand in those records to the secretary of the Department. During the last days I only managed to sleep a few hours per night. And that Monday, there was still a feedback class with the *English I* group at 7 a.m. Then, I'd have my first actual 2 weeks off since long. With over an hour to go, I decided to check my email and surprise, surprise…

To all postgraduate students enrolled in the holiday course on Optimality Theory and Linguistic Variation, Dr Walter Carpenter's classes start early Monday at 8.
I hope to see you all there,
Head of the Postgraduate Programme in Linguistics

I'd entirely forgotten Dr Carpenter's course. After rushing to the shower carrying the portable audiotape player with my favourite comedy in, as I heard the tape tangling during the news recorded at the start of the tape, I felt dispirited. I still tried pulling the cassette off the player carefully but the magnetic tape split inside. So, I simply sat half naked in a sofa and drifted off for a while to try and muster forces to walk to the campus.

That was the onset of a week of interesting events.

49

The Optimality Theory and Linguistic Variation course would last 5 mornings, 8 to 11 with a break. The tutor, Dr Carpenter, was an Associate Professor in the Education Department of Concordia University in Canada.

Despite my tiredness I felt a great excitement with the chance to study with an international tutor. That excitement grew stronger after the feedback class with the *English I* group as I hurried to the room where Dr Carpenter waited for the postgrad students to arrive.

The people enrolled in the holiday course were from different stages within the Postgraduate Programme in Linguistics: people still preparing themselves to officially enrol in the programme, students officially enrolled in the Master's programme like me, and students enrolled in the Doctoral programme, including one who used the Optimality Theory in his thesis.

Dr Carpenter's methodology was nothing like we normally had at the university. He used a web-based course management system called *Moodle* through which the students had been officially enrolled and where PDF articles and PowerPoint class presentations could be accessed by the students – quite similar to Nathan Bodington Building at the University of Leeds, only right there at our State University.

More than tutoring well, Dr Carpenter knew how to keep us students awake in those holiday mornings. During his class, Dr Carpenter would ask a question on the class topic. Whoever managed to answer correctly would be rewarded by Dr Carpenter with a memento from Concordia University. Of course, I coveted each memento, but Dr Carpenter had me really salivating when he explained about the course assessment.

"As you must've seen in the Moodle, to obtain the credits, students of this course need to undertake two assessments. The final assessment is a formal essay that has to be submitted within thirty days after the course ends. The first assessment is a Moodle-based online test that must be compulsorily answered between six p.m. on Wednesday and six p.m. on Thursday." Dr Carpenter paused to allow the students' grumbles to echo within the classroom. "I know. But it's less complicated than it sounds. And there's a sample test that you can try before. But, just so that you have one more reason to undertake the test: the student who gets the higher score will receive this memory stick."

Although I felt utterly weary, when Dr Carpenter showed the memory stick, the promise of such reward stirred my brain cells. "Oh yes, I never had a memory stick. This one's mine." I commented with my former undergrad classmate Renata.

"You wish. We don't stand a chance," mumbled Renata, who now, after much reluctance during the undergraduate course, ended up following my habit of using English to communicate.

"We'll see about that." I used a dismissive tone.

That chance of winning a memory stick turned me on totally. Still, that first morning under Dr Carpenter's tutoring, nothing worked better as an aphrodisiac to me like a casual comment he made during his presentation.

"...en passant, if any student of the programme is willing to study one semester at Concordia University under my supervision, an exchange can be arranged."

Boing! If that was a cartoon my head would turn into a wolf's head and I'd be howling mad.

Dr Carpenter's bid set my insides alight. I craved for another chance to be in touch with real English.

"Dr Carpenter," I declared myself. "I'm more than willing to go."

"Oh good, that's one for now."

Curiously, no other candidate seemed interested. Certainly, no one wanted to spend capital or stop working. I didn't think much about that. I just thought of seizing that chance. I could give notice of my position as substitute, save money, exchange my British Pounds for Canadian Dollars and take off to Concordia.

And to make sure that Dr Carpenter would be willing to accept me, I set myself up to impress him. I just had no idea how I'd possibly impress Dr Carpenter knowing so little on Optimality Theory. Besides, I was busy all afternoon until Wednesday attending another holiday course on Syllable whose tutor was my advisor himself. Well, there were still free nights for me to read the PDF articles available in the Moodle and get prepared to strike on each class.

So, that very Monday night, back at Helen's house, I printed the PDF articles for the next class and, holding a strong cuppa with my right hand and the articles with my left hand, I readily started reading. Minutes later, I dozed off on the sofa. My determination to enhance my knowledge on Optimality Theory was a daily fiasco. I was psyched up through the morning, up and about through the afternoon, and comatose through the night.

I waited until Thursday after Dr Carpenter's penultimate class and went to Helen's to do the online test. Perhaps because of Dr Carpenter's brilliant tuition, or the technical terminology of the OT was entirely in English, or I badly lusted after a memory stick, or I madly yearned for a semester in Concordia and wanted to impress Dr Carpenter, or a massive combo of all these factors, all I know is that I was the only student of the entire group to score a hundred percent in the test.

The memory stick was mine. And with Dr Carpenter properly aware of my intellectual reach, I should start packing to fly to Concordia University!

50

MEERWALD

Thursday night, the 21st of September.

Dr Meerwald came out of the South Shopping theatre where he'd just watched the premiere exhibition of *The Devil Wears Prada*.

"Splendid!" Dr Meerwald repeated in a state of ecstasy. "Simply splendid!" He insisted as he walked alongside his partner to the parking lot, where Dr Meerwald's Land Rover was parked.

Dr Meerwald delighted in feeling the warm breeze blowing gently on the light gray Armani suit he bought just for that occasion. It was worth every penny because advanced screenings of mainstream American films seldom happened in the local theatres – official national releases happened normally on Fridays.

Dr Meerwald managed to acquire two VIP guest tickets from an acquaintance who worked for the entertainment section of a local paper. In the theatre, among the guests were some tv presenters, radio hosts, journalists, columnists, local actors, artists, and a few staff of the State University where he taught.

Dr Meerwald couldn't help noticing that no one was as well dressed as he was. Well, they didn't know any better. Still, dressing Armani for that event wasn't enough. The night wouldn't be complete without a restaurant dinner where Dr Meerwald could extend that moment of bliss by sharing his thoughts on the film with his partner over a bottle of Miolo Merlot Terroir.

"Oh, I really wanted to have watched this film back in July in the States. Imagine that." Dr Meerwald said, a bit oblivious to his partner. He fancied himself praising the film to his colleagues much before they had a chance to watch it. But that was just beyond his possibilities. Especially now, busy as he was as the head of the Postgraduate Programme in Linguistics. At least he felt gratified by his work: all the hard labour did provide him with the distinction he deserved.

At the restaurant, Dr Meerwald gently asked his partner, "Order the wine, will you hun?" And with a twitch of his lips, he added. "I can't stand the smell of these waiters."

Whilst gnawing on a breadstick, Dr Meerwald eagerly scanned the other tables for someone who'd also attended the screening of the film or someone he knew from the campus. If he spotted any acquaintance, he could find an excuse to approach the table and say, "Just been to the premiere of *The Devil Wears Prada*." – He liked pronouncing the film titles in English instead of its translation; he especially delighted in how the *l* and *r* sounds rolled with his tongue and loved even more when his interlocutors cracked an expression of confusion, so he'd translate the title using a rising intonation of surprise and end with "Haven't you heard of it? It's *sooo* New York."

Dr Meerwald was careful to choose a table near the entrance so he could have a better view of arriving guests. Yet, there wasn't anyone known to him that night apart from his partner. And to be honest, his partner didn't seem all interested. "Hun, will you ask the waiter to bring the bill, please?"

That night, he barely slept waiting to go to work early morning. At work, he'd have a chance to tell someone how Meryl Strip was fabulous in the film and that she'd surely win an Oscar for her perfect portrayal of Miranda Priestly. He couldn't avoid feeling a bit upset thinking on how his colleagues of the Classic Languages Department showed little interest in talking about American films.

Most of the staff of Classic Languages Department taught literature and yet they frowned upon tv or commercial cinema; certainly they forgot that literature formed the basis of many tv shows and films. With luck he'd meet someone of the Foreign Languages Department. Over there they were more into pop culture, mainly American and European. That reminded Dr Meerwald that if he ever regretted something it was never having pursued a career in English before he got academically committed to the area of linguistics.

The department where Dr Meerwald worked was crowded with squares. Most of his colleagues of that department were so unambitious and uninspiring. They had a mediocre sense of accomplishment, and were satisfied with where they were. Not that Dr Meerwald cared, mind! Their complacency actually gave him the opportunity to stand out from the crowd and make a difference within the Classic Languages Department. Hard work and adroit strategy made of Dr Meerwald a successful leading presence at that small department.

Frankly, in the film *The Devil Wears Prada* the character of Miranda Priestly, as a successful editor of the fashion magazine *Runway* who had everyone at her feet, could well be homage to himself. Dr Meerwald thought of himself as the Ms Priestly of the academic realm. Yes, just like Miranda Priestly there was nothing on him that didn't scream style. Although the clothes he wore at work were more casual and from national lesser known designers, his accessories made justice to his sense of distinction.

Dr Meerwald only signed cheques and important documents with a silver ballpoint pen from Gucci Accessories Collection; he never went outside without his Dolce & Gabbana sunglasses on; he loved shaking his left forearm, which was wrist cuffed with a flashy D&G watch that he bought at *Saks 5th Avenue* during his unforgettable trip to New York; and during his constant flights to other universities he always paraded carrying a Luis Vuitton leather luggage set with him. Besides, more than just a sense of style, Dr Meerwald also possessed Miranda Priestly's sense of leadership and control. With the genuine dedication he devoted to academic affairs he could make things happen to reach and remain on the top.

51

Just recently Dr Meerwald had developed an essential role in the foundation of a new postgraduate programme at the Classic Languages Department. Actually, he was the main intellect behind the proposals to segregate the already existing programme.

The original postgraduate programme offered courses in the areas of literature and linguistics equally. In the last years however the increasing number of teaching staff being admitted in the programme generated disputes for the limited scholarships offered by the Government. The dissatisfaction was higher among the staff from the area of linguistics because whereas this area grew in demand and importance in the national academic scenario, linguistics tutors remained undervalued considering the number of scholarship available for them. Amongst the most dissatisfied members was Dr Meerwald who, aware of his unmatched academic curriculum in the postgraduate programme and of his importance as the head of the *Circle of Linguistics Studies of the Northeast*, plotted along other tutors to form a representing group and sign a proposal for an independent postgraduate programme. Dr Meerwald triumphant endeavour made him the head of the new Postgraduate Programme in Linguistics by the unanimous vote of his colleagues.

This vital achievement endowed Dr Meerwald with unprecedented influence within the university; from then on, he counted with the compliant loyalty of most staff from both departments who were clever enough to cooperate with whatever project he had in mind.

The academic success that Dr Meerwald benefitted from was hard earned through disciplined work and his ability to deal with numbers. His Master's dissertation was in the area of Quantitative Sociolinguistics and that required him to stay endless hours in front of a pc screen typing on a keyboard nearly half-dozen thousand code strings. Such code strings correspond to each of the multiple utterances of a grammatical or phonetic feature (linguistic unit) in the speech from different speakers – a single analysis may comprehend around a hundred hours of speech. Each string contains letters and numbers corresponding to the speakers' age, level of education, social class, gender, and to where the linguistic unit is contextualised within the word, sentence, or speech. These series of code strings are entered as input data to a software package named *Varbrul* that processes a statistical analysis of the distribution frequency of the alternative forms of a specific grammatical or phonetic feature in the vernacular of a speech community.

Besides teaching Dr Meerwald also researched in the sociolinguistic area and supervised nearly a dozen other researches, including undergraduates' research projects and postgraduates' ongoing research. Dealing with quantitative sociolinguistic research throughout the years made Dr Meerwald assimilate the weight of respect those data and numbers imposed to linguistic analysis. The force of those numbers was also present in his academic work. Dr Meerwald knew that in the academic realm numbers and quantity made a difference in the curriculum of a researcher.

The State Government offered financial incentive awarding scholarships proportionally to the scientific production of tutors and researchers. So, his intellectual efforts were applied into multiplying the number of his academic production and enhancing the excellence of his curriculum. Students, Department, University, and the State profited with the efforts of Dr Meerwald.

So it was with mathematic meticulousness that Dr Meerwald consciously calculated the actions which took him to the top. He'd lived through economic hardship half of his existence and knew the worth of opportunities in life. When success came into consideration there were no half measures. He accurately distinguished the quick from the weak and, knowing that the world never pardoned the unfit, he wasted no time to dispose himself from those who couldn't cope with his rhythm.

"The State doesn't award excuses," Dr Meerwald often repeated. "It awards academic production." As a researcher, he wanted people willing and ready to add to the numbers he aimed at, and share the burden of, academic production. Unwilling students and colleagues equal failure. The moment he estimated someone wasn't eager to cooperate was the moment he turned his back on them. Naturally, on his way to the top, Dr Meerwald learned how to tackle the two-faced, the back-stabbers, and the shine-grubbers – those whose only interest is to nourish themselves from the successful light of others.

The academic realm was a seedy nest of shine-grubbers and Dr Meerwald knew how to bargain with them. One of the most coveted assets within the academic community is the publication of an article in a journal. And since the name *Dr Meerwald* bore great weight in the process of academic publishing he often signed, as co-author, articles produced by researchers and students at the beginning of their careers so everyone profited from that practice. As time passed, he gained more and more influence and as the head of the new postgraduate programme there were no limits to him.

52

In the morning after he'd watched the premiere of *The Devil Wears Prada*, when Dr Meerwald arrived at university and parked in the space reserved for his Land Rover he gave a good look around and saw that no tutors had arrived at the postgraduate headquarters yet.

"Slackers!" He murmured.

Dr Meerwald approached the caretaker for the keys. He opened the postgraduate headquarters' front door and thought on how that Postgraduate Programme in Linguistics was no doubt his master piece. If left to the will of his colleagues they'd still be complaining about in the old postgraduate programme.

Shortly after he sat at the computer desk of the main office, a tutor from the programme entered.

"Oh hello, how are you doing in this beautiful morning?" Dr Meerwald greeted with a smile.

His interlocutor felt lucky to find Dr Meerwald so happy. Yet, she herself didn't share of that same mood. "Morning, I'm a little worried to bother you so early."

"Not at all, is it about the article?" Dr Meerwald knew what she wanted but preferred to continue setting the mood to talk about the premiere.

She tried not to sound so eager. "Yes, the deadline closes tomorrow by 5 p.m. and…"

"Listen, one of the organisers personally assured me the deadline will be extended for another week. So, there's no need to panic. I'll have a look this coming week. Relax… Would you like a strawberry tea?"

"Oh, thank you. I know the routine here is madness, so I really don't want to interrupt anymore. I'm sure this article will add to our programme. I have class at seven now. Have a good morning." The tutor, seeing that two students had just entered the office, made her escape as quickly as she appeared.

This article is a goner, Dr Meerwald thought. "So, what brings you here?" He turned to the students.

"Actually…" One of them spoke hesitantly. "We came to ask about the selection process for student researchers this coming semester."

"That is a matter to the secretary, and she only arrives later." Dr Meerwald answered dryly, without looking at the students, very aware that what they really wanted was to ask if he'd be willing to accept them in the research group.

Grubbers, Dr Meerwald thought. "Will you ask the caretaker to lock the office, please?" He said, already making his way to leave the main office.

Since his class started in minutes, he decided to hang around in the classroom organising a few papers until the students arrived. Instantly a group of girls entered the classroom. Soon after they exchanged "Good morning," Dr Meerwald threw the film topic in the chat as the girls turned their coloured mobiles off.

"Oh my God, I'm dying to see this film." One of the girls said, while they all perched to listen to their tutor's review of the film.

Dr Meerwald left his enthusiasm fill the classroom. He didn't forget to mention the VIP guests, his Armani, and the restaurant dinner with his partner. The girls couldn't stress enough how chic Dr Meerwald was. He was genuinely happy and liked sharing a little of that happiness with them. Other students arrived and, apart from a few shy ones sat at the back of the classroom, they had a shine in their eyes as Dr Meerwald talked.

Dr Meerwald knew just how those students admired him. Indeed, he knew just how every person at that university coveted his academic prestige and the social status that such prestige entails.

That moment, observing the mesmerised expression of his students, Dr Meerwald repeated to himself the words of Meryl Strip, that is, Miranda Priestly in the end of the film: "Everyone wants to be us."

53

Just a month into a new semester, I was on top of the world and loving it. Teaching English as substitute at the Foreign Languages Department and getting great marks at the Postgraduate Programme in Linguistics.

I'd already submitted the essay from the holiday course on Optimality Theory to Dr Carpenter and not long after the feedback flashed in the Moodle.

...your work is excellent. I'd like to see the development of these ideas in a future work – in a PhD thesis or an article for a journal (great potential here). Your work shows you have an excellent knowledge on OTheory, its place in phonology in general, and its use in the linguistic analysis. You have an analysis already!

All final marks were posted in the Moodle; mine was just 1% beneath the highest grade – from a lady who was writing her doctoral thesis. I forwarded the feedback to my advisor and he promptly congratulated me. So far, so good.

Then, I wrote to Dr Carpenter, who was back to Canada, thanking and reminding him I was willing to accept his invitation to go to Concordia University.

Dr Carpenter replied telling that he was happy with that and that he'd have a final word with my advisor.

And that was the last I heard from Dr Carpenter.

54

My essay on *OT* hadn't been perfect as there was a minor note at the end of Dr Carpenter's feedback regarding a sentence which wasn't clear. Still, first in the online test and just second to a Doctorate student. I couldn't have been more qualified than that.

Perhaps, Dr Carpenter wasn't expecting a student to actually accept the challenge. Willy-nilly, the seeds had been sown. The fire to get in touch with real English was burning again. Besides, a semester overseas during the Master's degree would make a difference in my academic curriculum. So, after having the doors of Concordia University smashed on my nose, I set myself to dig another opportunity in a more fertile soil.

At that time, a tutor of the postgraduate programme informed me about the programme called AlBan.

The AlBan awarded scholarships to Latin American students who could choose a Higher Education Institution (HEI) among 17 European Union member states to conduct their Master, Doctorate, or advanced Specialisation training. To be awarded with a postgraduate scholarship from AlBan applicants should first be accepted by one eligible host HEI and should be supported by an eligible HEI in their home country. That meant the applicant should be working in a HEI as a teacher and that the department in which the applicant worked had to agree with the absence of the teacher.

Well, I was teaching in an eligible HEI from Latin America and by the time the next academic year started in Europe the Foreign Languages Department would gladly let me go. The best revelation was that sandwich projects were eligible for AlBan scholarships! That meant that I could do the final phase of my Master's degree in a HEI from Europe.

With everything going for me, I emailed the AlBan office to inform them of my status and plans to apply for the programme. The application process closed by December and I had just over two months to do it.

A few emails later, I was left to choose between either a British or a Dutch university. First, I had to research for tutors whose research interests included quantitative sociolinguistics because my current research project was in this area. There was one tutor at the University of Leeds who I knew; but my academic performance under his tuition didn't favour me. There were still two tutors at Vrije Universiteit – one of them had advised my current advisor during his postdoctoral research in the Netherlands. I took my chance.

The AlBan office staff efficiently put me in contact with a lady named Eva de Bruijne at Vrije Universiteit who informed me that she'd consult if the tutors would be interest to accept the project. A few more emails exchanges and Ms de Bruijne wrote:

I forwarded your message to the right persons within our faculty. With the information you gave us Mr Hinskens and Mr Wetzels would be prepared to be your advisers during your study period in The Netherlands. Herewith you find information on the Linguistics Master that might be interesting. In order to see how the program can be adapted to the courses you have already done in your country.

With the tutors' favourable response I should start preparing myself to Vrije Universiteit!

The next move was to make my advisor aware of that by email. He'd sure be proud. No other student of the postgrad programme would have that courage. I'd be a pioneer student of the Postgraduate Programme in Linguistics and that could open further doors.

Before I took further action, I learned that European

institutions required an official certificate of English proficiency from overseas students – Vrije Universiteit is in the Netherlands, but subjects in the area of linguistics were conducted in English.

The most suitable standard test available was the International English Language Testing System, aka IELTS, to which I applied by mail.

Regarding AlBan, there were application forms to be filled, a research project to be translated into English, and a dozen documents I should begin gathering to meet the application deadlines set by the scholarship programme. The marathon was about to start when I received an email from my own advisor.

I was in touch with Prof. Wetzels and he informed me that he and Mr Hinskens will travel to France next year and so won't be able to accept you.

55

That had to be a nightmare. Or my advisor couldn't find another way to tell me he didn't approve my enterprise. In any case, even with the remote chance of contacting and obtaining a favourable response from a tutor overseas, my advisor would have the final word.

I was a little confused, but strongly suspicious that my advisor wasn't very pleased with my independent academic attitude. Having those plans frustrated dragged me down to earth… momentarily.

There was nothing much to do about that just then. So, I diverted my focus to the IELTS – I'd paid all the application fees and acquired all the pricey didactic material; now I had to go through with it.

Now, the events around the IELTS test can convert any sceptic into believing that some supernatural force should be pulling the strings to make me choose the right path towards English.

56

It all started with IELTS test date.

The IELTS results should be provided with the application form to the programme AlBan: that is, by December. I was informed that the next IELTS test still available would happen in the 25th of November and the results could be informed within 3 weeks.

Just a week before the IELTS test date – 25th of November –, I received an email informing me of a detail that I'd neglected.

There are 2 formats of the IELTS: **General Training** *format is structured for non-academic purposes and applies to prospective immigrants and professionals;* **Academic** *format is structured for academic purposes and applies to prospective higher education students, medical doctors, and nurses. On the application you've ticked* **General Training** *format whereas on the 25th of November* **only the Academic** *will be administered.*

I'd completely ignored that distinction. And yet, I'd actually applied for the right format of the IELTS without realising that.

To make things better, while the General Training format was available every month the Academic format was available every 3 months or less, depending on the demand. So, that little detail was solved by accident. Serendipity! *What are the odds?*

Still, there were two minor complications. One, the IELTS test took place at the British Council office in the neighbour State's capital city (Recife), where I'd been only once before, in the occasion of my flight to England. Two, the IELTS test date clashed with a 4-day linguistic conference I had to participate in yet another capital city distant from Recife at least 4 hours by bus.

But I had all planned beforehand.

I could miss the final day of the conference, take a bus to Recife in the day before the IELTS test, visit the British Council office, and spend the night in a nearby hotel. I'd already invested almost £200 for the IELTS and the specimen exercises material, then, just a little extra spending would make no difference.

All set: the epic IELTS odyssey was about to start.

57

I arrived at the conference site on Tuesday afternoon and stayed in a hostel room with 2 other students.

The bus journey, all the way to the hostel, did last around 7 hours. I'd spent the previous night awake, planning classes for the final week of the semester and putting together the material for my presentation at the conference. During the bus journey, in a state of near-stupor, I made a concentrated effort to revise the specimen exercises for the IELTS.

During my stay at the hostel, at the end of each night – when conference activities had ended –, as my room-mates hit the pillow, I hit the listening exercises using a CD player and a set of headphones that I'd borrowed from the hostel reception. And I wouldn't surrender to exhaustion before going through a few writing exercises until the world fade to black.

During the conference, apart from when I presented my work on the subject of my Master's research, I tried to approach other students who were interested in practicing English. I wouldn't speak Portuguese, unless it was really necessary. That behaviour garnered me the usual spooked looks from some students at the hostel; But I had no time to explain to them what was going on and couldn't care less about what they were thinking.

There were quite a few conference participants who gladly engaged in pleasant chats in English. I let myself get involved in the intellectual mood of the conference without ever losing my focus on the approaching date of the IELTS: the 25th would be on Saturday morning.

According to plan I'd leave the hostel on Friday morning; I'd get to Recife just after noon; then, follow my planned route. On Thursday night, I went to the bus station to buy the ticket for Friday morning but changed my mind: I bought a ticket for Friday night instead. It'd be simple and economic. I could sleep on the overnight journey to Recife and pay a taxi to the British Council.

Things didn't go to plan, however.

58

When I returned from the bus station that Thursday, my hostel room-mates were waiting to moral-bash me about something that had happened in the previous day.

Wednesday afternoon, on the way to the conference I caught sight of a young construction worker who appeared out of the blue across the street and came towards my direction. For some reason in this world he greeted me with over-familiar spontaneity. *Beautiful stranger...* Within seconds the construction worker had my promise that I'd be back to that same spot 4 hours later – time when he'd leave the construction site where he was working at.

I just couldn't take him off my mind that afternoon.

Later, on the agreed time, I found myself in the company of the construction worker at the hostel room.

There was a cocktail at the conference that evening, so none of my room-mates would return at that time.

We had a good conversation, a better time, and all went swell.

Some other students at the hostel had seen me chatting to the construction worker on the balcony of the room and the gossip gained ridiculous proportions. Apparently, to what my room-mates were saying, an air of collective hysteria spread around the hostel. *Tough*!

That Thursday night, my room-mates promised that they'd have a serious talk with my advisor regarding that outrageous incident and, a sign of protest, moved out to another room.

I could spend some time thinking about what had happened, perhaps be ashamed, or perhaps be angry with those room-mates; still, I couldn't see how that would do any good toward the IELTS. So I went down to the reception, borrowed the CD player and took advantage that I had an empty room to go through the listening exercises without the headphones.

When my head hit the pillow that night, my entire body was alight with emotions. I was resolute to leave the hostel at 5 a.m.

59

6 a.m. I was at the ticket counter of the bus station trying to change my ticket for the next departing bus.

"There are seats available on the bus leaving at ten a.m. only." The gentleman behind the counter told me. "Just wait over there and I'll tell you if any passenger cancels a reservation."

"Oh, I'd appreciate it greatly." I thanked, more hopeful than grateful.

"I cannot promise anything though." The ticket clerk emphasised.

What other option? I was going to one of the largest cities in the country, without knowing the place, without a hotel reservation, and carrying a hand luggage. Time was precious.

I stood by the ticket counter for nearly an hour. Just minutes to the departure of the 7 a.m. bus, a passenger rang. I saw the ticket clerk making a motion to me.

"Excuse me. You're lucky." The ticket clerk smiled.

"Oh, thanks so much!" I said as I paid the ticket difference.

Soon as I boarded the bus I bumped into a postgrad classmate named Louis Castor; he'd attended the conference as well and he lived in Recife.

"Hi, aren't you in the wrong bus?" Louis Castor asked, knowing that I didn't live in Recife.

"No. I'm doing the IELTS tomorrow in the British Council."

"You never told me that. I live twenty minutes from the British Council. Are you staying with some friend?"

"No, I'll find a hotel when I get there."

"You'll certainly not. You'll stay with me. I insist."

To avoid further annoyance or embarrassment I explained what had happened at the hostel during the conference and told that I preferred to go to a hotel.

"Listen. What kind of Christian would I be if I forsook you in a moment when others have thrown stones at you? You're coming with me."

Stones, huh? I smiled. But it was no time for jokes.

Luis Castor lodged me at his residence, provided me a good meal, took me in his car to see the British Council office that afternoon, took me to the beach to drink coconut water and talk; later he prayed with me for a tranquil test and for successful results.

At the end of the night, we watched *Willy Wonka and the Chocolate Factory* with his wife and daughter, and in the morning he drove me to the British Council.

Weeks later, the IELTS results arrived by mail. The band score on my IELTS test report form showed an average of 7.0 (good user) which is the band score required by most universities overseas.

60

The evening tinted the light blue firmament with pinkish tones. Yet the clock marked nearly 9 p.m., already a waning daylight still entered through the wedged-open door of the fish and chips shop.

Clifford was queuing to order one large portion of chips and curry sauce for him and one small portion of chips and a fishcake for me. The air was completely still and the vertical grill that toasted the rotating lamb meat on the skewer was doing nothing to alleviate the temperature. Everyone was boiling inside the shop. Still, the men queuing seemed to enjoy that warmth.

I gave in and went outside to breathe some fresh air.

The large sign above the entrance read *Bawtry Fish Bar* 'Traditional Fish & Chips Doner Kebabs.'

Just past a convenience store, across Scot Lane, was the place of *Bawtry Motor Auction* where Clifford and Ewan went to bid on used cars every Friday evening.

We usually took a ride on Ewan's car to Bawtry, but the return journey depended on Clifford's success at the auction.

"So, did you manage to buy one?" I asked Clifford, soon as he came outside with my portion of chips.

"Ah'll try the next; otherwise, we'll go wi' Ewan."

"And if Ewan buys one?"

"If 'e manage to outbid, he's paying t' deposit only. So we can't take the car yet."

I was happy to wait for Ewan to finish his biddings. Friday at *Bawtry Motor Auction* was always a pleasant experience. During the Big Freeze, a large vent on the wall blew warmness and cosiness into the salesroom. But on that summer evening, a combination of weather condition and body heat set the temperature in the salesroom.

After a whole day toiling over (and dancing around) cars, that was my chance to unwind munching on chips and fishcake and, to feed the habit, paying attention to the auctioneers' fast and furious English.

Over a year ago Clifford had taken me for the first time to a motor auction, sited in between the A 63 and the Thorns Farm Approach, called Scottish Motor Auctions (Leeds). In such occasion, amid the rapid succession of sounds from the auctioneer's speech, I could only distinguish one word: "Sold!!!" – And that because it was uttered at the fall of the hammer.

I blamed that language unintelligibility to the noise from the cars' engine and the quality of the sound from the amplifiers. Still, what truly intrigued me was the way how Clifford, and the crowd of bidders in the salesroom, could understand the auctioneer perfectly well and also inform the biddings to the auctioneer using a system of subtle signs to which I was completely blind. I couldn't understand the auctioneer's English and couldn't see the bidders' signs.

I usually sat among other members of the audience on the seats facing the rostrum where the auctioneers stood. Traders and brokers circulated around at the floor level, in between the audience and the rostrum, where the cars crossed through the duration of the sale. The auctioneer remained urging on the bidders from the auction rostrum, moving his head swiftly to the left and then to the right, and back again to the left, and bang!

"Sold!!!"

Lately, by my request, after the shift at Ewan's garage, Clifford brought me along to all motor auctions in Leeds and Doncaster. In the auctions, I sat among the audience, reading a paper, a textbook, or a novel, listening to the dissonance the auctioneers delivered.

Auction after auction, night after night, I began tuning into the frequency of those auctioneers' speech.

Gradually, from a few isolated words I began to understand full sentences, mainly before the bidding started, when the auctioneer formally stated the details of the car, and certified that the car had been examined by the auction engineer, or mentioned any particular defects notified by the seller. Eventually, I understood every word of the auctioneers' speech, including when they specified the various makes and models of cars.

Particularly at Bawtry I enjoyed following the two auctioneers' speech.

"Lot five o six, registration t two o eight k a j, from car people; this is a Rover two hundred s e... hatchback, petrol, manual; mileage shows sixty-seven o fifty. M o teed till August." After presenting the car on sale, one of them started by setting the minimum bid, then verbalising the values of bidders' offer, initially in slower rhythm and stretching the vowel of the first numeral. "...Ooone hundred, eleven hundred, twelve hundred. I've got thirteen hundred pounds. Don't go away." Then, when the value of the bids stopped rising, the auctioneer kept repeating the value of the last bid increasing the rhythm of speech. "Thirteen hundred, thirteen 'undred, thirteen, thir'een..." He moved his head quickly towards two or more bidders at the floor, threatening to bang the hammer.

The auctioneer then turned to the audience, searching for potential bidders and sometimes teased them. "Wakey, wakey, thirteen 'undred, anybody..." Often, to provoke bidders to outbid each other, the auctioneer proposed slightly higher values towards the losing bidder. "Thirteen hundred and fifty, thirteen hundred and twenty-five, I take a tenner..." He insisted until the bidder's battle ceased. Bang. "Sold, outright!"

Just as a result of having tuned into the frequency of the auctioneers' language, I also developed a natural proficiency in recognising the signs the bidders made to the auctioneers. Something inside my brain or my mind seemed to have slowly altered as I became familiarised with the whole system of procedures of the motor auction protocol.

As to that proficiency improvement, and based on my view on the constant development of one's English, I came up with the following idea: perhaps it wasn't the English precisely that became intelligible to me, but actually the routine to which that English related to. Naturally, becoming familiar with the words that each auctioneer uttered frequently helped the process of adjustment.

One curious thing to notice was that the English one of the auctioneers in Bawtry used gave the impression to pulse along the engine of a moving car. At the start of the bidding routine, the slow rhythm and the stretched vowels that he used sounded like he was changing gears from neutral to first. "Heere we goow…" Then first to second. "This car had a lady owner; nice and clean upholstery." Third gear as the bids started. "Giv' us a bid… fourteen hundred bid, fourteen hundred, twenty-five? I've got fourteen twenty-five, four two five, fifty… fourteen and a half, fifteen hundred, fifteen bid." Then, the cadence of the auctioneer's articulation speeded up and reached fifth gear as he approached the maximum bid offer. "Fifteen hundred, fift' hundred, fifteen bid, fift' bid, fift' bi'…" The auctioneer's speech became a sequence of 'f' and 'b' and 'd' sounds, which only reminded the words which identified the last bid. "Fiftbid, f'ftb'd, f'ftb'd, fdb, fdb…" And just like an engine stall, the hammer would come down and bang!

"Sold, to Bodyshop Doncaster." The auctioneer referred to Ewan.

Ewan had finally outbid another bidder from a local garage. As he was an old customer, Ewan paid the deposit and filled the paperwork at the office. He'd collect the registration document, the keys, and the car only on Monday morning.

And just like so, in that hot summer evening, our routine was over at Bawtry.

I followed Clifford and Ewan to the parking lot across High Street, jumped on the back seat of the Vauxhall Omega and Ewan drove towards the A638 through Doncaster Road and Great North Road.

During the journey Clifford and Ewan always talked as I listened quietly. However Clifford had been silent since the morning when we came from Wakefield.

From the deep silence in the car Ewan spoke. "So, Jonesy; tell oos wha' really brough' ye to work with oos at t' garage?"

61

Aw, not this again. Would he ever tire of that?

Ewan came up with that question because earlier on Daniel was hanging around Unit twenty insisting on winding me up by asking "Wher' ye come from, 'ow old ar'you." The first time Daniel had asked that I told him that such information meant nothing to me because thinking about my age would make me age faster and thinking about my nationality would make my English more distant from the local English. But Daniel often repeated the same questions anyway.

Ewan normally joined Dan or, like in that journey from Bawtry, he teased me to begin a chat that could lead me to give away information about my nationality.

Once, I mentioned that ripe mangoes dropped off trees in the summer at my hometown, and afterwards, – Clifford told me – Ewan printed off the net a list of countries where mango trees were cultivated. From then on my chats with Ewan were less personal.

Yet, I didn't want to provoke Ewan's dislike with my constant refusal to give him personal information. So I made an effort to please him with honest answers. "Well, this is something that even I cannot be sure. I could tell you a sequence of facts that led me to seek for a job at the garage. But they wouldn't inform what really brought me to the garage."

"So, tell's t' sequence o' facts..." Ewan always found a way to imitate my intonation and my choice of words when I refused to answer things directly to him, "...that brought you to the garage."

"Ok, I'll tell if you convince me it is worth knowing it." Haggling that question would distract Ewan some extra miles until Doncaster. "Can you tell what brings *you* to the garage?"

"Pay me bills obviously; to make money..." Ewan promptly replied. And before I had a chance to say more he ended, "...n' 'cos I choose t' work on cars."

I did expect an answer as such, and I had another query prepared. "An' what would you do if you hit the jackpot in the lottery?"

Ewan was quick. "I'd go on vacation to a ski resort in Ports du Soleil t' practise my French."

"Ah you see. Your first answer doesn't really inform me what brings you to the garage. I might say that you don't choose to work on cars; you choose to go on vacation instead. I might also say that money cannot be a reason either 'cause you could be doing something else for a living. So you think you know what brings you to the garage but you don't really know it." – Ewan didn't contest. – "But I could tell you perhaps the most genuine reason to what brings *me* to the garage."

"Go on then," Ewan replied with a challenging tone.

"I am at the garage probably for the same reason why you are there: that's the way God wants." I told this knowing that Ewan was a declared atheist.

"Is that your final answer?" Ewan used an odd tone, looking through the rear-view mirror with a naughty smile. "Just admit y' don't wan' to say it as you do."

"I can't tell you something I don't actually believe. I don't believe in other reasons to what brings me to the garage or anywhere else in this world." That was a genuine way to understand it and, so, an honest answer.

"If it's come to this I say that God 'as nowt to do wi' me being at t' garage. Ah'm ther' becos' I made a choice in the past based on financial need. Any other choice would 'ave the same base – *loot*; summat to do wiv *money*, wi' surviving, no' wiv God. That simple. Y' know wha'. Jus' say money brought ye t' work an' I swallow it, Jonesy. We're slaves to money anyway."

That would be Ewan's final remark which, I had to admit, was a good one. Also, I should stay quiet not to annoy Clifford, whose silence prevailed for the rest of the ride to Doncaster.

62

Clifford was worried with the business at his garage. His business was quiet that week.

During the time I'd followed Clifford around, all motor auctions started streaming the auctions live on the Internet. Along this process the bidders who were present at the auction gained a distinguishing name: they became *floor bidders* and were contrasted with *internet bidders*. Although Clifford didn't complain, he was being constantly outbid by the internet bidders in the past weeks. Clifford had to bid on the cheapest cars available and increase their trade value by repairing, refurbishing, and painting them in order to generate enough income to compensate the warehouse rent and continue conducting his business.

Clifford, as a floor bidder, besides having to bid against other floor bidders, still had to outbid too many net bidders who targeted the cheapest cars as well. That increased the price of the cars he targeted. Clifford's disadvantage was also in the way he advertised. More and more traders updated their adverts online in real time as their stock was ready for sale; whereas Clifford still depended on a weekly system of online adverts – if he had a car ready for sale on Friday it wouldn't be advertised online until Monday. That weekly system made Clifford lose sales and, consequently, affected his performance on auctions as he wouldn't have enough money to cover higher bids. Sadly the years of constant toil on the motor trade business promoted modest progress on Clifford's skills with internet resources.

Another reason of concern to Clifford concerned to where I'd continue living. The flat lease at Springfield Mount was reaching its end and we'd discussed recently if I should continue living in Leeds, move to Doncaster, or just return home. Clifford knew that my routine at the garage and auctions left nearly no time for me to focus on my purpose to write which was the main reason I'd decided to stay basically.

Considering all that happened until then I just couldn't surrender myself to difficulties or doubts.

Interestingly, right that morning I felt so sure of myself, waxing cars, dancing around, all sweaty, enjoying a remix of Leo Sayer's *Thunder in My Heart*, and singing along to the words that I could understand. "Am I in too deep or should I swim to the shore, is this the real thing? I hear a thunder in my heart that I just can't control. Should I walk away or follow my soul?"

Then, that silence on the way to Doncaster only made Ewan's question on what had actually brought me to the garage keep echoing inside my thoughts.

63

Ewan was right when he insinuated that 'what brought me to the garage' was a million pound question. Yet he was wrong when he insinuated that I deliberately concealed the answer. If that was simply a multiple-choice question *writing a book* would be just one of the possible right answers. If I phoned a friend, Mr Reasonable perhaps, he'd remind me that pride and pretence held me dreaming of a feat in England. Or perhaps the audience would indicate that I was simply mad and, as a matter of fact, they could be correct.

Ultimately, what had brought me to the garage was a strong need, call it material, call it spiritual, to pursue a passion for – and to be in touch with – English.

A question remained: where to that passion could lead me to?

If curiosity killed the cat, so, meow!

It was such feline curiosity that gave me the impulse to return to England a second time; mainly after the events surrounding the IELTS that left me thinking if I should ever mistrust my impulses regarding English.

Until then, I'd been successful in my aspirations to do with English; a corresponded passion, it seemed.

Still, my final decision to embark on a flight to England only happened after another stimulating event.

64

At the start of the new academic year, my advisor called me to the postgraduate office to talk about the progress of my Master's dissertation. By then, I'd completed the course credits and still had a year to write it; but I was only halfway through the process of codifying 6 thousand language occurrences, aka *tokens*.

I planned to complete the dissertation by September so it'd be ready to be formally presented to a judging board at some point after that. There was a reason why I wanted it done by September: the circumstances in which two opportunities to study abroad were snatched off my hands just made me more determined to attempt another prospect, and I had one in sight for September.

I'd been enrolled in a new undergraduate major, and this entitled me to take another chance in the exchange programme offered by the I.A. Office team. It was the only option left, and so, I applied to the University of Leeds a second time. The band score on my IELTS report exempted me from further proficiency test; all I had to do was to submit my new undergraduate average score for the I.A. Office team. The places available at the University of Leeds hadn't been confirmed so far, but chances were positive. Fortune favoured me, at last.

But my advisor had sniffed around my good fortune.

"...Hi, just take a seat for a sec, please." My advisor said whilst he ended a phone conversation. "So, how are you in this beautiful morning?"

"Busy, busy. Just came from a class now."

"Excellent, let's get to business, shall we? I've had a look through the data you're working on and... I'm thinking that you have to do a slight change of focus in the object of study."

"Wha... what change?" I was caught by surprise.

"Instead of focusing on the preceding palatal consonants and glides like you're doing now, you should include all the set of vowel sounds to observe how they function as triggers of the phonetic process."

Oh, the bitch had to be tripping! That *slight* change of focus that my adviser referred to essentially entailed going through 60 hours of transcribed interview again, selecting around further 6 thousand different tokens in which the linguistic feature under focus occurred, typing new code strings to each of the new tokens, and re-listening to good part of the 60 hours of audiotape interview to discriminate which phonetic variant the speaker had uttered.

Why, after a full year, he wanted a change of focus?

"Eh, I don't think so because the current focus already reveals original data," I tried to protest without using a defiant tone. "And no other current study in the country has addressed this phenomenon the way I'm doing. So, to be honest…"

Before I could go any further my advisor stood from his ergonomic chair projecting himself 3 meters above my sight level. "Listen," He raised his voice. "I'm not here wasting my time. I called you to give an informed direction, and you come with this attitude as if I didn't know what I'm saying."

"No. I do trust your judgement. But I know for sure that the current focus is authentic of a linguistic study. We didn't even have a proper look at the data. And this change of focus is basically another study."

"You know what…" My advisor began huffing and puffing. "If you're not ready to accept your academic responsibility, you should consider finding another advisor. Or else, see yourself disconnect of this postgraduate programme immediately…"

As usual, my advisor spurt his words loudly enough so that the office secretary and the tutors in the adjacent office could listen to his little spectacle. I'd seen him re-enacting that scene with at least three other students and having them cut off from the linguistics laboratory.

But my advisor's thespian act wasn't new to me. Just as he began putting on his diva show, I recalled my smile coaching drills at Upper Crust in Leeds Station, and opened a gentle smile.

65

Just before I classified as substitute teacher, I had a revealing conversation with Ms Miles, who'd been promoted from secretary of CLSN to secretary of the new Postgraduate Programme in Linguistics.

After my graduation in the course of Letters, my student researcher scholarship had to be passed on. At the time, Ms Miles casually asked me how I intended to support myself economically without the scholarship. Ms Miles' interest was thinly disguised as a concern with my economic prospective; her real goal was to offer me an unofficial job as her assistant in the new postgraduate programme. Of course, Ms Miles was just following instructions from my advisor, who apparently assumed that all I could do after my graduation was to carry out routine tasks in an office.

I turned Ms Miles' offer down, not telling her about my plans to apply for the place as a substitute position. Since my advisor was used to having control over every person around him, when I classified as substitute teacher at the Foreign Languages Department, he began to realise that he was losing his grip to control over my academic ventures. And he wasn't happy with that.

So, after he learned that I'd applied for the exchange programme again, since he couldn't interfere with that directly, he found a way of turning things a little less easy for me: by demanding that *slight* change of focus in the object of study of my dissertation.

In the second that my advisor began his hissy fit at the postgraduate office, I had a full glimpse of a much less subtle display of his obsession with my autonomy. And as I beheld my convulsive advisor losing control of himself, I smiled as if I was about to serve him a skinny cappuccino topped with creamy froth, chocolate sprinkles, and a spoonful of the sweetest sugar.

"Professor," I started with a soothing tone. "You know well I recognise your authority as one of the best linguists of this country, and regardless, I trust your judgement as my advisor. If you say this is what should be done, I'll do just that. We don't need to go through a row." With those words I managed to take the steer of whatever my advisor tried to control at that moment.

Though my advisor had no more argument to justify disconnecting me from the postgraduate programme, he looked at me amid shivering spasms and said in a defying tone: "You should try something more in your area…" – By that he referred to English – "…Perhaps a postgraduate course in a British university." By saying that he grabbed his bag, hitched it higher up on his shoulder, and strutted off the office.

66

What a she-devil! If not for his academic titles my advisor would've made a career out of his sharp tongue alone. He knew that enrolling in a British postgraduate programme was indeed a major ambition of mine; and he knew just how beyond the bounds of the possible such deed was for someone like me.

Yet, my advisor wasn't the first person who doubted me to achieve something; and he wouldn't be the last. It didn't take long until a less personal challenge inflamed even more my will to return to Leeds. It happened just after my advisor's spectacle in the postgraduate office, whilst I waited in between classes at the tutors' lounge in the Foreign Languages Department.

"Oh hello there; how're things going?" Dr Austen greeted me, whilst taking a seat opposite to me.

"All's going well. Busy as usual."

"Listen. I actually wanted to tell you how surprised I

am to hear that you applied to the exchange programme again." Dr Austen sounded intrigued.

As member of the assessment team of the I.A. Office, Dr Austen probably wanted to know my reasons to return to the University of Leeds for the second time.

"Yes, I... think that going to the University of Leeds will improve my knowledge on English further. I sure need that. And honestly, once I end the Master's course here, being already in Leeds will increase my chances to contact tutors over there and try for a Doctorate."

When I finished saying those words with my natural enthusiasm, Dr Austen remained silent, staring at me as if questioning my sanity. For a split second, it felt like she was about to stand with her jaw hanging open, point to me, and emit a piercing shrill. I still hadn't grown accustomed to that well-known stare.

Without question, it wasn't the safest way; but what other chances I had to pursue a Doctorate in England? I'd waited 25 years for a contact with English overseas, and, then, had been nearly 2 years without speaking English in a non-pedagogic setting. In fact, I still had a safe and formal option to try a Doctorate England: first, I had to get a permanent job in a State University, then teach during a 2-year probation period, then wait in a list with other teachers willing to be excused from work to pursue their own postgraduate degrees either abroad or within the country, to finally have my chance. Until there, my spirit of adventure could be tired and my English could be as dead as a dodo. No can do, Madam.

Of course, Dr Austen had no reason to see things my way. Her reaction didn't stem from jealousy either. But her stare pillaged my self-esteem harder than my advisor's bitching words; and it made my guts recoil.

Perhaps noticing my dread, Dr Austen made up for our awkward silence with a change of topic.

67

Months passed. The places at the University of Leeds hadn't been confirmed yet. I had what felt like forever to ponder the pros and cons of returning to Leeds.

Initially, being coerced to accept my advisor's terms left me struggling to write the dissertation within my schedule; returning to Leeds before completing it would leave me dependent on my advisor's will to keep advising me via email. *As if*.

Then, came my father, asking where was my head at to play with my future like that. *Papa, give me a break*.

Even my former partner William urged me to finish the dissertation by any means and get a permanent job or else he wouldn't help me if I got in trouble. *Boohoo*.

And finally, some tutors of the Foreign Languages Department wasted no time to begin backstabbing me. *Oh, sod them all*.

When the places available at the University of Leeds were confirmed, I quit my substitute teaching job, and packed the suitcases.

68

The memory of those days filled my thoughts as Clifford kept introspect on the road from Doncaster to Leeds. The feelings of doubt and hesitation of yore came back to haunt me right there at the murky A1.

I sought to exorcise my fears by recalling each event that likewise strengthened my faith and conviction on the decision to return to England: when I obtained my scholarship, when I found free cable, when I passed in the I.A. English test, when the Jobcentre assistant took me to Georgetown restaurant, when I classified as a substitute teacher, and when I made the IELTS test.

All that had pointed to one direction and I hadn't been let down to follow that path. Still, seeing Clifford so concerned made that faith and conviction wane. Clifford was struggling with his car trade business and I was struggling with my writing business. If there was a way to turn that situation around I fully failed to see it.

The situation that I found myself into (and so did Clifford, apparently) recalled some ideas I had whilst watching the film *Quest for Fire*, 2 months earlier, in a special 80's exhibition at the National Media Museum.

Quest for Fire is based on a Belgium novel of 1911. It tells a story set on the Palaeolithic Age depicting fire as an extremely precious element to the Neanderthals who possess no knowledge of firemaking techniques. As fire is a basic element for these primitives' survival, as a source of warmth and protection against wild beasts, it is coveted by tribes that don't possess it and promote assaults on the tribes that keep a source of fire. In the film, 3 Neanderthals from a tribe that had their fire stolen go on a long dangerous journey in search for fire and come across an advanced tribe who knows the hand drill technique to make fire; when they behold fire being crafted they become amazed in disbelief. The 3 Neanderthals depicted in the film uses a great amount of strength to go on a journey searching for fire because they have no science of how to make and control fire.

What I took from *Quest for Fire* was that human's burdens result mostly from a similar kind of ignorance. Clifford's main source of struggle came from his lack of skills with internet resources that clearly were used to other car traders' advantage. But human's burdens had to do with more than just that. The burdens don't stem from the ignorance of how to control a technology but from the ignorance of the nature of the technology. If the primitive humans of the film understood the nature of the fire they'd know a mean to replicate fire.

This idea may apply to Ewan's remark on work that 'we're all slaves to money.' What Ewan said earlier on could be rephrased to 'we're all slaves to our ignorance of how to make and control money.' I believed that, ultimately, there must be a way – a technique – to create and control all aspects of reality in this world; something to do with how we understand the nature of reality in this world itself, something within the mind, something within the heart, something within. Something everyone intuitively understands in different measures and associates to different elements.

To the Neanderthals in *Quest*... controlling fire was a mean to control their reality. Presently, money can be a mean to control one's reality. Yet, thinking carefully, money is an incidental element as a mean of control. To comedians, humour is a mean to control their reality; the money comedians earn is incidental to how well they control humour to audiences. To someone with health issues, it's a doctors' science on medicine that can bring healing; money paid to a doctor is incidental to the process. In my case, I believed that creating and controlling all aspects of the reality around me should be linked to English; hence, English was my element.

Alas, until then I still struggled on my own quest for English and struggled to understand how to control and improve that situation around me. And to complete I'd begun struggling to understand Clifford.

When we neared Leeds I tried to get a chat started.

"Clifford... I've never seen you so quiet." I said, a little afraid to anger him.

"Just knackered..." Clifford sighed those words.

Oh God, *just knackered*, no subject pronoun, no copula *be*, no one to sleep with me, no internet. Oh no... nother lonely night at flat 7, 6 Springfield Mount.

Part Three

1

The hall was immersed in silence and darkness. It was late night. I had to grope around to find the doorknob.

As I scrabbled for the light switch on the wall, I recalled the general mood at the Foreign Languages Department before I quit my job as substitute teacher.

Some permanent tutors were all excited because new language-specific modules would be introduced in the undergraduate curriculum, starting from the following semester. In the English Major the new subjects included Translation Studies (in English), Semantics (of English Language), Pragmatics (of English Language), History of English, Anglo-American Culture, and others. In the last meeting that I attended, the tutors discussed the prospect of the new modules and considered the discrepancies regarding the students' skills in English. Claire, for instance, a permanent tutor who'd just returned from Sweden, where she finished a Postdoctoral degree in Linguistics, had keenly prepared herself to make basic English lessons a thing of the past and start exploring up to date research studies on English in her classes; yet, she stumbled on the usual scenario of students with distinct backgrounds of education in English – half with elementary skills half with advanced skills. The tutors spent hours in the tutor's lounge deliberating if a more advanced syllabus should be implemented in the assumption that least proficient students would make an effort to cope with it, if the traditional workbooks' syllabus should be followed to favour the least proficient students, or if two distinct syllabi should be devised to attend the needs of a split group. Each solution had its pitfalls when the standards of assessment came into consideration. Although those meetings led to questions rather than answers what was latent about the discussions was that the official syllabus of the English-specific modules, which was based around the contents of grammar books and workbooks, lagged behind the tutors' growing awareness of English as a living language and not as a set of restrictive norms. Even Mr Harrison, who never took part in those department meetings, seemed to have been affected by that new awareness – weeks before I left the department I attended one of his classes and, among other examples, he mentioned that whereas English folks would say '*the car needs washing*' the Scottish equivalent was '*the car needs washed*.' That was a start. Still, Mr Harrison's newest mote was "English is all about collocation; if you don't know which words collocate with another exactly you cannot speak English." Old habits... That growing awareness was the outcome of a new wave of permanent tutors being recruited by the State right after I went to Leeds in 2004. Recently recruited tutors came from the Southern States, where postgraduate programmes in English are more in tune with the latest developments of linguistic research on English as a foreign language.

For a brief while, recollecting those events reassured me that I'd taken the right step investing the savings of my substitute teacher income in a second exchange programme; in the worst scenario, if I failed to find a chance to do a Doctorate, I'd still finish my Master in Linguistics and add modules of the University of Leeds to my curriculum. Permanent jobs at State universities back home were rather disputed and required applicants with flashy curriculum and excellent knowledge of English. Surely, being back at the School of English could improve my knowledge of English and prepare me better for a permanent job in a State university.

"Yes...!" I reassured myself, exhaling a drowsiness-charged puff of carbon dioxide from my lungs as the tip of my fingers flipped the switch on. "I'm finally here."

The light cast out all shadows from inside room 2, White Lodge.

2

Room 2 was filled with the distinctive crisp scent of fresh paint of a refurbished student accommodation.

The curtains had been drawn open. The brisk cold air passed through the panes of glass of a large sashed bay window forming a thin layer of condensation that blurred the already dim moonlit view of the hedges surrounding the gravelled area in front of the residence. Room 2 was spacious, with hardwood flooring only half carpeted, and furnished with wardrobe, bed, chest of drawers, and a large oak desk facing the window.

"So, this is the beautiful White Lodge." I talked to myself, recalling the online brochure description and the time I first heard of it when I was still back home.

"...It's really beautiful," A lady informed me by the phone. "It's the most economical alternative among the smaller residences at the Accommodation Office."

"How much exactly?"

"Two thousand, three hundred and fifty pounds." She sounded like she was telling me the price of a latte.

"That's almost twice more than my old shared room at North Grange Road!"

"Well, it's really a bargain luv, 'cos that's a single."

Just the memory of that itself could have brought water to my eyes. Still, the real first tear-jerker moment that first night happened after I plugged the radio into the electrical outlet and turned the dial to *BBC Radio 4*.

After over 2 years listening to repeated news and shows recorded in cassette tapes, listening to the clean, lilting, soft, sweet sound of real time English in live radio sent chills down my spine that left me weak in the knees – perhaps a symptom of a 6-hour coach journey to Leeds or, rather, the effect that the sound waves of genuine English had to make me feel in 7th heaven.

Heart pounding, I threw myself on the orthopaedic mattress inebriated by those sounds wishing that instant lasted forever. No fear, doubt, regret, or remorse had a chance to surface like in that first night at North Grange Rd. Such feelings had been deservedly consigned to oblivion in the M1 through the journey from Victoria Station in London to National Express Station in Leeds.

Being back to Leeds had left me numb with pleasure to that instant. After collecting the house keys at the University Security Office at Woodhouse Lane – as all late night comers do –, and having searched the White Lodge for nearly an hour going up and down North Hill Rd. and circling around James Baillie Park dragging a suitcase and a hand luggage in the cold air of the night, being safe and sound inside what were to be my lair for the next 11 months just made me feel home and happy.

The steel radiator had been on, so the warmth in the room slowly brought my body temperature up as I lied quietly with the lights on.

A soothing light music started playing on the radio.

"...*Sailing By*... And now the Shipping Forecast issued by the Met Office, on behalf of the Maritime and the Coastguard Agency at double o one five on..." The hypnotic rhythm of those words finally knocked me out that night at White Lodge.

3

When I came to, daylight had broken into the room.

"The weather forecast... Northern England, a mild day with scattered clouds, occasional rain showers early morning, and sunny spells throughout most of the afternoon; mean temp of twelve degrees Celsius, fifty-three point six Fahrenheit, with highs of sixteen…"

Hearing of a good weather day and understanding clearly all words of the forecast made me rise and shine with a bright smile. *Time to explore the ground floor.*

Just a couple of steps apart, room 3 stood opposite to room 2. In between these, to the right, was the bathroom, which had a toilet and shower. *Good.* I could sneak to the shower and put on a fresh mug with little chance of being seen with a flushed out morning look.

Refreshed, I grabbed the portable radio, a box of PG Tips and a can of evaporated milk – the last 2 bought at Heathrow – and went left across the hall to the kitchen. I gazed around: large table, fridge, freezer, oven, sinks, washer, microwave, toaster, and my fave, the kettle.

I plugged the radio on, put the kettle on, and brewed the first pyramid tea bag of which I hoped to be the first of many breakfasts to come. Browsing through the radio stations I tuned in *The Chris Moyles Show*.

Similar to the weather forecast it was easy to understand the presenters' English; still, the topics they talked on – celebrity gossips and last night tv shows – escaped my knowledge. It just wasn't part of my world.

Sean Kingston's *Beautiful Girls* started playing. Back home that song never struck me as anything to be keen about, yet then, it sounded as a perfect soundtrack to that student house setting; it minded me the type of music Shay used to enjoy back in 47 Clarendon Rd.

I feel so young! In that upbeat mood, as I fiddled with the radio dial, I went through a mental 'to do' list: *contact Shay, sign the accommodation contract, enrol at the School of English, explore the old Leeds, apply to my old post at Upper Crust.*

After ending my breakfast, I unplugged the radio, and off I went to face a different kind of music.

4

Under broad daylight it was easy to see why finding the White Lodge could be deemed a mission impossible to newcomers.

It is sited behind the end of both North Hill Rd. and Cumberland Rd. – yet none of these roads lead directly to it – and is surrounded by other houses' backyard. The main pathway that leads to White Lodge is located at the very end of North Hill Rd. between the last house on the left and the parking area in front of James Baillie Park. And to really challenge newcomers, the pathway is camouflaged by a row of tall leafy trees that basically makes it invisible. No signs indicated the existence of houses situated beyond that area. Even if it sounds like a fictional site amid a real scenario, this house is real.

North Hill Rd. is parallel to North Grange Rd., just further down Headingley Lane towards the University. After trekking down North Hill Rd., I followed the old route to the University of Leeds: Ashwood Villas, Cumberland Rd., Grosvenor Rd., the same old signs emblazoned with *Sam Widges* and *Cellar Vie*, Regent Park Av. – some shops on the left had changed –, Hyde Park Corner pub, Woodhouse Lane, Robovideo was still there (with the same range of 3 gay erotic films), Hyde Park, still with its majestic paradisiacal green, the Victorian buildings, Queen Victoria on her pedestal, The Library, The Eldon, St. Mark's Street, the Quakers Meeting House, and finally, the Parkinson Building with its Clock Tower reaching the sky.

It was just past 9 a.m. The hubbub at the Parkinson Building steps hadn't started yet. I'd walked there along a wave of students and we were all going straight to the main entrance. This time, it was like a live *Total Wipeout* course set within the University of Leeds.

The qualifier involved dashing through the Christian tent pitched opposite the Union building to get some refreshments with biscuits, then paying the £200 deposit at Accommodation Office, signing the contract, setting up a direct debit fee payment of 8 instalments at the NatWest branch across Woodhouse Lane, and swinging from there to the International Student Office just to have some hot drinks and the cakes they offered. The registration and module enrolment was a sweeper, consisting of 20 min. queuing at the School of English where the study abroad officer, Mr Burkhard Hauder, checked with each student that the modules had been suitably chosen online and stamped the enrolment document. From there, we students played dizzy dummies sprinting through the Red Route to the E. C. Stoner Building just to get another stamp from the Accounts Receivable Office to qualify for the next round. In the final course, way less tough than the real *Wipeout Zone*, we had to rush to the Sports Hall, stand on a queue for a few minutes, and have our digital photo shot printed in the student card.

This time, amid other necessary queues and proceedings, I finished the whole process by Thursday. I'd eaten at the Christian tent, at the International Office, at the Emmanuel Centre in an international students' meeting, and bought vital ratio at the Union Building. Lectures would start on Monday, so Friday was the day to rediscover the city centre and get myself sorted at the train station: I'd apply to a job at Upper Crust, hoping they had a position available.

4

Friday morning, whilst I snoozed a little longer under the covers, the radio started playing *Grace Kelly* by Mika. That song – something like nothing I'd heard before and that I mistook for Freddie Mercury – made me jump from bed with so much joy and will to live that I tap-danced my way to the shower and to the kitchen. There, I literally bumped into Nicole – the Austrian housemate who I'd met that week.

"Morrrning!" Nicole held firm to her plate, after I almost hit her with the door as I entered the kitchen. "Are we in a dancing mood today?"

"More like stumbling mood. Sorry. And you?"

"Bit tirrred. Damien kept up till late yesterrrday." Nicole referred to the English lad from room 1, who was her boyfriend.

"Hum… Are we in a loving mood today?"

"Not really. We stayed up organising the barbecue for today."

"Till late? Romantic barbecue, I see…"

"No. We bought everything over the internet."

"That's new. They sell food like that now?"

"Amazing right? So, I've texted Ummer already." Nicole referred to the Pakistan lad from room 3. "And I'll tell the girls upstairs. I see you around five, right?"

Holding the door for Nicole, I answered. "Aye, aye. I'll be here."

What a great first week! Weather was perfect. No worries with money. I knew where to buy low-priced food and where to find a job. That morning I went to Leeds Station and met my former manager Antonio, who told me to assume my old job the next day.

On the way back I bought 2 packs of audio tapes at the pound shop underneath Leeds Shopping Plaza at Albion St. Then, up the road at the Merrion Centre, after admiring *The Flying Machine* for a while I made my first trip to Morrisons and loaded a carrier bag with the stuff I'd craved so much during those long years away from England: Thai sweet chilli Sensations crisps, raspberry donuts, Morrisons double chocolate cookies, muffins, bread, strawberry jam, Irish butter, scones, sparkling peach flavoured water, Robinsons barley water, banana flavoured milk. I put on at least 2 kilos that weekend.

The initial two weeks at the School of English were easy-going. I was enrolled in 2 modules, *20th-Century Fiction in English* and *Foundations of Language Study*, and was keen to have lessons on English in a British university setting again. I started updating my DVD collection, ordering recent releases of my favourite American sitcoms and introducing to that collection the Radio 4 comedies newly released in CDs. And as *Radio 4* had new comedies on the audiotaping rage was back.

That mad atmosphere of nostalgia was complete when an old housemate from Clarendon Rd. phoned. "Hello Jonesy. It's Valle."

"Hello Valeria. How you doin'?"

"I'm great. I got your email. Listen, me and Ben are coming to Leeds this weekend."

"Oh my, I'm so happy. Where are you now?"

"Warwick, two hours south from Leeds; we're doing a Master's course at Warwick University."

"Ah yes, I remember. So, I'm waiting."

"Perfect, I'll text when we get there…"

That 3rd weekend, Valle and Ben came as promised. We went to the Dry Dock and to the Corn Exchange to take pictures. Before they left to Warwick we called at Shay's place and learned that he'd moved to London.

Into the 4th week nostalgia found no slot in the tight schedule of lecture attendance and seminar preparations that the university compelled to all students' routine. At White Lodge, housemates became shadows that moved swiftly through the hall to meet their academic obligations. We met in the kitchen only casually and quickly enough to exchange a few sighs of exhaustion.

I worked a couple of 7-hour shifts on weekends. With a little sleep deprivation I could keep up with the seminar preparations and the compulsory readings from *20th-Century Fiction in English*, whose tutor was Dr Clare Barker. Essay 1 of this module was scheduled to the end of October; from 8 questions, one dealt with 'representations of *home* and *abroad* in James Joyce's *Dubliners*' and was formulated around the quotation "*But real adventures, I reflected, do not happen to people who remain at home: they must be sought abroad*" from the short story *An Encounter*. Naturally, I threw myself wholeheartedly into that assignment. In this essay I considered how some short stories from *Dubliners* depicted characters stranded between home (Ireland), facing a life of obligation, lack of perspective, and immobility, or paralysis, and abroad (away from Ireland), facing a life of adventure, opportunity, and liberty. Dr Barker's corrections on the essay underlined a few typos, some phrasing mistakes, and a few formal and argumentative flaws. But she also emphasised her appreciation with the essay and marked it with a good grade.

All things considered, it'd been a good beginning.

Following the essay submission I even treated myself with a visit to the National Media Museum to watch, for the first time in life, a film in IMAX 3D – *Space Station 3D*. There, I still watched some classic British comedies in the museum's viewing facility called *TV heaven*. October had me over the moon until November came and... Houston, we have a problem. After verifying my NatWest Step account balance I realised that working 13 hours per week on a minimum wage of £5.52 wouldn't see me through the 3rd accommodation instalment.

That was when this young blond mannequin-looking stunning lady came to the rescue.

5

"Hiya, I'm Rebecca, manager from Pumpkin." She approached me during a shift at Upper Crust. "Antonio told me t' talk t' ye."

"What's happened?"

"Right, this Monday is Bonfire Night an' I 'av a staff on t' roster who wants to tek 'is offspring to see t' fireworks at Hyde Park." Rebecca rolled her eyes. "Can y' cover 'is shift for me?"

"Surely, anytime!" I replied, all excited to work for a proper leodensian manager. After that, Rebecca, who for some reason took a shine on me, invited me to move permanently to Pumpkin and work the full twenty hours per week allowed to students.

Working in Pumpkin did wonders to my English.

Pumpkin unit was located inside a quiet warm waiting area where customers normally would sit until their train arrived. The contact with customers there was less frantic than with the hurrying customers from Upper Crust. I could listen better to the customers' English and just that itself was a plus. Again, I was plunged into a slightly new universe of words.

The Pumpkin menu had a wider variety of hot drinks starting with the decaffeinated coffees, which customers asked prefixing the word *decaf* to coffee names; lattes and cappuccinos served with an optional shot of mint, orange, vanilla, or cinnamon syrup, were referred to by customers as *mint cappuccino*, *vanilla latte*, and so on; and there was an assortment of fruit and herbal infusions like *lemon tea*, *peppermint tea*, *camomile tea*, *green tea*, and *strawberry tea*. Snacks sold at Pumpkin also differed from Upper Crust. There were buttered scones, fruit scones, shortcakes, chocolate chip shortcakes, butter croissants, almond croissants, ham and cheese croissants, cinnamon swirl or cinnamon Danish, pain au chocolat, lemon drizzle cake, and Victoria sponge cake. The muffins had curious names printed in small signs behind the counter glass: *blissful blueberry muffin* and *scrumptious strawberry muffin*. It was at Pumpkin as well that I learned chocolate names like *Aero*, *Bounty*, *Boost*, *Cadbury Dairy Milk*, *Galaxy*, *Kit-Kat*, *Mars*, *Minstrels*, *Snickers*, *Twirl*, *Twix*, *Wispa*, and *Yorkie*. Customers usually asked, "Jus' a Mars bars, please" or "Can a 'av an Aero, please?" I learned also crisps' brand names like *Walkers*, *McCoy's*, and *Kettle*, and the flavour types such as *ready salted*, *cheese and onion*, *salt and vinegar*, *prawn cocktail*, *roast chicken*, *smoky bacon*, *Worcester sauce*, *Mexican chilly*, *flamed grill steak*, *sizzling king prawns*, *cedar and onion* (the last 4 excusive McCoy's flavours).

I was in charge of selling and stocking an endless variety of gummy and jelly sweets, mini wine bottles, can of beers, soft drinks, still and fizzy mineral water, cold pasties, vegetarian wraps, and wrapped sandwiches. As those products became part of my routine so the vocabulary that referred to them became part of my English. I improved my pronunciation of those words or the chunk of words which sounded like one, like *chees'n'onion*. More importantly, I learned to recognise them as well. Before that I just ignored those words; even if the products they referred to were visibly on display in shops and supermarkets, I hardly understood when people used them in sentences.

Working at Pumpkin made wonders to my English; but not without a price, naturally.

I had to work at least an extra hour all shifts for free, and Rebecca had me on the roster Monday to Friday, closing shifts. Closing duties included signing the shift diary, counting the till money, checking the safe hard cash, making a list of wastage, wiping off the counter, polishing the sneeze guard, cleaning the sink area and the coffee station, washing the coffee machine arms and tray, ticking the cleaning checklist, refilling the fridges with soft drinks and fresh sandwiches, stocking the chocolate and crisps stands, sweeping and mopping the shop floor, setting the fire alarm, and leaving everything absolutely flawless for the next shift.

I had a hard time to accomplish all the tasks within the hour the company paid, mainly because I had to make the till readings and to fill and sign reports. After everything there was still a large bag of rubbish to be carried across 3 platforms to the south concourse and dumped in the rubbish cage. Still, the job had to be done and the English experience at Pumpkin paid off.

I started at 5 p.m. and clocked off just after 10 p.m. in easy shifts. Then I had to walk from the train station upwards Park Row, go through The Light to Albion St., and follow through Woodhouse and Headingley Lane, and finally, just after 11 p.m, reach the White Lodge.

Being responsible for the closing the shift during all weekdays really started getting into my nerves.

6

Under the stress of those working hours there were 2 more essays to be submitted by the end of November. This time, a few fuses in my brain started to blow.

20th-Century Fiction in English essay had to focus on 2 or more novels on the module. Among others a question considered the use of metaphoric imagery in Ken Kesey's *One Flew Over The Cuckoo's Nest* – a novel set in a psychiatric asylum whose narrator sees the world as controlled by a complex system of surveillance machines.

I wrote an essay on how in Ken Kesey's novel and George Orwell's *Nineteen Eighty-Four* the figures of authority, Big Nurse in the former and Big Brother in the latter, are portrayed as omniscient human-computer hybrids who sit at the top of a hierarchical system which ultimate goal is to standardise behaviour by transforming humans in machine-like creatures.

Dr Clare Barker's feedback still commented briefly on misspellings and grammar inconsistencies but what was really prominent on her observations was that she was impressed by my essay. On the side of the conclusion, Dr Clare Barker jotted a large handwritten '*Excellent*!'

When this essay was done, I had precisely 4 days to compose the *Foundations of Language Study* essay.

The tutor of *Foundations...*, Dr Alison Johnson, had been very considerate accepting me in her seminar group; so, though I felt unprepared, I wrote the essay to just have something to submit to the tutor. Surprisingly, despite the usual problems with my written English, Dr Johnson's feedback pointed it was a well observed analysis and marked it with a good grade.

It sounded like a modest success to whom had already graduated in English; yet, the assessment criteria at the School of English were much more strict than at my previous undergraduate course. Such grades demanded a heroic effort: from 5 p.m. to 10 p.m. I worked behind a counter dealing with the hardship and stress of the hectic routine of the closing shifts from Pumpkin Café; after that I summoned a super-human strength studying through the small hours and going to Irene Manton North cluster to type the essays on a PC.

Meanwhile the Masters' dissertation – which I'd planed to continue writing whilst in Leeds – remained abandoned inside a suitcase waiting for my waning brain energy.

7

December brought longer nights and the Christmas break. As non-European students are allowed to work full-time during this period my shift hours at Pumpkin doubled. And I still had to study to semester 1 exams.

Until then, I'd explored the university website and collected some brochures searching for prospects of Doctoral degrees and potential scholarship available. Sadly, the prospective for Doctoral degrees, with or without scholarship, was not promising.

Inevitably, considering that my Master's dissertation wouldn't see much of me in that routine in Leeds, I reluctantly began to lose faith in myself and to admit that trying that 2nd exchange experience hadn't been a bright move after all. Midway through Christmas break, I humbled myself and emailed my advisor to tell him about the possibility that I might return in February, after semester 1 exams, to finish the dissertation.

As the reply to that humiliating email never came I felt doubly ashamed: one for having tried a pretentious academic feat, two for having showed a weak nerve.

A week later my inbox email flashed a collective email from my advisor.

Congratulations to all postgraduate students of the Postgraduate Programme in Linguistics for your accomplishments this year. Wishing you this holiday season all the success you really deserve.

Dr Meerwald

Well, I didn't have either the refinement or the chance to craft an equivalent vengeance email. So I turned to my imagination and saw myself announcing the Academy Award in the category *biggest bully bitch*. My advisor approached to accept the accolade, and I gave the statuette to him... right on the top of his bald Bob Flag head. The paparazzi flashed away as the audience applauded relentlessly.

That image relieved me for a hilarious minute until I really stopped to consider the effort I'd employed in my dissertation and how much I'd studied at the Masters to that point. Then I thought: *Oh shuts, here we go again.*

08

ROBERT

Season 1 of The X Files is back on tv Monday night. It's been more than five years after the final episode aired on the satellite channel Fox in Dec 2002. Robert wrote in the msn chat box.

Promptly a reply popped up. *Cool. I never managed t watch it properly.*

Reruns were on till around 2 years ago.

A friend of mine told he can download it off the net.

He's a witch!

Yes internet is magic uncle. I'm sending these messages from my mobile.

I'm on a PC powered by coal.

Cool... Have fun with The X Files.

Ok. God bless...

Robert ended the online chat remembering that almost 15 years had passed since the adventures of the FBI agents Mulder and Scully around cases involving extraterrestrial and paranormal phenomena aired for the first time on a terrestrial channel. In those days, he was single and attended night classes at Secondary School.

On Monday nights, after classes, Robert had to dash down the road, to make in 10 minutes the way that he normally did in a half-hour walk to watch *The X Files*.

Robert usually missed the episodes' intros. That was the only chance Robert had to watch them; the series aired on Fox channel other times through the week but only half a dozen people could afford satellite tv in the small town where Robert dwelt. Also, the few people who had a VCR never bothered to record *The X Files*.

Back then, released VHS copies had only a selection of episodes and were seldom available at video stores. Now entire seasons could be found on pirated DVDs. Time had really gone by. In the meantime, *The X Files* became a classic, and Robert became the father of a little boy named Wilbert and a faithful husband. Satellite tv also became so cheap that recently Robert could afford the basic package that included Fox.

Robert never managed to buy any copies of the classic seasons; that's why he was eager for Monday night to remember the younger and innocent days when he was literally mad about extraterrestrial phenomena. Such madness had subsided some time before little Wilbert's birth at the beginning of the 3rd millennium.

During those days, Robert had gone through pretty stressful times. He'd married few years before and, under the protest of teachers and classmates, Robert decided to drop out of Secondary School in the final study year to do extra work in his upholstery workshop. He decided to accept more sofas and armchairs to refurbish so that his wife could graduate Secondary School without having to seek for a job herself.

Robert had always been known as an intelligent and sensitive person, with an outstanding skill to improvise poetry within the flow of conversation, and an eccentric sense of humour characterised by nonsensical speeches on politics, science, and philosophy. He enjoyed an audience; in one occasion, his audience was formed by one of his nephews, and three nieces, all of them who'd come on holidays from the capital to stay with him.

"...The new millennium actually started in two thousand and one," Robert said, whilst they gathered in the porch. "And according to Nostradamus, the start of this millennium would coincide with a revolution in mass communication."

"Serious?" One of his nieces asked a bit sceptic; she knew that Robert read a lot about Nostradamus, but wondered if he was up to one of his jokes.

"True. What's more cutting edge than the arrival of internet in this town in January this year? The mayor acquired internet with public funds and installed it in the Town Hall and in his residence." Robert kept straight-faced. "Even more revolutionary this year was the inauguration of the town's first cybercafe with *two* computer terminals. Don't laugh, 'cause the reach of internet here is impressive. These days I was browsing a webpage there and I was contacted by an alien entity via a message on the screen."

"You're still being contacted, uncle Bob?" His nephew chuckled.

"Yep, it's high-tech contact now. The message said: Congratulations, you've won an interplanetary voyage to Zeta Rediculi!"

"Ah, that's the internet space lottery." His nephew fuelled the topic.

"True. But I turned it down 'cause of my travel-sickness." Robert then put on a smug face. "No, I'm joking. I knew all along that aliens' web invitations are scams. Old scam by the way."

"From radio days..." Another niece added.

"True. In the fifties, American residents were tricked by entities named Kanamits into boarding a flying saucer in the promise of an exchange experience. In the end, these Kanamits transported the Americans to serve them as main courses in their planet." Robert told that with a grievous face as everyone laughed.

At times, his silly talk made Robert feel immature. Still he found it hard to engage in serious chats about anything in this universe where everything seemed so controversial. Besides, he knew how eccentric his ideas and beliefs were, mainly considering how a small town like that one where he dwelt restricted its inhabitants to a rather limited mindset. Just to stay on the safe side, when Robert wanted to express an eccentric opinion he often created a persona to make it tricky for others to discern if he was being serious or funny; depending on each person's reaction he'd pick up from there.

That camouflage had improved over the years as Robert developed a forthright fascination with matters dealing with the unknown. Such fascination made him talk passionately on certain subjects that often attracted flustered looks and caused awkward silences.

Already as a teenager, Robert grew captivated by stories about possessions and hauntings after watching *The Exorcist* and *The Amityville Horror* on tv; he also read the original novels, by William Peter Blatty and by Jay Anson. He found these novels gathering dust in the small library of the local Catholic Church where he served as acolyte for 3 years. Led by such American cultural influence and empowered by the heat of youth, Robert intended to embrace the priesthood aiming at fighting evil spirits. After some time such religious inclination dwindled and his interest in the unknown shifted from the inner to the outer space – specifically to all things concerned with UFO and extraterrestrials.

09

Robert's conversion started after he'd dug through the church library in search of a book on deities for a Latin literature assignment. Among others works, he borrowed Erich von Däniken's *Chariots of the Gods*.

In *Chariots of the Gods* the author hypothesised that throughout world's history extraterrestrial astronauts have contacted humans and shared their technology with ancient civilizations. It hadn't much to contribute with the assignment on Latin literature, but once Robert flipped through a few pages he couldn't stop reading it.

Robert was mesmerised by the descriptions of how archaeological monuments like the Pyramids in Egypt, Stonehenge in England, the monolithic statues named Moai in Easter Island (Chile), Machu Picchu in Colombia, Cusco in Peru, and many others seemed to have been engineered with highly advanced technology that supposedly evidenced extraterrestrial intervention. He became thrilled with the author's statement that volumes of Tibetan Kanjur make references to Gods appearing in the sky, that the Indian epic Mahabharata depicts flying machines called Vimānas, and that the Dead Sea Scrolls mentions sky vehicles and 'sons of heaven' whose arrival and departure were accompanied by clouds of smoke and fire. Still, those accounts from ancient texts could simply be a product of human imagination. Then, it was the mention of the *Holy Scripture* that essentially bewildered Robert.

Soon as he had a chance Robert scanned the books of the Bible in search of specific references to heavenly sightings and there they were. In Exodus there's a pillar of a cloud that turns into a pillar of fire by night and floats above Moses and the Hebrews leading their way through the desert. In Second Kings, a chariot of fire and horses of fire whisk up to heaven the prophet Elijah, who's never to be seen again. In chapter 1 of Ezekiel among other bright images the prophet's visions of God include a great cloud with fire infolding itself, wheels the colour of a beryl hovering upon the earth, and rings with eyes round about them, and living human-like winged creatures that were lifted up from the earth along with these wheels, and a firmament stretched upon the head of these creatures the colour of a crystal – Robert had to admit that it was much easier to visualise such images from a sci-fi perspective. In Mathews, a star appears in Bethlehem in the East and goes ahead the wise men until it finally stands over the place where the baby Jesus was.

Though Robert was familiar with the Bible those images never struck him as something as earthly as a spacecraft or any other flying device. He regarded himself as an unfaithful and sinful blasphemer for even considering the Scriptures in that way. Yet, the more he read those verses the more used to the idea he grew.

Robert continued serving as an acolyte, helping the local priest with the mass service, to make up for the guilt of renouncing his former religious convictions. By then he also started working for a small retail store and using some of his hard earned salary to buy issues of *UFO Magazine* and other literature on ufology. Along with these he also kept a folder with newspaper cuttings and jottings he made. It was mainly based on this material that Robert began to develop a new view of the world.

10

What started as an innocent approach soon became a replacement for Robert's faith in the divine. And like with his former passion for spiritual matters his new approach on the unknown also counted with American cultural influence.

Most of the material Robert found epitomised the American UFO culture developed in the last half of the 20th century when the phenomenon of Unidentified Flying Objects captured American's imagination and a UFO sighting epidemic started.

Robert turned into one of those who *want to believe* and accepted any information that evidenced the existence of humanoids from other planets. His enthusiasm echoed that of a naïve UFO hunter.

UFO sightings became Robert's immediate interest. He learned that the term *flying saucer* had been coined when an American journalist interviewed the American aviator Kenneth Arnold, who reported the sighting of 9 saucer-shaped flying objects during a flight near Mount Rainer in Washington in 1947. Initially, these UFOs were thought to be secret military aircraft. Speculation over the extraterrestrial origin of these airships gained popularity after 1950 when a veteran naval aviator, former member of the US Marine Corps, named Donald Keyhoe published *Flying Saucers Are Real* in *True* magazine stating that the government suppressed the truth behind sighting reports. Then the US Air Force launched a series of systematic investigations in 1952 called Project Blue Book that nearly 20 years later reached no definite conclusion on the nature of UFOs; since by then it seemed evident that UFOs represented no imminent threat to national safety the investigations were terminated. In the 70's, scepticism grew among former believers because flying saucers and lights in the sky had become more of a myth. In the previous 2 decades, UFO sighting accounts were frequent, but nothing concrete, like a clear authentic picture, would support witnesses' claims. Even recent articles in the 80's, when portable cameras became popular, brought no more than colour illustrations and dodgy montages.

Robert lost some of his initial enthusiasm when he read articles stating that 90% of UFO sightings were misinterpretation of explainable phenomena.

This is when Robert turned to closer encounters.

Robert's interest gained steam after he watched *The UFO Incident*, a film based in the first famous case of alien abduction occurred in 1961; the case was reported by the abductees Betty and Barney Hill, who during hypnosis regression recalled how they were taken into an alien craft and submitted to physical examination. Most of the reported abduction cases that were referred in magazines dated from after the Hill's testimony.

Again, abductees provided incredible accounts but no credible memento. Yet, if abductees weren't enough to confirm that human kind isn't alone in the universe, there were still the *contactees* who affirmed that, on a regular basis, they received messages from aliens.

The first famous modern contactee was a Polish-born American man named George Adamski, who claimed to have been contacted in 1952 in the Mojave Desert by a being from Venus. Another interesting one was a London cabbie named George King, who began channelling messages from a Venusian entity in 1954 and in the following year founded the world's first UFO based religion: *Aetherius Society*. Following the encounter template set by Adamski and the spiritual approach set by King, contactees multiplied in a pretty similar pattern, most of them publishing books, seeking media attention, and some forming sects based on their extraterrestrial channelled messages.

Whilst reading on contactees Robert saw the picture of a flying saucer filmed by Adamski that looked like a prop from the 1959 film *Plan Nine from Outer Space*.

Indeed, the information Robert learned about UFOs gradually gained qualities of a Hollywood film plot.

In 1984 an American tv producer received a 35mm film in the mail that contained an 8-page document with information about a secret research committee named *Majestic 12*, composed by scientists, military leaders, and government officials, allegedly formed in 1947 under executive order of the president Harry Truman to investigate UFO-related information. In

1989 a man named Bob Lazar came on tv to state that he'd worked briefly as a physicist in an area named Sector 4 – a secret military facility for the analysis of reverse engineering of extraterrestrial artefact.

Nearly two years on into Robert's conversion to ufolicism, he became increasingly frustrated and bored with the lack of evidence behind so many stories. Only few cases still sounded intriguing.

There were cases of death of horses and cattle involving mysterious circumstances connected to UFO sightings in the vicinities; in some there were precise cuts, as if made by laser, in others some of the carcasses had been totally drained of blood. There were cases of enormous circular designs that appeared overnight in crops of barley, maize, rye, or wheat.

Still, the boundaries between official accounts, fictional narratives, and genuine mistakes were pretty much blurred. UFO sightings could be anything from weather balloons, Chinese lanterns, artificial satellites, planet Venus itself, to lightning, seismic lights or earthquake lights, parhelion, etcetera. Abductees could be imagining things or just utterly lying. Contactees could be cashing in on a new social craze. *Majestic 12* could be an elaborate campaign of misinformation promoted both to instigate scepticism and stimulate the UFO publishing market. And in that same year the tv news affirmed that Bob Lazar had been debunked by the *Los Angeles Times*.

Robert begun to wonder what was left for him to believe when *The X Files* pilot first aired on tv. After seeing some episodes he understood that much like in the series many earthly events could be submitted to different views which not necessarily invalidated one another. He knew that in the middle of so many stories and theories about the UFOs and extraterrestrials there should be something closer to the truth.

By this time, a younger more pious lad had replaced Robert as acolyte. So he spent some time distant from the church dedicating himself to his little intellectual world.

11

After so much reading and watching on the UFO and extraterrestrial matter, Robert wrote down some hypotheses that could provide a general background explanation for the mystery surrounding that mishmash of stories about sightings and encounters.

Hypothesis 1: *The American government started spreading rumours in the late 40's and, supported by literature and mass media, pushed the UFO and extraterrestrial imagery into social consciousness. The government used this facade to conduct experimental use of top secret technology. So, abductees had never been boarded onto spaceships yet they might have had sham memories implanted in their minds by hypnotherapists – who, by the way, generally had profiting purposes like publishing books, writing articles, or gaining free of charge media exposition. Several sightings and encounters certainly came off the creative individual's mind who profited from disguising fiction as genuine incidents and feeding them to either the publishing market or the sensationalist media. That eliminated real life in other planets and brought the spiritual dimension and the Divinity back to earth.*

Hypothesis 2: *UFOs and extraterrestrials existed in a parallel abstract dimension and now and then they made contact with people, individually or collectively, through their minds without really materialising themselves on earth. Thus, sightings happened 'cause some more sensitive persons had glimpses of these parallel abstract dimensions and abductions were no more than a mind experience, a dream that people remember as an actual experience 'cause it occurred in unusual circumstances, that is, not during sleep. This still disregards the cases of abductees who presented themselves with implants under their skin, in which case the hypothesis would be that aliens exerted control over materialisation, converting matter from an abstract dimension to a concrete one. In this case, parallel abstract dimension hypothesis is replaced by contiguous concealed dimension hypothesis. The latter explains how UFOs appears and vanishes without a trace. That eliminated the spiritual dimension and the Divinity and put the UFOs and extraterrestrials back into the ends of the universe.*

Obs. Whether visitors are deities or aliens, genuine or imaginary, the important thing is that documented testimonies referring to visitors are encountered throughout human history in ancient scrolls, sacred scriptures, modern press, and that such testimonies are produced by a considerable number of humans, from simple farmers, urban junkies, to holy prophets, and dodgy contactees. Come what may, considering the supernatural incidents and apparitions mentioned in the Bible and other ancient texts, the anachronic sophisticated tech evidenced in the architecture of historical monuments, and the contemporary accounts of UFO sightings and alien visitations, it's reasonable to think that some kind of powerful being (or beings) must wield some control over creation and damnation on earth and its inhabitants. Either divine or extraterrestrial whatever has control is not supposed to be conspicuously perceived or does not want to be conspicuously perceived by humans - at least not lately.

Whatever truth was out there, it needed faith to be

believed and Robert needed to believe in something, otherwise he had to face himself as an empty shell, a carcass bearing nothing more than goo and guts.

Eventually, Robert came full circle, going from having faith in an abstract spiritual world to believing in a concrete extraterrestrial world, just to become aware that this extraterrestrial world was essentially as intangible as the spiritual one, or being the spiritual one itself under a different view. Thus, he embraced his religion back and continued praying and exercising his faith in the expectation that whatever inhabits beyond this world would hear his prayers and respond to them with benevolence.

Assuming a sceptical mindset towards UFO and extraterrestrial phenomena, Robert went on researching on the subject with moderation, slipping more philosophy into his reading list. He'd also grown more conscious of his interest as in the small town where he dwelt no one could be bothered with that. Not even *The X Files* had an audience; locals were more enticed by the films that aired at the same time in another channel.

The only solace to Robert was to know that other folks in the world shared of his interest, like the more than 3 thousand members of the Mutual UFO Network (MUFON) which is the world's largest UFO organisation formed by people from varied intellectual and educational background. Here and there he met someone who took some interest on the subject after he managed to introduce the topic as a joke or in the flow of one of his nonsense speeches. At times Robert needed to talk on the matter as a way to organise his thoughts and he found no mate with an informed view.

When a black and white grainy footage of an alien autopsy, allegedly found in the 1947 Roswell UFO crash, aired on national news, the townsfolk only talked about that for a week.

"That alien is a dummy!" Robert heard from many neighbours – their scepticism would be vindicated a decade later when British film producer Ray Santilli, after making a fortune selling the film to tv networks, confessed that the footage was indeed a hoax.

After the alien autopsy sensationalism, 2 years on, the townsfolk experienced another furore – this time instigated by an interview granted by a retired captain of the national Air Force; this captain came on prime time news and told what he witnessed at the command of a military mission assembled to investigate a case of mass UFO sightings in 1977, in the north of Brazil.

12

The incident had happened in the small island of Colares at the mouth of Amazon River, where over 80 residents alleged that a strange beam of light came from above and struck them, immobilising their limbs and sucking their blood. The doctor of the local health care centre at the time of the incident, Dr. Wellaide Carvalho, also appeared on national news and stated that she attended dozens of patients who presented similar symptoms: skin showing what appeared to be round radiation burns that had puncture marks at the centre and seemed to have been instantly cauterised.

The captain of the national Air Force, Uyrange Hollanda, was assigned to lead a team of officers to investigate the incident after island officials and the mayor contacted the regional air command of the national Air Force army. He told how during surveillance shifts the military officers had their own encounters. 4 months into the operation, codenamed *Operation Saucer*, Capt. Hollanda was commanded to surrender all materials and withdraw the operation.

Then, the strange lights in the island of Colares ceased, the incident turned into local legend, and the Operation Saucer remained under wraps for 30 years until Capt. Hollanda appeared on national news.

After that interview the townsfolk were really excited. "It was collective hallucination," one stated.

"It's a sign of the apocalypse!" Others affirmed.

Some even told personal accounts of strange lights in the sky. Robert amused himself thinking that with a little extra push the whole town would be engulfed in mass hysteria. So he seized the opportunity and added to the folks' repertoire an experience of his own.

"…Just another night – it was pissing down – and I heard a thunder that made my hair bristle. Then, I heard a humming noise coming from the backyard. When I went there to investigate, I saw this amber light gleaming underneath the canopy of the mango tree. True, I was covered in gooseflesh. But I got courage, went near the mango tree holding a stick, and used the stick to move a branch and uncover whatever was hiding there. Then, all of a sudden, a flash burst." Seeing his audience paralysed in suspense, Robert completed. "It was a lighting that had been stuck in the branches of the tree." Everyone called him names and laughed. "True. I still have the shoes I was wearing that night; all covered in soot…"

Good times. Little after that, Robert became a family man, ventured his own business, and brought little Wilbert to earth. Since Wilbert's birth, Robert referred to him as the chosen one. When people asked what Wilbert had been chosen for Robert replied: "Wilbert was chosen to redeem the intellect of his father, who didn't finish proper education."

Robert affirmed that he'd been in contact with a pal who belonged to a better breed of beings and had promised him to obtain a scholarship to an intergalactic university that would be granted to little Wilbert when he reached adulthood.

Together with the bachelor life Robert had left the intellectual pursuit of unknown mysteries behind him. The books and magazines he bought during those years went to the church library, and the cuttings and jottings he made ended up in a cardboard box.

What was left from that pursuit was basically a man who believed in everything and nothing equally, a man who understood that the spiritual world was real to whom believes in the spiritual world, that Gods were real to whom believes in Gods, that UFOs were real to whom believes in UFOs, and that anything would become real as long a person believes that thing is real.

Robert believed that once a person believes in a thing this thing can materialise on earth and become visible to others who in turn would also believe and that triggered a process of materialisation in a chain; so, the more people believe in one thing the more this thing strengths its concreteness on earth, to the point that this something may remain lingering on earth even without no one to believe. In summary, believing generates an energy that sparks the creation of something.

Naturally, that was just another hypothesis. Robert had that as his ultimate hypothesis – one that covered the speculation over what's fact and fiction on earth.

A weak point to his hypothesis was that Robert could never explain why he believed in a lot of things yet he only saw them through stories or illustrations.

Well, if there was a God on earth it certainly wasn't him, so he couldn't have all the answers. And if there was a God on earth perhaps that was part of God's master plan: to confuse people on what they can believe since certain beliefs can be proven right at a time and then wrong at another. Perhaps God used this strategy to lead humanity into a state of confusion that would ultimately lead them back to a condition of innocence similar to that of Adam and Eve.

That thought reminded Robert of H. P. Lovecraft's *The Call of Cthulhu*, a short story that impressed him greatly and that begins stating that humans dwell on a placid island of ignorance in the midst of black seas of infinity.

In the midst of his ignorance, all Robert knew was that he'd believed the classic episodes of *The X Files* would be back on the schedule and after many years there they were. And watching *The X Files* remained as the last breath of his past fascination with the unknown, a fascination that indeed had been an attempt to navigate away from the ignorance to which Robert knew he'd be doomed to as a dweller of a small town in that godforsaken corner of the world.

So, that Monday night Robert put little Wilbert to bed earlier because the chosen one was still too young and could have nightmares if he stayed up to watch. He gave a gentle kiss on his own home-made little human and hastened to the couch to sight some flying saucers and extraterrestrial beings that only quality American tv could make.

13

Another beautiful summer day and I'd gotten up with a heavy gloom weighing upon my chest. Even before the work at Whittington St. started I already breathed with difficulty.

To begin at the garage I prayed for inspiration. "Oh Madonna, I beseech thee, bring me some glee."

Then, inside Unit twenty, a whispery voice echoed. "What are you looking at…" It was followed by a pulsating beat that replicated the rhythm of a ticking clock and made vibrate some still string within me.

Synchronised with that rhythm my hips swayed left to right like a pendulum following the circular motions of my hand as I rubbed the wax over the paintwork of a Peugeot. No melancholy could stand against the sound of *Vogue* that played on and on as I waxed on and off a couple of cars in succession, moving wildly around them, shaking my woes off.

It took a few cars, some stretching, flexing, and other body movements, until the sweat started washing down my distress about the situation I got myself into.

I'd stayed in England with a purpose: writing.

I reminded myself of that all the time; yet, apart from jotting down drafts, I had no progress with actual writing, and the few chapters I'd created didn't seem to render the spirit of what I had in mind. The fear of giving up and returning home was nothing compared to the fear of admitting that I'd failed to live up to my literary aspirations. But listening to that upbeat tune helped me to purge that distress.

"Go Jonesy!" Ewan shouted as he passed in front of Unit twenty – probably to remind he was watching me than to actually encourage my frolicking. "Ah come in a bi' to 'elp ye."

In Ewan's English that translated as *I have a new assignment for you.*

I waxed off the last car and waited for Ewan, resting in a passenger seat that had been stripped from a scrap car. As I started reading a paper, I noticed someone entering the unit: it was Luke.

Luke was a young English lad who was staying at Unit ten temporarily. Unit ten was rented to his father and housed a plastering workshop.

"Ar'ya all right, Jonesy?"

Luke always used that same greeting which to me sounded much more British than Ewan's *Aye up, cock*!

That impression probably stemmed from the fact

that Luke had been born and bred in Peterborough, a city located further down in the south, halfway between Doncaster and London. Southern accents, mainly those around London, gave me that impression of Britishness.

Though northern accents sounded to me much more beguiling, wild, and spicy, I found southern accents particularly beautiful, polished, and smooth. And that is how Luke sounded and just how I wanted to sound like. I'd die to sound that British.

In all truth, despite the intellectual and practical reasons that I generally alleged, deep inside what had driven me another time to England and what motivated me to stay was an incontrollable irrational yearning to sound as natural and spontaneous as a native like Luke – this doesn't make other reasons less genuine though. I lusted for Luke's fortune in having English all around him through his entire life; a gift offered to him at birth and that I, under my visa constraints, so well knew its value. With English skills similar to Luke's I'd rule the world. *My precious…*

Luke surely was unaware of his luck. Just shy of 20, he'd been going from job to job before he joined his father's business of manufacturing plaster architectural mouldings and fitting the end product into homes.

I learned that when I, to listen to Luke's English, asked him to let me into his trade. Then, Luke patiently introduced me to another world of English to which I was oblivious.

14

"What we make here is called fibrous plaster work 'cause we mix a fibrous element to the pieces made so to give more strength, right? In some cases we need to make stronger pieces, so to add more strength we mix pieces of wood. Originally the fibrous element used to be horse hair; but the standard now is fibreglass. Now, this is how we do exactly…" – Luke proceeded showing me the tools he referred to. "We take a mould, then pour layers of liquid plaster and whatever we mix to add strength until the mould is full; then we leave it to set, right? Then, once it hardens, we peel the piece out of the mould. Actually, before that we have to pour this vegetable oil here (he held a gallon containing a yellow fluid) to grease the inside of the mould; we call the oil a release agent 'cause it make sure the pieces come off nice and easy. The plaster we use here is a fine gypsum plaster. The mould can be wood, fibreglass, foam rubber; foam rubber is the most expensive. We only use it when loads of details have to show on the finished piece. We make moulds also if a customer need to match up to something they have already. In this case we take a squeeze; this is when we brush a rubber compound onto whatever we wish to copy then we put plaster onto the back of the rubber, leave it to set, then peel off, and we have a mould of the piece we need. We can also do what we call running mould; this is to make cornices – that bit that go around the top of a room; we do nice ones. To do this we get a flat bench, pour plaster onto it, mixing layers of fibreglass and timber as we go then running a shaped piece of metal – used to be tin now zinc – along the top of the slowly setting plaster to give the shape we want. This is more out of date now; people used this technique to make the piece in situ, actually making the shape into plaster onto the wall where it would stay. The pieces we make here in the shop are fireplaces, columns, pillars, ceiling roses, which is mounted on the ceiling and a light fitting dangle through them, and ceiling mouldings, which is not popular today but was big in the twenties to make faux beams, and the cornices I told ya."

Luke pointed, showed things, and emphasised some words, but it was still hard to follow him. Sure I tuned out a few times paying attention to how round his vowels sounded, and how his "t" sounds were flap or glottal. I'd asked him to tell me when he finished a piece and, judging by how the overalls Luke had on was entirely splattered with plaster, that is why he came that morning. "C'mon Jonesy, ya may like to see this."

I followed Luked to Unit ten just to be amazed.

"Wow! It's beautiful." My jaw was hanging.

"Do ya like it? It's a fireplace." Luke didn't make a big thing of it, but he patently took pride of the final product. "We're fitting it today in a living room."

"You're definitely an artist, mate." I admired the beautifully designed flowery details sculptured on that fireplace. Around that beautiful piece, portions of dried plaster were scattered through the floor.

It was difficult to ignore the mess inside Unit ten. It was filled with dust, plastic, wood, tools, old furniture, unfinished pieces, and rubble. And Luke lived there!

I thought of my cosy flat at Springfield Mount, with a bathroom, bedroom, living room, an inbuilt wardrobe, cupboard, washer, microwave, fridge, sink, sofa, table, desk, and a panoramic window. I felt ashamed of my earlier distress. Luke had an artistic talent that didn't garner him much in terms of social status and he didn't seem miserable about that.

"With your talent you can probably get rich."

"Not much, I'm afraid."

"Well, I'm sure this beauty is worth gold."

"Thank Jonesy. I wish our customers thought like ya." Luke smiled.

I left Unit ten thinking that the beauty of that fireplace should be the kind of beauty that I desired with my idea of writing. Teaching and being an academic had its charms, but before reaching that obligatory path I wanted to do something aesthetically romantic out of my knowledge. Something not as beautiful as the song *Bohemian Rhapsody* by Queen, or the *Mission to Mars* OST by Ennio Morricone, or the western *The Good, The Bad and The Ugly* by Sergio Leone, but at least something unique.

That's what being gay sometimes is all about: being unique. And that is probably why Daffyd Thomas, from *Little Britain*, wanted to be the only gay in the village.

Talking to Luke that morning reminded me that everyone has issues – a lesson I forgot from time to time and that I began to grasp better after my Christmas at the White Lodge.

15

"Oh, I really wanted you to spend Christmas holidays in the Netherlands with us." Claudia's tone over the phone sounded disappointed.

"I'm truly thankful, but my manager could not give me the week off." In truth, I couldn't afford a week off work.

"Well fancy pants. If you get the chance, at least come for the New Year's Eve."

"I promise." I lied again; even if I had the chance, I couldn't afford a flight ticket.

"So, b'bye fancy pants. Take care."

"Bye…" I hung up the phone heartbroken, knowing that the White Lodge would become so deserted up to Christmas that I might open the front door and be knocked down by a rolling tumbleweed.

At least, I had contact with humans at work. Such comfort came at a cost, of course. I'd been scheduled from 2 to 9 p.m. with a half-hour break, Monday to Saturday – that is, 39 hours per week. Adding the extra hour I took to do the closing shift tasks – sign shift diary, tick cleaning checklist, count till money, check safe, list wastage, clean counter, sink, and coffee station, refill fridges, stock stands, sweep and mop floor, set fire alarm, and dump rubbish – I was on that working routine no less than 44 hours per week.

After a daily journey of almost 8 hours standing at Pumpkin, topped by a 40-minutes walk from the station to the White Lodge, even the sheep I counted to sleep were shattered. I was immersed in an atmosphere of depression that combined exhaustion and loneliness.

In the 24th of December Pumpkin closed at 5 p.m. So I clocked off earlier and click-clacked all the way to the White Lodge where I found a table laden with Christmas goodies and where I slept warmly to wake up to a white Christmas. Actually, make it more like, I clomped to the White Lodge, where I laid the table with the end of the leftover snacks of Pumpkin and where I dropped dead freezing to wake up to a shite Christmas.

On Christmas and Boxing Day, Pumpkin closed – on holidays, employees get double pay and business wouldn't be busy enough to make a profit.

Room 2 was still dark when my mobile phone woke me up. It was before 8 a.m. "Hello…"

"Merry Christmas." It was my former partner. "Sorry for calling this early. How are things going?"

"Not as I've planned. I'm working a lot. Stressed."

"Haven't you talked to your advisor yet?"

"I've emailed him, but he didn't reply."

"Well, if I were you I'd insist. This isn't time to be proud. I heard that the State University will be recruiting permanent tutors of English this semester. If you finish your Master you'll be able to…"

"I can't believe you called for this."

"No. I did call to wish you a merry Christmas. It's just that… you're missing an opportunity."

"Please, don't tell me what's an opportunity to me."

"Listen, I just want you to be…"

I cut him short. "Nothing enrages me more than anyone presuming what my social place, my ambitions, and my prospects should be."

"Listen, I didn't call to upset you. I just care about you. Hearing that you're stressed out worries me."

"Well, I must trust my intuition. And I'm paying the toll to follow my heart through. And I'll stick to it till the end. But you wouldn't know what this feeling is."

"…Ok, enjoy your Christmas. I need to go now."

Tell me about the ghost of Christmas past.

To purge its haunting influence, I jumped off bed, got on my knees, and prayed the Psalm 23. *The Lord is my shepherd…* With my senses more awakened I had the impression that the White Lodge gained life: whistles and bangs travelled around the house's walls.

Some student might have returned, I thought. I could swear that a person was strolling on the floor above. Slightly scared, I jumped back to bed and turned the radio on.

"…fresh gales will blow through some areas around West Yorkshire, and snow is expected still this week."

One of those winds broke into the room and filled my body with vigour. I jumped off bed again, this time firm on my feet, turned the lights on, and drew the curtains open. The light of the fluorescent lamp inside the room shed some lively whiteness against the dead darkness that filled the gravelled area beyond the bay window. That brightness travelled the nightly stillness lighting up a million minuscule particles of icy-crystals of the thin-layered hoar frost on the shrubs; those gleaming sparkles outlined the hedges around the parking area. The chilled air puffed against the window causing the glass panes within the frame to vibrate. Gooseflesh rippled across my skin making me reach for a warm jumper.

I picked up the radio, the portable DVD, a few goodies, braced myself and sprang across the dark hall into the kitchen.

It was freezing there. To warm up, and to muffle any odd sound in the house, I tuned to *Radio 1* and let *The Chris Moyles Show* presenters cheer me up. It was easier than usual to understand what they were saying as their exchanges were mostly about Christmas topics and to the Secret Santa they played – I only struggled to understand them when they made reference to celebrity names, tv shows, or events that I wasn't familiar with.

Next, I started preparing a recipe of mulled wine that Nicole had taught me: half a bottle of red wine, a pint of orange juice, a hint of vanilla, a few cinnamon sticks, and a handful of cloves. *Great*! As the mulled wine boiled on the stove swirls of vapours rose from the saucepan filling the air with a spicy scent that made that Christmas morning distinct. That Christmassy feeling was further characterised by the way the radio presenters highlighted in their chat words like *presents, surprise, shiny paper, giving, receiving, wrapping, chimney, Santa's sac, guess, Christmas food, messages, Santa's helper, elf,* and *fairy*. The mood wouldn't be complete without the Christmas pudding that I bought from the pound shop – it came with a tiny bottle of brandy and instructions on how to flame it.

The morning was brighter by the time the table was set with a bowl of Thai sweet chilli Sensations crisps, leftovers from Pumpkin, a steaming mug of spicy mulled wine, and the flaming Christmas pudding. That table reminded me of the Christmas supper scene from the film *The Dead* in which Gretta, played by Angelica Huston, transfers the pudding alight with a blue flame to the table and the guests give a round of applause.

Before watching *The Dead* for a class presentation I'd never heard of Christmas pudding; that morning, I had a Christmas pudding covered with a blue flame on a table in front of me. I remembered how passionately I'd prepared myself for that presentation of *The Dead*, so hopeful of travelling to England for the first time. I couldn't refrain from bursting into an emotional sob.

To avoid thinking of what went wrong thus far, I turned the portable DVD on, and began to enjoy that Christmas, shoving crisps, pasties, pastries, pudding, and mulled wine down my gob whilst watching the Christmas edition of *Whose Line is it Anyway* of 1989.

Light-spirited, and a bit tipsy, I went to my room to dust the furniture and vacuum the carpet, hoping to cleanse the dirt and myself from the sin of gluttony.

Carried away by the inebriating feeling of hygiene, I went on through the toiled, hall, and back to kitchen. I dusted, vacuumed, and swept, dragging the radio along, laughing about, and writing down a list of the comedy shows that I'd recorded after my return to Leeds: debut series of *Bleak Expectations*, series 3 of *It's That Jo Caulfield Again*, series 6 of *Old Harry's Game*, series 3 of *Genius*, series 23 of *The Now Show*, series 2 of the sketch show *The Hollow Men*, reruns of series 2 of *Count Arthur Strong's Radio Show*, a rerun of series 3 of *That Mitchell and Webb Sound*, series 2 of the sketch show *Recorded for Training Purposes*, and series 4 of *15 Minute Musical*.

I still mopped the kitchen floor dancing with the mop to the sound of The Shangri-Las. By the time I finished, not a sip of mulled wine remained in the pan.

After 3 p.m. I went to the phone booth at the end of North Hill Rd. to phone home before the colours of that beautiful Christmas day faded into darkness again.

I ended that night comfortably warm on my bed munching crisps and listening to a traditional ghost story called *The Tractate Middoth* by M. R. James that aired on *Radio 4*.

16

In the morning of Boxing Day I went for a stroll at city centre.

First, I went to Albion Street to the pound shop underneath Leeds Shopping Plaza to get a pack of audio tapes. When I arrived there most shops from that area were boarded up – that commercial block was going through refurbishment. A bit frustrated I went to Leeds Corn Exchange to drink some coffee and take pictures to send home. This time I was surprised to see that most of the independent traders had gone off there and that the remaining ones were ready to shut down.

I approached a lady who worked in a fragrance shop. "Why is it so quiet in here?"

"Ah, traders can't bovver t' come no more. We'v been told this place's goin' t' be turned into a food emporium." The lady sounded dissatisfied.

"Oh, that's not good, right?"

"Indeed, luv. Indeed…"

From there, I headed up through Briggate, just to give a look at the *Time Ball Buildings*. Naturally, I felt more attracted by the rainbow flag fluttering in front of Queens Court. I wanted to go there, sit in a pub, and flirt with some Englishman, but I didn't have the guts.

What an excuse for an out and proud gay I am. That thought was quickly dispersed when I reached Merrion Centre and saw that *The Flying Machine* in front of Morrisons had vanished. Oddly, from the time I'd left Leeds, in 2005, such places had been unchanged until my return; suddenly that chain of changes emerged as if triggered by something – the end of the year I guess.

While some refurbishment in the commercial area of Leeds city centre was happening I'd failed to perceive those changes until then. Perhaps in a subconscious level I insisted on seeing the same Leeds that I'd left before; then, possibly as the plans that had brought me back to Leeds had taken a different turn, something was modified inside of me, and subconsciously I'd sought for those changes in the outside.

Indeed, changes seemed to be disclosing themselves to me lately. In the end of November, when I asked Damien, the British lad, to record *The Now Show* series, he introduced me to something new.

"Er, did you know this show's available on podcast?

"Pod what?" My intonation went hideously high.

Damien smiled. "Podcast. It's basically an audio file posted for download on the Radio Four website."

"Oh... internet..." I said, judging that Damien was giving an excuse not to record the show for me. "I'm terrible with the internet."

"No worries mate." Damien replied, maybe thinking how stupid I was for still be dealing with magnetic tapes in a world of digital podcasts.

Nevertheless, I learned later that my archaic habit of recording radio shows on tape was still worthwhile because only Friday broadcasts of Radio 4's *half-past six comedies* were available on Podcast.

I went on thinking about those changes on the way to White Lodge, recollecting how only years ago my universe of English was restricted to cinema and video, satellite tv, and didactic material. Finally, back at White Lodge I focused on reading through the rest of that Boxing Day.

Until the exams week I followed a similar routine: get up early, read, study, and work. The housemates returned to White Lodge before the New Year and followed a pretty similar routine, apart from working.

Before semester 2 started we all left our rooms, met more often in the kitchen, and gathered once or twice to go to pubs and relax – we even went to Queens Court!

At the end of January we said our goodbyes to 3 girls, including Nicole, and welcomed new housemates from Europe. When semester 2 began, all housemates retreated themselves to their commitments. I was enrolled in 3 modules at the School of English and back to a working routine of 20 hours a week, Wednesday to Saturday, and Mondays, on closing shifts.

Already during January the work burden at Pumpkin had become unbearable. The staff from the previous shift left the morning takings unchecked so I had to count a great amount of money at the end of my shift.

Every day the cash in the till drawer didn't match the system figures so I had to fill a discrepancy report explaining the reason for that. I had no way to determine who had made a mistake. The previous shift staff also left the fridges and stands empty, so there was more to refill and stock for the next shift, left the unit all messy, so there was more to clean, and left all the rubbish behind, so there were two or three large bags full to be carried across three platforms and dumped in the rubbish cage in the south concourse. I still needed what was called the *bin key* to open the rubbish cage and I had to borrow it from *The White Rose* bar. To top that saga, as I closed late night and worked alone, it was difficult to find someone available or willing to sign as a witness and drop the end of the day takings in the general safe. Closing shift must be the staffs' worst nightmare and I am pretty sure that it is called *closing shift* due to a spelling mistake.

By then, having searched many university websites and failed to find any postgraduate prospect in England that I could possibly afford until September, I felt extra miserable. Most days I dragged myself to Pumpkin thinking about my unfinished Master, my academic pretension, and mainly about returning to my parents' empty-handed at that age. *Why is all this happening?*

17

During that break season, on the way from the White Lodge to the train station, I always took a short cut through the University of Leeds and passed by the Tetley Round Garden. There, by the feet of a tree, candles and flowers were placed beside a photo of 21-year old student named Meredith Kercher – a student of the University of Leeds who'd been murdered in Italy in the past November during her exchange programme.

Every time I passed by the Tetley Round Garden and saw Meredith's photo I contemplated it, with a heavy chest, thinking on how the dreams of such a young and beautiful girl were terminated by an irreversible misfortune. I imagined her family's distress and prayed: *Oh Lord, forgive me for being so sorrow for my little troubles.* And even though I realised the pettiness of my troubles I still wallowed in self-pity.

In the beginning of February, just 2 weeks into the new term, I was on the verge of a nervous breakdown with my situation and the stress at Pumpkin. Exactly at this time, my Leodensian manager, Rebecca, turned up.

It was nearly time to shut the unit. Rebecca helped me to serve the last customers and close the shutters.

Rebecca hardly spoke a word to me until we found ourselves alone. Then, she uttered, "Jounz..." slowly, with a falling intonation, and a freaky creaky voice. "...Can you count t' wastage and put t' sam'widges in t fridge whilst I do the till, please?"

"Yes," I replied waiting for her to go to the point.

After a silence, Rebecca creaky voiced again. "Jounz... ye know whe' the till discrepancy forms ah?" As I nodded, she went on. "D'you know y' 'af t' fill wan when the'z a discrepancy?" Again she waited. "An' why ye don't put'em together with t' cash bag?"

"Er…, I don't know a reason for the discrepancy."

"Y' still haf to state a reason. It's our policy." After some more silence, Rebecca spoke again. "Jounz… D'you know you haf t' leave the unit stocked up an' neat for t' next shift?" Again, I nodded. "So, why ah'f had complaints from the morning staff about the state of the unit in the morning?"

"It's that, I can't manage to do everything." I answered as I stocked up and moved on to cleaning the coffee station. I couldn't tell Rebecca that I'd just had it with putting up with the whole mess from the previous shifts myself. There were cameras, so she should know.

"…Right, off my own experience, I'll show you how t' speed things up…" Rebecca started instructing me how to begin closing each station an hour before closing the shutters. Also, since she realised a few things on her own, she told me to report when the till wasn't checked as I started my shift, and she assured me that all staff would comply with the tidiness.

I realised Rebecca's disappointment. She managed both the Pumpkin and the Upper Crust at the Coach Station, and already had enough on her plate. It was terrible to see her taking time to handle a situation that I wasn't capable of solving myself. To a native English in her position, having to tell a foreign grown man how things should be done was surely delicate, if not awkward. I felt stupid, useless, and utterly humiliated.

When I returned to White Lodge that night I just threw myself under a freezing shower expecting that the pain I was feeling inside subsided under the shock that the biting water caused to my body.

There was a seminar preparation set for the next morning that I still had to finish. *What was the point*?

Succumbed to that pain, I threw myself under the covers, with the radio on to help calming my nerves.

I was light asleep when *When You Believe*, sang by

Leon Jackson, began playing. The song talked of prayer and hopefulness, of apprehension and doubtful feelings, and of moving mountains and miracles. As those words began making sense to me, a wave of sobs ripped from my chest; each sob felt like a stone being lifted off me.

The difficulties I'd had until there flashed across my mind. That gave me strength to get up and finish the seminar preparation, as a few tears still flowed, making the printed letters of the textbook all blurry.

Yet, I felt calmer.

Minutes from then I had the impression to hear, coming from above my window, a chilling scream.

18

Outside the windowpane a hazy twilight veiled the surrounds of the White Lodge intensifying the suspense generated by the silence that followed from that high-pitched scream.

I wasn't startled by that. Perhaps some girl from James Bailey Park or Devonshire Hall was playing daft. Still, the tension on the muscles of my forearms made me clutch the textbook with so much strain that the words on the page were trembling.

A moment from then, the sound of thuds came from the hardwood floor above me. Another second and the night hush within the walls of the White Lodge was interrupted by a muffled sound of sobs and of a second voice in a non-English language.

Hesitant on whether to offer help or to be discreet, I climbed the stairs to the 1st floor. There, Luciana – the Italian housemate of room 5 – with two non-residents of the White Lodge gathered in front of room 6.

"Wh-what happened?"

"It's Matilda..." Luciana informed, referring to the

German lady of room 9. "She came downstairs and passed out in front of Gundula's room."

"Oh, what's wrong with her?" I could hear Gundula, who was also German, speaking inside room 6.

"She had a breakdown, I think. Gundula is trying to calm her down now."

"Ah…" I stood there, not knowing how to act. No housemate from the ground floor bothered to come upstairs; and frankly there wasn't much we could do.

"Don't worry. Anne is with them," – Luciana referred to another German housemate. "And an ambulance is on its way. We called the emergency."

"Alright." I went down to room 2, heavy hearted, a little ashamed for being so miserable just before, and thinking how my troubles shouldn't be great after all.

It never seemed apparent that anything wrong was happening to Matilda, mainly because as a housemate from semester one she'd always kept herself to herself.

I heard the NHS ambulance and remained inside the room to respect Matilda's privacy at that moment. Calling at the General Infirmary the next morning after the seminar seemed a more reasonable attitude.

It was past 3 a.m. when I, struggling to concentrate, managed to end the seminar preparation. I knelt down, prayed for myself and for Matilda, turned the radio on, and jumped on bed. As my head hit the pillow, I had the sensation that the night had been a long unpleasant dream. And indeed, the incidents to follow from that night on, like a continuous dream, would be remarkably surrounded by surreality – a surreality that seemed to spring from my mental state and behaviour as I sought to withstand dejection and strive against defeat.

Whilst still awake, I thought about a series of beliefs that I'd cultivated so far; beliefs that, similar to my own approach to English, were fostered by a sense of self and pride, but that also hint at a bloodline inheritance.

19

I grew up hearing my father often making references to the ambiguities within the Christian scriptures, to the writings of Allan Kardek on Spiritualism, to the mediumistic letters of Chico Xavier, to the occultism in the *Great Book of Saint Cyprian*, to the secrecy surrounding the Rosicrucian Order and the Freemasonry, to the foundation of UFO sects like *Aetherius Society* and *Heaven's Gate*, to the voodooism in the macumba cults of Candomblé, to the exorcisms practiced in many local Protestant temples, to the mass suicide at Jonestown, to the grisly murders committed by the Mason Family, and a miscellany of controversial religion related subjects – along with the odd myth of supernatural happenings.

Other influence came from the maternal family line, precisely from Uncle Bob, a pious man and a true intellectual who believes in intelligent inhabitants from outer space.

My father and Uncle Bob bequeathed their interest in such matters to me either directly with the genetics or accidentally with the influence of their suggestions. Their influence must have led me to mistrust any kind of religious dogma or unanimous creed. Still, what ultimately pushed me to cultivate a more personal set of beliefs was a strong desire to achieve something that could make my life a little more meaningful.

As a gay man living in a community that often marginalises their homosexuals and with little prospect of rising socially amid a majority of underprivileged individuals, I felt myself doubly pushed to the bottom of society. The only problem with trying to achieve something meaningful is that getting a stable job that pays a bit more than the minimum wage is pretty much the main ambition within the society that I grew up in. Naturally, I shared of that same thought, but I also thought that the way to escape from an empty existence was by doing something intellectually outstanding.

Alas, trying to do something outstanding and not belonging to the upper crust are antithetical conditions that usually prompt people to say: "This is impossible!"

I've heard this often, and it always made me cringe.

Contemplating this scenario led me to seek out any information that supported the thought that *anything is possible* in this world, especially if this possible applied to my prospects in life.

I had thrills to hear acknowledged stories regarding weird and wonderful phenomena that transcend the commonplace understanding of this world; stories like the one of the hundreds of small frogs that poured over Trowbridge (Wiltshire) in 1939, and over Croydon (South London) in 1998, and the flounders and smelts that fell off the sky on Newman (East London) in 1984, and the golf balls that showered down on the region of Punta Gorda (Florida) in 1969, and the shower of coins dating from the 16th century that happened in the village of Meschera (Russia) in 1940. I didn't believe when I first read about the incident that happened in Tewksbury (Gloucestershire) in 1996, in which workers at a printing factory witnessed a tennis ball-sized glowing orb to fly into the building, whizz around the girders, hit the printing machinery, send sparkles everywhere, and finally explode in a flash. Another impressing story came from a group of passengers who were sailing up the English Channel and witnessed what appeared as upside down ships hovering over the horizon in 1957.

The important facet of these incidents is that the impression of strangeness they cause is just a deception to our common understanding of the world.

Though extraordinary, the freaky rains sound rather less impressive under the explanation that they are caused by tornados that suck creatures or objects up from lakes or the ocean miles away and after they have been frozen in the atmosphere for some time they are dropped back to earth. And the spooky floating ball of light that sounds like a FX of a summer blockbuster is identified as a phenomenon called ball lightning; it's been reported around the world and is regarded as nothing much but an unusual electric effect occurred during thunderstorms. And as to the ships, these were indeed real ships, yet, just a mirror image projected by the refraction of light as a result of the air conditions that work as a giant reflective glass in the sky revealing places hidden by the horizon; it's called *Fata Morgana*.

These phenomena come to show that no matter how weird something on the surface of this world appears to be, once the principles underlying its workings are understood, what initially may sound unreasonable or unbelievable is ultimately possible. What I learned with these stories is that the realm of impossibility must lie in the human lack of understanding of this world and not in the world itself. Naturally, the truth of this idea is open to debate; yet, one thing is out of question: this idea was fundamental to suppress any thought contrary to the possibilities of my future prospects. And, with little to guarantee the fulfilment of such prospects, holding on to this idea sounded like a good start.

Convinced that anything is possible, I sought to understand the *principle* underlying such infinitude of possibilities to perhaps understand how to trigger a specific possibility – that is, generate a desired result.

Having been brought up in a Catholic family, I learned that the Creator, an abstract being all-seeing, all-knowing, and all-powerful, was behind anything; I learned that having faith in this Creator and elevating the thoughts towards this Creator through prayers could trigger and generate miracles, i.e. a desired results.

But I still wondered to what extent the Creator acted independently without human conscious intervention, and to what extent faith and prayer effectively inspired the Creator's will. I also learned that the Creator sat at the top of a spiritual world that's intrinsically related to this material world and that contains the source of the energy that animates the human body. Thus, I implied that a path to understand the *principle* underlying the infinitude of possibilities in this material world would be to understand how the spiritual world works.

Based on the aforementioned intrinsic relation, the workings of the spiritual world was to be disclosed in the workings of the material world. So, at some point I formed a thought regarding the *principle* in these terms: everything in this material world, from physical matter to natural behaviour, follows a recurring pattern; somehow this pattern must replicate the spiritual world, ergo, must replicate the *principle*.

A known pattern is manifested in the dimensions of the *golden ratio*, which is a recurrent measure found equally in the Pyramids of the Egypt, in the facade of the Parthenon at Athens, in the gothic structure of the Notre Dame de Paris and other historical architectures, in the paintings of Leonardo da Vinci, in the music of Frédéric Chopin and other classical musicians, in the proportions of plant parts, of animals' skeletons, of the human body, of chemical compounds, in the geometry of crystals, of honeycombs, in the spiral shapes of sea shells and galaxies as well, just to name a few.

The significant point here is that the recurrence of a pattern must be an indication of a spiritual principle operating in the material world. This thought led me to a further interpretation of this operating principle; this happened as I came across with the *Myth of the Cave*.

20

In the *Myth of the Cave* the human perception of this material world is compared to the perception of prisoners who, having lived from birth in a cave, can perceive in front of them nothing but shadows projected by a source of light behind their heads.

Considering the golden ratio through the perspective of the myth would mean that the multiple dimensions of the material world share proportional similarities because they are all generated by the same source of light, i.e. the spiritual principle. Again the significant point here is that just like the golden ration may offer a glimpse of a spiritual principle under mathematic interpretation, other patterns may offer glimpses of a spiritual principle under different interpretations.

Until here my individual glimpses hadn't led me to understand how to generate a desired result.

Another influence that brought me closer to an understanding came from *The Matrix*, a film that depicts the material world as a virtual reality to which humans are bound to in a permanent dream state; the laws and limits of physics are generated by a computer programme that computes variants of the virtual world to maintain the humans engaged in a virtual existence and unaware of their non-virtual state. A specific scene of *The Matrix*, in which a child bends a spoon, addresses a concept that sounded to me like the closest thing to what generating a desired result should be: to bend the laws and limits of physics in the virtual material world one has to bend one's belief of the laws and limits since the material world is ultimately generated to make one to abide to these. In a sequel, the film also introduces a character named the Architect who is just an avatar of the main programme generator.

Seen through the perspective presented in *Cave* and *Matrix* the Creator's omnipresence, omniscience, and omnipotence in our material world made more sense. In this way the Creator isn't quite an emotional being with bad or good will; he's a mathematical, logical principle. This clarified why so many sad and unjust things happens in the world without a fair divine intervention.

Until here, I'd understood that desired results could be generated through conscious prayer. Yet, if the Creator was a non-emotional principle so a conscious prayer, being an emotional pleading, wouldn't instigate a response. What triggered a response had to be something incidental to praying. So, I hypothesised that people could manage to generate a desired result by establishing an intuitive connection with the *principle* even without being conscious of that act. The result generated from this intuitive connection could be quite ordinary, like keeping a situation undisturbed, or performing a work routine successfully, or obtaining cooperation from another person; but extraordinary results could be equally generated. Such intuitive connection could be established through a number of approaches as long as people engage their mental efforts towards the desired result – the physical effort becomes a mere effect of such mental engagement.

This idea stemmed from the fact that religious institutions and spiritual leaders often include a set of behaviour in their teachings and prioritise faith, which ultimately is a mental attitude, as a way to obtain blessings (results). The association "mental effort and the ability to generate a desired result" is also the focus of non-fiction books like in *The Miracles of Your Mind* written by a church minister named Joseph Murphy, or in *The Infinite Power of Your Mind* written by a priest named Lauro Trevisan, or yet in *The Alchemist*, a novel by Paulo Coelho, in which the author affirms that when a person wants something, the universe conspires in helping this person to achieve this something. The same association is explored in the documentary *The Secret*, produced by Rhonda Byrne, which refers to the principles of the *Law of Attraction* to state that thought and emotion can project real situations.

So, perhaps the mental engagement should be the connection that interacted with the workings of the *principle* and controlled its forms in the material world.

Unluckily, I sensed a problem with this hypothesis: I lived in constant prayer, applied a great amount of mental effort towards my desired targets trying to keep an optimistic thought and attitude, and, not to be called a philosophical layabout, worked like a mule; yet, that night at White Lodge, I seemed to be utterly defeated. Had I tried to push my prospects a little too far then?

Anyhow, on that journey pursuing English I'd crossed the Rubicon and the die had long been cast. And since English had never really come to my life to bring peace, I had no option but to carry on battling to fulfil my desired prospects in English in the UK. For that, I desperately needed to figure out why my return to Leeds had been so mired in turmoil and what was missing for me to understand how to trigger a specific possibility (generate a desired result).

Here is where one of Uncle Bob's conjectures on aliens lit a further light on my understanding of the workings of the spiritual world and of the *principle*.

21

Last time I visited Uncle Bob, we spent time talking about films that dealt with aliens. As we went through a list of titles that we had found particularly interesting, Uncle Bob asked, "*Fire in the Sky*... Seen it?"

"Uh-uh, remind me."

"It's based on the events surrounding the alleged actual abduction of a lumberman named Travis Walton, from Northern Arizona, who was seen by five eyewitnesses being struck by a beam of light in the woods before he went missing for five days."

"And he was found alive…?"

"Yep. What got my attention was a scene that shows Travis waking up inside a cocoon-like cell of what looks like a giant beehive structure. Then, when Travis wanders off from this cell, he's caught by eerie beings, held down on a table with an organic-like sheet, and the scene is cut just as a probing machine full of wires is plugged to his mouth and a drilling needle descends straight upon his speculum-opened eyeball."

"And this Travis claimed that?"

"No, but what matters is that this scene resembles *The Matrix* when Neo escapes from the virtual world." Uncle Bob referred to the scene that the protagonist awakens in the non-virtual world within a goo-filled pod connected by wires to a gigantic power plant that consumes human bioelectricity.

"I see. But that can't be an actual event."

"True. I read this scene was created for dramatic effect. These films actually have the same director of photography; hence, the coincidence. But when I saw it after *The Matrix* I thought: if the Earth is a virtual world it's certainly controlled by extraterrestrials…"

Recalling that particular idea of Uncle Bob made me think of a number of new questions. Still, his idea seemed to be the penultimate piece to fill my understanding on how to generate a desired result.

The final piece was an idea that I'd contemplated as I read George Orwell's *Nineteen Eighty-Four* for the module *20th-Century Fiction in English*.

22

Nineteen Eighty-Four tells of the struggles of civil servant Winston Smith to preserve his identity and free thought from the ultimate control of an omniscient and omnipresent government, embodied in the virtual figure of Big Brother – whose ultimate purpose is to maintain a totalitarian control over the population of Oceania.

The idea that had me thinking came from the novel's depiction of such control.

Big Brother manages to control the population by manipulating people's perception of reality, either by manipulating factual information of the world through the media or by manipulating the thoughts of the individuals through coercion. Big Brother isn't human; Big Brother is a picture of a human face in a monitor – a human-computer hybrid as I'd highlighted in my *20th-Century Fiction* essay from semester one.

By manipulating individuals' perception of reality Big Brother functions as an invisible/ abstract principle generating the forms of the material world; not much generating the forms themselves but determining individuals' perception of these forms. The narrative tells how members of the government rewrite historical information and destroy previous historical evidence to determine a single, even if not factual, historical truth.

The final part of *Nineteen Eighty-Four* describes a direct process of determining an individual's perception of reality. In this part, a member of the government named O'Brien controls Winston's perception of reality by inflicting pain and suffering on him through physical and psychological torture. O'Brien has the power to control Winton's pain and suffering, so Winston, to avoid being inflicted with pain and suffering, surrenders to O'Brien's suggestions to the point of genuinely accepting them as the truth.

Orwell's novel enlightened me not much for the parallels from the novel and my understanding of how the principle determines the material world, or the human perception of the material world, but rather for the notion that pain and suffering could generate a shift in the perception of reality. After reading it, I remained contemplating that if pain and suffering could generate a shift in the perception of reality then perhaps pain and suffering could generate a shift in the reality itself.

And so, that night at the White Lodge, as I found myself so gloom, thinking on all these ideas lit a bulb above my head – or just blew it up for good. I came to a conclusion on how to generate a desired result.

I had to start from the belief that the material world is a shadowy or virtual illusion inflicted on human perception, like in the *Cave* or *Matrix*, and that aliens exert control over the properties and physical laws of our reality just as Uncle Bob suggested. In order to keep humans engaged in this illusional material world, unaware of the source of this illusion, these aliens must exert this control – i.e. operate the principle – from a place which cannot be perceived by human physical senses, a realm invisible to humans, namely the spiritual world. The aliens need humans to remain unaware of this illusion because the material world must be designed with the purpose to maintain humans continually stressing, struggling, and suffering, both physically and emotionally. Under circumstances of stress, struggle, and suffering humans must produce some sort of energy – perhaps bioelectricity like in *The Matrix* – that must be fundamental to the aliens and the spiritual world. This fundamental energy may perhaps be interpreted by the human body in the form of a rush in the mind, a lump in the throat, a crush in the heart, a thrill in the stomach, an intense anxiety or sexual excitement, and other similar sensations.

The recurrent proportions of the golden ratio found throughout the physical world might be as much an indication of a spiritual principle as the recurrent emotional and physical circumstances of stress, struggle, and suffering found throughout the human history and throughout the daily lives of humans.

Humankind also seems to be specially designed to prompt and engage in circumstances of stress, struggle, and suffering; sign of this is in the oppressive and fraudulent practices of most governments, the barbaric nature of some nations and social behaviours, the prejudice and intolerance between individuals, the fact that many forms of amusement lead to vice and dependency, and that most means of enjoyment involve some form of physical endurance, human antagonism, some risk of hazard, or a sadistic act. Aliens must give that extra little push as well by, from time to time, making themselves conspicuous in the material world, without really revealing their nature, driving peoples' beliefs into different directions, and consequently promoting scenarios for confusion and war – stress, struggle, and suffering naturally follow on from this.

Through this perspective the aliens' purpose seems full of wickedness. Fortunately this perspective doesn't match the fact that the material world is also a realm full of beauty and a setting of beautiful stories. Perhaps the aliens' ultimate purpose is to generate beauty, to prepare humankind to surmount their illusory problems and become more perfected. I was also inclined to believe that the aliens make no distinction between wickedness and beauty and thus generate any illusory reality to stimulate the production of the fundamental energy. Submitting humans to stress, struggle, and suffering must be the most efficient mean to stimulate the production of the fundamental energy; yet there may be other means. Aliens might be perfecting other efficient means to stimulate the production of the fundamental energy in humans without generating the usual circumstances of stress, struggle, and suffering.

Submitting humans to laughter and love, for example, may have a similar function.

This perspective might cast a different light on the grounds for aliens' conspicuous visitations throughout history. Instead of promoting confusion and war their aim might be to instruct nations of such different means to stimulate the production of the fundamental energy, to instruct humans to induce their illusions into a certain direction that will still maintain them producing the fundamental energy. This might be main function underlying the religious principles of faith and belief.

In this thought, I understood, should lie the solution to the question of how to generate a desired result.

The illusion of the material world is designed with properties and physical laws that potentially present infinite variations, i.e. possibilities, so as to suit multifarious circumstances. These circumstances are inflicted upon a collective perception but specific variations may be filtered to suit individuals. One doesn't need to have a high level of spiritual awareness to perceive some possibilities; individuals may discover certain possibilities through their life experiences in the material world. Being more aware of these possibilities, though, must facilitate individuals to generate a desired result. I was aware of the possibilities and, hopefully, in the right direction to generate my desired result.

So, if illusions are inflicted upon individuals to make them produce a fundamental energy, maybe when an individual decides to pursue a desired result, this individual is actually choosing the illusion that's worth to stress, struggle, and suffer for. And the more this individual stresses, struggles, and suffers, the more this individual induces the illusion to a certain direction.

This happens because when a person is stressing, struggling, and suffering this person is producing the fundamental energy and thus establishing a connection with the *principle*. At this moment if this person is strongly focused on the desired result, this person is actually communicating to the *principle* what illusion will motivate him or her to produce that amount of energy. This is how a mental engagement in a thought interacts with the workings of the principle and filters a specific possibility in the material world. And this is why passion is fundamental to trigger a specific possibility (generate a desired result) since passion strengthens the interaction with the principle.

Well, it should be that or having read *Nineteen Eight-Four* under the deadline pressure of the School of English loosened my last screw. Still, that belief made sense to me; mainly as I thought back to the difficult situations that I experienced from the moment I'd made my mind to pursue what I truly passionately desired.

Since, willing or not, I lived in constant distress, I embraced that principle. If something went wrong and caused me to stress, struggle, or suffer I'd repeated: *Don't think of the pain, think on the purpose.*

And my purpose in Leeds was to do a postgraduate – if not a Doctorate, any other that could save me. By instinct I followed that belief when I threw myself under the cold shower after arriving from Pumpkin. Under cold water, with my body in shock, I focused on my purpose of returning to Leeds, and thought of the emotional and physical discomfort as a vital element in the workings of the *principle* which I had to endure to fulfil that purpose. Even if I had doubts about how close to the truth that belief was and how deep into a state of insanity I was, cold showers became just one of the enduring habits that I included in my daily routine after that night.

23

"…In Northern England, patchy fogs and occasional hail showers are expected until noon; the mean temperature is eleven degrees Celsius, forty-nine point one Fahrenheit, falling to nine degrees into the evening…"

The radio had been on all night. Early that morning, it woke me up from the dark abyss of a deep sleep with that brilliant weather report.

A little yawning and stretching and my knees went straight on to the carpet for my morning prayer. After that, I tottered to the bay window and drew the curtains open just to catch sight of the weather forecast words projecting themselves in their full length, breadth, and depth beyond the pane, around the White Lodge.

Another miserable cold morning, I thought, hardly suspecting that the most wonderful time of my life was about to begin.

I'd slept a few hours only. I'd failed to die by fatigue once, so a little sleep deprivation should pose no serious threat to health. The exhaustion that weighed on my head and shoulders should be enough to keep me struggling and fulfil the demands of the *principle*.

A tepid shower was all I could endure that morning. I should fast too, but there was no way I'd stay hungry and not end up collapsing later. So, I went for a lifesaver tea and toasts in the kitchen, where I met Gundula. "Morning…"

"Hi, morning…"

"I went upstairs last night. What's up with Matilda?

"She had a breakdown." Gundula replied. "She's at the General Infirmary now."

"Should we visit her?" I more suggested than asked.

"Yeah, I mean… this early?"

"No. I have to type and print a preparation at the Edward Boyle before a seminar at eleven. But there's a break at noon." Seminars of the *Forensic Approaches to Language* module happened in the Office House 5 at the School of English. I had an hour to hasten myself to Leeds General Infirmary and be back to attend a lecture in the Roger Stevens at 1 p.m. "So, I got time then."

"I'm busy this whole morning as well, but I'll find out which warden she was admitted to and text you."

"That's fine." I thanked Gundula whilst she already made her way out of the kitchen.

I waited until I had to turn the mobile off during the *FAL* seminar. Gundula's message never flashed though.

23

Matilda's in ward 38, Brotherton Wing. Gundula.

The text flashed, when I turned the mobile back on.

I left the Office House 5 at Cavendish Rd., crossed underneath the car park straight to Willow Terrace, turned right to Calverley St., and reached the entrance of the Brotherton Wing.

Ward 38 felt comfortable. Not warm though. It had around a dozen beds, all occupied. Matilda was lying there under the covers, a little quiet but awake.

"Hello there." I stood near her bed. "Hope you don't mind me coming. Feeling better?"

"I'm alright." Matilda replied as I sat on a chair by the bedside.

"Just attended a seminar. It's a bit chilly here isn't?"

"A bit…"

I was trying to avoid any remarks or questions that reminded us the fact that we were in an infirmary ward. "Well, you're must be used to the weather surely."

Matilda just smiled.

There was a bit of silence as another patient next to Matilda, who didn't seem well, said to an approaching healthcare assistant that it was past the time to leave the infirmary and the assistant amiably threatened to call the doctor. Matilda seemed visibly unquiet with that.

I couldn't avoid thinking that indeed my troubles should be smaller than I deemed them to be.

The assistant then approached Matilda with a smile. "How are you feeling?"

I kept hushed for a moment, but began humming the tune of *Relax, Take it Easy* by Mika – which stuck like an earworm in my head – to give Matilda some privacy.

"Excuse me." The assistant addressed me. "Would you sign this, please?"

"I'm just a housemate, is that alright?"

"Yes, just sign it, please…"

As I signed it, the assistant commented to Matilda on how charming my continental accent sounded, then left without telling when Matilda would be discharged.

"See? At least my accent is charming." I made Matilda smile. Then, I noticed near the bed a blue tray with a mini-pot of jam and marmalade untouched. "Are you still eating that?"

"Uh-uh."

I grabbed the mini-pot and uttered, "Buy none, get one free!" I felt happy to see Matilda amused. I'd been target of housemate's comments due to that habit of living on free food past the sell-by date from Pumpkin.

"Did you see any other housemate today?"

"Only Gundula knows I'm here, I think."

"Everyone's busy really. I'm between lectures now." I carried on, making small talk until the time to return to the university came. I recalled how the White Lodge often felt awfully lonely and shivered to think of how worse staying in an infirmary ward should feel. So before leaving I asked, "Can I call again after lecture?"

"Yes, if you want." Matilda seemed happy with that.
"Fancy anything off Morrisons?"
"I'm alright…"

Two hours later I headed again to Brotherton Wing, this time with a Morrisons carrier bag in each hand. But by the time I reached the ward 38, Matilda had left.

I assumed that Gundula, who had a rented vehicle, had come to drive Matilda back to White Lodge. I rang Gundula but the call went straight to the voicemail.

A bit disappointed, I was making my way out when Matilda, who seemed to be waiting, called my name.

"…Here!… I'm leaving now."

"That's great." I said, feeling a little awkward.

The shopping at Morrisons had blown my weekly budget and, as usual, I'd walk to the White Lodge.

Matilda didn't mention anything about Gundula, or how she intended to return to the White Lodge, and all that she had on her was a blue woolly hooded jumper – not the warmest fashion choice for a 30-minute stroll under a weather that felt less than 11 degrees Celsius. The time had come for me to reach for the emergency funds. So, I fished deep in my pocket and asked, "You mind if we get a bus and get off at Hyde Park Corner?"

"Not at all."

The Hyde Park Corner stop was one stop before the North Hill Rd. stop. We'd pay only £1 each, instead of £1.60, if we walked three streets up the road and went to White Lodge via Cumberland Rd. "Let's go, then."

We crossed the Millennium Square, went through Cookridge St., and made to Woodhouse Lane. There we waited at the bus stop in front of the Leeds College of Technology. A smooth bus ride took us to the foot of Headingley which at that time was bustling with young students coming back from the university – a view that transmitted a feeling of enthusiasm and cheerfulness.

Unlike me, Matilda wasn't touched by that scene;

she still sounded apathetic as we reached White Lodge.

Luckily, that evening I was off work. In evenings like that I'd unwrap a frozen baguette, heat it, and eat it whilst listening to a half-past 6 comedy on *Radio 4*. But that was no ordinary evening, and thus, a perfect one to prepare an instant chicken consommé that had been stocked in the cupboard for a special occasion.

It wasn't difficult to bring smiles to Matilda's face. It felt fabulous to have a guest for dinner in the ground floor kitchen – especially Matilda, who spoke native English; though Matilda was German from birth she'd lived in Ireland from the age of four. We had the consommé watching *The Oblongs* on the DVD player, then we ate double chocolate cookies from Morrisons, and still shared a Thai sweet chilli Sensations crisps.

Other housemates turned up to talk to Matilda but didn't linger over long. I asked no question about the nature of Matilda's problems or bothered her with my personal dramas; but made sure that she knew that should she need help I'd be glad to oblige, and that she should help herself with anything from my cupboard.

As the night drew to a close, before Matilda went to her floor upstairs, we lingered a little longer in the hall of the ground floor, a bit reluctant to retreat to the solitude of our chambers. Finally, we bid "Good night."

Once into the room, I turned the radio on to dissolve the silence. The English coming from the radio sounded quite less interesting though.

I threw myself on the mattress with a full stomach but a light head. The pillow felt so fluffy and cloud-like that I had to muster a great strength of mind to get off bed again and do the compulsory reading for next day.

The minutes on the phone display leaped whilst I caught myself staring blankly at a paragraph, thinking about that evening. I felt proud for being supportive in a moment that I found myself wanting support, and for being able to felt compassion when other housemates passed by that situation somewhat indifferently. In all honesty, being such a gentleman to Matilda that evening involved a bit more than altruism of my part; as I felt dejected myself, offering support to a mate entailed a therapeutic impulsion. I usually sympathised with others in their hard times; it was no different with Matilda. Without doubt, whatever misfortune had led Matilda to that infirmary, it'd also brought along a full-blown friend. In between paragraphs, I kept thinking of all things we could do together, like enjoying a trip to a local fish and chips shop in Headingley, having a *Früli* at Fab Cafe, and going out Monday to Queens Court!

Finally, I hit the mattress, trying not to think of the outcome of my inefficient reading – an early morning lecture would tell me all about it.

24

The weather forecaster announced another gray day, making no effort to enliven the languor of an early routine.

To get me going that early, and to atone for the sin of being so distracted in the previous night, I threw myself under a full flowing cold shower. In the second the biting water poured over my skull, I shrieked. "Ooohhh! Oh mah good."

Afraid that the blood rush would burst some clogged vein within my brain, I adjusted the water temperature to tepid. That should lighten my slumberous state.

On the way out of the bathroom, I met Damien in the hall. "Good morning!"

"Brilliant morning." Damien sounded cranky.

"Yes, this will be one of those days that a dark cloud hovers over us."

"Tell me about it." Damien agreed.

I was wrong; when I stepped outside, the cloud was engulfing me – that, or a veil of smoke hazed my sight. The lecture, for example, was a blur as I strived to hold my eyelids up. I went on through the afternoon semi-alive, languid, and sensing the world in slow motion. I followed to the Edward Boyle Library, to use the Net in the level 10 PC cluster, and read a little for Thursday.

Holding on to my belief about stressing, struggling, and suffering, I thought: if human life meant sacrificing and if sacrificing oneself for a purpose would indeed yield that purpose no matter the odds, that would be an opportunity to undertake the acid test of that principle. I'd arrived at the assumptions on that principle by trailing a painful pathway, but had been reluctant to actually commit to its implications consciously, even if I'd done that sometimes intuitively.

So, that afternoon, I kept my bloodshot eyes opened, through nodding off and all, on a chapter of the textbook *An Introduction to Forensic Linguistics*, by Malcom Coulthard and Alison Johnson – the latter being my tutor for the second time. When the fatigue became unbearable, I thought on my purpose of doing a postgraduate course in the UK and perched my chest. That wrestle went on, until the time to go to Pumpkin.

Rebecca had assigned me to cover closing shifts from 4 p.m., Wednesday to Saturday, and Mondays. After the frustrating events of Monday, I promised myself to do anything to keep in control at Pumpkin, and endure any distress, thinking on my purpose. Shifts at Pumpkin would bring the usual burdens anyways, whether I obliged to them or not.

I reached Leeds train station half an hour before the shift started as I usually had to get cakes and savouries in the kitchen next to platform 8 before crossing the footbridge pathway to platform 15B – where Pumpkin

Café was located. At the end of the shift I didn't focus on the frustration caused by the discrepancies between the cash in the till drawer and the till reading figures; instead I recounted the pound notes and coins, signed the discrepancy forms, and then refilled every shelf and fridge, sanitised every counter and lower surface, and left a spic and span Pumpkin right behind me. But not without packing a bag with savouries past the sell-by date to dine later at the White Lodge.

Committed to that ritual routine I didn't see Matilda until Saturday afternoon.

Matilda used the upstairs kitchen and only came to the ground floor to cross the hall, either to leave or enter the house. Apart from when all housemates went on a night out, my chances of seeing Matilda were slim. That afternoon, however, as I washed the dishes before going to work, Matilda entered in the kitchen with Gundula, both carrying bags from Wilkinson.

"Good afternoon." I addressed Matilda, rather enthusiastically. "How are you?"

"Oh I'm fine actually." Matilda replied, distantly.

"We've just been to Otley Road. Will you join us for dinner later?" Gundula invited me with her well-paced German accent.

"I'll take a rain check; got work tonight." I said whilst Gundula began emptying the carrier bags on to the sink counter, displaying a colourful and organised array of groceries labelled with different organic certification logos. – Most girls at White Lodge had a thing for organic food and, to some of them especially, the habit of 'eating organic' had a sacredness that they persistently preached about. Sometimes, as I innocently enjoyed my artificial meals in the kitchen, two or more girls would flock to bash me about how non-organic food was contaminated with synthetic pesticides and chemical fertilisers, and were processed using industrial solvents and chemical additives, and had genetically modified organisms; if I was drinking black tea they would talk on the benefits of herbal infusions, if I was eating a baguette they'd talk on the benefits of whole wheat bread, and so forth. Mealtime at White Lodge often felt like a crossover between ITV's *Loose Women* and Channel 4's *Hell's Kitchen*. – So, seeing Matilda and Gundula together next to that amount of organic labels made me a little diffident to invite Matilda for lunch on Sunday. I couldn't come up with any reason to get together with Matilda other than… "Hey, are you free to watch *The Oblongs* after lunch tomorrow?"

"Oh, I'm afraid tomorrow I'm going with Gundula and the girls to The Bear Pit in Cardigan Road…" – I didn't have the slightest idea where this Bear Pit was. I kept silent, waiting for her to add something to that. After a while, Matilda added. – "Do you mind watching it a bit later… tea time possibly."

To what I feigned a smile, to hide my frustration and jealousy, and replied, "That's alright with me."

"I'll make an Irish apple crumble." Matilda had a gentle smile that I instantly replicated with my own.

I had no idea what kind of food was Irish apple crumble. *Some traditional titbit from Ireland*, I implied. Just the thought of that stirred my expectations for it. "Great! See you tomorrow."

"Great, see you." Matilda's ominous tone, though, somewhat indicated that her Irish crumble wouldn't be all that great.

25

Sunday dawned, living up to its name: clear sky and light winds. Unfortunately, that Sunday wouldn't live up to my expectations.

As usually I did on Sundays, I phoned home.

Bad news: my mother had been hit by a bicycle in the street and ended up with some broken teeth and cuts on her mouth that needed stitches. I couldn't feel more impotent; so far from mom, with no means to assist her. My father told me not to worry and not to mention anything, as she'd made him promise he wouldn't tell.

Such news left a lump strangling my throat.

This lump'll dissolve with Matilda's apple crumble. I hoped. But then again, the apple crumble just made the lump bigger. Not that Irish apple crumble – which, as I learned, is a kind of pie made with pastry dough, peeled and chopped Granny Smith apples, and a mix of flour, sugar, butter, and cinnamon on the top – tasted bad; but being with Matilda that evening turned out to be an unsavoury disappointment.

First Matilda brought Gundula along and they began talking in German more than in English; then I had a strong impression that they should be talking about me as they giggled every time I opened my mouth; finally they brought to my attention that I consistently used the word *mud* instead of *mould*, and that whenever they corrected me I just uttered the word *mud* louder; and to make sure that they'd leave my self-esteem for dead they said that my English sounded like that of Kazakhs journalist Borat Sagdiyev. For someone who aspired to a Doctorate in English that was rather humiliating.

Well, the English idiom to learn from that event was a follow-up to the expression *hit rock bottom*; this time I learned the meaning of *sinking to a new low*. And having learned that, I gave those German ladies my good night smirk, gathered my unheeded DVD player, my last piece of apple crumble, my last crumble of dignity, and crumbled on to bed to drown in tears.

At the end of that Sunday an overwhelming sinking feeling dragged me down to the depths of a nightmare. And a thought scared me to death: *I'd gone mad.*

26

I plugged the radio on, turned the lights off, and curled up under the covers, shaking, thinking that in my delirium I'd misguidedly resorted to believing in supernatural intuition, in spiritual principles, in science fiction, and trusting that fasting, sleep deprivation, and cold showers could generate miracles. Worst of all, I'd brought that shame upon myself for having too much pride of my intellect, for my wrath against those who challenged me. Things were just not working and my life was stripped of sense.

I remained in that state through the week, dragging myself to the University of Leeds, on to Leeds station, and back to the White Lodge. Sitcoms and cartoons made me nostalgic and radio comedies gave me nausea. I did the seminar preparations through watery eyes.

One night that week, I was lumbering back from Leeds station, through the usual poorly lit short cut from the South entrance to the North entrance of the University of Leeds, absorbed in that melancholic haze, when all of a sudden, I found myself surrounded by a chav, a patch-eyed pirate, a constable, a rugby player, a harlequin, a ballerina, a winged angel, a teletubby, and a pussycat. They were beating on a small drum, spinning a wooden rattle, blowing a plastic horn, as well as dancing, jumping around, and frolicking graciously. I felt embarrassed to be wearing the orange uniform top from Pumpkin, holding a paper carrier bag, and with an awful dull look right in the middle of that parade of fancy-dressed students. Before I had time to move to one side, they slowed down their rhythm and some of them greeted me with jovial gestures – the harlequin making a chivalrous bow and the ballerina making a curtsey – as I passed undisturbed.

As that frolic ensemble of students acknowledged my presence with such affability, they made me feel like one of them for a moment, and that cheered me up.

When I arrived at the White Lodge I felt enough less miserable to go and slip a note under Matilda's door.

Would you like to have lunch together on Saturday?

Earlier on at the university, I'd met Matilda at the entrance of the Student Union building and she looked distressed again. Luciana, the Italian housemate, who was accompanying her, gave me a look of discomfort as if saying "How to solve a problem like Matilda."

I felt hurt with what had happened on Sunday but, that night, with a lighter spirit, I let go of that grudge.

This time Matilda came alone. We ate baguettes and pastries that were stocked in the fridge, watched my traditional DVD player, and chatted until the time to go to Pumpkin came. We'd been given flyers advertising a 24-hour marathon of performances starting on Monday from 8 p.m. in the Riley Smith Hall – the theatre of the Student Union building.

"*Entry just a pound*, that's my kind of price. C'mon, I'll pay yours."

"Are you off Monday?"

"No but, if you're up to go, I'll ask to work tomorrow instead."

"Go on, then…"

All worked out.

Monday, at 8 p.m., we were at the Riley Smith Hall, where there'd be a presentation each hour.

We'd made plans to see the stand-up routine that'd be performed in the second hour slot. Before that, they had a performance from a local production of *Songs for a New World* – an off-Broadway production by Jason Brown from 1995 but that I'd never heard of until then. That unfamiliarity with the musical forced me to make a considerable effort to understand the meaning of the lyrics in the opening musical number. But when the second number began the lyrics became instantly intelligible to me as the meaning of its verses seemed to dodge my linguistic cognitive limitations and reach straight into my heart.

In the next minutes I'd witness the manifestation of something hard to explain; something that's been called *Thinking Substance*, *subconscious power*, *infinite mind*, *Universal intelligence*, *secret*; I called it, the *principle*.

27

The lights on the stage had faded at the coda of the opening number; everything was pitch-dark. Then, the pianist struck the first chords of the second song.

A dim blue light came up on the stage and this young lad dressed as a ship captain began singing with a powerful tenor voice. *"Lord, we take this journey, To find a promised land. And we believe in your power..."*

I held my breath, awed with the beauty of that voice.

It was 1492. The captain was on the deck of a Spanish sailing ship navigating in the middle of the ocean under a stormy sky, leading a crew of outcasts. The captain sang, staring blankly at a distant horizon, as the chords of the piano grew more thunderous. When a harmonising slow paced bongos' beat was introduced, my heart pounded more intensely. *"Lord, these men are hungry. There just hasn't been enough. And the journey's been so rough."*

The captain went on, claiming that he was starving, and hurting, and lost. The rhythm of the music intensified and the captains' claims reached higher notes, each note pulling thick tears right off my chest. *"Have mercy, Lord... shine your light on these children who have faith in your guiding hand. I'm just begging Lord, cause there's no place else to go."*

Other characters appeared on stage, among them a woman carrying a baby and a man with a suicidal gaze, and they all appeared to be in a turning point of their life, searching for guidance, pleading to the Lord to give them the strength to survive the journey; these characters joined the captain in a unison supplication. "*Lord, give me hope. I am not strong enough... I am unworthy.*" As the song reached its coda, they all claim to see that "*a new world calls across the sky.*"

My own plead at that moment was that the Lord kept the lights in the Riley Smith Hall away from the audience for another number since there was no way to disguise my convulsions. I'd been caught unguarded.

I expected that a musical would be something like *The Phantom of the Opera*, *Grease*, or *Mamma Mia*! But when I began listening to such emotional lyrics that seemed to be uncovering the uncertainties and anxieties of my heart, speaking so intimately to me, a flood of tears streamed down my beautiful cheeks. Those lyrics made sense of my journey to that moment, made sense of my determination despite the fact that there was absolutely nothing to guarantee my success in Leeds; that made me cry because I understood in my heart that such determination didn't come from a feeble mind like mine but from something higher than me, most powerful, against which no doubts dare to stand. Just as I felt like a total wreck a song about a ship on the verge of breaking up made me regain strength to keep trusting in the ideas that'd brought me a second time to Leeds.

Hopefully, Matilda hadn't seen me weeping like a girl; perhaps she'd wept herself, but I had no courage to look. I only gathered courage to face Matilda again just before the stand up comedians' presentation started.

"Did you enjoy the musical?"

"Pretty much... Were you crying during the ship song?" Matilda asked smiling.

Bugger! "What? No. The performance was so real that the water beneath that ship splashed on my face."

"Hum-well, let's go with that."

When the comedians came on to the stage, I laughed my head off whenever I understood what they were saying.

It was a fantastic night out. We cried, we laughed; we passed by the fish and chip shop and vowed to come there another night. That night marked the real beginning of a beautiful friendship.

That night also foreshadowed a turning point in my plans regarding the postgraduate course: not long from then a new world of prospects would disclose itself to me. This new world would make me better understand why Humpty Dumpty, in *Through the Looking Glass* by Lewis Carol, says that when he uses a word that word means just what he chooses that word to mean – and how that short sentence carried a spiritual principle behind this material world. This new world would also reveal to me the distinction between two Greek words: one that came into English around the 17th century, *agape*, and the other that came through Latin, *Eros*.

28

"Cast t' ship on t' righ' side o' the net, and ye shall find, inni' bruv."

This unknown eye-catching Caucasian lad casually uttered those words as if he was quite familiar with me. He looked pretty young and skinny, was wearing a baseball cap, flashy earrings, a white shell suit that screamed polyester, imitation designer-label trainers, and he kept playing with his hands underneath his trousers in a very distracting manner whilst repeating that sentence to me.

I knew there was something not right with his utterance but couldn't tell what. "What do you mean?"

The lad just grinned, saying, "Inni' bruv... Innit?"

Then, another voice interrupted us. That other voice came from the radio next to my bed. It was half past 7 and the sun had just risen. There was a bit more than a week to the end of February. I didn't pay much heed to that dream until a few hours later when I was at the PC cluster at the Edward Boyle library.

As usual, if I didn't have to go straight to Pumpkin after the lecture, I stayed an hour or more logging into the Nathan Bodington Building to download texts and exercises, checking emails, and browsing through websites looking for postgraduate opportunities. I'd done that regularly for the last months, and found no affordable postgraduate programme.

More than anything, browsing through university websites again and again had become an act de résistance. Yet, in the past weeks, under a despondent mindset, I'd concocted a stalling ritual: I did all that had to be done online and then remained reading Wikipedia before finally going through a few online postgraduate prospectuses. I stalled because I'd begun to disbelieve that at that late date any suitable and affordable opportunity would show in the monitor. I had qualifications that met the entry requirements from most postgraduate programmes in English but the tuition fees weren't within my financial reach. I had nearly £1.000 in the bank back home and could save a bit until September. But that still would be beneath the target.

The annual tuition fees depended on the modality of postgraduate programme and subject chosen, on whether the programme was full-time or part-time, and on whether the applicant qualified as Home, European, or International student. Part-time programmes cost around £1.000 and £2.000 but there were rare options of part-time programmes. Full-time programmes cost around £3.200 and £5.000. Such fees were applicable exclusively for Home and European students. Overseas students were allowed to apply only for full-time programmes and were required to shell out two times as much the cost of the tuition fees for Home students. So, applicants who qualified as International had to pay around £9.000 and £15.000 for a full-time programme.

There were two or three options of full or partial scholarships for overseas students. Information on these scholarships had to be accessed from other websites and the application process was described under complicated instructions; the scholarship availability was unclearly stated and the eligibility criteria seemed simply unattainable. Just looking at those instructions made me so nervous that cramps in my stomach started kicking in. After reading all instructions, I understood that I didn't qualify to any of them because either the application deadline had passed or the qualifying restrictions were simply too many.

So, that afternoon after the lecture, whilst I browsed the Internet, I remembered what the skinny chavvy lad in the dream had said. In the morning after seeing *One the Deck of a Spanish Sailing Ship, 1942* I'd searched for the full lyrics of that song entering a combination of words that I could recall – among them *ship* and *Lord* – on Google and ended up being directed to a version of *John 21*. Revisiting the final chapter of the *Gospel of John*, which I knew from early school years, made me understand that though logical reasoning impelled me to surrender, as I'd browsed through many websites time and again and found no affordable option of postgrad programme, I insisted in browsing through the same websites because I had an unconscious faith that something like the miraculous draught of fish could happen. That unconscious faith wouldn't let me abandon the PC without browsing for an opportunity one more time.

That stalling ritual should be by-product of reason and faith pulling in opposite directions. An unconscious faith wouldn't abandon me not even during REM sleep whilst I dreamt with dashing English lads. Recalling that I navigated through the net chasing a miracle, that afternoon I understood why the words *net* and *ship* were swapped in the lad's utterance. I just couldn't think that "the right side of the net" would be closer than I suspected. Still that same week, I followed the Coursefinder link for postgraduate courses in the University of Leeds website and found a full-time programme that cost £4.850. The course was a PG Diploma in Applied Translation Studies from the School of Modern Language and Cultures.

It's my miracle! I had to try that one.

29

Early on Monday I climbed the stairs of the Michael Sadler Building, knocked at the G35, the Postgraduate Admissions office, and talked to a lady at the desk.

"Excuse me. Could you confirm this information?"

"Yes, sure." The lady replied gently.

I showed her a PDF brochure printed from the web page of the Centre for Translation Studies. "Er… is this PG Diploma a postgraduate course?"

"Yes, this is indeed a postgraduate qualification."

"And, just another thing…" I showed her a PDF brochure that listed all fees from the previous academic year. "I compared these fees with the current ones and I saw that in all courses the fees increased at least a thousand pound, but this PG Diploma actually decreased over a thousand pound. Is this right?"

The lady examined for a moment. "Yes, this information is accurate."

"Oh, thank you. I'll email if I decide to apply."

"You're welcome."

I knew that a new adventure had begun.

I phoned home, euphoric. "Mom! Listen, I found a chance... Yes, like I told you. I have a thousand pound on my bank account there, plus three hundred and twenty pound in the NatWest here, plus two hundred of my accommodation deposit... Listen, until September I can save from the wages I earn here, and can do some extra work on holidays. Also, dad can take a bank loan. All this will make forty-eight hundred and fifty pound. After the course I can stay another year, earn back this money, and pay dad... Right... Talk to him then. Bye."

Later, my mother emailed me, telling that my father couldn't make a bank loan but that she could still take all she had – nearly £1.000 – and send to me. *Bummer*.

But nothing could defeat my optimism that day.

Perhaps, I'd talk to the manager from the university branch of the NatWest and tell him about my journey until then; the manager would be sensible enough and understand that I had all for my success and approve a loan. Still, one step at a time; first I had to apply and be accepted, then there would be time to think of funding.

I urged mother to send a translation from my degree transcripts. The transcripts needed to be submitted with the application along with an IELTS certificate and two references from academic lecturers. Along these, there was a translation into English test that should be submitted as well. The application could be done online but I believed that handing over all documents sealed in an envelope would make the application more real.

That afternoon, I run straight to Pumpkin and didn't stop until I got there, eager to tell the news to my manager Rebecca, who knew my plans.

"…That's great." Rebecca patiently expressed her support as she finished labelling sandwiches in the kitchen.

Before I dashed off to platform 15B, carrying the labelled sandwiches, I handed to Rebecca a short letter. "Please, read after I leave."

30

Dear Rebecca. Feel free to add hours to my roster this coming Easter. I'll work with pleasure because this will bring me closer to my dreamed postgrad course.

When Rebecca came later to the unit, bringing fresh muffins for the next day, she replied my request.

"I promise you'll be on full-time during Easter, in 'ere or Upper Crust in t' coach station."

"Thanks," I said before she left.

I had to calm myself down not to quake with excitement that shift. I almost forgot that I had a student party to go still that night. The party's host was Teri: a lovely Londoner lady, who I'd met through the language exchange scheme from the Language Centre.

Taking advantage of the multicultural mix of students within the campus, the Language Centre offered a language exchange scheme that puts language learners in contact with native speakers of the language they wished to learn. So, every week I met London-born Teri in the second floor of the Parkinson Building, and for a full hour we had a proper chinwag – as Teri used to say –, during which she drew attention to a few English mistakes I made; given that the language scheme worked under a reciprocity agreement, Teri also took advantage of my native linguistic abilities to improve her spoken Portuguese.

In our last chat Teri had told me that her housemates were throwing a party and that she wanted me to come to their house at the end of Cliff Lane, just off north of the Hyde Park corner. Being invited to a student party like that was quite unusual to me, so I had reasons to be two times cheerful that night.

At the end of the shift at Pumpkin I darted up the road to the White Lodge, took the uniform off, put a fancy with tight T-shirt on, and met Matilda in the hall.

"Oh, I've been a pile of nerves. Thank heavens we have a night to celebrate." I told as we were off the White Lodge. "And thanks for coming."

"I'm glad to come along." Matilda sounded pleased.

For the first time ever, under a 5 degree temperature, I dared to wear, besides my usual black trousers, just a T-shirt. I was totally showing off, without a jacket. I felt so fancy, so utterly different, like I wasn't myself.

As we walked to Headingley Lane, I became all excited with the night freshness, and started declaiming. "Tonight I'll be jolly, like the students I see at Woodhouse Lane when I come back from work; and I'll be merry, like the lads I see walking down Lower Briggate. Tonight I'll fun and gay. Indeed gay… with *hag* and all." I pointed to Matilda.

"How dare you call me hag?" Matilda faked anger.

"Wait… a hag with the lures of a princess."

"That's more like it."

"Yes, and this will increase my chances of getting the attention of straight blokes in the party."

"Cheeky you…"

"It's nothing I can't do myself with my Shakira-style hip shake and my Beyoncé booty bounce."

"You'll nick all t' *gaze* off me, so you will." Matilda giggled, as if saying something I couldn't really grasp.

I was glad to make Matilda smile with my daft chat. Still, what really had me grinning was having that chance to talk with a native speaker of English at will, with no time constraint.

We stopped at the *budget booze* shop to buy some cheap ciders and after taking a wrong turn towards Cliff Road we found our way to Cliff Lane.

At the party, Matilda spent most of the time eschewing the advances of a shaven-headed Southern bloke, who was wearing ragged jeans and ear-piercing. I kept shaking the stress away by the sound of Rihanna, and trying to wow some straight lad by the sound of Kylie Minogue. We both got a little tipsy and left the party just after midnight.

"This has been the most perfect night out." I said, whilst Matilda skipped on the pavement. "Woo… I saw you naughty, with that hottie."

"You could have that slimy bald bully all to yourself." Matilda feigned indifference to conceal that she'd secretly enjoyed the bloke's attention.

I felt happy to see Matilda well.

When we arrived at the White Lodge we lingered in the kitchen microwaving a couple of chicken and onion pasties. Then, we went to eat the pasties in my room to stretch the chat. I told Matilda about the *PG Diploma* course and she encouraged me to apply. We continued talking like there was an endless backlog of untouched matters to be discussed. I didn't want to stop chatting; Matilda didn't seem in a hurry to go up to her room.

31

"…You know, this night reminds me of a novel that I read ages ago about some insights from a manuscript dating from centuries BC. *Celestine Profecy*, that's it."

"Yes. May I know what it reminds you of exactly?"

"It's one of the insights; it stated that people carry energetic fields around them and that a person can develop addiction on another person's energy."

"Never heard about..." Matilda sounded puzzled.

"Well, if these insights are true we must be getting addicted to each other."

Finding that idea amusing, Matilda observed, "I do have an addictive personality."

"Woo... overconfidence. I like that!"

Matilda and I carried on chatting until nearly 4 p.m.

After Matilda left, I slept so soundly, that four hours later I felt fresh enough to jump out of bed a take a cold shower. It was the first morning in two months that I woke up without a stomach cramp or a chest crush.

But I had another reason to be thrilled that Tuesday: I had to go to Leeds Crown Court to watch a cross-examination session as part of a seminar preparation for the module *Forensic Approaches to Language*.

Indeed, I'd grown enthusiastic with *FAL* because, amongst other modules that I attended at the School of English, it was the one that provided me with the most revealing insights on the intrinsic interrelation between language and the physical reality around us. And if my state of mind then didn't lead me to misread the teachings of *FAL*, I was inclined to think that Dr Johnson's tutorial greatly promoted such insights.

Dr Johnson organised her lectures and seminars around the chapters of the enlightening introductory textbook that she and Dr Coulthard, a professor from Aston University, had jointly worked on. Furthermore, Dr Johnson, a self-declared Trekkie, certainly had sufficient imagination to bestow us students with a unique manner to understand the language and reality interconnection. This was evidenced in how Dr Johnson included into her teaching schedule that visit to Leeds Crown Court at Oxford Row – a setting where the English tongue, as I found out, is regimented by slightly unique laws.

32

Just before we entered into the courtroom, Dr Johnson told us: "The defendants in this case are on trial for committing the crime of *conspiring to pervert the course of justice*."

"Sounds like a line right off a thriller film." One mate from the seminar group commented.

"You're just about right. What it actually means is" – Dr Johnson turned to the whole group – "that the defendants acted or plotted to prevent justice from being properly executed. In this particular case, the defendants are being accused of intimidating witnesses and giving misleading testimony."

Conspiring to pervert the course of justice... That was just a sample of a few, quite Hollywoodean, sentences that we'd hear, and jot down, whilst the cross-examination proceedings developed.

After we all entered in the courtroom, we sat silently on the wooden pews in the public gallery and started watching the action unfold in front of us like a neatly choreographed stage musical.

As the judge entered, the usher cried, "All rise, the court is now in session."

We all stood up, naturally.

Then, the twelve members of the jury entered and one of them took an oath upon the *Bible*.

The usher and the barrister made reverential bows before they addressed the judge directly.

The witness, who was Islamic, was summoned and asked to take an oath upon the *Qur'an*.

The politeness of their body language had a counterpart in their verbal language as they always referred to each other by their titles or using terms of respect. The judge, particularly, was addressed as "my Lord" and referred to as "your Lordship."

The cross-examination started with "I put it to you that in the date of..." It sounded so cinematographic that I almost could hear incidental music.

The barrister always introduced questions with "I'd like to ask you," or "May I ask," or "Please tell us," and even a combination of these, what left me thinking if he wanted to be polite or just buy time before formulating the questions. Judge and barrister spoke with moderate rhythm, and in one occasion, when the witness started speaking hurriedly, the judge apologised saying, "I'm sorry, I'm taking notes." A few times, questions were rephrased. The barrister, mostly, seemed exceptionally careful with his phrasing.

And the witness repeatedly started his answers with, "To be honest, I can't remember..." as if not really willing to cooperate with the judge's question; the witness even coughed after a certain question, possibly, as a subterfuge to hedge his answer.

I couldn't help but notice that the precise gestures and measured English of the court staff were only matched by the flawlessness of their outfits: the judge wore a silk black gown and a bar jacket, and a fabulous white bench wig, full of weaves, that reminded me of a Georgian aristocrat; the usher wore an immaculate black velvet robe; and the barrister wore a dark suit, topped by an open-fronted black gown decorated with buttons and a gathered yoke, and short white horsehair wig, with lovely curls at the side and two ties down the back.

With my attention driven by those theatrical gestures, and luxurious costumes, whilst still struggling to focus on the peculiarities of the English within the courtroom setting, I found myself gasping for breath, as if suddenly struck by Stendhal syndrome.

Luckily, the trial soon had to go into lunch recess and the judge announced: "The court is adjourned."

33

That visit to Leeds Crown Court unearthed a moment of linguistic epiphany.

During the courtroom session, the impression I had was that the English used by the judge, the usher, the barrister, and the witness, transmitted their personal intentions, their social identities, their institutional roles, and most of all, it transmitted the quintessence of that environment along with all its etiquette and dressing protocols.

Such realisation echoed my former encounters with Sociolinguistic concepts, which regard language structure as a symptom of discrete social settings. Still, it was Dr Johnson's seminars on Forensic Linguistics that triggered, and eventually led to, that realisation.

Dr Johnson had mentioned how linguistic analysis became a significant element in the investigations of the Yorkshire Ripper hoaxer – the man who sabotaged the investigation on the Yorkshire Ripper by sending hoax letters and tapes recordings, and who was identified through DNA analysis and caught in 2005. 26 years earlier Stanley Ellis, a phonetician, dialectologist, and lecturer at the University of Leeds, had carried out a linguistic analysis of the hoax tape recordings to identify the accent of the speaker and inferred that the hoaxer should come from the Castletown district of Sunderland – half a kilometre away from the hoaxer's revealed residence.

What amazed me about the Ripper hoaxer case was how language carried marks so distinctive so as to allow such a close identification of an individual's geographic background. But, I still learned that the intrinsic connection between language and reality went beyond geographical / physical aspects.

This happened when Dr Johnson talked on how linguistic evidence played a central part for the conviction Derek Bentley – the man who was hanged in 1953 for participating in a burglary attempt jointly with an underage accomplice, Christopher Craig, who wounded a sergeant and murdered a police constable at the crime scene in Croydon. On the night of the crime, according to the officers' statements, Derek was heard shouting "let him have it, Chris" before the constable was shot. The accusation claimed that by shouting "let him have it" Derek incited and instigated the murder. The defence claimed that by shouting "let him have it" Derek actually urged Chris to hand the revolver over to the officers.

What attracted me about the Derek Bentley case was how the meaning attributed to an English sentence completely affected individuals' interpretation of a circumstance. Indisputably, just as individuals may attribute different meanings to an instance of language, individuals may have different interpretations of an instance of reality too. But the "let him have it" debate demonstrated this principle operating on language and reality simultaneous and mutually.

In my view, that was evidence that language and reality were linked by some metaphysical fundament that made of them an indivisible whole.

Naturally, my knowledge limitations wouldn't allow me to go much beyond that assumption. Still, this assumption gave me an invaluable insight into writing my essay that should be submitted within a week.

In the essay I addressed how the UK statute laws used different terms to encrypt slightly different interpretations of *theft* (the act of thieving). The terms *robbery*, *burglary*, and *aggravated burglary*, for example, appear in the *Theft Act 1968*, the term *hijacking* appears in *The Aviation Security Act 1982*, and *take* in the *Aggravated Vehicle-Taking Act 1992*. Within the limits of an essay, that was the most straightforward way of putting into a written work my understanding of how language, particularly English here, captured interpretations of a reality – or likewise, how interpretations of a reality were reproduced into a language counterpart.

The *FAL* essay, of course, had a more complex theoretical approach and demanded a substantial effort to be done within the deadline.

Again, it was an opportunity to put my belief to test: time to add intellectual effort to suit the principle of physical endurance and wilfully *think on the purpose*.

34

After the courtroom rush I hardly had time to catch my breath before being drawn into the ruthless rhythm of a hectic routine.

I dashed from Pumpkin straight to the Irene Manton North PC cluster to type the essay as I went through the reference texts; then, I staggered back to White Lodge and dropped on the mattress, just to be, a few hours from them, on my feet and on my way to attend the lectures and start all over. I only managed to complete that essay because, Rebecca rescheduled me so I had Tuesday to Thursday off work to focus on the essay.

By the time I submitted the essay, a haze of exhaustion engulfed me. I had applied my heart into that essay because Dr Johnson would be one the two tutors to whom I'd request an academic reference for the postgraduate application – the other one would be Dr Clare Barker, from *20th-Century Fiction in English*.

I had only two weeks to deliver the application documents at the Postgraduate Admissions office, before the university closed 4 weeks for Easter break.

Until there I waited for the English translation of my degree transcripts that my mother had posted the week before. I still had to do a Portuguese into English translation exercise that should be provided by all applicants of translation courses.

I started my Sunday off going over the non-assessed assignments for that week; then, later, I focused on the translation exercise without further ado. Firmly holding the exercise printout, I proclaimed: "By the power of Grey-matter!" Alas, within the first lines I felt defeated.

My future depends on a 500-word text translation!

Such thought made my stomach cramps kick off.

Exhausted, I fought against my droopy eyelids and tried to stop the pen from wandering off the translation draft. The translation needed improvements, but right then, I shouldn't stop translating. I had to exercise the principle of physical endurance that, as I'd grown to believe, could generate a desired result on reality. Thus, I carried on translating, feeling quite a few times that I was all Portuguese and no English, and a few words short of a grammatical sentence.

Over that weekend, I corrected the translation to the best of my skills and filled all the documents required for the application in the postgraduate course.

When I began to worry that my degree transcripts would delay, just 4 days left to Easter break, I received a brown envelope with my mother's handwriting on.

Brimming with enthusiasm, I ripped the envelope open just to find that my mother had sent the wrong degree transcripts. *This nightmare cannot be real.*

I tried to breath but no air went into my lungs. I began to suffocate.

34

A gulp of tears ripped through my throat. I breathed.

Not to alarm the whole White Lodge I buried my face in the pillow, and stayed like that for a long time, thinking, *why, why, why*.

It was official: there was no principle of physical endurance. Things had started off on the wrong foot. Worse yet, I'd probably gone mad. *Why had I returned to Leeds*? Here I went again, on that misery loop that, like an underwater vortex on a riverbed, continued digging an emotional-cut basin into which I always ended up sinking.

I calmed down and called home to solve that situation. Though I made an effort not to sound edgy, my mother noticed how upset I was and started crying.

Then, my aunt picked the phone up and admonished me. "You'll end up killing your mom; she's elderly and feeble."

Then, my 18-year old cousin picked up the phone and followed my instructions until he found the right transcripts; he assured me that the transcripts would be posted in the following morning.

I apologised, thanked, sighed, and collapsed on the mattress. *You'll end up killing your mom; she's elderly and feeble*. I turned the radio on to hear something other than my thoughts.

"...An official website for the *Shannon Matthews Appeal* is being officially launched this evening; more than three hundred policemen continue the investigations – the largest search since the Yorkshire Ripper inquiry – to find the nine-year-old girl from Dewsbury who's disappeared for three weeks... The American exchange student Amanda Knox, accused of taking part in the murder of the British exchange student from the University of Leeds, Meredith Kercher, continue under the Italian police custody waiting for the result of her appeal... Two months exactly had passed since the disappearance of Gavin

Terry, a 19-year-old student from Leeds Metropolitan University, who's been last seen in the Revolution nightclub."

I recalled Gavin Terry's picture, which was all over the city centre; a ginger lad, so young and beautiful; where would he be at that moment; how painful should it be to his mother. The radio reminded me that my problems were nothing at all. I remained trying to fall asleep. *Dear Lord, what a mad world was that.*

All my muscles were feverish, and my head and eyes hot. All the sleep deprivation had made me so weak that if I blew a candle I'd go out. Eventually, I was plunged into the penumbral world of slumber.

Then, from a distance, there came a tapping, as of someone gently rapping. Still light asleep, I came towards the door, just to find, standing there, a bird.

"Hi Matilda…"

35

After the party at Cliff Lane, Matilda and I'd become much closer.

We started having breakfast and walking together to university every morning. It was great to talk in English with a native speaker well early; I felt so English.

Sadly the tight schedule of those weeks didn't give me much time to fully enjoy Matilda's company. In the weekdays that I was off, I returned to the White Lodge after the lectures and, during tea time, I'd come to her room upstairs and have a quick chit-chat over a strong coffee before heading off to Irene Manton PC Cluster. Matilda had assignments too; but she had a laptop that saved her the trouble of walking through the cold night to a PC cluster. So, our academic routine maintained us more or less distant; depending on our plans for the day, we let each other know if we'd have tea together.

Because that Tuesday night I was off, we'd agreed to meet in the upstairs kitchen. But with all the frustration of that afternoon, I'd forgotten that.

"I'm so sorry. I forgot. Come in, please." I turned the lights on and pulled the desk chair for her.

"Are you all right?"

"So so. My mother... She sent the wrong degree transcripts." I couldn't hide an anguished tone.

"Oh, don't be so upset." Matilda said, motherly.

"I know. But now I can't apply before Easter. Ah... I hate being poor." I threw myself on the mattress.

"There, there, you're acting like a queen of glum. Calm down." Matilda sat by my side. "Can I do anything to help?"

"Hum, thanks. Unless you can do magic to make my transcripts appear."

Matilda stared blankly for a second. "I can do better; I'll make ya bad mood disappear." With a naughty smile, Matilda grabbed a pen from the desk, and made a charming movement. "Hocus-pocus, change your focus. Pif paf poof! There... you're all gay now."

Even though I didn't get the joke with the word *poof*, I gave Matilda the first smile of that evening.

To hear Matilda joking made me forget a little more about the application. During the tea, Matilda talked about a few mail incidents that she'd experienced herself, and told me about her own application process for the University of Leeds.

After tea, Matilda brought her inflatable mattress to my room downstairs, so she wouldn't have to return hers. That would be the first night after the party at Cliff Lane that we stayed up late again, chatting like there's no tomorrow – even if we both had lectures early morning. We watched a *Family Guy* episode which featured a song called *Shipoopi*.

"What Shipoopi means?"

"I don't know. Never heard it before."

I opened the *OED*. "*Ship of the line, shipowner, shippen...* there's no S*hipoopi*."

"It says in the words *the girl who's hard to get*. That may be it."

"Possibly..." I said, not quite convinced. "You know, I still think that because you've been educated in English from your infanthood you know the meaning of all words. Actually, I think that all words uttered by an English speaker, English, American, whatever, are known to everyone. And this is coming from someone linguistically open-minded. Sometimes I forget that words are created, and recreated, all the time. I think it's the way I learned English; I'm still conditioned to believe that each word has an equivalent meaning..."

After minutes of uninterrupted speech, I played *Shipoopi* again and started imitating the choreography from the cartoon. I kicked my legs up high, making Matilda laugh real hard.

Matilda started clapping her hands. "Come on, dance Michael Flatley!" She said aloud.

I had no idea who she was talking about. But I couldn't care less because I was having the most unrestricted chat in English ever, and that felt blissful.

Right then, my earlier sorrow made little sense; I could only see reasons to be happy: all the assignments for that week were done, and yet the postgraduate application had to be postponed, I had extra time to have another go at the translation exercise.

Matilda went on clapping as I danced and clowned about by the sound of *Shipoopi*. Then, she joined me, spinning, tap-dancing; with genuine Irish dance moves that I didn't understand really. Bliss!

Unknowingly, Maltilda and I were conjuring magic. And the product of such magic would start to show soon after that night.

36

In the following nights that week, after work I'd go straight upstairs to call Matilda to watch a cartoon or a sitcom and eat sandwiches and pasties from Pumpkin.

Before Matilda went back to her room we conversed until the early hours. I talked about the lectures, about Pumpkin, and went on to read some funny headlines from the *Metro*; that spanned into other chat topics.

Matilda revised the translation exercise with me.

I didn't apply but managed to get confirmation from both Dr Alison and Dr Barker about their reference letters.

Friday finally came, marking the official beginning of the Easter break.

When I arrived from Pumpkin that Friday, I dashed upstairs. "Matilda, you won't believe this."

"What...?"

"The police found Shannon Matthews! The missing schoolgirl from Dewsbury."

"You're joking!" Matilda sound incredulous.

"No, Shannon is alive!" I held Matilda's hands and skipped around, making her laugh with my theatrical gestures. "And you know what else is good...? The refurbishment starts Monday and the White Lodge will be crawling with builders!" I skipped again.

That humorous mood would improve during Easter.

Most housemates left the White Lodge. The ones who stayed, like Matilda and I, were asked to vacate the room during a specific period because all carpets and windows were going to be replaced.

Within a week, the White Lodge facade was entirely girded by scaffolding. Since the refurbishment started from the upper floor, Matilda moved to my room right that week.

37

Matilda and I had assignments, but had four weeks to complete them. Even though Rebecca changed me to a full-time roster I still had plenty time to enjoy Matilda's company.

Each single morning, we had tea and toasts together. There was never a minute of silence, English usually being the dominating topic. One particular morning, as we prepared breakfast along with stonefaced Damien, I heard a voice on the radio that sounded Irish to me. Matilda didn't have a marked Irish accent – at least, not when she spoke with me; she had an educated tone of voice, uttered her syllables clearly, and, unlike the Irish that I knew from *Father Ted*, didn't pronounce the rhotic *r*. But I knew she could distinguish Irish English.

"Is this an Irish accent?"

"No."

"This is Marcus Bentley from *Big Brother*. He's from the North." Damien interfered.

"But we're in the North and people here don't sound like that."

"He's from Gateshead, a town in Tyne and Wear, 'round hundred miles North from Leeds."

"That's like Irish."

"No, it's not..." Matilda asserted.

"So imitate an Irish speaker then."

Matilda then mocked some marked features of Irish English. "He's an Irishman, *so he is*. I *no* all *aboit* him, *so I do*... '*Tis* a *shem* he's a culchie an' doesn't *no* me *becoz* I'd *loik* to *gev* 'im a *beg* squeezy *hog*."

I'd never noticed such peculiarities of Irish English until Matilda highlighted them to me. That made me happy that morning; but not for long... Soon as a song started, I asked, "Is she singing *chasing ravens*?"

"I think it's *chasing pavements*."

"It doesn't make sense. How's she chasing a thing that doesn't move? Is it like *Dancing on the Ceiling*? Only make sense if you watch the video." I stated, noticing that Damien couldn't keep a straight face.

At night, when I returned from Pumpkin, our chat took another tone. I had a world of ideas to share with Matilda. I narrated my glories as an English undergrad student, my anger with for those who challenged my intellectual ideas, and my longing to become a graduate from a British university.

But, to a late night bed session, my academic saga became a bigger flop than Mankiewicz's *Cleopatra*.

Within the initial nights we delve into conversations of a more intimate nature. The bulk of my romantic adventures didn't go beyond a couple of frustrating relationships and a few disappointing flings. Matilda though – considering she was 5 years younger than me – had stories that were true jaw-droppers. Among them, she'd had an affair with a married man and almost caused his divorce.

Talking about romance and, of course, heartbreaks, triggered my speculations on the nature of suffering. I shared my thoughts on how life on earth prompted situations of suffering and hardship to humans and that humankind seemed to be bound to a higher spiritual authority through suffering and hardship. Matilda listened patiently. I then told my hypothesis on free will and on how all individuals could exert control over their fortune through suffering and hardship.

At this point, Matilda interrupted me. "I can't agree that we all can actually control our fate by making an effort to overcome hardship. You see, my brother is sixteen but he's chair-bound and can move his left arm only because there's a tumour growing in his brain and basically he isn't aware of what's around him."

"I had not thought of that actually…" I felt stupid. "I really feel for your brother."

"Some are more privileged than others, I think." Matilda saved me from shame.

Once the morning dawned, no matter how late we'd stayed up, our slumber was never sound enough to defy the noise that the construction workers produced. The banging and clanging travelled through the structure of the building making vibrate walls, floor, bed, skull, eardrum, hammer, anvil, stirrup, and brain.

Whilst I listened to the unintelligible shouting of the men labouring around the White Lodge, my lethargic imagination pictured an outdoor opera, with loud drilling intermezzi, performed by steamy muscular shirtless Caucasians hanging from the scaffolding.

Matilda always remained immobile on her inflatable mattress, cuddling a little teddy bear. If I didn't tiptoe off the room, sometimes I carefully snatched the teddy off Matilda and waited for her to awaken.

"Where's my teddy?"

I held my laughter and solemnly stated, "Shannon? I took her for a walk."

Matilda laughed every time. "Give my teddy back."

Unfortunately, the fun and laughter didn't last long.

38

Within the second weekend of Easter break I called home and talked to my father; he asked how much the postgraduate course cost, and how I intended to finance that; then, he draw attention to my age and to the fact that the State was recruiting teachers for permanent jobs and that I was missing that chance. I couldn't go against his reasons. Clearly my father gave expression to apprehensions that my mother also had and that they should have discussed at home. I had no right to put my parents through that pressure at that age.

I felt alone. Still, I had this conviction that all was worth the risk because I was aiming at something much bigger, more meaningful. I tried not to upset Matilda with my qualms, but ended up venting my frustrations during our night chat. Matilda gave me so much attention that I, having gotten all that stress off my chest, just passed out on bed.

In the next morning we kept snoozing longer, not really bothering with all the refurbishment hoo-ha. I got up earlier than Matilda, showered, and got smart for work. Then, I heated buttered croissants, boiled the kettle, and brought the breakfast to the room.

Over the breakfast, as I mentioned the postgraduate course again, Matilda reminded me: "Maybe you can apply for a student loan from NatWest."

"I got a NatWest brochure on loans but, as a student immigrant from Latin American, I don't qualify for any type of loan. But honestly, funding is the least of my troubles now; I need to apply and be accepted first."

Matilda then mentioned with a casual tone. "You wouldn't have problem to get a loan as a spouse of a European citizen…"

That flicked a light on my head. Was she serious?

A heat of excitement travelled up and down through my body. "Would you do that?"

Matilda then opened a naughty smile, like she was having a laugh at my expense. "I'm quite fond of your surname; it suits me well.

I preferred to believe that Matilda wasn't joking. "Right, think well about that; we talk when I return."

I went to Pumpkin that afternoon thinking: *Something new had just started*!

38

When I arrived at night, Matilda showed me on her laptop the information that she'd gathered from the Home Office website.

As Matilda explained, my heart pounded hard.

"I wouldn't know where to start." I said.

"I'm doing this for the sake of your surname. Fair trade."

We continued talking almost the entire night, considering what made a union like that less truthful than any other official union. I understood that Matilda should love me to do something like that. I couldn't love her less for the same reason. I had my concerns but, frankly, couldn't refrain from embracing such blessing.

With the lights already off, I still asked. "Maltilda... And what happen if you meet your prince?"

"Poor naive boy..." She replied with a sarcastic, calm tone. "There are only frogs."

39

The next day, I was off.

Despite the chilling air Matilda put on a black pinafore dress, I put on a wheaten T-shirt and olive short trousers, and we made ourselves all hippies to enjoy the sunny weather with a picnic at Hyde Park.

Sitting on the grass, Matilda and I talked on the odds that brought us together, on how a wedding could affect our friendship, and on who could be our witnesses. Well, I talked actually.

Whilst Matilda listened, she plucked fresh daisies from the grass, weaved them together into a chain, and made a delicate wreath that she put on her head.

Wearing that string of white daisies around her golden blonde hair, Matilda quietly sauntered under the spring sunshine towards an emerald hillock. I remained there, speechless, admiring the splendour of that instant – Matilda had figured out a way to make me shut up.

It was like Matilda could wilfully hold all the colours of the scenery around her with her thoughts.

Indeed, though I saw Matilda as a fragile girl, she'd still surprise me with how much she could manage to keep under her control when she really wanted it.

During that Easter recess, for example, Matilda took care of everything regarding the marriage. She phoned the Home Office to obtain an application form for a Certificate of Approval for the marriage. Later, she also introduced me to two reliable acquaintances who would be our wedding witnesses: a university mate called Hannah, and Hannah's boyfriend, George.

Hannah had seen me during the few times that she'd been to the White Lodge. Hannah learned the reasons of our marriage when Matilda arranged a meeting to formally invite her and George to be our witnesses.

Hannah and George shared the ground floor of a house near Hyde Park Terrace. When we arrived there, the instant George shook hands with me, I became enthralled by his English. George's well articulated English sounded like that of Ben's from *I am Alan Partridge*, with precisely pronounced syllables.

Just as George uttered a sentence I couldn't refrain myself from flattering him. "Wow, your English is so beautiful. If I could speak English like this I'd be the richest man alive."

George replied with a polite "Thank you."

George was a perfect model of English gentleman; but not with the looks one may expect. He had nothing of Hugh Grant; he was a slim, not so tall lad who, as Hannah told us, had had elocution lessons in school.

Hannah, who spoke English with plenty glottal stops and shortened syllables, had just dropped out of university and was set to move back in to her parents' in London – she already had purchased a train ticket.

Sadly enough, George and Hannah were in the imminence of breaking up, but George understood my situation and accepted our invitation. Hannah herself guaranteed that she'd travel back from London for our wedding ceremony.

I was happy George and Hannah were willing to be our wedding witnesses; but with Hannah's moving to London, something warned me she'd never show up.

40

The recess ended; the refurbishment continued.

By then, the workers had started renewing the rooms from the ground floor, and so, when the room 2 had to be vacated, I brought the inflatable mattress upstairs and moved in to Matilda's room.

During the recess I received the envelope that my mother sent; this time, containing the right transcripts.

In the first Monday after the Easter break, I climbed the stairs of the Michael Sadler Building, knocked at the G35, and personally submitted all the forms and documents of the application. Dr Johnson reassured me that her references would be posted by that weekend. But I was a little afraid to bother Dr Barker with another email to remind her about the references.

That same week, whilst I served coffee to a long queue of customers in Pumpkin, I lifted my eyes from the till screen to shout, "Next!" and the person I saw right in front of me was Dr Barker.

"Oh, that reminds me!" Dr Barker looked surprised.

"Oh, so nice to see you; how can I help…?"

After a standard exchange routine, which resulted in Dr Barker being served a skinny latte, she assured me: "I'll post the references within the next week."

Within another week I submitted all assignments.

During those days, I returned from the university to the White Lodge under great expectancy, hoping to find a large post envelope with the Certificate of Approval for the marriage; but Matilda found it first.

Right away, we went to the Leeds Register Office at the Town Hall and booked an appointment for the legal preliminaries, otherwise called *Notice of Marriage*.

For the first time all was working perfectly well.

I was living a beautiful dream.

Two weeks into May, on the way back from Pumpkin Café, I entered at the Irene Manton PC Cluster to check my email. Finally, it was there:

Sender: *School of Modern Languages and Culture*.
Subject: *Regarding your postgraduate application*.

41

"We regret to inform you that your application for the above MA programme has been unsuccessful.

As you may know, there is considerable competition to gain entry to the course and unfortunately we have not been able to offer you a place..."

Why bother to read it through? A life opportunity and I'd failed miserably. So much had I endured with the translation, thoughts on the desired result; for what? At least I had a marriage to focus on and, perhaps, other opportunities to apply in the future.

As I left the PC cluster behind me and walked to the White Lodge, I made a prayer and a promise: *nothing would have the power to bring me down anymore.*

42

By this time, in Pumpkin, I'd learned how to complete all the closing shift tasks within the paid hour.

By the time the rolling shutters had to come down, I'd have washed, wiped, sanitised, and polished mostly everything in sight; that gave me a full hour to count the wastage, stock the fridge, cash up the till, fill all forms and reports, and do the safe check.

Finally, all was under control at Pumpkin Café.

Then Rebecca turned up at the end of a shift.

After helping me with a few tasks, Rebecca kindly asked: "Would you like to work at Millie's Cookies?"

Oh sh…ugar. A whole new routine to learn? "Yes!"

43

Millie's Cookies routine included waking up at half past 4 a.m. to shower, put on the uniform by the sound of the shipping forecast, and dash to Leeds station.

Fortunately, I didn't have to climb up and down stairs across platforms; Millie's Cookies unit was next to the ticket counters in the South concourse. I had to start an hour before Millie's Cookies opened at 7 a.m.

"Mornin' luv." My new manager Joanne was a Leodensian born and bred. She was waiting for me at the unit in the first morning to guide me through my initiation rite into the opening routine and into the doughy world of cookie baking.

I had an hour to complete the opening procedures.

First, check the safe and turn the coffee machine on. On went the oven too. The following steps were to take the boxes containing the frozen slabs of cookie dough off the fridge, take the slabs off the boxes, and break the small sections of dough that will go into the oven;

24 portions went on a baking sheet, and 4 baking sheets at a time should be baked for 12 minutes – 8 baking sheets should be prepared for the opening shift.

Then, it was muffins time; the muffins dough should be baked for 15 minutes, and that gave me 21 minutes to bake the mini cookies, aka *mini bites*, and the cookies on a stick, aka *cookie pops*, which should go into the oven together for 10 minutes. With the 11 minutes left I had to polish the display glass, dust the counter, fill the flip-top cash drawer, and organise a flawless array of a 192 cookies, 24 muffins, 36 *mini bites*, and 8 *cookie pops*.

At 7 p.m, whilst the shutters started rolling up, there I was, behind the counter, with an impeccable smile on, as if that was the commencement of a performance at the West Yorkshire Playhouse.

"Can a'av a coffee n' a choc chip cookie, please?" Promptly asked the gentleman ahead of a queue of customers who, drawn by the sweet smell of freshly baked cookies, were already pointing their greasy index fingers towards the glass and ogling at the front row of cookies, where the classic flavours were displayed.

In minutes the counter glass was all smudged with digital prints and so I constantly had to polish the glass to wipe them out. Still, I was glad that the customers pointed towards the cookies because during my start at Millie's Cookies I couldn't understand them well when they simply uttered which cookie flavour they wanted.

"Al laugh a chokl'tchip cookie, pleiz." That is how *I'll have a chocolate chip cookie please* sounded to me.

All the names of the cookie flavours were engraved on acrylic red labels. But the customers' pronunciation of those names confused me still. I needed a few sales to realise that most customers referred to the cookies using a combination of words slightly different from those in the labels.

The 'milk chocolate cookie' was often referred to as *chocolate chip*, *choc-chip*, and *chocolate chunk*; 'double chocolate cookie' and 'white chocolate cookie' were usually clipped to *double choc* and *white choc*.

These words I learned fast, as they named the most sold flavours. It took me longer to get used to how the customers referred to the flavours that didn't sell so often. With 'chocolate and toffee, raspberry and white, oatmeal and raisin, almost no one bothered to utter *and*; chocolate orange, cherry, banoffee, which is a compound word formed with *banana* and *toffee*, and dark chocolate, aka *plain chocolate*, were easier to understand; and double chocolate fruit and nut was abbreviated to *fruit 'n nut*.

Within the universe of Millie's Cookies the English peculiarities didn't stop at the word level; a few times customers would sound pretty much like they were using a new language.

"We'll 'af a chokachoka, a chocaroka, 'n four chokl'tchunk cookies, pleez."

Well, understanding *we*, *four*, *cookies*, and *please* was a good start. But with the miles at Millie's that consonance soon became part of my English too.

"U kudchuz a darkchok 'n a cookiepop, 'n drink a hotchok or a chokamoka."

Such tricky tongue-twisters revolved around the names of Millie's chocolate flavoured hot drinks like *chocca chocca*, *chocca rocca*, *chocca mocha*, and of course, *hot chocolate*.

Within a month I acquired full proficiency in Millie's English, becoming fluent in the skills of listening, speaking, and writing. Yes, writing.

One of the main products from Millie's was the celebration cookie, aka *cookie cake*, which is a pizza-sized cookie decorated with icing and chocolate beans on the border, and topped with a *Happy Birthday*,

Happy Valentine, or *Happy Whatever* message; I had to write those messages, with beautifully designed letters, using a piping bag and a choice of chocolate, caramel, vanilla, or raspberry icing.

The time that I worked in Millie's Cookies was the sweetest moment of my entire life.

Perhaps because my daily consumption of cookies and muffins increased greatly I was just going through a long sugar rush. Then again, I had to admit that something other than cookies and muffins must have fuelled me with a constant state of bliss.

It started in the morning. During the hour I had to complete the opening routine, I listened to *Radio 4* comedies. It also felt great to design coloured messages on top of cookie cakes, and prepare creamy chocolaty drinks topped with squirty cream and marshmallows, and stimulate smiles on the customers' faces.

Such happiness lasted after the working hours. Millie's had a policy of selling cookies and muffins freshly baked all day; so, at the end of every shift I had to, like Joanne worded, "chuck'em cookies and muffins from the morning in the bin."

I bagged them, of course, to eat with Matilda later.

With the summer nearing and no academic pressure we promoted backyard picnics at the White Lodge.

Hannah and George usually joined us – whilst they were still together – and we all gorged ourselves on cookies, muffins, crisps, and tea.

Also, after the postgraduate application refusal, I felt less pressure to save money. I used to walk looking toward the ground, collecting pennies; then I spend my earnings with CDs, DVDs, and other entertaining and soothing activities. This was when I found out about *Movies That Matter Festival* at Vue Cinemas that was on at the Leeds Kirkstall Road venue; every Monday, at 6:30 p.m, this cinema showed a classic film.

To make things perfect, with the purchase of an individual ticket another free entrance was given away. So, I took Matilda to watch *East of Eden*, *The Wild Bunch*, *The Searchers*, *The Good The Bad & The Ugly*, *Death in Venice*, *Dial M for Murder*, *Rebel Without a Cause*, *Gone with the Wind*, and *The Wizard of Oz*. I wanted Matilda to feel the glory of classic cinema. I also took her to watch 80's films at the Fab Cafe.

Where I failed as a straight partner I tried to balance with friendship and anything within my reach to make Matilda happy. Seeing Matilda happy made me blissful.

Despite my efforts though, Matilda began to show signs of discontentment.

44

During this time Matilda told me that in the night she was taken to the Brotherton Wing she'd attempted suicide by ingesting a handful of hypnotics; she also told me that, after that, a university mate attempted to abuse her. That's how I learned the nature of her woes.

I assumed that Matilda's personal issues and her depression caused her to grow unhappy at moments.

I couldn't be unhappy along; I had to play the strong link. I couldn't think of a way to thank Matilda for giving me a chance to carry on pursuing my love for English other than bringing her along with me on a merry-go-round of emotions.

But the merry-go-around was nothing compared to the roller-coaster of our marriage ceremony.

We went through the legal preliminaries in the Leeds Register Office at the Town Hall, which included an interview to measure how well we knew each other, and verify the authenticity of our union; yet we'd been close to each other just for months, during the interview it seemed that we knew each other from infanthood.

The ceremony was confirmed to the end of June. Hannah's and George's names were given as the official wedding witnesses.

When the great day came, Hannah, who'd been back to London, let us know only hours before the ceremony that she wouldn't be able to make it to Leeds. But George, with his beautiful English, told me to calm down that a lady friend of his, called Imogen, would be willing to be our witness.

And then there were four: I, the groom, Matilda, the bride, George, the witness and best man, and Imogen, the surprise witness. We all assumed our roles in the the Brodrick Marriage suite of Leeds Town Hall where the wedding ceremony happened.

The wedding ceremony didn't make me nervous; but I was petrified during the marriage vows.

I didn't want my English to sound foreign or commit any pronunciation mistake.

"I solemnly vow to give myself to you to be your husband, to share my life openly with you, to speak the truth to you in love. I promise to honour and tenderly care for you, to cherish and encourage your own fulfilment as an individual through all the changes of our lives." I had to recite all this whilst looking at Matilda, holding her left hand, and putting a ring around her digitus annuláris, aka ring finger.

It felt like a neurolinguistics active distraction task and I must have sounded like Latka Gravas.

When the wedding ceremony ended we left the Brodrick Marriage suite through a door on the side that opened to the stairs of the Town Hall.

It felt like there should be a party there; but there were only the four of us under a blue sky. We proceed through The Headrow, taking pictures of George and Imogen, and of Matilda and I showing our marriage rings, standing next to Henry Charles' War Memorial in front of Leeds Art Gallery. Then we followed to Swan Street to celebrate our marriage in a pub near the City Varieties Music Hall.

I wholeheartedly thanked Imogen and explained why Matilda and I had married. I talked a bit about my beliefs to Imogen and debated with George, who was a convinced atheist, on how could that marriage be something less than a divine intervention.

Matilda kept quiet and I was a little anxious about our future together and if Matilda would be happy.

After the pub, we said our goodbyes to George, I thanked Imogen again, and we were back to our final days at the White Lodge.

45

By then, we were just over a week from the end of the student accommodation contract.

We'd said our farewells to most of the housemates. One by one they went, leaving behind, on a table at the hall, unwanted clothing, toiletries, kitchen appliances – most of which we silently accepted as wedding gifts.

Matilda vacated her room in the start of July and moved to my room - I'd paid for a week of extension.

Within days that we had to vacate the White Lodge, we signed a 12-month lease on a flat: 42 Clarendon Rd. Being married to a European national was fundamental for me to reach an agreement with the landlady; we agreed on bimonthly payments, directly debited from our bank accounts, at the onset of each 2-month period.

Matilda feared that she couldn't afford staying in Leeds as she didn't have a job. She relied on a student loan but wouldn't be able to reapply because she'd failed all her modules. So, I went around the city centre with her, searching for job vacancies. I knew how searching for a job could be daunting.

Then, I asked Joanne to talk to the other managers to find a place to Matilda. In no time, Matilda started in small coffee shop in the South concourse called Taste.

In our new flat we lived a usual newlyweds' routine; we shared a double bed, but, without physical intimacy.

During all this time I focused on prayers. I'd learned by heart the *Psalm 91*. I also focused on my physical endurance practices, staying long hours awake, having cold showers, and when I had the strength, fasting.

To that point, I had no chance to let doubts affect my actions. When my postgraduate application was refused, the marriage arrangements had already started, so willing or not I had to remain in Leeds.

Certain that I'd lost the postgraduate challenge, I was surprised when, days later, I read the refusal email again and realised that I'd disregarded an important part of the message.

...Depending on your background, you may want to apply for some of the other programmes offered in Leeds, in the School of Modern Languages and Cultures.

In particular, the MA programme in Linguistics and English Language Teaching may be of interest to you.

There I went again, up the stairs of the Michael Sadler Building, knock at the G35, and ask information on how to apply for the MA in Linguistics and ELT.

46

It was easier this time: I filled another application form and resubmitted the same documents.

By the end of June, after the wedding had happened, another email arrived. *We would be unable to accept you onto this programme... unless you provide details of any teaching experience you may have.*

Without further ado I called my mother and begged her to urgently post my substitute teacher contract and the payslips, so to meet the programme requirements.

An agonising wait of 14 days and presto!

I received an email from the admissions director of the Department of Linguistics and Phonetics.

"After consideration of your application, I have recommended to the Office of the Registrar that an unconditional offer be made to you for a place on the MA programme. I hope that you will accept, and look forward to welcoming you in September 2008."

I didn't know whether to laugh or cry.

I'd applied to a postgraduate programme that cost £4.850; now I'd been accepted to one that cost £9700!

This happened right after I'd paid the flat deposit and 2 months' rent. But, at least then, I had a chance of getting a bank loan. Or so I thought.

47

Matilda and I went to NatWest to talk about a loan. But, the bank wouldn't even consider a loan unless I had a visa that recognised me as a spouse of a European national. Matilda again helped.

Matilda took me to the Citizens Advice Bureau and there we obtained all the information needed to apply. Then, we printed all the visa application forms, filled, signed, and sent all papers together with the marriage certificate and my passport to the UK Border Agency.

So, I waited, and waited, every day feeling like a fortnight. And my passport never returned.

September approached and I went from sad, to sadder, depressed, hopeless, and then looped to nutter optimist. During this time I developed an irrational certainty that I'd obtain that money.

Virtually everyone I spoke with must have heard me repeating "Nine thousand and seven hundred pounds... I don't know how, but I'm going to make it."

I woke up, went to Millie's, baked cookies, iced cookie cakes, made chocca choccas, served customers, went to watch the classics with Matilda, and stayed up till late in bed chatting to her, and all I could think was *nine thousand and seven hundred pounds*.

Until one night, more than a week into September, I had to step down from my cloud and decided that in the following morning I'd go down to the Department of Linguistics and Phonetics and tell them that I wouldn't be able to afford the programme.

In that very morning, 11th of September, a day I was off from Millie's, whilst I remained snoozing on the mattress trying to delay a bit more the awful truth that waited for me, my mobile phone rang.

No ID caller.

Matilda had got up early and already gone to university. *Why would she hide her ID?*

On the other side, I heard an unfamiliar voice from a gentleman who identified himself as calling from the International Student Office.

"...here is to inform that you have been qualified to receive a scholarship of nine thousand and seven hundred pounds to cover your tuition fees. Are you willing to accept the offer...?"

48

"...Yes, that's real." The lady at the reception of the International Office responded when I asked her if that offer was real.

Before accepting the scholarship I was naturally eager to know about that offer. "Can you tell how I was chosen to receive this scholarship?"

"Let me check here." A few clicks of the mouse, and the lady replied. "Ah, right... Let me read for you. In December of two thousand seven the University of Leeds and the Abbey Santander Group signed a co-operation agreement that included the setting up of scholarships for prospective postgraduate students. The scholarships were available to nationals from Argentina, Brazil, Chile, Colombia, Mexico, Puerto Rico, Uruguay, and Venezuela willing to undertake a full-time postgraduate taught study or MA by research within the Faculty of Arts..." – This included MA in Linguistics and ELT – "...who would commence their studies in September two thousand eight."

"Right but... I've never seen information on this scholarship online and I never applied to start with."

The lady clicked the mouse again. "There was actually no separate application form for these scholarships; so all students applying for any of the courses with the Faculty of Arts were considered via their application form."

I thought for a second. "Is this scholarship agreement by any chance called Alban?"

"Yes actually, but the agreement that the Abbey Santander Group had with the institutions from Latin America ended in two thousand and six. It shifted to European institutions last year."

"Wow, you won't believe this... I actually tried to apply for this scholarship in two thousand and six to go to the Vrije Universiteit in Amsterdam."

The lady raised her eyebrows. "Seriously?! What are the odds...?"

49

Thanks for popping into the International Office to confirm that you are glad to accept the scholarship and sorry that I was'nt here to speak to you.

As I read the email from Mr Hodgson – the man who offered me the scholarship – that morning, the chat I had with the lady at the reception of the International Office lingered on my mind.

Being awarded a scholarship that allowed me to register for the MA in Linguistic and ELT meant salvation to me. In the moment that I'd returned to Leeds, having quit my position as substitute teacher, I'd entitled myself to ostracism back at my home university. And having been cut off my previous MA stripped me off of the last thing that could make anyone in that academic community still treat me with respect.

All that relief surfaced when I met Matilda home at 42 Clarendon Rd. "You won't believe what just happened…!"

We went out to celebrate with a lunch in an Irish Pub in Great George Street called O'Neill's. We took pictures, I made her laugh, and she seemed happy.

In the following morning, after having attended a meeting with the new postgraduate group at the Department of Linguistics and Phonetics, I sat down in the sofa from our flat at 42 Clarendon Rd. and sighed.

"I have the feeling that we are going to live in this flat for a long time." I said those words looking at Matilda, believing that soon we'd have a chance to have a better and quieter future.

At that point I didn't know how wrong I was.

50

Palace Picture Hall was an 800 hundred seater cinema situated in the Armley district – two miles off the city centre of Leeds – that began screening films in 1912.

The building that housed the Palace Picture Hall cinema was originally the venue of a roller skating rink that continued to operate, as a dancing hall as well, alongside with the film presentations. So, besides the filmgoers, Palace Picture Hall also attracted the folks who enjoyed roller skating, flirting, dating, dancing to loud music, and getting their jollies. Whilst the skating rink and dancing hall remained attracting the public, after the 50's the Palace Picture Hall had its filmgoers snatched by the expansion of television. In 1964, Palace Picture Hall closed and had part of its premises converted into a bingo club: New Western Bingo Hall.

Back in the days of the Palace Picture Hall, its building attracted many individuals willing to hide themselves from the harsh boring reality of the outside world; many of whom, under the dim light of the cinema, let their imagination fly watching the romantic black-and-white films of the time. In the beginning of the 21st century, the building of the old Palace Picture Hall still continues attracting individuals willing to hide themselves and set their imagination free; but the films showing currently are more of the blue type.

After having been turned into a squash court and a bar, the old skating rink within the Palace Picture Hall eventually became the venue of a gay sauna, which has two medium sized cinema screens showing adult films.

No wonder that, as a classic cinema enthusiast, I felt so attracted to a building that had been the setting of many old films presentations.

Well, four months before the postgrad course started I'd never stepped into a gay or any other kind of sauna. But one night, whilst I rushed through the closing tasks in Pumpkin I had my attention drawn to a tiny calendar with a picture of a slim toned lad.

"Boy, oh boy, who's this?" I murmured, reading the captions in the pic. *Daniel Broughton Mr gay UK 2007*.

Other prints on the side read, *Basement Complex – your gay sauna just a minute walk from Leeds station.*

On my next day off I went to the address printed in calendar. *Spending a few pounds won't make a difference*, I thought.

Lost and a bit embarrassed, I asked for directions to a young lady at the reception of a hotel near Heaton's Court. "Excuse me. I'm looking for this address here."

"Oh," The lady opened a friendly smile. "Just follow me." She left the reception and came a few metres off the hotel to ring the bell of a discrete door with no handle that reminded me of the strange door in *Dr Jekyll and Mr Hyde* novella.

As a man answered the door, the lady winked at me and said, "There you are, enjoy it…"

51

Three weeks later, there I was again. This time, a gentleman told me about the sauna in Armley.

Another couple of weeks and, on my day off, I set foot to the Armley district. There, I found paradise.

It had a gym area with a big screen TV set showing BBC! Since no one there cared about exercising or watching BBC, I had the big room with TV just for me.

Naturally, I explored the other areas like the jacuzzi, the steam room, the hot sauna, the adult cinema, and enjoyed the adult entertainment.

I'd never had intimacy with an Englishman before those days. Having a chance to have an open talk with some of them felt fantastic. I heard and learned things that were absolutely new to me.

There was this man who talked with me and every time that I said the word *tension* he repeated "Shun!"

"Churn? Why churn?" I asked.

"No, ah didn't say churn."

Then, as I continued, he came again. "Shun!"

"Why you say *shun*? What it means?"

"Oh, you mean *sion*." The man corrected me. "It's because ye saying t' world revolves around *tension*, and I'm stressing the word *ten-sion* to agree wi' ye."

Another occasion, as I talked with another local regular, I asked. "Can you understand the chorus of this song?"

The man listened for a second. "Clearly, yes."

"All I hear is *ah-tchoo-jee-tchoo-ray*. Is that something?"

He looked at me funny. "No, 'e's saying *ah predict a riot*."

"What… but he's not saying like you."

"Of course 'e is…" The man asserted.

That moment, I had a further glimpse of the light years of distance between my proficiency in English and the proficiency of whom had lived around English an entire life. Realising that I'd never have the experience that a man like that had with English, I felt a painful longing. That realisation and longing persisted whenever I talked with other regulars.

"…Where are you from in England?"

"Castleford…"

"If I had a mobile phone, would you provide me a sample of your English for my records?"

"Your records? Wha' ah' ya, a copper…?"

Copper?! So long learning English and I still found hard to understand a third of what those men uttered.

Those men liked referring to things with odd words.

I had a Vulkan jockstrap that I always kept on whilst cruising and going into the Jacuzzi area. Other cruisers often repeated the same thing to me.

"Why don't ye get yer *knickers* off?"

I was easily enthralled by such language subversion.

I never missed a chance to overhear, with discretion and deference, the cruiser's conversations. And I asked the cruisers I met to speak as much as possible.

Never had I felt so much fulfilment in life like I did talking to the cruisers I met at the sauna in Armley. As well as that full contact with the English, I had years of loneliness and unrealised fantasies to make up for too.

In August, knowing that I'd either get the loan for my tuition fees or have to start saving for the next year for a new academic enterprise, I began coming back to Armley more often. Armley became my hiding place, where I could watch *Dickinson's Real Deal*, blow off steam, take cold showers, fast, pray, and put my mind on my goals.

Everything was running smoothly until I met this big, brawny, butch, blonde, and a proper stonefaced British (Yorkshireman actually).

"…Call me Clifford."

"So, being in control turns you on, you say." I tried to learn that about Clifford's, using a humorous tone.

"Aye." Clifford didn't have a hint of a smile.

My heart raced with anticipation. "Oh my…"

52

Clifford seemed to have taken his form straight from my thoughts; each bit of him awakened my desires.

We met once. Then again a week later, by chance; this time, we spend a full night together. Then, after losing sight of each other for two weeks, we met again. I usually went home early; this time however, I phoned Matilda to tell that I wouldn't return that night.

Clifford dropped me at Leeds station in the morning and we negotiated a suitable meeting in Armley again.

We met twice again that week. During our meetings, Clifford didn't mind talking as much as I wanted him to; he didn't mind me making videos of him speaking; he told me the story of the British trade union movement and the miners' strike in the 80's, and how that story was related to Margaret Thatcher's famous phrase *this lady's not for tuning*; he also shared some misfortunes that happened to his family.

We'd marked other meetings without exchanging numbers, until Clifford, just as walked away off his car without mentioning a sixth meeting, shouted. "Hey… 'ow can I reach ya later?"

This way, Clifford got my number and trust, to the point that I introduced him to Matilda.

53

Matilda and Clifford met in the week that I received the scholarship offer. Around this time, Matilda herself was seeing this young lad from Wakefield. Hannah had also returned from London and was staying some nights with us at Clarendon Rd.

I'd always talked to Matilda about the sauna, my meetings, and that had never affected our life together. We kept going to watch classic films in Kirkstall Rd., and still watched DVDs, being happy together.

All that order, however, seemed to have been orchestrated to make me fall prey of a new trap: Matilda had grown depressed again.

In two previous occasions, without warning, Matilda simply sulked. Sometime after the new semester started, I noticed Matilda distant again.

"C'mon, cheer up. They'll show *The 39 Steps* in Bradford tomorrow. We'll go together. It'll be fun."

"Leave me alone." Matilda had a sweet tone.

"It's the undergraduate results, isn't it? Just apply to resit the exams, you'll make it."

"You don't understand. I failed badly. Now, without attending seminars, how am I going to pass? But this isn't the problem."

"Is it your boyfriend? I'll text him."

"No." Matilda stayed quiet a bit. Then, as I insisted, she spoke. "I think I'm pregnant. And I don't want him to know…"

Oh God. It took me time to realise the implications of that.

54

The lad Matilda was seeing hadn't showed up lately.

Gladly, Hannah was there to make some company to Matilda.

In the next Saturday, when I returned from a closing shift at Millie's, I didn't find Matilda home. I assumed that she'd gone out with Hannah. Then, Clifford called and asked me to go out. To avoid bringing him to the flat, I went to his house in Wakefield.

The next day, when I returned, I found a puddle of vomit on the floor and, next to it, an empty bottle of prescription pills.

Clifford walked down to the Leeds General Hospital with me. I found Matilda in a ward, conscious but sick.

What was I doing wrong? I thought. That was the beginning of the end of my love story with Matilda.

55

At my request Clifford stayed away for some time.

To cheer Matilda up I invited her to come to attend a *Moday Classics* in the Cineworld in Bradford, to watch *The Apartment*.

I'd never watched that film; it was a bad mistake to invite Matilda to watch it along: in *The Apartment* a heartbroken young Shirley MacLaine ingests an overdose of sleeping pills.

After that, Matilda distanced herself yet more from me and we no longer shared the same room or bed. Despite me begging Hannah to stay and make company to Matilda, Hannah returned to London.

In between working and studying I still tried to cheer Matilda up as I could. Under pressure, I quit from Millie's during the first assignments.

I understood that Matilda was seeing her boyfriend again, but he refused to come around to our flat.

I kept trying to cheer Matilda up through November.

"Hey, remember I told you that they're showing films of Paolo Pasolini in the Hyde Park Picture House midnight tonight? Let's get changed and go."

I'd just arrived late from Irene Manton PC cluster. After telling that to Matilda, who was lying in her bed, I went to the kitchen to eat something.

Matilda then came to the kitchen over tears. "Listen. I want to move in with my boy in Wakefield."

That hurt a little.

"…And I want to divorce you."

That hurt a lot.

Already fearing the answer, I asked: "And what happens to my visa application?"

That's when the mercy shot came.

"I don't care." Matilda replied.

All my bowels revolted; I made an effort not to hurl.

"I'm sorry. It's your right. You know I'm thankful for all you've done." I tried to suppress my anger, feeling truly betrayed.

I still went to Hyde Park Picture House alone, and watched *Il Decameron* through laughter and tears.

Days from that night, Matilda walked out the door.

56

I'd failed with Matilda. And yet I resented her.

Why she'd disregarded my situation like that? Her boyfriend had something to do with that, maybe. Or Clifford could the reason.

After I asked Clifford to stay away, apart from when we met at the university so that he could proofread an assignment, we'd kept contact via text message only. But one night, in the middle of November, I'd stayed at the Edward Boyle PC cluster working on an assignment until midnight; when I entered home Clifford knocked at the front window – he'd been waiting opposite Clarendon Rd. inside his car. I allowed him to enter and, trying not to sound ungrateful, explained that we should keep texting until my next assignment had to be proofread in a few days. So, Clifford agreed.

With all assignments off the way, I started working again; this time at Whistlestop – a convenience store and off-license in the North concourse of Leeds station. I covered shifts from 2:30 p.m. to 11 p.m. At the end of every shift, Clifford would show up and offer me a ride home. He'd always come inside for a little chat and tea.

Matilda never voiced, but she possibly grew jealous of Clifford. Yet, I had no courage to tell Clifford to leave me alone. And just as Matilda refused to go to the Hyde Park Picture House, Clifford found a chance to follow me to the other screenings of Pasoline's films.

In the imminence of going through a tough time, having just been given verbal notice of divorce, I had no reason to distance myself from Clifford.

So, after Matilda left me, I found myself in tatters, emotionally dependent on Clifford's support.

Luckily, Clifford was the most caring man that I'd ever had an affair with. Of course, being that lucky would be a little too much for me. Clifford was all I wanted, but with a minor crippling detail.

After the first meetings in Armley, Clifford warned me that he had a secret. "…Ah'm married to a woman."

57

"Extra, extra! Read all about it!" I tried to mimic the classic inflection of the newsboys from yore. "Listen, quite a few men in here say they either have or had a wife. Can I be honest?"

"Go on then." Clifford didn't blink.

"In Rock Hudson's days this may have been a bombshell, but in the third millennium it's a squib."

"I get t' gist."

"I just don't know why you have to tell me about your private life."

"Right…" Clifford said, calmly and stonefaced.

Alas, it didn't take long for me to learn.

First off, Clifford was a second-hand car trader and salesperson. And yet it is true that the reputation of car dealers and salespersons are to a degree unfairly coloured, Clifford justified a negative stereotype. In all truth he was a genuine and considerate person but these characteristics came second to his personal gratification and economical comfort.

Nothing preceded Clifford and his self satisfaction. Rightly he'd determined that to his life. He'd been jobless before and learned how harsh the world could be to the bankrupt geezer. Getting into the car trade business wasn't easy either. The little pleasures that he could afford and all he possessed hadn't come to him without hours of uninterrupted hard labour over the surface of many vehicles. Not to mention the verbal juggling that he had to make, haggling with customers to convince them to pay the price that, he knew, was well beneath the value of his sacrifice. Clifford always got the best of everything, and when he approached me, he definitely wanted best of that affair. And to have that best he knew how to make me fall for his kindness.

But Clifford needed a backup source of valid alibi to have time for himself when he pleased. And by making me aware that he was family man he made me aware that once I admitted that situation I'd be stripped of reasons to complain afterwards.

So, Clifford sometimes just vanished and if I ever troubled him with questions he stated: "I needed to go home early and couldn't answer the mobile."

Clifford had no time for drama. He had an offspring of three children to cater for and a wife who he wouldn't separate from to circumvent the prospect of losing the comfort of his house in a divorce settlement.

That's how Christmas arrived and Clifford left.

Before vanishing during the holidays he surprised me arranging on a small table a stack of presents, including a small HD TV with a built in DVD player.

With a new TV set, my long term affair with my so loved portable DVD player came to an end.

I learned then the meaning of the word *freeview* and delighted myself with hours of free digital channels, including all the BBC channels. Truth I was alone and watching life pass me by, but at least I was watching it in colour, and on BBC.

Who cared if Matilda and Clifford were away; I had the company of Richard Hammond, Amanda Byran, James May, Stephen Fry, David Tennant, Jeremy Kyle, Trisha Goddard, Ricki Lake, David Walliams, Matt Lucas, Tim Wonnacott, David Dickinson, Jenny Frost, Davina MCall, Kim Woodburn, Aggie MacKenzie, Richard McCourt, Dominic Wood, Barney Harwood, the Chuckle Brothers, Basil Brush, and other lot of odd faces that kept me entertained.

Not to say that I was forgotten Clifford sent a few happy New Year messages. And on the New Year's Eve, early in the evening, Matilda called to inform me that she had a miscarriage.

58

On New Year's Day, dejected, I went to Armley.

Soon as I entered, a member of the staff, an old warm-hearted Scotsman, known as Bob, greeted me at the bar. "Happy new year. How's it gaun?"

"Alright, and yourself?"

"Guid. Whaur's yer loove?" Scotsman Bob referred to Clifford, as he knew us both.

"He's not coming." I replied, a bit annoyed with his curiosity.

"That's the problem o' bein the mistress…" Bob said and bit his tongue. "But ah'm just bein a nosy auntie."

I knew he didn't mean to offend, so I responded to his comment. "You know. I don't like playing such role. But that's not the first time I come second to a woman."

"We've all been thaur. But it's nae season to be sair-hertit. 'av a lager on me an' be jolly."

"Thanks." I accepted the Bob's offer and said, "I'll be jolly." Then, I quietly repeated, promising to myself. "Indeed, I'll be jolly."

59

Soon as the Edward Boyle reopened in 2009, I applied myself to an essay on *error correction*, and so the photocopied texts and books kept me company.

Clifford returned soon.

"…And what's mah angel up to?"

"Reading for the essay."

"I'm here t' giv'ye a hand."

"I can't complain about that."

Clifford proofread the essay and continued helping me with the English through the new semester.

Until then, no trouble dissuaded me from enjoying the bliss of being a student in the MA in Linguistics and ELT at the University of Leeds. Every time that I attended a lecture and a seminar felt like I had a golden ticket to enter into the scrumdidilyumptious world of research and knowledge on English and English language teaching. And like every world I entered into, this one was full of words that I learned, and relearned.

Such words sprung from the concepts brought forth by decades of hypotheses and theories on the nature of language and of language learning – especially foreign language learning. And unlike what some may suppose, learning a foreign language entails more than memorising all of its grammatical rules off a grammar book and all of its words off a dictionary.

One may start grasping the complexity of learning a foreign language by considering that children can utter complex sentences in their native language without having been formally taught grammar or semantics. Besides, children's grammar normally is more complex than the grammar they've been exposed to; a fact that the American linguist Noam Chomsky formally acknowledged with the term *poverty of stimulus*. So, learning a language, native or foreign, must be more than a question of parroting.

Pursuing to optimise the efficiency of learning a foreign language, scholars have proposed different methods to foreign languages teaching. Each method, being grounded in different beliefs and assumptions on the nature of language and of language learning, brought forward varied variables – variables attached to labelling words (or short phrases).

Grammar-Translation Method, for instance, aka *Prussian Method* in the USA, is the most traditional teaching method, practised at the end of the 1800s and beginning of the 1900s and modelled after the classical method of teaching Latin. Here, instruction basically consists of detailed presentation and analysis of grammatical rules, presentation of translated vocabulary, and subsequent translation of sentences and texts. Also, instruction is conducted using learners' native tongue. Although there isn't a formal theory that justifies this method, it implies the belief that language is a set of prescribed grammatical rules and defined vocabulary and the assumption that learning a foreign language is a question of learning such rules and vocabulary.

Essentially, this is the method through which I started learning English at State school in the 1990s; and its principles are surely followed today to different degrees. Naturally, foreign language teaching methodologies came a long way from this through the 1900s.

Audiolingual Method, as well, aka *Army Method*, was developed mainly for training of American military personnel during the World War II and became popular in the USA through the 1940s to 1960s. It's grounded in the theory of language formalised by the American Structural Linguistics which establishes that language is a system of structurally related elements that codify meaning. Here, learning a foreign language is assumed to be a question of mastering the elements of its system. And to prompt such mastering, the Audiolingual method draws from a formal theory of learning: the *Behaviourism*. This theory defines all human learning as a mechanical process of habit formation triggered by a sequence of stimulus, response, and reinforcement – to either encourage or suppress a response. So, instruction consists of presentation of verbal behaviour to be followed; this involves repetitive presentation (called *drills*) of dialogues and language structural patterns to be imitated by the learners. To suppress the formation of wrong habit, learners' language mistakes (called e*rrors*) are promptly corrected. Though overt presentation and analysis of grammatical rules isn't essential, this method has an implicit orientation towards grammar. Naturally, instruction is conducted using the target foreign tongue.

Essentially, this is the method through which I studied English in the 12-book collection *English at Home*; the commands *listen and repeat* heard throughout the audio tapes embody the imitation fundament; and sentences like *the book is on the table*, *the dog is under the chair* epitomise the presentation of patterns which highlights alternant structural elements.

Still, the words that labelled the most interesting variables on the question of foreign language learning came from the *Natural Approach* – a philosophy of foreign language teaching developed in 1977 by the teacher of Spanish Tracy D. Terrell and the linguist Stephen Krashen.

60

The *Natural Approach* already is a development of a new trend of methods, commonly referred to as the *Communicative Approach*, which started after the 1960s with the *Communicative Language Teaching*.

This new trend of methods is actually a corollary of the Generative theory of language formalised by Chomsky at the time; he criticised structural theories of language for failing to account for the creativity and uniqueness of certain individual sentences. Hence, Communicative Language Teaching emerged as a rejection to previous teaching methods that were grounded on structural theories of language.

Here, the focus of learning a foreign language shifts from mastering its structural system to mastering its communicative dimension. However, despite following some learning principles in its teaching practices, Communicative Language Teaching fails to account for a formal theory of learning a foreign language. And that's where the Natural Approach stood out.

In the Natural Approach, following Communicative Approach principles, instruction basically consists of inducing learners to use the foreign language to engage in genuine communication in a meaningful and purposeful way. No language drills or reference to grammar is needed, since learning a foreign language here is assumed to emulate the naturalistic language learning of children – thus the name *Natural*.

Though the Natural Approach addresses no particular formal theory of language, it implies the belief that language is a vehicle to communicate meaning. Still, when it comes to a theory of learning, the Natural Approach is unique, as its proponents developed its own theoretical rationale. It indirectly refers to Chomsky's theory of *Universal Grammar*, which states that humans are endowed with a specific faculty for language acquisition; hypothetically, a specific module of the human brain, called *Language Acquisition Device*, functions to generate and store language. This implies a distinction on how the brain processes language knowledge and other types of knowledge.

From this ground, the Natural Approach establishes an enlightening distinction on the question of foreign language learning: whilst *learning* refers to gain of language knowledge through conscious reasoning, like memorising grammatical rules, *acquisition* refers to gain of language proficiency through unconscious processing, like when children start speaking.

Putting simply, even if learners have no difficulty to learn and remember the 3rd person singular present rule in English – suffixation of *s* to verb forms – they may fail to apply the rule during spontaneous production. The *learning* v. *acquisition* distinction is the fundament to justify why language proficiency is only truly gained when language is truly used for communication.

The *learning* v. *acquisition* distinction is a ground to further hypotheses, like the *Interface Hypothesis* that considers if explicit knowledge (learning) can become implicit knowledge (acquisition) – i.e., if learning is a path to acquisition. Actually, throughout the history of foreign language teaching, all methods have somewhat dealt with the *interface* issue, both before and after it was formally identified.

And under the prism of the *interface* issue, two variables become fundamental: *explicit instruction*, i.e. explicit presentation of linguistic forms, and *corrective feedback*, i.e. response to learners' language mistakes. In practical terms, methods can be labelled by how they approach these two variables: whether teaching focuses on the presentation of linguistic forms and emphasises grammar accuracy rather than meaning (*form-focused approaches*) or whether teaching focuses on the use of language for communication and emphasises meaning rather than grammar accuracy (*meaning-centred approaches*).

Naturally, the variables that affect efficiency on foreign language learning go beyond these. As I read on past and ongoing research on ELT, I became familiar with many more of these variables – and with the related words. That's also how I learned names like Rod Ellis, Tom Hutchinson, Jack Richards, Theodore Rogers, and Alan Waters. And after learning them all, I knew that I'd hardly scratched the surface of the world that I visited through the MA in Linguistics and ELT.

61

Easter came and another break started.

In a period when the assignments accumulate, the Easter break comes to lighten the academic burden and, allied with the spring, disperse the clouds that hover over the students' head. If the previous Easter relieved my worries by bringing Matilda closer to me, this one comforted me by bringing her for one last meeting.

After Matilda left Clarendon Road, I'd seen her just once as I worked on Whistlestop at Leeds Station: she happened to walk by, with her boyfriend, just a few feet from the counter. Busy and not knowing whether to call her or not, I stared. For a moment, as she paraded, Matilda stared back. Was it humiliation, indignation, or jealousy that I felt? Besides sisterly affection I hadn't really understood the feelings I'd nurtured for Matilda.

In the past months, it was certainly preoccupation. The times that Matilda had phoned she always sounded unquiet. I'd earnestly asked her to return home and proceed with the divorce from there. Sadly, she seemed resolute to hurt me, and herself, by not returning.

But this Easter, as I struggled through composing four essays, Matilda sent me a message one afternoon.

Cn u meet me in d Union. ma...

62

Matilda had a suitcase with her in the Union.

She was ready to return to Ireland in the company of her mother, Frieda. Matilda's mother had been against our wedding, but right then she was quite kind with me.

Frieda maybe saw how distressed I was with all that.

The three of us had tea together at the Terrace.

"I apologise for all concerns I caused... I'm sorry for failing to make Matilda happy."

After a silence, Frieda replied. "It takes two, you know."

Matilda remained quiet, drinking a herbal tea.

"Perhaps Matilda told you about my beliefs. I say that what happened between Matilda and I can only be part of a miracle."

"Yeah. I too have my beliefs." Frieda was dry.

"Apart from me being gay, our union was perfect. We could've been happy."

"That's not how things worrrk. But you two will solve this legally." Frieda hesitated for a moment. "And talking about legal issues... what you're doing about yourrr visa?" Frieda had a careful tone.

"I've seen a legal adviser at the International Student Office and he said that I should withdraw my current visa application and apply again for a tier four Student Visa."

"Well, I'm glad you seem to have this sorrrted."

None of us added a word to that.

After another moment of silent, whilst we all sipped a bit of tea, Frieda asked a question that seemed to have been playing on her mind.

"What you doing when you graduate? Staying?"

"I'm thinking of... Actually, I want to write a book about this story."

Matilda, having been quiet until then, abruptly burst into laughter. Frieda kept serious, though. "Well. If you got a strrrong goal, considerr yourself successful..."

We continued talking for about an hour.

Eventually, I escorted Matilda and Frieda to a Bus stop at the top of Clarendon Way. It pained on me to realise that this time Matilda was going away for good.

With Matilda gone, I'd have to wait a formal notice of divorce.

63

Over 6 months had passed from my visa application. At work my manager had already asked me if I'd heard from the UK Border. Having to concentrate on essays, thinking of Matilda, and fretting about my visa, I finally cracked.

It couldn't be normal. Every time I promised myself to be happy something happened to bring me down.

That afternoon, after Matilda departed, I went to the flat, closed the curtains, turned the radio on, and danced like Karen wearing her red shoes. Then, I revamped my promise: from today, if I ever had a thought that made me upset, I'd shake that thought off with a bop, until I could think only of blissful things.

White snowflakes falling, red brick houses, classic films in Kirkstall, Bradford, and Hyde Park, half-past six Radio 4 comedy, sitcoms and cartoons, tea and toasts, Thai sweet chilli crisps, apple pie, fish and chips, dashing English lads, and Clifford's sturdy arms. All these weren't once distant from me and just that was enough reason to subdue any bad feeling.

When all is said and done, everything must happen for a higher purpose, and such purpose cannot be anything less than beautiful. I shouldn't attempt to how unattractive my current situation looked but to embrace the beauty of the melody put together by the conditions that had led me to my so desired MA.

Who cared if I'd gone barmy? I felt marvellous.

I was beholding a new beginning in the blossoming colours of the English spring. That was the spring that would bring pretty to the ugly and high prospect to the short of hope. That was the spring of those who have a dream and believe they have got talent to fulfil it. After all, that was the spring of Susan Boyle.

64

I held that mood as the end of the MA approached.

After the Easter break, I applied myself heart and soul to write the dissertation. The dissertation had to be on a linguistic subject, but the language under analysis didn't have to be English. I could just translate the dissertation that I'd almost finished back home; but it analysed data from a dialect of Brazilian Portuguese. That would spoil the fun of analysing a topic essentially related to English.

I also wanted the topic to deal with a non-standard feature of English, preferably a feature that dealt with intelligibility. As a learner of English, I knew certain non-standard uses of English could be puzzling and I'd observed that watching or listening to comedy. Humour could make English sound rather tricky and bizarre. So I began researching on a linguistic topic related to jokes and language play.

Searching *humour* and *pun* in the index of Crystal's *Encyclopaedia*, I came across a linguistic phenomenon called *linguistic strangeness*; this labelled the rule-breaking and deviation from the normal standards of language which, as Crystal affirmed, is an essential feature of everyday conversation. *Gotcha*!

If strangeness was an essential feature of language, so I wanted to gather data from English that evidenced how frequently strangeness occurred and if patterns of strangeness existed.

I then started listening more attentively to speakers' utterances near me to identify instances of strangeness.

"…Oh, I did enjoy the gig last night… ish."

I heard this girl on the bus casually throwing an *ish* suffix detached from any word.

I couldn't believe my ears when two customers in

Whistlestop started saying something like "Oh yes, freggenchegged heggim leggoads. T'was leggush. Ah tell thee…" It was the so called *eggy peggy*, a disguised speech in which speakers add the *egg* sound in between word syllables; it's similar to but simpler than pig Latin that's formed by adding *ay* to the end of a mixed up word, like *ordway* for *word*.

I noticed how Kim Woodburn used rhyming slang on *How Clean is Your House*? "Ah, don' tell porkies!" And "Stop pork pieing me…" And still "I don't have a scooby-doo."

I'd have never noticed such uses before reading on these instances of strangeness in English. And there were many instances of strangeness that I read on, like the *baby talk* that mothers use with their babies, or the affectionate *silly talk* lovers use between themselves, or the *mock talk* people use to ridicule others; *back slang* used among young friends; there was also what's called *glossolalia* that's an apparent alien language used by people during spiritual realisations – something similar to the *scat* articulated by Scatman John in the hit *Ski Ba Bop Ba Dop Bop* and by the Hanson band with their *MMMBop* "ba duba dop ba du bop, ba duba dop ba du."

It was these types of evidence that I was looking for to use as linguistic data in the dissertation.

Here and there I noticed individuals using English in an abnormal manner but I couldn't walk with a recorder randomly pointing to them. Then, I tried to get data from radio shows that I had tape-recorded.

65

Radio comedies were ideal sources of linguistic strangeness. Milton Jones's shows were by far the most productive, featuring absurd exchanges like Milton's imaginary encounter with Leonardo da Vinci.

"I'm Milton Jones. Come to see da Vinci."

To what Leonardo asks, "Do you know the code?"

Milton and Leonardo then start a chat that mimics the words from Bohemian Rhapsody.

"…call me Dah. And in a moment, you may meet my friend Galileo."

"Galileo?" Milton asks.

"Galileo…" Leonardo replies.

"Magnifico!"

Their conversation ends when Milton says, "No… Mamma Mia!"

To what Leonardo asks, "Have you got tickets?"

This sequence makes no sense unless the listener is familiar with the references and understands that the incongruence of their exchanges is structured around such references. Comedy shows like this contained remarkable patterns of strangeness; but comedy shows were script-based usually and to demonstrate that strangeness could occur naturally in everyday English I needed something more spontaneous.

Then I turned to *The Chris Moyles Show* where the presenters often exchanged bantering remarks. In a show, for instance, Moyles interjected Jimmy Carr with "Hey, he's leaving Friday."

Jimmy then replies, "What do you mean he's leaving Friday."

And Moyles completes: "Robinson Crusoe."

The Chris Moyles Show was a good source of data; but gathering and quantifying data from random chats would need too much time and I had to be quicker to meet the dissertation deadlines.

Prudently I'd kept newspapers with interesting English examples of strangeness in their headlines.

Papers often brought headlines like *Get well roon*, referring to footballer Wayne Rooney; *ow now wild cow* about a dog walker who'd been attacked by cows;

Glow in the bark, on cloned dogs with glowing skins; *BBC iPayer*, on paying licence fee to online TV catch-ups; *Forget the porkers and pick up this corker*, using rhyming slang and referring to the MPs; *Order... order me a cab*, about the resignation of Mr Speaker during the expense scandals; *One small tweet for a man*, on the first man to use Twitter from space; *Jacko set Backo*, on Michael Jackson's O2 gigs, and so many more.

I decided to include these headlines as evidence of a more spontaneous production of linguistic strangeness in everyday English, and compare them with other uses of strangeness.

Following the guidance of my dissertation adviser, Dr Plug, the dissertation centred on headlines only; besides being more dynamic and spontaneous than scripted English, papers' headlines were productive, easily quantifiable, and considering the source of paper, they'd be representative of social class.

Clifford then helped me to gather 2 weeks issues of 4 papers, *The Times*, *Daily Mail*, *Daily Star*, and *Metro*; he further helped as a native English speaker to judge the language deviations. We went through 31 papers, analysed around 5.000 headlines, classified the types of linguistic strangeness by the patterns of deviation from the usual structure of English, and correlated these patterns to the papers, the papers' sections, and articles' topics. And that was just the data analysis.

Researching a theoretical fundament to justify and support an approach on a quite unusual topic such as linguistic strangeness was another part of the challenge.

Gladly, at the time, I moved to Springfield Mount, just a minute walk up the road from the Irene Manton North and Bragg PC clusters. To and fro between these places I strutted all day, carrying a stack of papers and books in a Morrisons reusable bag. I only had breaks to drink some tea and watch *Horrible Histories* on *CBBC*.

All the dissertation sacrifice was worthwhile: I lost a few pounds, and uncovered a few patterns of linguistic strangeness in the headlines of those English papers.

66

The function of the headlines' strangeness was to draw extra attention to the person or thing in the news. Some headlines deviated from what would be normally expected in a sentence using an incongruent word, like *Website drops a Barack*, referring to president Obama, altering *drop a bullock*; *The Ender faith, soap & glory*, referring to the soap *EastEnders*, altering *hope & glory*; *It ass to be Gaga*, referring to Lady and her buttocks; *Phoar play*, referring to a match in Wimbledon, altering *foreplay*; *Breast in Peace*, referring to a breast-shaped headstone, altering *RIP*; *Bangers and Crash*, referring to the car scrappage scheme, altering the dish name *bangers and mash*; *No- whinny situation*, altering *no- win situation*.

Some headlines used unusual blends, or neologisms, such as *Staycation? More like the holiday from hell!*, about staying in Britain for holidays, blending *stay* and *vacation*; *Police guilty of ploddledygook*, blending *plod* and *gobbledegook*; *Egg-norant kids*, on children who cannot boil an egg; *Twitchhiker is looking for you*, on a man who used Twitter to hitchhike; *Wimbledone*, *Wimbledoomed*, *THREEmendous*, and *Caulifloccoli* were other one-word headlines.

Headlines also inserted or made allusions to known titles in a sentence, as in *Jacko vows to Beat it* and *Wanna Be Startin' Somethin'... eventually*, on Michael Jackson and his O2 comeback concerts being delayed; *Meet my new fella, ella, ella!*, alluding to Rihanna's *Umbrella*; *Gr-ape escape*, about 30 chimpanzees which broke free in a zoo, alluding to *The Great Escape*;

Harry Potter and the Deathly Swine Flu and *Rupert Grint and the prison of Potter*, on the actor catching flu and having become a typecast.

Similar pattern of allusions to titles was also applied to known sentences, like in *Gurk, Guest & Stay*, on the Gurkhas' being allowed to settle in Britain, alluding to the advert *A Mars a day helps you work, rest and play*; *You've been Quango-ed! But Dave Bottles it*, alluding to the Tango advert *you've been Tango'd*; *Queenz Meanz Heinz*, on the Queen at the 50th anniversary celebration of the Heinz baked beans, alluding to the ad *Beanz Meanz Heinz*; *Baby due in 4mins*, on a woman who went into labour on the London Underground, alluding to a sentence used to announce the train times.

Other headlines used silly rhymes, alliterations, and consonance, generally clipping proper names and creating odd collocations, as in *One Ali of a man u fan*, referring to boxer Muhammad Ali; *A royal role for Royle*, referring to a member of the TV's Royle family; *Ron to rake in rent*, referring to Cristiano Ronaldo; *Stefan stuff sad Saints*, referring to Stephan Ratchford; *Falcons nab Bok Bobo*, referring to Springbok and Gcobani Bobo; *Big Bro book is a boob*, and so on.

Other unusual headlines had metaphorical phrases related to the news' topic, such as *Hitler's birthday oak tree is facing the axe – because its roots are in the Nazi past*; *Last laugh for comedy film silenced by censors*.

Not all patterns of deviations were neatly distinct in each headline; many headlines mixed different patterns, like in *The fur will fly over her purr-vy sex sessions* or *Clash of Internet Titans as Google tries to smash Windows' monopoly*.

The fact that such patterns appeared consistently and systematically across the headlines of all 4 newspapers corroborated David Cristal's statement that strangeness is an essential feature of everyday language use.

Yet the use of strangeness in headlines often added humour to the expression, not all uses were humorous; their main function was to enhance meaning by using words or phrases that evoked extra references as to connect and merge two meanings to the sentence. Like in the headline *Michael Jackson: 29/08/58 – 25/06/09. Jacko: this is it*, referring to the singer's death and the title of his O2 concerts, and implying that the funeral was Jackson's only performance of the *This Is It* tour.

By pointing this in the dissertation, I managed to show how strangeness had a genuine communicative function within the language – English in this case – since language users resorted to strangeness not just to be deliberately strange (or merely humorous), but to be economic and convey extra meaning.

After the dissertation, I began to notice patterns of strangeness everywhere in English, as if I'd discovered a sublanguage that's used liberally and unconsciously. I'd found a golden mine of English from which brand new patterns of words and sentences are always being generated. Writing the dissertation on linguistic strangeness in English was a liberating experience; it felt like I was being set free from all the limits of the Standard English from grammar books and dictionaries. It could be called *dissermission*: a compound of *dissertation* and *manumission*.

After having settled for conforming to a social standard with my pursuit to master English, my nonconformism with standards had ultimately led me to learn how to subvert it. And that felt blissful.

Though I truly respected and loved English, I also wanted to be sinful with it, to use it for pleasure, to fulfil my passion unrestrictedly.

And with such desires well consummated, it felt just right that I looked forward to officialise my passion for English with the forthcoming graduation ceremony.

67

"So you're no' telling us wher'you come from, then."

It was my last shift at the garage.

Dan and Dave had come inside Unit twenty for one last chat. "C'mon... Tell us." Dan actually gave voice to Dave, who despite being more reserved was just as curious as Dan.

Both son and father kept staring at me.

I didn't want to reveal that information; didn't want to be rude either. "Right, I cannot say it now but you'll know in a short time." I truly expected that.

"Y're joking." Dave let it out. "Well, 'av a nice flight, then. An' come n' visit us again."

"Will do."

Before they left, Dan still said. "Ah'll find out la'er."

A bit after that, Ewan entered the unit. "So you're going then."

"I need to. I wish I could stay, 'cause I really love working here; speaking English. You know."

"I know y're 'appy t' work wiv us, 'cos ye know wha' y' want."

"I hope so, I do."

"I know o' chaps who don't reckon the worth of our country or our tongue. If they 'ad the interest ye have, t' country would be much be'er than i' is now." Ewan made a brief pause to settle his flames down a little.

"It's good enough for me."

"Yeah boo', I judge by t' business 'ere in t' garage. I mean, Ah've seen a lot o' progress this year, bu' i' could b' be'er."

"Well, if you're committed to make business better, you'll make it. I believe there's something watching down on us, giving some sort of support to our goals."

"You know I don't buy these things."

"I know but... I've lived situations that... I wanted something really bad, and I got it. I can't explain right but, believe me... it starts with a strong desire; almost like a sexual desire."

"I believe in merit; 'ard work."

"Yes. It's part of it. Bu' there's something else, I think. I can only be sure when I achieve what I really want. Then I can tell it better."

Ewan usually didn't take anything I said seriously. So that was the only time I talked like that with Ewan and he didn't mock me back.

After some silent, whilst Ewan proceeded with his work, he turned to me again with an upbeat tone.

"Will ye miss us Jonesey...?"

It was interesting to see Ewan making that question as a subterfuge to actually saying "I'm going to miss you." That made me happy. "Of course I'll miss yous."

Ewan almost didn't spoke for the rest of that shift.

My emotions were high but I calmed myself down. I didn't want to go naturally, but, although I didn't admit it to myself, I'd made my mind up for a while; first because I wasn't making any progress with my writing, second because of my relation to Clifford. I gathered forces to tell Clifford that I wanted to go 2 weeks ago.

68

Like in other occasions, Clifford had to have a car that was advertised for the next day ready. So we'd stayed in the Bodyshop UK until late after Ewan left.

"Clifford. I was thinking... So far my appeals to the UK Border were dismissed. What should I do now?"

"We go on appealing." Clifford replied, not shifting his eyes off the engine of the car he was fiddling with.

"But the contract of the flat is about to end."

"We find a place here in Donny…"

After all that Clifford had done for me, I couldn't complain much. But I felt hurt and angry to see Clifford avoiding the subject so bluntly. "Babe. I can't stay like this. I'm thankful you've done so much. But it doesn't feel right that you help me without taking a position."

Clifford stopped fiddling with the engine and faced me, with a rather frustrated gaze. "What ya want me to do? Ah'av responsibilities, y' know it."

Weary, and frustrated myself, I struggled to hold my feelings. "I don't want this for me. I'm really, really tired of trying. N' you don't seem bothered about it."

"Right. Ah've been honest wi' you. I never hid ah go' my children. Ah luv'em to bits, n' I can't gamble like ye do." Clifford talked calmly. "I go' t' work t' earn enough to buy my freedom…"

"What? Don't come with *freedom*. For a white man you give a terrible meaning to *freedom*. It's downright wrong 'cos you actually mean get rid of your kids."

"Y' know wot. Ah can't be arsed wi' this." Clifford immediately buried his head in the engine again.

"Right. Ignore it. Pretend this will go away, like you been pretending your whole life."

Clifford looked at me. "Shoot oop, right now."

"I will. But just answer this: if you love your kids, why you spend the nights with me? Hey? Why…"

"Shoot t' foock oop, b'for' ah hit ya." Clifford said as he threw a screwdriver on the floor. "Ah warn ya, ah won't giv' a flying foock wot 'appn." He sounded willing to keep his word.

I wanted to cry. But there was no grand red-carpeted staircase for me to lean on and sob dramatically. So, I swallowed my rancour and shut up.

After we both calmed down, I thought that what happened wasn't so bad. At least Clifford showed some emotion – a rare display behind his stonefaced facade.

We made up of course. And like usual, Clifford was hands-on to help me on my decision to go. "...Here's what we can do: we sort out an extension of t' flat lease; then we bell n' come to an agreement wi' the immigration agent. We can manage t' ge' a departure deadline for t' date the flat lease ends. This will giv' ya time t' sort yourself out."

And that was the beginning of my departure.

69

First, I phoned my parents. "Mom... I decided to return..."

Hearing that, my mother sounded allayed and warm. I knew that it wouldn't take long, though, until I'd see that warmth turn into cold bitchiness and I'd hear her calling me a bum, a failure, a deviant... as usual.

When my father picked up the phone, he told me something new. "Your mom left a glass with her brandy half-full and quit drinking at all."

I was awfully happy to hear that; yet, I'd bet she didn't quit being a shrew who controls the house with her whinging.

Near to the date of my departure, I emailed some old mates to tell them of my return.

Helen emailed me back with surprising news: she'd recently met my first boyfriend, whom she knew from our younger days, when she was known as Joy. Helen told about that meeting in detail. She'd accidentally spotted him crossing the street; actually, she had her attention drawn to him as he flung a red silk scarf in the air and wrapped it around his neck just before entering a beauty salon. Helen went to talk to him. He then told Helen that he'd been sentenced to a 1-year jail term in the States after being accused of abusing a minor. It'd passed a few years that he'd been deported from there.

Now, after he managed to set up a beauty salon in a district better than that of former times, he was back on his feet and still kept his old confident attitude.

By the time I read Helen's email, I've already filled two suitcases with stacks of books, papers, audio-tapes, and DVDs. It was déjà vu all over. Times moved on and I kept trying to save my precious English before it slipped off my reach. Only one thing was new: I bought a TV recorder and recorded all I could; so, this time, I'd take with me the finest of the BBC and ITV shows.

Brand new technology! I thought – until the eve of my departure, when I read an email from Aristotle.

...I'm glad to hear such news. When you come back, I hope you don't have to work as much as I do: I work 3 shifts to make money. I have a new car to pay for and a family to provide! Btw, remember I told my wife was pregnant; so, I can't name my baby Kalel because the ultrasonography showed it's a girl. Yeah, I agree with your lines about my would-be Kalel: "Kalel will see the light of an ultra-modern world. He won't know the concept of writing letters and posting in the mail; or sharing the lyrics of that song; or recording a tape with a *Twilight Zone* episode. A touch in a screen and voila! He will be watching any episode – quite probably. We've been in the very boundary of two worlds. We saw the rise of video and its transition to DVD, and Blue ray. Now, Ipad is the new sensation in the UK. How many changes will your Kalel see?"

Let me tell a change you'll see when you're back. English's no longer distant as it used to be during our undergrad course. A huge variety of English words can be explored online. Just type 'domino' on Google, and many words related to the game are there. And if you have a go on YouTube, you'll be watching native speakers from USA or Britain playing! We can hear the slangs and the teasing remarks. BBC is on Youtube too;

I watch the Big Brother UK here! I can also download shows that have just aired on USA or British channels. I watched EastEnders *yesterday. And I'm watching the revival of* Futurama! *All the English radio stations are broadcast live online. And there are the podcasts that you told me. There's more yet, but I don't want to spoil it for you. I want to show you. See you soon…*

Again, technology had surpassed me.

During my MA, I'd noticed other students watching BBC shows via the BBC iplayer in the PC clusters; I didn't know how to use that. Perhaps then, the iplayer could be watched abroad. If so, I'd learn from Aristotle.

That reminded me of Uncle Bob, who referred to the internet saying, "A thing that transmits information and live images without wire; that's from the Devil!" What would he say about watching the BBC iplayer abroad simultaneously to the British audience? The last time I heard from Uncle Bob he'd got a job in the local water supply and treatment Company. He kept his upholstery business still and sounded busy. He didn't mention anything on his usual speculations on aliens. Either he didn't mind about that anymore or he'd found out the truth and decided to keep that secret.

Just after I finished reading Aristotle's email using Clifford's mobile at the garage, Clifford turned up and whistled. "Hoy! 'oorry oop."

"I'm coming!" I hastened myself and jumped on Clifford's banger.

Whilst Clifford started driving off Whittington St., I gave a long last gaze towards the cars parked in front of Unit twenty. All I could see was still cars with different colours, sizes, and shapes. I'd learned a few words that identified them: Amiga, Citroen, Corsa, Fiat, Fiesta, Mondeo, Peugot, Toyota, Vauxhall, Vectra, Ranger; but I still couldn't relate any of those words to them. To me, those cars had been no more than surface forms that I had to keep valeting until they were sparkly and shiny. I'd only started paying more attention to the cars lately; but it was to stare at their radiant paintwork and appreciate how beautiful my physique had become with the new slender muscles that I'd built up after months of splashing, scrubbing, vacuuming, and dancing around those cars.

I waved farewell to Ewan as he came out of Unit eighteen. As if reading my mind, Ewan shouted one last utterance for me to remember. "Ah'll seethee Jonesey!"

70

The M1 was the last leg of that adventure.

First, Clifford stopped at Morrisons to buy crisps and cookies. When we returned to the car, he said, "Remember when I took ye t' Alton Towers?"

"I'll never forget."

"This is wha' ah can do t'night. Ah want ye t' enjoy t' ride." Clifford had a grip on my chin, as he often did when he wanted me to pay attention to his words.

"I'll enjoy."

Alas, I couldn't avoid foreseeing the nuisance I'd face on my return. I prayed that I'd never come to meet again my former partner; the last thing I wanted was to give him a chance to say: "You could have a stable job now." He was entitled to preach. The last time he called he made me know that he'd secured a job in a State University; though he now worked and dwelt in a small district, he was earning an honest and decent salary.

Along the M1, *BBC Radio 4* helped to keep any glum thought off my mind. Clifford was quieter with each mile he neared the Heathrow. Being driven into the short stay parking was painful. I could hear Marcus Bentley to voice-over: "Jonesy. You have been evicted! Please leave the Big Brother country!"

I made an earnest effort to ward off that pain by engaging in happy thoughts. Maybe on my return, I'd walk down the airstairs by the cheers of a crowd. And with luck, I'd find out that the aeroplane had landed right on my former-advisor, leaving just his Armani shoes sticking out. Perhaps even, the cheering crowd would sing, "Ding-dong! The bitch is dead."

"Why t' silly smile?" Clifford interrupted my trance.

"Bi' nervy, I think." I replied, wondering how bitter I'd become to amuse myself with such thought. How sad. Almost as sad as knowing that such thought had no chance to become true. Just that week, I'd learned from Laura – who had married a Dutch and now lived in the Netherlands – that my former-advisor had started another Postdoctoral degree in the Netherlands.

"Wonders will never cease." I said over the phone.

"…He's following your steps, fancy pants."

"That's why, months ago, she emailed me enquiring about English courses at the University of Leeds."

"I think he wants you to invite him over to yours."

"I'm honoured, but no thanks. She can practise her English in the Netherlands. Besides, a mix of Brazilian and Dutch accent will suit her English well…"

That memory should be bad for the skin. And I wanted to look pretty during my farewell to Clifford.

"This is it mah angel." Clifford said, after helping me to carry and weigh the suitcases.

"Thanks for everything." I tried not to show any emotion. "And sorry for…"

Clifford interrupted me with a heartfelt farewell hug. "Lis'n. Ye won't stay there long. Ah promise."

I felt the impulse to say that I didn't believe him, like I said other times. *Why spoil the moment?*

"Thanks." I said, feeling the solitude that lied ahead of me until the check-in counter opened in the morning.

It wasn't a bright take off for my literary enterprise.

Going home would bring new challenges, but would allow me time and better resource to write. Besides, I'd embraced that journey to fulfil a passion for English, and to seek for a change too. And lately I felt that I was stuck in the garage routine, under Clifford's protection, losing my will to write. Apart from writing, I failed to see any other promise of change. Without that promise, I wouldn't bear staying in that situation for too long.

Into the small hours, whilst I waited for the check-in counter to open, the imminence of my departure hurt horribly. Going away from Clifford, from England, and from English, felt like losing all that I'd fought so hard to conquer. Still, as I'd grown to believe, all changes and achievements entailed sacrifice or endurance. I saw that in the Stonewall riots – and also in the behaviour of those who came out and fought strategically before and after Stonewall – without which the LGBT community wouldn't have ever left the gutter. I saw that also in the in the sociolinguistic work of William Labov on Black English Vernacular. So, for the progress of my literary enterprise, the pain of my departure was worthwhile.

I still feared that going away from England was a bad omen. I was being removed from the epicentre of English, from a physical reality connected to English. Through this journey, I'd grown to believe that physical reality and language are mystically connected. I'd considered this, time after time, reading on linguistics – particularly *Cratylus*, and works on Quantitative Sociolinguistics and Forensic Linguistics. I'd observed also how each environment seemed to bring about a particular selection of vocabulary, hyponyms, and expressions. And I thought to have experienced this connection by noticing certain aspects of reality more prominently after truly learning the words that named such aspects. So perhaps, by going away from England, I'd eventually lose my English itself.

Naturally, I considered the perspective that words/ sentences functioned as empty frames transmitted among individuals arbitrarily. Yet, as I understood, when words/ sentences are given the human breath they gained context, form (combinations), pronunciation, intention, and other features; only then words/ sentences are truly empowered and turned into fully fledged language. So, by going away from the breath that turned English words/ sentences into true English, I'd lose this true English anyway.

Still, that early in the morning, felling fatigued and forlorn, I let the pessimism soak in. After all, I'd started pursuing English with a dozen coursebooks, four tapes, and two hours of English on TV. Now, I had an MA in English, valuable knowledge on English, and two cases laden with takeaway English.

And I had to trust in my intuition; it was this intuition that led me to follow my own method to truly improve my English before I learned on linguistics and academic methods in foreign language learning. Much before I read on the principles of the Communicative Approach, I used English in the most real way imaginable: daily, as part of my life routine, making it part of my reality. Somehow I indeed felt the language and reality went together, and I sought to surround myself with anything at my reach that was related to English. I also used formal means to learn English, like studying books and grammars, writing down glossaries, and focusing on class lessons. Surely, any formal type of approach to learning a foreign language is subject of debate in foreign language learning theory (Interface Hypothesis); still, I believe that it's a path to start, especially if other means aren't at one's disposal. If my intuition put me in the right path to learn English, perhaps again my intuition was putting me in the right path to fulfil my literary enterprise.

Or maybe all had been a just a massive coincidence. Maybe I'd been misled to believe in abstract dimensions, mystical connections, and in the possibility to generate and control our fortune. Either way, I'd carry on writing... in English. I was stubborn and English made me feel loved-up. Writing would be a way to hold English as part of my reality, to persist on breathing English myself.

Becoming a full-blown published writer in English would be another part of the challenge. I'd failed to achieve this from within England as I'd desired; so, I was quite confused on how to generate a desired result. Still, as I understood, language and reality shared of the same divine code of creation, and both served the divine purpose of keeping humanity confused.

Hence, the human power to generate a desired result and control fortune couldn't be that easy to decipher.

When I felt the aeroplane lose contact with the English ground, I whispered, "Oh, my English. Gone." But I'd bring it back. I just couldn't think about that then. I just wanted to cry and sob. *Where the hell is that grand red-carpeted staircase*!? Well, I'd think about it tomorrow. What was there for me to do if not writing? It was either writing or perishing. Writing was the thing that I'd live for; the only thing that would matter; that would last. Writing... in English. After writing, I'd be back to England. England! Back to my English. The beautiful English of England. I'd find a way. After all, tomorrow would be another day.

Again I saw myself under that oak tree, surrounded by the red light, and by the grandiose music of Steiner.

Then, I started picturing how beautifully designed would be those two closing words of the book.

Acknowledgements

Thanks to William, Matilda, and Clifford – real characters who offered me a ride on the journey to conquer English.

Ewan, David, Daniel, for the attention and fruitful chats at the garage.

To my neighbour, Dr Victoria, who allowed me to take friends to her house, and her sons – Rodrigo, who often lent me his VCR/ DVD, and Rafael, who had his journey learning English interrupted by fate at the height of his youth.

Diogenes Figueiredo, Renata Monteiro (Undergrad mates); Fernanda Lima, Maja Kamprath, Valeria Nardi, Benjamin Ruschin, Nico Micarelli, Aida Aljam, Svatopluk Nevrkla, Shayless Patel, Sara Thelen, Emilia (Clarendon Rd. housemates); Javier Zapata, Vanessa Ignatova, Nicola, Emanuelle Spoleto, Martin (North Grange Rd. housemates); Dr Gloria Gama, Dr Sandra Luna, Dr Genilda Azeredo, Dr Michael Smith & Dr Selma Smith, Dr Juvino Junior, Dr Wilma Martins, Dr Mariana Perez (Undergraduate tutors); Mr Dharmendra, Mr Thillay, Chef Sukumar, Ajesh, Aju, Kannan, Rajaram (Georgetown Restaurant crew); Mr Antonio, Rebecca, Joanne, Sharon (SSP managers at Leeds City Station); Claudia Bolders and Luiz Castro (real Samaritans); and Uncle Valberto.

Dr Clare Barker, Dr Alison Johnson, Dr Leendert Plug (University of Leeds tutors)

Stuart Hodgson from the International Office (University of Leeds).

Abbey Santander Group.

www.ingramcontent.com/pod-product-compliance
Lightning Source LLC
Chambersburg PA
CBHW020321170426
43200CB00006B/231